SALESPERSON EXAM PREP

The state exam can change at any time.
Download updates to this book from our website
www.RealEstateCentre.biz

21st Edition

COPYRIGHT 2013
JOHN HENDERSON
ALL RIGHTS RESERVED

All rights reserved. No portion of this publication may be reproduced, transmitted, transcribed, stored in a retrieval system, or transmitted into any language in any form by any means without the written consent of John Henderson.

Published in the USA by
The Real Estate Centre

INTRODUCTION

About the Salesperson Exam

The Real Estate Salesperson Exam is a 3 hour, 15 minute multiple choice exam. There are 150 questions on the exam. You have an average of 78 seconds to answer each question. A passing score on the Salesperson Exam is 70% (105 correct answers out of a possible 150).

How to get the most out of this book

1. Please be aware that the state exam can change at any time, and without notice. As soon as you receive this book, go to www.Real EstateCentre.biz to register. When you register, you'll get access to weekly updates to the book, along with a handy answer sheet you can use when taking practice tests. When you register, we will also ask your permission to contact you for feedback on your exam. We take your feedback seriously; with help from students like yourself, we are able to make this course the best real estate exam prep in California.

2. **Read** the Salesperson Prep Outline, Math Workbook, Final Briefing, Glossary and the Update twice, taking particular note of information which is new to you.

3. **Chapter Questions**. There are questions at the bottom of each page of the Outline, testing your understanding of key concepts on that page. At the end of each chapter, you will find a Chapter Review with questions related to that specific chapter. These tests are important tools for you to use to gauge your understanding of the information in the chapter. When reviewing the answers to the Chapter Review questions, please note that there are page numbers following each answer. These page numbers will direct you to the page where you can find more detail about the correct answers.

4. **Practice Exams**. You will find additional practice tests in the back half of the book. These tests are designed to replicate the structure of the state exam. It's helpful to try and simulate the exam when you take these tests. Give yourself 3 hours, 15 minutes to answer 150 questions. Do not write your answers in the book (use the answer sheet you downloaded). After you complete an exam, grade yourself and try to determine why you had problems with the questions you missed. Then, take the test again answering only those questions you missed on the first try.

5. **Your goal** is to master all of the material. You can be confident that you've mastered the material when you score 90% (or better) on all the practice questions in this book.

6. **Time Crunch?** If you run short on study time, I recommend you divide your time as follows: **50%** of your available study time on the Salesperson Prep Outline, Math Workbook, Final Briefing, and Glossary, and the remaining **50%** working Practice Exams.

TABLE OF CONTENTS

SECTION I. SALESPERSON EXAM PREP OUTLINE

	PAGE
CHAPTER 1 - PROPERTY OWNERSHIP AND LAND USE CONTROLS	1-1
I. PROPERTY	1-1
II. ENCUMBRANCES	1-3
III. ESTATES	1-7
IV. GOVERNMENT RIGHTS IN LAND	1-11
V. JUDICIAL ACTIONS	1-12
VI. PUBLIC CONTROLS	1-12
CHAPTER REVIEW QUESTIONS	1-15
CHAPTER 2 - TRANSFER OF PROPERTY	2-1
I. DEED	2-1
II. TITLE VESTING	2-3
III. TITLE INSURANCE	2-5
IV. LAND DESCRIPTIONS	2-6
V. ESCROW	2-8
VI. TAX ASPECTS	2-11
CHAPTER REVIEW QUESTIONS	2-17
CHAPTER 3 - FINANCING REAL ESTATE	3-1
I. FINANCE DOCUMENTS	3-1
II. SOURCES OF FINANCING	3-5
III. GENERAL CONCEPTS AND DEFINITIONS	3-8
IV. GOVERNMENT LOAN PROGRAMS	3-12
V. LOAN CLAUSES	3-14
VI. FINANCING AND CREDIT LAWS	3-15
VII. ECONOMIC INDICATORS	3-17
CHAPTER REVIEW QUESTIONS	3-19
CHAPTER 4 - PRACTICE OF REAL ESTATE AND MANDATED DISCLOSURES	4-1
I. CALIFORNIA REAL ESTATE LAWS AND REGULATIONS	4-1
II. ADVERTISING	4-8
III. ETHICS	4-9
IV. VIOLATIONS OF THE REAL ESTATE LAW	4-9
V. ADVANCE FEE CONTRACTS	4-11
VI. SPECIAL RULES	4-11
VII. PROPERTY MANAGEMENT	4-12
VIII. MOBILEHOMES	4-13
IX. BUSINESS OPPORTUNITIES	4-14
X. FAIR HOUSING LAWS	4-14
XI. MANDATED DISCLOSURES	4-17
CHAPTER REVIEW QUESTIONS	4-21

©2013 John Henderson

	PAGE

CHAPTER 5 - CONTRACTS 5-1

- I. CONTRACTS 5-1
- II. LISTING AGREEMENTS 5-6
- III. RESIDENTIAL PURCHASE AGREEMENT 5-8
- IV. OPTIONS 5-10
- V. MISCELLANEOUS REAL ESTATE PRACTICE 5-11
  - CHAPTER REVIEW QUESTIONS 5-12

CHAPTER 6 - LAWS OF AGENCY 6-1

- I. AGENCY LAW AND DEFINITIONS 6-1
- II. CREATION OF AGENCY AND AGENCY AGREEMENT 6-2
- III. SCOPE OF AUTHORITY 6-3
- IV. RESPONSIBILITIES OF AGENT TO SELLER/BUYER AS PRINCIPAL 6-3
- V. DISCLOSURE OF AGENCY 6-6
- VI. DISCLOSURE OF ACTING AS PRINCIPAL OR OTHER INTEREST 6-7
- VII. TERMINATION OF AGENCY 6-8
  - CHAPTER REVIEW QUESTIONS 6-9

CHAPTER 7 - VALUATION AND MARKET ANALYSIS 7-1

- I. THE APPRAISAL PROCESS 7-1
- II. APPRAISAL REPORTS 7-1
- III. PRINCIPLES OF VALUATION 7-2
- IV. BASIC VALUATION DEFINITIONS 7-3
- V. ESSENTIAL ELEMENTS OF VALUE 7-4
- VI. FOUR GREAT FORCES INFLUENCING VALUE 7-4
- VII. ADDITIONAL FACTORS INFLUENCING VALUE 7-5
- VIII. METHODS OF ESTIMATING VALUE 7-5
- IX. APPRAISAL AND CONSTRUCTION TERMS 7-10
  - CHAPTER REVIEW QUESTIONS 7-15

SECTION II. MATH WORKBOOK MWB-1

SECTION III. FINAL BRIEFING FB-1

SECTION IV. GLOSSARY G-1

SECTION V. SALESPERSON PRACTICE EXAMS SQ-1

- SALESPERSON PRACTICE EXAM #1 .... SQ-1
- SALESPERSON PRACTICE EXAM #2 .... SQ-20
- SALESPERSON PRACTICE EXAM #3 .... SQ-37
- SALESPERSON PRACTICE EXAM #4 .... SQ-56
- BONUS QUESTIONS SQ-74

©2013 John Henderson

SECTION I.

SALESPERSON EXAM PREP OUTLINE

COPYRIGHT 2013
JOHN HENDERSON
ALL RIGHTS RESERVED

All rights reserved. No portion of this publication may be reproduced, transmitted, transcribed, stored in a retrieval system, or transmitted into any language in any form by any means without the written consent of John Henderson.

Published in the USA by
The Real Estate Centre

READY TO START STUDYING? REGISTER!

Wondering how to get the most from this book?

Your first stop should be registering at www.RealEstateCentre.biz.
When you register, you can:

Download Updates - we provide all registered students with weekly updates to our exam prep. Remember, the exam can change at anytime, and without notice so it's important to stay up-to-date with updates.

Download answer sheets - these are great tools to use when working on practice tests.

Access to new study tools - Get advanced notice about new study aids.

We want your feedback.
Our goal is to provide you, and all of our students, with the best real estate exam prep in California. To do so, we need your feedback. When you register, please let us know when you are taking your test so we can contact you for feedback. And, if you see anything strange or unusual on your test, please contact John Henderson. You can reach John by e-mail at 411@realestatecentre.biz.

Chapter 1

PROPERTY OWNERSHIP AND LAND USE CONTROLS
(Approximately 15% of Salesperson Exam)

I. **PROPERTY** - the owner of property owns a bundle of rights. Property is defined as **"the rights or interests a person has in the thing owned."** All property is either real property or personal property.

   A. **Real Property** (Land, Fixtures, Easements, Stock in a Mutual Water Company, etc.) - real property is generally immovable. Real property can also be defined as **"that which is immovable by law."** Real property includes:

   1. **Land** - includes surface, mineral, air and water rights. Mineral rights transfer automatically when land is sold. A land owner also has water rights. These water rights include the right to make reasonable and appropriate use of water on, under, or adjacent to the land. These water rights may be severed by voluntary transfer, condemnation or prescription.
      a. **Riparian rights** refer to **moving water (a brook, stream, river, or watercourse).** When a river or stream is the boundary of a piece of land, the riparian owner owns the land to the midpoint of the river or stream. If it is a navigable waterway, then the owner only owns the land up to the water's edge. A running stream is real property. The ownership of riparian rights may **not** be accurately determined from an examination of public records.
      b. **Littoral rights** refer to **non-moving water** (pond, lake, ocean).
      c. **Appropriation** - the government may give permission to a non-riparian owner to take water from another landowner or a public waterway.
      d. **Accession** - the acquisition of property by it being added to other property.
      e. **Accretion** - the process of gradual or imperceptible additions to land bordering a river or stream. An individual acquires title to land by natural causes as a result of accretion.
      f. **Alluvion** (alluvium) - the soil deposited by accretion.
      g. **Avulsion** - the sudden violent tearing away of land by the action of water.
      h. **Erosion** - the gradual wearing away of land by natural forces. Erosion results in the loss of title.
      i. **Reliction** - an increase in land by the permanent withdrawal of a sea or river.

Question #1: Legally and technically, property is defined as: (A) that which is capable of involuntary transfer; (B) things with buyers or sellers; (C) rights or interests which a person has in a thing owned; (D) only personal property.

Question #2: The owner of land owns riparian rights to water on, under, or adjacent to the land in which of the following? (A) oceans and bays; (B) rivers or streams; (C) underground caves with water; (D) all of the above.

Question #3: When an owner acquires land which includes riparian rights, such riparian rights: (A) give the owner absolute ownership of the water; (B) must be expressed in the trust deed; (C) may be determined accurately from an examination of public records at the County Recorder's Office; (D) concern the use of moving water, such as a stream or brook within the watershed.

Answers: #1-C; #2-B; #3-D

2. **Anything Affixed to the Land**
   a. **Fixtures (M A R I A)** - objects attached to the land may become real property (such as, homes, load bearing walls, built-in swimming pools). A **fixture** is defined as **something incorporated into real property.** This is determined by the **M**ethod of attachment or **a**nnexation, **A**greement between the parties, **R**elationship of parties, **I**ntention of the parties, and/or **A**daptability of the object. **The cost, size, or time installed are not factors** used in determining whether an object is a fixture.
   b. **Vegetation** is real property (grass, bushes, trees).

3. **Appurtenances - things used with the land for its benefit.** Appurtenances are **real property.** Appurtenances run with the land. Stock **in a mutual water company is appurtenant** to the land; it is considered real property.

B. **Personal Property (chattel, chose)** - generally movable; it includes leases, trade fixtures, business opportunities, and most mobilehomes. Title to personal property is not generally found by searching the public records. Personal property may be hypothecated. Most personal property is transferred with a bill of sale. A bill of sale must be signed by the seller.

Notes: 1. **Hypothecate - borrower retains possession** of the item securing the debt (like a trust deed, a mortgage, or a pink slip for a car loan).
2. A **trade fixture** is a fixture which is attached to leased property by a business tenant specifically for use in his trade or business. Trade fixtures remain the personal property of a business tenant.
3. **Crops** may be real or personal property. Crops which replenish themselves and do not require annual planting (orange trees, apple trees, etc.), are usually real property. Crops which must be planted annually (**emblements**) such as **corn and wheat are usually personal property** of the owner of the farm or of a tenant farmer who planted them. All crops when cut, mortgaged, or sold, become personal property.
4. **Severance** - the act of removing something attached to the land and, by doing so, changing its status from real property to personal property.

Question #4 What is **usually** considered real property? (A) crops which have been harvested; (B) minerals which have been mined; (C) stock in a mutual water company; (D) growing crops which have been sold.

Question #5 Which of the following would be considered real property? (A) a built-in refrigerator in a mobile home not attached to a permanent foundation; (B) trade fixtures installed by a tenant but which are removable without damage; (C) a mature grape crop which is under a sales contract and to be harvested later; (D) a load bearing wall in a single-family house.

Question #6 When the owner of a parcel of land cuts down a tree, it becomes personal property by the process of: (A) annexation; (B) mobility; (C) severance; (D) fixation.

Answers: #4-C; #5-D; #6-C

II. **ENCUMBRANCES** - burdens on property, including money burdens (liens - such as trust deeds, mortgages, taxes, judgments, etc.) and non-money burdens (zoning, easements, deed restrictions, leases, etc.). **Buyers commonly purchase encumbered property.**

Note: A homestead is not an encumbrance.

A. **Money Encumbrances (Liens)** - are placed against the property either **voluntarily** (with the owner's consent) or **involuntarily** (without the owner's consent). **A lien is a "charge against property."**

  1. **Types**
     a. **Specific Liens** - burdens on a particular parcel (**mechanic's lien, trust deed, mortgage, attachment, property tax, lis pendens**).
     b. **General Liens** - burdens on any and all real property of the owner in the county where they are recorded (**judgment lien and income tax lien**).

  2. **Voluntary Liens -** mortgages and trust deeds (See Chapter 3 - Financing Real Estate).

  3. **Involuntary Liens**
     a. **Mechanic's Liens** - money encumbrances recorded by people who have performed work or furnished materials for the improvement of real property and were not paid for their work. Mechanic's liens are the **only liens which must be both verified and recorded.**
        (1) **Priority of payment** - unlike most other liens, mechanic's liens take priority earlier than the date of recording. Mechanic's liens take priority as of the day work began or materials were first furnished (except for some government liens).
        (2) **Notice of Nonresponsibility** - recorded by the owner if someone else (like a tenant or vendee in a land contract) has work done on the owner's property. The notice must be recorded within **ten days** of obtaining knowledge of the improvement.

Question #7 Which of the following is **not** an encumbrance? (A) a lease; (B) an easement; (C) a lien; (D) a homestead.

Question #8 An owner employed Super Construction Co. to install a swimming pool at their home. If the pool company was not paid and it was necessary for them to file a lien for payment of the contract, the encumbrance created would be: (A) a specific lien; (B) a general lien; (C) a voluntary lien; (D) none of the above.

Question #9 Each of the following are specific liens, **except**: (A) judgment liens; (B) property tax liens; (C) attachment liens; (D) mechanic's liens.

Answers: #7-D; #8-A; #9-A

Notes:
1. Government liens usually have priority.
2. There is a **limited period of time in which to file** (record) a mechanic's lien. All of the following effect the filing of the mechanic's lien: notice of nonresponsibility, date of completion of the project, date of cessation of labor.
3. If a notice of completion is not recorded, the claimant has **90 days** after completion of the work of improvement to file a mechanic's lien.
4. The funds from a construction loan are typically released in a series of progress payments. Most lenders disburse the last payment when the period to file a mechanic's lien has expired.

    b. **Lis Pendens** - notice of pending litigation concerning title or possession of real property. A lis pendens must be recorded. Once recorded, it **clouds the title** pending the outcome of the lawsuit. Once recorded, a lis pendens is effective as long as litigation is pending.

    c. **Attachment Lien** - an attachment is created by recording a writ of attachment, which creates a lien on real property. The attachment lien legally holds real property to ensure it will be available to satisfy a judgment in a lawsuit.

    d. **Judgment Lien** - when an abstract of judgment is recorded it creates a **court-ordered general, involuntary lien upon all real property of the debtor located in the county of recordation.** A judgment lien is **valid for ten years** and enforced by way of an "execution sale." The court orders the sale of property by a **sheriff's sale** to satisfy a judgment with a **writ of execution.**

B. **Non-Money Encumbrances (Easements, Encroachments and Restrictions)** - affect the physical condition or use of the property. Non-money encumbrances do not include liens.

    1. **Easement - the right to enter or use another person's land within definable limits.** It may be created for any length of time, and it is **irrevocable** during the time limit specified. All easements are real property.

Question #10 Which of the following is true concerning a lis pendens? (A) a lis pendens can only be removed by a court order; (B) a lis pendens can be recorded against real property no matter what type of lawsuit is pending; (C) a lis pendens may affect title to real property based on the results of the lawsuit; (D) none of the above.

Question #11 Which of the following would be classified as a lien? (A) a notice to pay or quit; (B) an attachment; (C) a recorded declaration of homestead; (D) all of the above.

Question #12 All of the following significantly impact the physical use of real property, **except:** (A) an increase in the front yard setback requirement; (B) CC&Rs; (C) deed restrictions; (D) specific liens.

Answers: #10-C; #11-B; #12-D

- a. **Definitions**
    - (1) **Dominant Tenement** - the land that gets the benefit of the easement.
    - (2) **Servient Tenement** - the land that is crossed by an easement, the land that is encumbered (burdened) by the easement. Every easement must have a servient tenement.
    - (3) **Appurtenant Easement** - benefits the land of the dominant tenement. A buyer of a dominant tenement automatically receives the easement and has the same rights as the seller. The dominant and servient tenements of an appurtenant easement need not abut (touch) each other.
    - (4) **Easement in Gross** - benefits a person or corporation (like a utility easement for power lines). An easement in gross will involve at least one parcel of land.
- b. **Creation**
    - (1) **Express Grant** - agreement of the parties. A tenant may grant an easement, but it **may not extend beyond the term of the tenant's lease**.
    - (2) **Reservation** - an easement retained by a grantor when conveying property.
    - (3) **Prescription** - one may acquire an easement by **five years** of open, notorious, continuous, hostile use, under a claim of right or color of title. **No confrontation with the owner is required,** and the property taxes do not need to be paid.
- c. **Termination** - the holder of servient tenement cannot terminate or revoke the easement. An easement may be terminated by:
    - (1) **Express release -** when the holder of dominant tenement signs a quitclaim deed.
    - (2) **Merger** - an easement will terminate by merger when the owner of the easement acquires the servient tenement.
    - (3) **Non-use for five years - only** terminates an easement created by prescription.
    - (4) **Destruction** of the servient tenement may terminate an easement.

Note: An **unlocated easement is valid.** *For example, an easement for a path across a vacant lot need not specify where the path is located.*

2. **Encroachment** - wrongful placement of an improvement on the property of another, a type of trespass. An owner is allowed **three years** in which to sue his neighbor to have the encroachment removed.

Question #13 Gregory, who does not own any land in the area, has an easement to cross land owned by another person. This easement can be described as: (A) an appurtenant easement; (B) an easement in gross; (C) a non-occupant easement; (D) a license.

Question #14 All of the following terminate easements, **except**: (A) destruction of the servient tenement; (B) merger of the dominant and servient tenement; (C) non-use for five years of an easement created by express grant; (D) express release by the owner of the dominant tenement.

Question #15 Upon moving into the home they had recently purchased, Mr. and Mrs. Katz discovered that their neighbor had built a wall which encroached onto their property by three feet. When they purchased the home, they received a standard coverage title insurance policy. If a friendly settlement cannot be negotiated, who will Mr. and Mrs. Katz sue? (A) the title company; (B) the previous owner in the chain of title; (C) the neighbor, because the encroachment is a trespass; (D) the neighbor, if the encroachment has been in place less than five years.

Answers: #13-B; #14-C; #15-C

3. **Restrictions** - restrict the free use of land by an owner. All restrictions are either private restrictions or public restrictions.

   a. **Private Restrictions - created by the grantor or developer** in a deed or by written agreement (CC & R's). Private restrictions do **not** include **zoning laws.**

   Notes:
   1. **CC&R's** - *covenants, conditions, and restrictions are usually placed in a "declaration of restrictions," which is commonly part of a general plan created by a developer to restrict land use in a subdivision.*
   2. **Injunction** - *a court order restricting a party from doing an act (such as violating private restrictions). A court order saying* **"Stop that!"**
   3. *A* **covenant** *is a promise either to do or not to do a certain thing. A breach of a covenant merely results in a court action for damages or an injunction. A* **condition** *is a qualification of an estate held by a grantee. A breach of a condition affects the estate created, and the failure to comply with it may result in a forfeiture of title. The remedy for the breach of a condition is considered to be more serious (stringent) than a breach of a covenant.*
   4. **A deed restriction prohibiting "for sale" signs is illegal,** *but the signs may be limited to a reasonable size.*

   b. **Public Restrictions** (most commonly "zoning laws") are justified for the safety, health and general welfare of the public. **Retroactive zoning laws** are illegal. A "grandfather clause" allows an owner to continue to use structures which do not conform to new zoning laws as a "**nonconforming use.**"

Question #16 An occupant violated the CC&Rs of the homeowners association. The remedy for breach of a condition is: (A) less severe than the violation of a covenant; (B) more severe than the violation of a covenant; (C) the same as the breach of a covenant; (D) not related to the CC&Rs.

Question #17 Mr. Hayward has been burning leaves on his front lawn in violation of the CC&Rs of his subdivision. His neighbors have filed a lawsuit and have received a court order, ordering Mr. Hayward to stop burning the leaves. That court order would be called: (A) a lis pendens; (B) an attachment lien; (C) an injunction; (D) a writ of habeas corpus.

Question #18 An apartment building which was built prior to the enactment of a zoning ordinance prohibiting apartment units within the area where a building is situated is called: (A) a variance; (B) a violation of the applicable general plan; (C) a nonconforming use; (D) in violation of the zoning law.

Answers: #16-B; #17-C; #18-C

  c. If a landowner wants to use his property in a way that is prohibited by existing zoning, he may petition the planning commission for:
     (1) **Rezoning** to change the zoning for the area.
     (2) **A variance** for his piece of land. To obtain a variance, the owner must show that unique circumstances exist which do not injure the public.
     (3) Changes in public restrictions (zoning) may be initiated by a property owner, developer, subdivider, or by the government.
  d. **"Downzoning"** describes changing zoning from a high density use to a lower density use. For example, when a city changed the zoning from C-1 (commercial) or R-3 (multi-family residential) to R-1 (single family residential), the property was downzoned. No compensation is paid when downzoning lowers the value of property.
  e. If zoning conflicts with deed restrictions, the more restrictive of the two controls. **The most restrictive restriction restricts you.**

III. **ESTATES (what is owned)** - define ownership rights and interests, along with the degree, quality and quantity of interest one has in property. An owner of a condominium and a tenant who is renting both have an estate in property.

  A. **Freehold Estate** - an estate of indeterminable duration.

   1. **Fee Simple Estate** (estate of inheritance, perpetual estate, estate in fee, fee estate) - an estate which is indefinite in duration and can be sold or inherited. A fee simple estate may have encumbrances.
      a. **Fee Simple Absolute** - the greatest interest one can have in real property.
      b. **Fee Simple Defeasible** - conditions or limits on the use of the property. If the **conditions are broken,** the current owner is defeated, and the **property will revert** to the original owner (for example, a grantor gives title on the condition that there is no dancing on the premises; if dancing occurs, the title is defeated).

  Note: When a condition in a deed will cause title to revert back to the grantor if certain acts occur in the future, the condition may be described as a **condition subsequent.**

   2. **Life Estate** - a **freehold estate**, limited in duration to someone's life.
      a. **Life Tenant (holder of the life estate)** - may sell, lease or encumber the property. When a life tenant dies, the property reverts to the holder of the estate in reversion and any sale, lease, or encumbrance, is cut off. A life tenant cannot devise (will) her life estate when it is based upon her own life.
      b. **Estate in Reversion** - held by the original grantor if the property is to revert to him.

Question #19 The city planning commission recently changed the zoning for a neighborhood from C-1 to R-1. This change in zoning can best be described as: (A) spot zoning: (B) upzoning; (C) downzoning; (D) depressive zoning.

Question #20 The zoning for a subdivision said that each lot must contain a minimum of 10,000 square feet. The deed restrictions said that each lot must contain a minimum of 15,000 square feet. Which would control? (A) the most recent restriction; (B) deed restrictions; (C) zoning; (D) whichever restriction was created first.

Question #21 Jack owns a life estate based upon his own life. He leases the property to a tenant on a five year lease. Jack, the life tenant, dies two years later. What happens to the lease? (A) the lease continues in effect for the full five years; (B) the lease terminates; (C) the lease continues in effect, but the tenant must renegotiate the monthly rent with the holder of the estate in reversion; (D) the lease was always null and void, because a life tenant may not lease the life estate.

Answers: #19-C; #20-B; #21-B

B. Less-Than-Freehold Estate (leasehold estate or chattel real) - the legal interest in real property held by a tenant who is leasing or renting. A less-than-freehold-estate is personal property. **A lease is a non-money encumbrance against the property.**

1. **Types of Leasehold Estates**
   a. **Estate for years (lease)** - an estate for years must have a termination date.
   b. **Estate of periodic tenancy (month-to-month).**
   c. **Estate at will** - occupancy for an indefinite period.
   d. **Estate at sufferance** - one in which the tenant who has rightfully come into possession of rental property retains possession after the expiration of the term.

2. **Parties** - the leasehold estate creates a landlord and tenant relationship.
   a. **Lessor (landlord)** - transfers an interest in his estate for a term less than his own. He retains a "reversionary interest." A lease is the lessor's (landlord's) personal property.
   b. **Lessee (tenant)** - has a leasehold estate in real property. This leasehold estate is a tenant's personal property.

Note: The "or" "ee" rule - when a word ends in the letters **"or"** (lessor, offeror, grantor, etc.), it identifies the creator or giver of a document. When a word ends in the letters **"ee"** (lessee, offeree, grantee, etc.), it identifies the receiver of a document.

3. **Types of Leases**
   a. **Gross lease (flat lease)** - The lessee pays a fixed amount. The lessor pays expenses.
   b. **Net lease** - lessee pays expenses such as taxes, insurance and maintenance. The **net lease benefits** the lessor by giving him a **fixed income**.
   c. **Percentage Lease** - lessee pays rent based on a percentage of gross receipts of the lessee's business. A commercial parking lot would pay the highest percentage in a percentage lease.

Question #22 All of the following are less-than-freehold estates, **except**: (A) a leasehold estate; (B) an estate for years; (C) a life estate; (D) all of the above are less-than-freehold estates.

Question #23 Real property includes all of the following, **except:** (A) vegetation; (B) leasehold estates; (C) improvements; (D) minerals.

Question #24 When rent is based on a portion of the gross receipts of a business, the lease is called: (A) a gross lease; (B) a net lease; (C) a percentage lease; (D) a fixed lease.

Answers: #22-C; #23-B; #24-C

4. **Creation of a Lease (L A N D)** - no specific wording is required; however, there must be clear intent to rent the property.
    a. The following must be included in a lease:
        (1) **L**ength of time
        (2) **A**mount of rent and method of payment
        (3) **N**ames of the parties
        (4) **D**escription of the property
    b. You do not need the words "let" or "demise."
    c. **Leases** with a duration of **over one year** must be in writing.
    d. A lease for agricultural or horticultural purposes cannot exceed **51 years**. A lease of urban property cannot exceed **99 years**.
    e. A written **lease must be signed by the landlord (lessor) only**. A tenant (lessee) taking possession of a property and paying rent makes the lease enforceable. The sale of a property does not usually terminate a lease. The new owner of the property has no more rights than the prior owner.

5. **Transfer of Leasehold Interest**
    a. **Sublease** - the original lessee gives up a portion of his overall interest in the leasehold. A sublease **transfers possession** of the real property, **but not ownership.** A sublease is **subservient to the original lease**. The original lessee remains liable for the rent.
    b. **Assignment** - the tenant transfers all the rights and interests to a new tenant. When a leaseholder (tenant) assigns a lease, the assignee becomes the tenant. The assignment of a tenant's interest in a lease does not relieve the original tenant from liability under the lease, unless the landlord releases the original tenant from liability.

Note: A tenant may assign or sublease without the landlord's permission, unless the lease prohibits it.

Question #25 In a lease whose duration is greater than one year, what is not required? (A) writing; (B) signatures from both the lessor and the lessee; (C) termination date; (D) amount of rent and the method of payment.

Question #26 A sublease is: (A) the same as an assignment of lease; (B) a transfer of the entire leasehold to the sublessee; (C) a transfer of less than the entire leasehold to the sublessee; (D) limited to a term of ten years.

Question #27 When a leaseholder (tenant) signs a valid and enforceable contract with an assignee, the assignee who acquires the leasehold becomes a: (A) grantor; (B) tenant; (C) sublessee; (D) landlord.

Answers: #25-B; #26-C; #27-B

6. **Termination of a Lease**
    a. If a landlord fails to make necessary repairs within a reasonable time after written or oral notice to the landlord of problems (plumbing, heating, electrical, etc.) and these problems render the premises uninhabitable, the tenant may make the repairs as long as the **cost of such repairs is not more than one month's rent. The tenant can** deduct the expenses of the repairs from the rent when due, **or terminate the lease.**
    b. An owner is not required to give a notice to terminate to a tenant at the end of an estate for years (a lease) because the tenant has already agreed to a termination date.

7. **Definition of Terms**
    a. **Surrender** - landlord and tenant mutually agree to terminate a lease. Surrender is not the same as "accord and satisfaction." "Accord and satisfaction" is only applicable when the amount of a debt is in dispute. In the case of "surrender," the landlord and tenant mutually agree to terminate a lease without disputing the amount of the debt.
    b. **Abandonment** - a tenant voluntarily relinquishes possession of the rented premises without the landlord's consent and with the intent to never return.
    c. **Security deposit** - in residential rentals, the amount of the deposit a landlord may collect is determined by the terms of the agreement and whether the property is furnished or unfurnished. Security deposits on residential property may not exceed two months' rent on unfurnished dwellings or three months' rent on furnished dwellings. When a tenant vacates a rental unit, the landlord must return the unused portion of the security deposit to the tenant within **21 days**.
    d. **Quiet enjoyment and possession -** every lease has an implied covenant of quiet enjoyment and possession of the premises for the purpose for which it is leased, including compliance with all applicable building codes. The covenant does not protect the tenant from the acts of others over whom the landlord has no control. The right of "quiet enjoyment and possession" gives the tenant the right to possess the property without disturbance from someone claiming **"paramount title**." Paramount title describes title superior to the tenant's. A landlord may enter a rented unit after giving reasonable notice for the purpose of showing the unit to a buyer of the building.

Question #28 The hot water heater in an apartment breaks. The tenant has a $1250 month to month rental agreement. The tenant may: (A) deduct up to $312.50 to pay for the repair; (B) deduct up to $625 to pay for the repair; (C) deduct up to $1250 to pay for the repair; (D) deduct up to $3750 to pay for the repair.

Question #29 The amount of the security deposit a landlord may collect from a prospective tenant is dependent upon: (A) competition from other apartments in the area; (B) the term of the lease and whether the apartment is furnished or unfurnished; (C) the number of children occupying the unit; (D) the total number of tenants who plan to occupy the premises.

Question #30 The covenant of quiet enjoyment most directly relates to: (A) nuisances maintained on adjoining property; (B) possession of real property; (C) title to real property; (D) all of the above.

Answers: #28-C; #29-B; #30-B

    e. **License** - the personal and nonassignable right to do a particular act (or acts) on the land of another. Unlike easements, **a license may be revoked.**

IV. GOVERNMENT RIGHTS IN LAND

A. **Eminent Domain (Condemnation)** - the **power of the government to take private property** for public use. Eminent domain may be exercised by governments, public school districts, and utilities. The government pays fair market value for property taken under eminent domain. Eminent domain is **not part of police power or zoning.** If an owner objects, the government must bring a condemnation action in court. "Fair and just" refers to the **compensation** paid to the owner of property taken by eminent domain. If the property being taken is a commercial property, the owner or business tenant may also be entitled to compensation for loss of the good will value of the business.

Notes: 1. When a property is condemned under the Health and Safety Code (for example, because the structure is unsafe), no compensation is paid.

    2. **Inverse Condemnation** - *if a public work (airport, freeway, etc.) results in damage to property, a private party may bring a court action to force the government to purchase the property. Inverse condemnation is the opposite of eminent domain (condemnation).*

B. **Police Power (government regulation of property)** - the right of government to pass and enforce laws for the order, safety, health, morals, and welfare of the public (such as rent control, planning and zoning laws, building and subdivision laws).

C. **Escheat** - when a person dies leaving no heirs and no will, the state gets the property. An individual may never acquire land by escheat.

Note: *When the government sells land to an individual, it uses a patent to transfer title instead of a deed. Therefore, an individual may acquire property by patent.*

Question #31 All of the following are included in the laws governing the government power of eminent domain, **except:** (A) fair compensation at fair market value to the owner; (B) condemnation action in court; (C) the right of the government to take property from the owner for a legitimate public use; (D) the exercise of zoning authority.

Question #32 A large airport changed the flight pattern, extending the runways and creating excessive noise which made Mrs. Chang's home unusable. The legal proceeding by which Mrs. Chang may force the authorities to purchase her property is called: (A) inverse condemnation; (B) eminent domain; (C) police power; (D) quite title action.

Question #33 The legitimacy of zoning laws rests upon: (A) the fact that planning boards are local, and close to the neighborhood they regulate; (B) the government's police power to pass laws for the order, safety, health, morals, and general welfare of the public; (C) the ease of enforcing them; (D) the fact that their enforcement does not interfere with interstate commerce.

Answers: *#31-D; #32-A; #33-B*

V. JUDICIAL ACTIONS

A. **Quiet Title Action** - a court suit to perfect title, usually by removing a cloud on title.

B. **Intestate Succession** - occurs when a person dies without a will, but with heirs. When a person acquires property as the result of intestate succession, he acquires the property through the direction of the probate court.

C. **Probate -** When a person dies, there is a judicial proceeding to make sure the debts are paid and assets of the decedent are properly distributed. This proceeding is called "probate." Real estate may be sold while in probate. The **commission paid** to real estate agents in a **probate sale is determined by a Superior Court Probate Judge (court order).**

D. **Execution Sale** - property is sold under a "writ of execution" to satisfy a judgment.

E. **Adverse Possession** - acquiring title by **five years** of exclusive, open, notorious, continuous possession of the property, contrary to the best interests of the true owner, under a claim of right or color of title, and payment of property taxes for the same five year period. A **quiet title action** is used to perfect title when **property is acquired by adverse possession**.

VI. PUBLIC CONTROLS

A. **Subdivision Law**

1. **Subdivision Map Act** - grants cities and counties control over the design (physical improvements) of a subdivision (streets, sewers, etc.). Cities and counties develop a master plan (also called a general plan) showing the location of streets, freeways, commercial districts and seismic activity zones, etc. The primary tool used by the planning commission is zoning (police power). Master plans are implemented by zoning laws. A subdivision of **four or less** parcels is regulated by the Subdivision Map Act only.

Question #34 For more than three generations the Corderro family has owned the right to operate a gold mine on land which belonged to a neighbor. One day, the neighbor sold the land and the new owner immediately fenced in the property and padlocked the gate to the entrance. What should the Corderros do? (A) the Corderros should get a quitclaim deed from the new owner; (B) the Corderros should file a quiet title action in court; (C) the Corderros should give a quitclaim deed to the new owner; (D) the Corderros should do nothing.

Question #35 In the sale of real property which is a part of the estate of a deceased person, which of the following normally determines the amount of commission paid to the real estate broker? (A) the local multiple listing service; (B) the administrator or executor of the estate; (C) a court order; (D) the California Department of Real Estate.

Question #36 What is the primary tool used by planning commissions to implement a general plan? (A) zoning; (B) adverse possession; (C) eminent domain; (D) master plan.

Answers: #34-B; #35-C; #36-A

2. **Subdivided Lands Law** - designed to prevent fraud. It is regulated by the Real Estate Commissioner (State). To stop violations, the Commissioner issues a **Desist & Refrain Order**. A subdivision of **five or more** parcels is regulated by both the Subdivision Map Act and the Subdivided Lands Law.
    a. **A subdivider submits** all important information to the Commissioner, including:
        (1) Financial arrangements to assure completion of community recreational facilities.
        (2) Contracts, maps, and finance documents.
    b. When there is a **blanket encumbrance**, the Commissioner may require an **impound account** to **protect the buyers'** purchase money.
    c. **Final Public Report - issued by the Commissioner** when all of the Commissioner's requirements have been met.
        (1) A final public report **may be obtained by anyone** who requests it.
        (2) Buyers must be given a copy of the final public report.
        (3) A subdivider must give the final public report to a buyer and obtain a receipt from the buyer before entering into a binding contract. The receipt for the final public report must be kept on file by the subdivider, or his agent, for a minimum of **three years.**
    d. **Condominium Subdivisions**
        (1) A condominium is an undivided interest, in common, in a parcel of real property, together with a separate interest in the airspace in a particular unit. A condominium may be residential, industrial, or even a commercial building.
        (2) The common area of a condominium includes the sidewalks.
        (3) The seller must **give the buyer a copy** of the condominium's bylaws and CC&Rs, along with the most recent copy of the homeowner's association financial statement.
    e. **Mobilehome Park** - is any area or tract of land where **two or more lots** are rented or leased to accommodate manufactured homes, mobilehomes, or recreational vehicles.
    f. **In-Fill** - a kind of real estate development which consists of vacant parcels or dilapidated structures in an urban area targeted for new construction.
    g. **Miscellaneous Information**
        (1) The **three phases** involved in building a single family dwelling are **land acquisition, development, and construction.**
        (2) A **comprehensive market analysis** is vital in **planning a subdivision.**
        (3) The housing and construction industry is controlled primarily by:
            (a) **Local Building Codes**
            (b) **State Housing Law** (Health and Safety Code)
            (c) **Contractors State License Law**

Question #37 After several lots have been sold in a subdivision, the Real Estate Commissioner was informed of misrepresentations being made by the developer. The Commissioner may stop the sale of more lots by:
(A) revoking the final public report; (B) issuing a writ of prohibition; (C) filing an accusation in court; (D) issuing a desist and refrain order.

Question #38 "In-fill" is a kind of real estate development which consists of: (A) older, lower density housing, which is targeted for newer, higher density housing; (B) vacant parcels or dilapidated parcels in an urban area targeted for new construction; (C) underdeveloped suburban fringe property targeted for small scale commercial development; (D) industrial toxic waste area scheduled to be cleaned up for recreational use.

Question #39 Which of the following best identifies the three phases normally involved in building a single-family dwelling? (A) construction proposal, map approval, and buyer qualification; (B) financing, building and resale; (C) land acquisition, development, and construction; (D) syndication, subdivision, and relocation.

Answers: #37-D; #38-B; #39-C

    (4) When an owner sells apartment units to tenants and the tenants own the parking areas, halls, walks, etc. in common, it can be described as a subdivision.

    (5) The purpose of the State Housing Law is to set minimum construction standards. The State Housing Law is required to be substantially the same as the Uniform Building Code.

    (6) When comparing federal, state and local building codes, **local building codes** usually set the **highest construction standards.**

    (7) The Department of Building and Safety issues building permits. Minimum construction standards are enforced by inspectors for the Department of Building and Safety (also known as local building inspectors).

    (8) A developer is responsible for assuring completion of streets, curbs, sidewalks, and other common areas in a new subdivision.

    (9) Sanitation, sewage, and occupancy regulations are enforced by local health officers.

    (10) Flood Hazard Report - **Flooding** is considered "frequent" if a flood occurs **on average more than once in 10 years.**

B. Environmental Quality Act - a **negative declaration** indicates that the subdivision does not harm the environment; therefore, a negative declaration is good. The Environmental Quality Act also allows the conversion of existing rental units to condominiums.

Question #40 There are multiple building codes regulating construction. Which code usually sets the highest construction standards? (A) Local building codes; (B) State building codes; (C) Federal building codes; (D) Uniform building codes.

Question #41 A "negative declaration" in a discussion of environmental impact means that the proposed subdivision: (A) has been disapproved by the Real Estate Commissioner for the issuance of a public report, and the developer may not proceed with the construction; (B) will have a negative impact on the environment and create an environmental hazard; (C) will have an insignificant effect upon the environment and the developer will not have to pay for a full environmental impact report; (D) has been disapproved because of other environmental hazards in the neighborhood.

Answers: **#40-A; #41-C**

Chapter #1 Review Questions

This exam contains 22 questions. You have an average of 78 seconds per question on the Salesperson Exam. 22 questions x 78 seconds per question = 1716 seconds. Please give yourself 28 minutes to complete this practice exam, and take the exam in one sitting.

1. When the government has granted permission to a nonriparian owner of a ranch to use a nearby lake, the owner has received this right by: (A) eminent domain; (B) prescription; (C) appropriation; (D) percolation.

2. Each of the following factors determine whether an item of personal property has become real property, **except**: (A) method of annexation or attachment; (B) cost of the item; (C) relationship between the parties; (D) agreement between the parties.

3. Real property includes: (A) chattel mortgages; (B) trust deeds; (C) vegetation; (D) chose.

4. In addition to a grant deed, is a separate contract required for the sale of stock in a mutual water company? (A) yes, stock is always personal property and must be transferred with a bill of sale; (B) no, stock in a mutual water company cannot be sold; (C) yes, because stock in a mutual water company is chattel real; (D) no, water company stock runs with the land.

5. Which of the following is not a lien? (A) taxes; (B) restrictions; (C) trust deeds; (D) judgments.

6. A trust deed was recorded against a property on 1-5-12. Work started on remodeling the property's kitchen on 2-1-12. A mechanic's lien was recorded on 3-15-12. Which lien has priority? (A) mechanic's liens always have priority; (B) the mechanic's lien has priority if the lender was notified of the remodeling project; (C) the trust deed has priority because it was recorded before the work began; (D) none of the above.

7. A subcontractor was hired to install hardwood floors on a home under construction. If the subcontractor had to file a mechanic's lien to get paid, the mechanic's lien would take priority as of the date: (A) the installation of the hardwood floors began; (B) the entire project began; (C) work was completed on the entire project; (D) work was completed on the hardwood floors.

8. When a project of improvement on real property has been completed and the owner has not filed a "notice of completion" how many days do claimants have to file mechanic's liens? (A) 30 days; (B) 60 days; (C) 90 days; (D) unlimited.

9. All of the following are required for the existence of an appurtenant easement, **except**: (A) two parcels of land owned by two different persons; (B) the dominant tenement and the servient tenement must physically abut each other; (C) the easement is transferred with the transfer of the dominant tenement; (D) the easement benefits the one tenement and burdens the other.

10. The grant of an unlocated easement in a transfer of real property is: (A) void for lack of certainty; (B) valid; (C) invalid because an easement must be specifically located; (D) voidable because a deed cannot be used to create an easement.

11. Clyde purchased one of 40 lots in a subdivision and signed a contract which stated, "No owner of a lot in this subdivision shall put a 'for sale' sign on his lot until all of the lots owned by the subdivider are sold." If Clyde wants to sell his lot before the subdivider has sold all of his lots, he may: (A) not use a "for sale" sign because of the statement in the contract; (B) use a reasonably sized "for sale" sign because the statement in the contract is illegal; (C) use a "for sale" sign of any size if he pays a fee to the developer; (D) may be sent to jail for violation of the contract.

12. The method by which a local planning commission permits an inconsistency to the construction, systems, or standards within applicable building codes is best known as: (A) a variance; (B) an exemption; (C) a permit; (D) spot zoning.

13. John gave Mary a grant deed transferring title to Mary "upon condition that" the title would be forfeited and revert back to John if alcoholic beverages were ever consumed on the premises. The title held by Mary can be described as: (A) an estate in jeopardy; (B) a fee simple estate; (C) a less than freehold estate; (D) a fee simple defeasible.

14. When a condition in a deed will cause title to revert back to the grantor if certain acts occur in the future, the condition may be described as a: (A) condition precedent; (B) condition subsequent; (C) null condition; (D) none of the above.

15. In the usual percentage lease, rent is calculated as a percentage of: (A) the assets of the lessee's business; (B) the net sales of the lessee's business; (C) the gross sales of the lessee's business; (D) the net taxable income of the lessee's business.

16. When a lessee assigned his lease to someone else, the lessee: (A) is no longer obligated for the rent only; (B) is no longer obligated under the lease; (C) is no longer obligated for the maintenance fee; (D) may be obligated to pay the rent and maintenance.

17. When leasing an unfurnished apartment, a lessor may not take a security deposit exceeding: (A) $1000; (B) one month's rent; (C) two months' rent; (D) three months' rent.

18. Title to real property can be acquired by an individual by all of the following ways, **except**: (A) prescription; (B) patent; (C) intestate succession; (D) escheat.

19. The court action used to settle ownership issues related to ownership of a parcel of real property is called: (A) a partition action; (B) an interdiction; (C) a quiet title action; (D) a lis pendens.

20. How is title perfected by someone who has met the requirements to take property by adverse possession? (A) by a quiet title action in court; (B) by recording a writ of execution; (C) by prescription; (D) by paying the current year's property taxes.

21. The law which gives cities and counties control over the physical design of subdivisions is: (A) Subdivision Map Act; (B) Architecture Control Act; (C) the City and County Act; (D) Subdivided Lands Law.

22. The regulation of the housing and construction industries is accomplished by: (A) local building codes; (B) State Housing Act; (C) the Contractor's State License Law; (D) all of the above.

Chapter #1 Review Questions - Answers

1. Ans-C Appropriation describes when the government gives permission to a nonriparian owner to take water from another landowner or a public waterway. Pg 1-1

2. Ans-B Cost is not a factor which determines when something has become a fixture. Pg 1-2

3. Ans-C Vegetation is real property. Pg 1-2

4. Ans-D Water company stock runs with the land and does not require a separate contract. Pg 1-2

5. Ans-B Restrictions are non-money encumbrances. Liens are money encumbrances. Pg 1-3

6. Ans-C The trust deed has priority because it was recorded before the work began. Pg 1-3

7. Ans-B A subcontractor's mechanic's lien would take priority as of the date the entire project began. Pg 1-3

8. Ans-C When a project of improvement on real property has been completed and the owner has not filed a "notice of completion" claimants have 90 days to file mechanic's liens. Pg 1-4

9. Ans-B The dominant tenement and the servient tenement are not required to physically abut (touch) each other in an appurtenant easement. Pg 1-5

10. Ans-B The grant of an unlocated easement is valid. Pg 1-5

11. Ans-B The courts have held that a prohibition of "for sale" signs is unconstitutional. However, the signs must be a reasonable size. Pg-1-6

12. Ans-A The method by which a local planning commission permits an inconsistency to the construction, systems or standards within applicable building codes is called a variance. Pg 1-7

13. Ans-D When the deed contains a clause which may cause title to be lost if something happens, the ownership by the grantee may be defeated (fee simple defeasible). Pg 1-7

14. Ans-B When a condition in a deed will cause title to revert back to the grantor if certain acts occur in the future (subsequent to the transfer of title), the condition may be described as a condition subsequent. Pg 1-7

15. Ans-C A percentage lease is based on a percentage of the gross receipts of the tenant's business. Pg 1-8

16. Ans-D Assignment of a lease does not relieve the original tenant from possible liability under the lease. Pg 1-9

17. Ans-C Security deposits on residential property may not exceed two months' rent on unfurnished dwellings or three months' rent on furnished dwellings. Pg 1-10

18. Ans-D An individual can never acquire property by escheat. Escheat is when someone dies with no will and no heirs. The property goes to the State of California.   Pg 1-11

19. Ans-C The court action used to settle issues related to ownership of a parcel of real property is called a quiet title action.   Pg 1-12

20. Ans-A Title is perfected by someone who has met the requirements to take property by adverse possession by a quiet title action in court.   Pg 1-12

21. Ans-A The Subdivision Map Act is the law which gives cities and counties control over the physical design of subdivisions.   Pg 1-12

22. Ans-D The regulation of the housing and construction industries is accomplished by local building codes, the State Housing Act, and the Contractor's State License Law.   Pg 1-13

CHAPTER 2

TRANSFER OF PROPERTY
(Approximately 8% of Salesperson Exam)

I. **DEED** - the written instrument which, when properly **executed, delivered, and accepted,** conveys title to real property from one person (the grantor) to another person (the grantee). If a deed is recorded, it is recorded in the county where the property is located and **indexed by the names of the parties (grantor and grantee).**

   A. **Essentials of a Valid Deed**

   1. **Grantor Competent to Convey** (18, married, or veteran). A deed signed by a minor who is not emancipated is void.

   2. **Adequate Description of the Property.**

   3. **Grantee Capable of Receiving** (not a fictitious person).

   4. **Action Clause (Granting Clause)** - must say "grant," "transfer," or "convey."

   5. **Proper Description of the Parties.**

   6. **In Writing.**

   7. **Grantor's Signature (Executed)** - a deed is deemed by law to be executed when it is signed by the grantor. A deed may be signed by a witnessed "X."

   B. **Delivery and Acceptance** - necessary for the deed to be effective.

   1. **Intention - of the grantor** to pass title immediately must be present. A deed **cannot be delivered upon death.**

   2. **Acceptance** - grantee must accept the deed.

   3. **Possession - of the deed** by the grantee, **or recording, presumes a valid delivery and acceptance**, but such presumption is rebuttable in court.

Question #1   Deeds are indexed at the County Recorder's office by: (A) legal descriptions; (B) sales price; (C) names of grantor and grantee; (D) tax assessor parcel number.

Question #2   A valid deed may be: (A) assigned to another grantee; (B) foreclosed by the lender; (C) revoked at a later date by the grantor; (D) signed by an "X."

Question #3   A valid grant deed passes title when the deed is: (A) notarized; (B) signed; (C) delivered; (D) recorded.

Answers: #1-C; #2-D; #3-D

C. Acknowledging and Recording

1. **Acknowledgment** - declaration before a notary by a person (grantor) who has executed a document stating that he did in fact sign the document. A deed must be acknowledged to be recorded. Once acknowledged, a deed is accepted as "prima facie" evidence in court. It is not legally required to acknowledge or record a deed for a deed to be valid or transfer title.

Note: An **employee of a corporation who is a notary may notarize a deed** involving the corporation **as long as she does not have a personal interest** in the subject matter of the transaction.

2. **Recording** - very few documents must be recorded to be effective **(some documents which must be recorded include mechanic's liens, homestead exemptions, lis pendens, and abandonment of homestead).**
   a. **Notice** - can be actual or constructive.
      (1) **Actual Notice** - a person actually knows something (for example, you know someone has taken possession of a property).
      (2) **Constructive (Legal) Notice** - events which by law put people on notice regardless of whether they actually know of the events or not. Recording a document gives constructive notice. The act of taking possession of land, while holding an unrecorded deed, gives constructive notice.
   b. **Priority of Valid Deeds** - the first valid deed that is recorded determines the owner unless that person, prior to recording, had either actual or constructive notice of the rights of others. A deed signed, delivered and accepted, but not recorded, is valid between the parties but invalid as to subsequent recorded interests without notice.

D. Types of Deeds:

1. **Grant Deed** - **most commonly used deed**. It contains **two implied warranties:**
   a. The grantor has not conveyed title to any other person.
   b. The estate is free from undisclosed encumbrances. This is warranted by the grant deed and is not covered by title insurance.

Question #4 Which of the following is **not** essential to a valid deed? (A) the parties are competent to convey and capable of receiving title; (B) a granting clause; (C) the deed must be acknowledged; (D) the deed must be in writing.

Question #5 The recording of a deed gives what type of notice? (A) actual notice; (B) positive notice; (C) negative notice; (D) constructive notice.

Question #6 Adam sold his home to Tim, but negotiated a two year leaseback and remained in possession. Tim immediately placed the deed he received in a safe deposit box for safe keeping. Adam then sold this same home to Sally. Sally recorded the deed. Who owns the home? (A) Tim, because he received the first deed; (B) Sally, because she recorded her deed; (C) Adam, because he still has three more deeds ready to be sold; (D) Adam, because both sales were improper.

Answers: #4-C; #5-D; #6-B

2. **Quitclaim Deed** - contains no warranties. It is usually used to quiet title or to clear a cloud on title (for example, a vendee who has defaulted on a recorded land contract could record a quitclaim deed to clear title for the vendor). It merely conveys the rights of grantor, if any.

Notes:
1. In California the warranty deed has been replaced by the use of title insurance.
2. Trust deeds and reconveyance deeds are loan documents, not deeds.

II. TITLE VESTING - how property is owned, also called "tenancy."

Note: Tenancy is a mode or method of holding title to real property by a lessee or owner.

A. **Ownership in Severalty (individual ownership)** - ownership by one person, individual, or corporation; sole ownership.

B. **Concurrent Estates** - ownership by two or more persons. They hold title jointly and severally.

1. **Joint Tenancy** - created when two or more persons elect to take one title as joint tenants. **Four unities** are required for joint tenancy (**T - T I P**): **T**ime, **T**itle, **I**nterest, **P**ossession. A joint tenancy in real property can be legally created with the execution of a deed by a husband and wife who deed the property to themselves as joint tenants; existing joint tenants who deed the property to themselves, along with a new joint tenant; and/or existing tenants in common who deed the property to themselves as joint tenants.
   a. **Right of Survivorship** - the most important characteristic of joint tenancy. Joint tenants can do almost anything with their interest except will it. The surviving joint tenants receive the decedent's interest automatically. They are not liable to creditors of a deceased joint tenant who hold unforeclosed liens.
   b. A joint tenant may sell his/her share without consent of other joint tenants. The new owner usually becomes a tenant in common.
   c. Recording a lien against a joint tenant's interest does not sever that interest from the joint tenancy until the lien is foreclosed.

Question #7 Each of the following deeds will contain at least some implied covenants from the grantor, **except:** (A) grant deed; (B) warranty deed; (C) quitclaim deed; (D) gift deed.

Question #8 A brother and sister held title to an apartment building as joint tenants. Other than this building, their business and personal affairs were conducted separately. At the time of the brother's death, he was insolvent and owed creditors substantial unsecured amounts of money. Title to the apartment building would now be held by the sister: (A) subject to the processes of a probate sale; (B) subject to the claims of the unsecured creditors; (C) free and clear of the debts of her brother; (D) as tenant in common with the creditors of the deceased brother.

Question #9 Which of the following would **not** terminate a joint tenancy between two owners? (A) foreclosure on one of the joint tenant's interest; (B) the sale of one joint tenant's interest; (C) one of the joint tenants deeding his interest to a third party; (D) one joint tenant having a trust deed or mortgage recorded against his or her interest in the property.

Answers: #7-C; #8-C; #9-D

2. **Tenancy in Common** - two or more people may elect to take title as tenants in common.
   a. Each tenant in common has a right of possession and does not need to pay rent to the other owners. Tenancy in common requires only one unity - the unity of possession.
   b. Tenants in common may hold **unequal ownership interests.**
   c. **Tenants in common may will their interest.**
   d. One tenant in common cannot grant an easement.

3. **Community Property** - the basic rule of community property is that **each spouse owns 50%**. Community property is assumed when title says **husband and wife.** Community property is also assumed whenever a husband and wife buy property, unless they specifically take title as joint tenants or tenants in common.
   a. The purchase of real property encumbered with a loan by one spouse is voidable within one year by the nonconsenting spouse.
   b. Either spouse can lease community real property for one year or less or list it for sale. A **listing contract** (placing a home on the market) **signed by only one spouse is enforceable.**
   c. Signatures of both husband and wife are required on a contract to sell community real property (deposit receipt); one signature alone creates a cloud on the title. The contract to sell community real property signed by only one spouse would be voidable (unenforceable). However, if the sale is voided by the other spouse, the broker may sue for the commission.
   d. Either husband or wife may leave their 1/2 interest by will, unless the deed says "community property with the right of survivorship." When a married person dies intestate, the other spouse receives all interest in the community property by intestate succession – separate property goes 1/2 to the spouse and 1/2 to an only child, or 1/3 to the spouse and 2/3 divided equally among two or more children. **Separate property** is most commonly distributed according to the **Statute of Succession** (intestate succession).

   Note: The term "et al" in a deed means "and others."

Question #10 When a young couple decided to purchase their first home, they elected to take title as "John and Marsha Buyer, husband and wife." How did they take title? (A) sole ownership; (B) joint tenants; (C) tenants in common; (D) community property.

Question #11 John and Debbi, husband and wife, own a home as community property. If only one spouse signed a listing contract to sell the property, the listing is: (A) an enforceable contract; (B) an unenforceable contract; (C) an unbinding contract; (D) a violation of the Statute of Frauds.

Question #12 John and Martha, husband and wife, own a home as community property. If only one spouse signed the agreement to sell the property, the agreement is: (A) an illegal contract; (B) an unenforceable contract; (C) a binding contract; (D) a violation of the Statute of Frauds.

Answers: #10-D; #11-A; #12-B

III. TITLE INSURANCE

A. Title Policy - an insurance policy insuring that a policy holder (grantee) and his heirs have received **marketable title** (reasonably free from doubt in law). The title company searches the records of the **county recorder, county assessor, county clerk, and federal land office.**

B. Chain of Title - the **record of prior transfers** and encumbrances affecting the title of a parcel, usually searched by a title company employee. A recorded instrument that does not appear in the chain of title still gives constructive notice.

C. Cloud on Title - items effecting title, which may prevent transfer. (For example, if a woman bought a home prior to marriage, but sold it during marriage, signing her married name to the grant deed creates a cloud on title.)

D. Color of Title - that which appears to be good title but isn't.

E. Abstract of Title - **written summary** of the chain of title.

F. Title Plant - records of recorded documents maintained by title insurance companies.

Notes:
1. The **seller** of a home appears as the **trustor in a preliminary title report.**
2. The buyer who discovers a mechanic's lien in a preliminary title report will insist it be removed before close of escrow.
3. Title companies set their own fee schedules and costs of services provided to customers.

G. Types of Title Insurance Policies - title policies insure title as of the date of issuance of the title policy. Policies do not insure against events which occur after the policy is issued.

1. **Standard Coverage (CLTA) Policy - most commonly purchased policy**, it covers:
   a. Matters of record.
   b. Lack of capacity (such as damages resulting from a recorded deed signed by a grantor who was legally incompetent).
   c. Forgery.
   d. Defective delivery of a deed.

Question #13 On May 1, 2011, Dick offered to buy Bob's home. The offer was accepted and escrow opened. Bob purchased the home in 1991, using an FHA loan, on which he is currently making payments. A preliminary title report dated May 9, 2011, will: (A) include exactly the same information as a future CLTA policy of title insurance issued on the close of escrow; (B) show a deed of trust with Bob as the trustor; (C) obligate the title company for insurance in an amount equal to the purchase price; (D) show title vested in Dick.

Question #14 Which of the following items in a preliminary title report would the buyer insist be removed from title before the close of the escrow? (A) CC&R's; (B) quitclaim deed; (C) mechanic's lien; (D) property tax lien for the upcoming property tax year.

Question #15 Which of the following is correct concerning an ALTA title insurance policy? (A) it protects against a lessee who occupies the property after the date shown on the title insurance policy; (B) the protection is limited to conditions affecting title as of the date of the issuance of the title policy; (C) it protects against encroachments that occur after the date of issuance of the title policy; (D) it protects against easements created after the issuance of the title insurance policy.

Answers: #13-B; #14-C; #15-B

Note: The standard coverage title insurance policy does not include a site inspection or a survey. The title company does not check boundary lines when preparing a standard title insurance policy. It does not protect against unrecorded events, such as rights of parties in possession or encroachments.

2. **Extended Coverage Policy** - includes the protection of a survey and protects against most unrecorded events.

3. **American Land Title Association (ALTA) Policy - includes the protection of a survey** and **provides the lender** with extended coverage protection.

4. **Policy Exclusions** - no title insurance covers everything.
   a. Defects known to the buyer and the seller which are not disclosed to the title company.
   b. Acts by government (such as, zoning, eminent domain, etc.).

IV. **LAND DESCRIPTIONS** - **in California, three methods** are commonly used to create legal descriptions of real property. A sales agreement for rural property requires a legal description, because it usually has no street address.

   A. **Metes and Bounds** - is created by a survey. Metes and bounds merely describes boundaries, metes and bounds does not measure land. When a description reads, **"Beginning at a point...,"** it indicates a surveyor is using metes and bounds. A metes and bounds description starts at a fixed point of beginning and follows the boundaries of the land from one point to another until returning to the point of beginning. "Metes" are measures of length, and "bounds" are measures of boundaries.

Note: The use of monuments in a legal description of real property is usually considered to be less desirable because monuments may be moved or destroyed.

   B. **Recorded Tract Map or Lot and Block System** - a legal description can be created by reference to a recorded tract map.

Question #16 What type of title insurance policy covers everything? (A) ALTA; (B) extended; (C) standard; (D) no title insurance policy covers everything.

Question #17 A contract for the sale of rural property requires a: (A) rural P.O. Box number; (B) parcel number; (C) legal description; (D) amount of acreage.

Question #18 Reference to a monument in a legal description is usually considered to be less desirable because: (A) monuments are difficult to describe in writing; (B) monuments may be destroyed; (C) monuments may be hypothecated; (D) monuments are may not be mentioned in a recorded document.

Answers: #16-D; #17-C; #18-B

C. Township and Section Method (U.S. Government Rectangular Survey System) - used to describe very large pieces of land (desert land, ranch land and farms). The starting point for a township and section system of land description is the intersection of a line running east/west called a base line and a line running north/south called a meridian line.

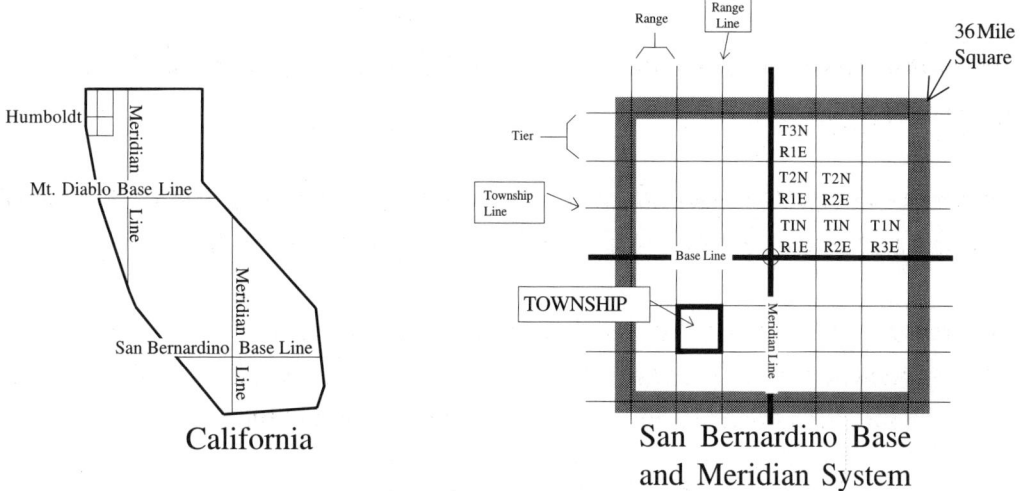

California

San Bernardino Base and Meridian System

1. **Townships** - all of California is divided into **six mile squares** (containing **36 square miles**) called townships. **A 36 mile square contains 36 townships.**

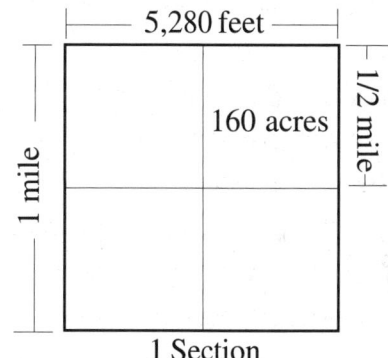

2. **Sections** - townships are divided into 36 one mile squares called sections.
   a. There are 18 sections (18 square miles) in 1/2 of a township.
   b. Each section is one mile square and contains one square mile.
   c. Each section contains 640 acres. **Remember**, a township made up of parcels of land containing 640 acres each would have a total of 36 parcels.
   d. A quarter section is 1/2 mile by 1/2 mile and contains 160 acres.
   e. An easement along one side of a section which covers an area of 3 acres would be approximately **25 feet wide**.

Question #19 How many square miles are there in 1/2 of a township? (A) 9; (B) 18; (C) 36; (D) 144.

Question #20 How long is each side of a 1/4 section? (A) 1/4 mile; (B) 1/2 mile; (C) 3/4 mile; (D) one mile.

Question #21 When an easement runs the full length of one side of a section and covers an area of 3 acres, approximately how wide is the easement? (A) 10 feet; (B) 20 feet; (C) 25 feet; (D) it is impossible to answer.

Answers: #19-B; #20-B; #21-C

V. ESCROW
the deposit of instruments and/or funds with a neutral third party who has been instructed to carry out the provisions of an agreement or contract. The **purpose of escrow** is to make sure that the **conditions of transfer are met** prior to closing.

- **A. Agent for Principals** - escrow officers act as agents for the principals. They are dual agents for both the buyer and the seller until the close of escrow. After the close of escrow, they may become the separate agent of either party.

- **B. Broker as Escrow** - a real estate broker can escrow a transaction and charge a fee for doing so only if he is an agent for a seller or a buyer in the transaction being escrowed. If a broker wants to handle escrows in which he is not acting as an agent in the transaction, the broker must be incorporated and licensed as an escrow company by the Department of Corporations. An incorporated broker's escrow activities are regulated by the Department of Corporations, instead of the Department of Real Estate.

- **C. Termite Reports** - The seller should order a **termite inspection before the property is listed for sale**. The broker must be certain that the buyer receives a copy of the structural pest control report as soon as practical before close of escrow. When a termite report recommends **preventative work**, the **buyer usually pays** for the work. If the escrow officer receives two termite reports, she should submit both reports to the buyer and the seller and let them decide which report to use.

- **D. Escrow Instructions**

    1. **Changes** - Escrow instructions can be changed by written mutual consent of both buyer and seller. They can change the terms of the financing or even cancel the escrow. These changes can be made without the broker's approval. An escrow officer may encourage the buyer and seller to alter escrow instructions which have already been approved by the parties.

    2. **Conflicts** - if escrow instructions contain terms in conflict with the original contract, the **escrow instructions will usually prevail.**

    3. **Recording** - escrow instructions are not usually notarized or recorded.

Question #22 When a trust deed is sold, the parties often use an escrow in order to: (A) obey the real estate code; (B) make sure that the terms and conditions are met prior to the closing of the transaction; (C) provide evidence as to the terms of the transaction; (D) provide recourse against the escrow company when there are disputes over the disposition of the deposit.

Question #23 A real estate broker may escrow a transaction: (A) if he or she is involved as an agent for the buyer or the seller in the transaction being escrowed; (B) whenever he or she is requested to do so by another broker; (C) under no circumstances unless he or she is acting as a principal; (D) only if he or she is incorporated and licensed by the Department of Corporations.

Question #24 Escrow may do which of the following? (A) act as a mediator when there is a dispute between the buyer and the seller; (B) change the selling price with the agreement of the buyer and seller; (C) change the terms of the financing with the consent of the seller; (D) decide when the escrow will close without the agreement of the buyer and seller.

Answers: #22-B; #23-A; #24-B

4. **Execution** - escrow instructions may be carried out (executed) by buyers, sellers, and/or third parties.

Note: In addition to escrow instructions, escrow can prepare simple standard documents necessary to complete the transaction, including a grant deed, but escrow cannot prepare complicated documents resulting from negotiation of the parties such as a wraparound trust deed or a lease with an option to buy. These complicated documents require a lawyer.

E. **Loan Funding** - escrow officers are usually authorized to call for the funding of the buyer's loan.

F. **Possession** - the buyer of a home will take possession of the property at the time agreed upon by the buyer and the seller. **Only the seller can give the buyer permission** to move in or make repairs to the property prior to the close of escrow. When a seller giving a buyer permission to move in before close of escrow, the real estate agent should have both buyer and seller sign an **interim occupancy agreement.** When the parties to an escrow enter into an interim occupancy agreement, their relationship in that agreement is as landlord and tenant.

G. **Income Tax - escrow is responsible for reporting the sale to the IRS.**

H. **Completion of Escrow** - all of the terms of the escrow instructions have been met.

I. **Interpleader Action** - escrow should **not act as a mediator** in a dispute between the buyer and seller. Escrow can file an **interpleader action** in court to settle an unresolved dispute between a buyer and a seller which prevented the closing of the escrow.

Notes: 1. If a broker is holding a deposit and there are conflicting instructions from the buyer and the seller concerning the deposit (prior to putting it into escrow), the broker can file an interpleader action.
2. The funds held by escrow may be released at any time by mutual consent of the parties or court order.

Question #25 Escrow can legally prepare which of the following? (A) a wraparound trust deed; (B) a lease with an option to buy; (C) escrow instructions and grant deed; (D) all of the above.

Question #26 In the purchase of a home, when would a buyer take possession of a property? (A) midnight of the day of closing of escrow; (B) morning of the day of closing of escrow; (C) at the time agreed upon by the buyer and the seller; (D) when the loan is funded.

Question #27 When the buyer of a home wants to move in before close of escrow, what should the broker do? (A) deny the buyer permission to move in; (B) grant the buyer permission to move in; (C) make the buyer sign a lease before granting buyer permission to move in; (D) prepare an interim occupancy agreement, and get the seller's consent before allowing the buyer to move in

Answers: #25-C; #26-C; #27-D

J. **Escrow Closing Statement (Final Accounting)**

1. **Purchase Price** - appears as a **debit on the buyer's closing statement.**

2. **Prepaid Taxes** - appear as a **credit on the seller's closing statement.**

3. **Interest on a Loan Assumed by a Buyer** - will appear as a debit on the seller's closing statement and a credit on the buyer's closing statement.

Note: Interest on a loan assumed by the buyer **will not be a debit on the buyer's closing statement.**

4. **Recurring Costs** - mentioned in the closing statement include **impounds.**

5. **Different Numbers** - the debits and credits on a seller's closing statement and the buyer's closing statement are usually different since each party pays for different expenses; it is also possible that they can be the same.

K. **Proration** - escrow usually prorates expenses like taxes, insurance, interest on an assumed loan, and rent, at the close of escrow. Most proration problems can be answered in **two steps:**

1. **Step 1** - Establish who is going to pay.

2. **Step 2** - Calculate the money using a **30-day month** and a **360-day year** (banker's year).

Note: Title insurance fees are non-recurring fees and are **not prorated** in escrow.

L. **Insurance** - When one party agrees to indemnify another for a named loss in return for periodic payments, it is called insurance. A property owner who carries the proper amount of fire insurance coverage should **neither gain nor lose** in the event of a claim.

M. **Short Rate Refund** - when a home is sold and the fire insurance is cancelled, the seller receives a short rate refund which is less than received by proration. The fire insurance policy is said to be "short rated."

Question #28 Which of the following items would **not** normally be listed as a debit on a buyer's closing statement? (A) discount points on a new FHA loan; (B) homeowner's insurance premiums; (C) prorations for property taxes; (D) interest on a loan assumed by the buyer.

Question #29 The seller of a home has paid the annual property taxes of $1,380; escrow will close on May 1. If the buyer and seller agree to prorate the property taxes as of the sale date, the buyer's portion of the taxes would be most nearly: (A) $115; (B) $230; (C) $345; (D) $1,380.

Question #30 When one party agrees to indemnify another for a named loss in return for periodic payments, it is called: (A) insurance; (B) a fidelity bond; (C) performance agreement; (D) none of the above.

Answers: #28-D; #29-B; #30-A

VI. TAX ASPECTS

A. **Documentary Transfer Tax** - is collected when a deed is recorded.

   1. **Consideration** - the tax is based on consideration (selling price minus any existing loans assumed by the buyer). Consideration is the **new money** created in the transaction. An existing loan being assumed by the buyer is old money; it was already taxed.

   2. **Tax Rate** - the tax rate is 55 cents for each $500 of consideration or fraction thereof.

B. **Property Tax** - an "ad valorem" tax (according to value). Real, tangible personal property is subject to taxation; intangible personal property is not.

   1. **County Tax Assessor** - assesses the value of all taxable property in the county every year. The annual assessments are published in the assessment roll. The purpose of the assessment roll is to establish the tax base. Property is assessed at 100% of taxable value (100% of fair market value or 100% of full cash value).

   2. **County Board of Supervisors** - sets **the tax rate which is limited by Proposition 13 to 1% of the purchase price** (assessed value taxable value, full cash value, fair market value), plus an amount to cover existing bond debt.

   3. **County Tax Assessor** - calculates the amount of tax each property owner must pay. The Tax Collector then prepares the tax bill. The tax bill assesses land and improvements separately, but they are taxed at one tax rate.

   4. **Assessment Appeals Board** - hears appeals from property owners who believe they have been over-assessed.

Question #31   A home sold for $210,000. The buyer agreed to a total down payment of $50,000. A new loan from the bank for $130,000. The seller agreed to take back a purchase money second trust deed for the balance of the purchase price. If the Documentary Transfer Tax rate is $.55 per $500 of consideration or fraction thereof, what would be the total Documentary Transfer Tax? (A) $55; (B) $198; (C) $231; (D) $462.

Question #32   For property taxes, the tax assessment roll, showing the assessed value of property in a county, is used to: (A) determine the proportionate share paid by each property owner; (B) establish the property tax rate; (C) establish the tax base for the county; (D) equalize the taxes paid by the property owners in that county.

Question #33   If a property owner believes that the assessed value on his property has been set too high, the owner may file an appeal with the: (A) County Board of Supervisors; (B) Assessment Appeals Board; (C) Tax Collector; (D) State Board of Equalization.

Answers: #31-C; #32-C; #33-A

5. **Property Tax Calendar**

```
                  No      Darn     Fooling   Around
   JAN. 1  JULY 1  Nov. 1  Dec. 10  Feb. 1   Apr. 10   JUNE 30
   |-------|-------|-------|--------|--------|---------|
   Lien    Start   1st.    Delinquent 2nd.   Delinquent Starts 5 yr. period
   Date            Due                Due
```

   a. **Property Tax (Fiscal Year)** - July 1 through June 30, or July 1 to July 1.
   b. **January 1** - lien date (precedes tax year).
   c. **November 1** - first installment due, **December 10** - first installment delinquent.
   d. **February 1** - second installment due, **April 10** - second installment delinquent.
   e. **June 30** - starts the running of the **five year redemption period**. If property taxes are not paid, the property is sold to the state. However, the owner remains in possession of the property and can redeem it during the next five years by paying all back taxes (plus interest and penalties).

6. **General Information**
   a. **Property is reassessed when it is sold** which results in a supplemental tax bill. For example, if a home was sold and the escrow closed on October 1, the seller would pay the first three months of the property tax year (July, August, and September) by proration in escrow. The buyer pays for the remainder of the tax year plus supplemental taxes based on the reassessment that was triggered by the sale.
   b. **Property Tax Bill** - does not contain a legal description, instead it uses an assessor's parcel number.
   c. **Homeowner's Exemption** - of the first $7,000 of assessed value applies to each residential property that is owner occupied.
   d. **Senior Citizens** - should contact the **State Controller's Office** for information about a program to defer payment of property taxes.

Note: Recording a "declaration of homestead" has no impact on property taxes.

Question #34 The due date and delinquent date of the second installment of real property taxes in California, are respectively: (A) November 1 and December 10; (B) July 1 and November 1; (C) February 1 and April 10; (D) January 1 and March 10.

Question #35 Which of the following are property tax exemptions stated in the California law? (A) single family residence; (B) occupied single family residence; (C) owner occupied single family residence; (D) any of the above.

Question #36 Which of the following would have the least impact on property taxes? (A) new development; (B) compacted population density; (C) tax deferment; (D) a recorded homestead.

2-12   ©2013 John Henderson

Answers: #34-C; #35-C; #36-D

C. Special Assessments - under the **Street Improvement Act of 1911,** cities, counties and even developers may use special assessments against property to pay for specific local improvements such as streets, walks, curbs, etc. Special assessments may be used to finance "off-site improvements," but may **not be used for financing the construction of homes or to buy land.**

1. **Priority - assessment liens have priority over all private liens** such as trust deeds or mechanic's liens.

2. **Local Improvements** - special assessments pay for specific local improvements, they do not go into the general fund to pay for the general support of government (as property taxes do).

3. **Escrow** - assessment liens (if any) are usually paid by the seller in escrow. Therefore, **assessments** for street improvements do **not appear as a lien** against the property at close of escrow.

D. Mello-Roos Act - provides for a wider variety of facilities and services than other improvement bond acts and has no requirement that such improvements will specifically benefit individual properties. The seller of one-to-four dwelling units subject to a Mello-Roos lien must make a good faith effort to obtain a disclosure notice concerning the special tax and give the notice to a prospective buyer.

E. Federal Income Tax - taxation should be considered before property is bought or sold.

1. **Progressive Tax** - the federal income tax is a "progressive" tax. The higher your income, the higher percentage tax you pay.

2. **Marginal Tax Rate** - the tax rate applied to the next dollar earned.

Question #37 Special assessments levied under the Street Improvement Act of 1911 may be used for any of the following purposes **except;** (A) new drainage and sewer systems; (B) to purchase vacant land; (C) build off-site local improvements; (D) improve street lighting.

Question #38 The difference between property taxes and special assessments is that: (A) assessment liens are always subordinate to property tax liens; (B) assessment liens can only be levied by local improvement districts; (C) foreclosure of assessment liens can only be achieved by court foreclosure; (D) special assessments are levied for the cost of specific local improvements, while property tax revenue goes into the general fund.

Question #39 The marginal tax rate: (A) is the total income tax a person must pay; (B) is the minimum income tax rate a person must pay; (C) determines the tax rate applied to the next dollar earned; (D) none of the above.

Answers: #37-B; #38-D; #39-C

3. **Cost Basis** (also called "basis" and "unadjusted basis") - the purchase price. The cost of building a wall is a capital improvement. The cost of a capital improvement cannot be deducted as an expense. A capital improvement is added to the cost basis of the property when calculating the adjusted cost basis.

Notes:
1. The term **"tax shelter"** refers to income taxes. A "tax shelter" is an investment; such as real estate which for income tax purposes allows an investor to defer payment of taxes on current income to a later year.
2. Benefits of the ownership of real estate under the Federal Income Tax law include depreciation, 1031 tax deferred exchanges, and installment sales.
3. The gain on the sale of real property owned by a **corporation** may be subject to **double taxation,** unless it is an "S corporation." An S corporation (subchapter S corporation) is exempt from corporate income taxes. All gains and losses pass directly to the individual shareholders.

4. **Personal Residence** - a taxpayer's principal residence.
   a. **Allowable Expenses** - property taxes, interest payments, and some uninsured casualty losses may be deducted as an expense. The owner of a unit in a condominium can deduct interest on a debt against the common areas of the condominium. A prepayment penalty can be deducted as an interest expense. No depreciation or maintenance expenses are allowed.
   b. **Losses** - losses cannot be used as deductions.

5. **Income Property** - property which produces income for the owner.
   a. An owner of income property **may deduct** interest, depreciation, taxes, insurance, management, maintenance and utilities on his income tax return, but not **vacancy losses**. Prepaid rent is taxable in the year received by the property owner.
   b. **Loss On Sale** of income property, **including residential income property,** may be deducted from other income subject to certain limitations.

Question #40 Mr. Smith purchased an apartment building for $180,000. The listed price was $200,000. Mr. Smith considered this a good deal on his part, since he only put $18,000 down and acquired a new first trust deed for the difference. The tax assessed value was indicated at $130,000. Mr. Smith's cost basis for income tax purposes would be: (A) $18,000; (B) $130,000; (C) $180,000; (D) $200,000

Question #41 The term "tax shelter" refers to: (A) mortgage relief; (B) real property taxes; (C) interest income; (D) income taxes.

Question #42 A homeowner sold his personal residence and took a $30,000 loss on the sale. For federal income tax purposes: (A) he may not deduct the loss on the sale of his personal residence from his income tax; (B) 40% of the loss is tax deductible; (C) he can deduct the $30,000 capital loss from any capital gain received during the tax year; (D) $10,000 of the loss is tax deductible.

Answers: #40-C; #41-D; #42-A

---

    c. **Depreciation** - allowed on improved income, trade, or business property. It is based on the cost of improvements (buildings). A disadvantage of taking depreciation is that every dollar taken as depreciation gets subtracted from the cost basis and is therefore recaptured as gain when the property is sold. **Land never depreciates.**

       (1) Minimum Depreciation Periods - residential income real property (apartment buildings) can be depreciated over a minimum of **27.5 years.** Nonresidential income property (commercial buildings) can be depreciated over a minimum of **39 years**.

       (2) Straight Line Depreciation (under current tax law) - calculated by dividing the value of improvements by the depreciable life (27.5 or 39 years).

       (3) Adding a capital improvement to income property increases the annual depreciation.

6. **Tax Deferred Exchange (1031 Exchange)** - when property is exchanged the taxes may be deferred. The properties exchanged must be "like for like" properties. They may be any combination of income, trade or business, or investment properties.

    a. When the values of properties are not equal, the **party "trading up" will defer the tax.** The **party "trading down" may have tax liability.** One party may defer the tax, while the other party does not.

    b. **Boot** - cash, other "unlike" property, or "**debt relief**" used to balance the equities of the properties for income tax purposes.

    c. **Actual Gain (Profit)** - determined by subtracting the adjusted cost basis from the exchange value of the property.

    d. **Taxable (Recognized) Gain** - is the smaller of the actual gain or the boot. Taxable gain is taxed in the year of the exchange. The receiver of boot will have a recognized gain.

Question #43 Which of the following is true regarding the depreciation of land under federal income tax law? (A) land may be depreciated by the 125% declining balance method; (B) an owner may deduct the accrued depreciation of land over time; (C) land may be depreciated by the sum of the year digits method; (D) land cannot be depreciated under federal income tax law.

Question #44 Tom recently bought a commercial office building. What is the minimum period of time in which he may depreciate the building for federal income tax purposes? (A) 27.5 yrs; (B) 39 yrs; (C) 40 yrs; (D) 50 yrs.

Question #45 Albertson owns a large apartment complex that he wants to exchange for another property so he will be able to defer paying income taxes in the year of the exchange. He should exchange his apartment complex for: (A) a personal residence with a loan on it equal to or greater than the mortgage on his apartment complex; (B) a less valuable apartment complex and assume a smaller loan than the mortgage on his current apartment complex; (C) a more valuable apartment complex, assuming a larger loan and paying cash boot to balance the equities; (D) a less valuable apartment complex, receiving money from the other party to compensate for any difference in equities.

Answers: #43-D; #44-B; #45-C

7. **Sale-Leaseback** - in a sale-leaseback, the seller (holder of a freehold estate) becomes a tenant (holder of a less-than-freehold estate). This allows the seller to deduct all future rent payments as a business expense. (For example, if the owner of a grocery store sold the land and improvements to an investor and leased it back, he would be able to deduct 100% of his rent payments as a business expense.)
    a. In a sale-leaseback, the seller retains possession of the property, receives an infusion of cash, becomes a tenant, but **does not** guarantee the mortgage payments.
    b. The buyer of a commercial building in a sale-leaseback transaction would be **least concerned with the seller's depreciated book value of the improvements**. The depreciation schedule for the improvements starts whenever the property is sold.

Question #46 The buyer of a commercial building in a sale-leaseback transaction would be **least** concerned with: (A) access to transportation for the property; (B) zoning of the property; (C) physical condition of the improvements; (D) the seller's depreciated book value of the improvements.

Answer: *#46-D*

Chapter #2 Review Questions

This exam contains 25 questions. You have an average of 78 seconds per question on the Salesperson Exam. 25 questions x 78 seconds per question = 1950 seconds. Please give yourself 32 minutes to complete this practice exam, and take the exam in one sitting.

1. A grant deed has been executed once it has been: (A) signed by the grantor; (B) delivered to escrow; (C) recorded; (D) delivered to the grantee.

2. Mr. Johnson executed a grant deed to Mr. Green and recorded it. Later, Mr. Johnson changed his mind and sought to set the conveyance aside, claiming that there had been no delivery to Mr. Green. Why was Mr. Johnson unsuccessful in his effort? (A) he was unsuccessful only if Mr. Green can prove he also took possession of the property; (B) delivery and acceptance is presumed with recording; (C) the recording validates the deed; (D) recording establishes the priority of lien.

3. Why are warranty deeds are rarely used in California, but commonly used in other states? (A) the buyer may recover double damages when a grant deed is used; (B) warranty deeds are illegal in California; (C) recourse against a title company works better than trying to collect from the grantor; (D) the law favors the use of the grant deed because the express covenants run with the land, while covenants of the warranty deed are personal to one particular buyer.

4. Who signs a quitclaim deed? (A) the property owner; (B) the occupant; (C) the seller; (D) the grantor.

5. Martha and David, single people, owned a home as joint tenants. Martha borrowed $10,000 to pay medical bills without the knowledge or consent of David. She secured the loan by recording a trust deed against the home. Shortly thereafter, Martha died, with the debt still unpaid. Which of the following best describes the subsequent title vesting? (A) David and the lender would become tenants in common, each owning a one-half interest in the property; (B) David would own all of the property free and clear of the trust deed; (C) David would receive ownership in severalty, but would still be liable to the lender for the $10,000 trust deed; (D) David and the lender would own the property as joint tenants, each with a one-half interest.

6. Concurrent ownership of real property by two or more parties, each of whom has an undivided interest (not necessarily equal) without right of survivorship, would be described as: (A) community property; (B) joint tenancy; (C) tenancy in common; (D) ownership in severalty.

7. Which of the following is the most commonly distributed according to the Statute of Succession? (A) community property; (B) joint tenancy; (C) tenancy in common; (D) separate property.

8. An uncle bought a home two years ago and purchased a standard title insurance policy. The uncle died and willed the home to his nephew. During probate it was discovered there was a defect in the title to the home because the grantor who sold the home to the uncle had been legally incompetent at the time of the sale. The title company denied any liability under the title policy. The probable outcome of the lawsuit will be: (A) the title company was liable because its obligation under the policy is not terminated by the death of the uncle; (B) the title company was not liable because the standard title insurance policy does not cover damage resulting from an incompetent grantor; (C) the title company was liable if the nephew filed his lawsuit within one year of the uncle's death; (D) title company was not liable because the death of the policy holder terminated the obligation to defend the title.

9. The ALTA policy of title insurance (insuring the lender) goes beyond the protection afforded to the grantee by a CLTA policy in that the ALTA policy also insures against damages caused by:
(A) existing liens and encumbrances as disclosed in public records; (B) the location of property lines according to a formal survey; (C) a reconveyance deed issued by a minor; (D) an error in the sequence of recording trust deed loans.

10. Which of the following is incorrect in regards to a "metes and bounds" description? (A) using a watercourse as a boundary; (B) metes and bounds is a method used to legally describe land, not measure it; (C) using a boulder as a boundary; (D) "metes" are boundaries and "bounds" are measurements.

11. A 36 mile square contains how many townships? (A) 1 township; (B) 6 townships; (C) 18 townships; (D) 36 townships.

12. How long is each side of a square parcel of land containing 160 acres? (A) 1/4 mile; (B) 1/2 mile; (C) 1 mile; (D) 6 miles.

13. In the typical escrow, once all the conditions of the escrow have been satisfied, the escrow officer becomes: (A) an advisor to both the buyer and the seller; (B) an advocate for the best interests of both principals; (C) a separate agent for each party, whereas during the escrow, the escrow officer was a dual agent for both parties; (D) none of the above.

14. A real estate broker placed a deposit received with an offer to purchase property in his trust account. After the seller accepted the offer, but before escrow was opened, the buyer informed the broker that she had terminated the contract and demanded the return of her deposit. The broker, unsure of what was the proper course of action, turned the deposit over to the court. This would be an example of: (A) a surrender action; (B) an interpleader action; (C) an equitable assignment; (D) an estoppel disposition.

15. When examining a properly prepared escrow closing statement, a broker would discover that the purchase price would appear as: (A) a debit to the buyer; (B) a debit to the seller; (C) a credit to the seller and to the buyer; (D) a credit to the buyer.

16. A property owner who carries the proper amount of fire insurance coverage will be indemnified in the event of loss. In such a case, the insured: (A) might gain, but definitely will not lose money; (B) should neither gain nor lose; (C) might lose, but certainly will not gain; (D) should gain or lose a little.

17. A home sold for $90,750. The buyer assumed an existing $30,000 trust deed and paid cash for the balance of the purchase price. If the documentary transfer tax rate is $.55 per $500 of consideration, what was the documentary transfer tax? (A) $33.00; (B) $66.83; (C) $67.10; (D) $100.10.

18. For property tax purposes, when is property normally reassessed? (A) whenever the property is sold; (B) only when the building is remodeled; (C) every year; (D) every three years.

19. Senior citizens may be able to defer the payment of the property taxes on their residence. In order to find out if they qualify for the program, the senior citizen should contact the: (A) Real Estate Commissioner; (B) State Controller; (C) State Housing Authority; (D) County tax assessor.

20. A young couple purchased a home for $200,000. Shortly after moving in they discovered they had a problem. Their dog kept running away because the backyard was not enclosed. "Dog gone!" they exclaimed. They built a wall at a cost of $5,000. For federal income tax purposes: (A) they have a $5,000 deduction that year from their reported income; (B) the $5,000 expense of building the wall has no impact on federal income taxes; (C) the $5,000 cost of the wall is subtracted from their cost basis in the home; (D) the $5,000 cost of the wall is added to their cost basis in the home.

21. Who is responsible for the disclosure of Mello Roos bonds against the property? (A) seller; (B) seller's agent; (C) buyer's agent; (D) both buyer's and seller's agents.

22. A benefit of ownership of real estate under the Federal Income Tax law is: (A) depreciation; (B) 1031 tax deferred exchange; (C) installment sale; (D) all of the above.

23. Debbi recently bought a 10 unit apartment building. What is the minimum period of time in which she may depreciate the building for federal income tax purposes? (A) 27.5 yrs; (B) 39 yrs; (C) 40 yrs; (D) 50 yrs.

24. Laura currently has a freehold estate, which of the following would result in her having a less-than-freehold estate? (A) leasing her property to a tenant for 5 years; (B) selling the mineral rights to a third party; (C) a sale-leaseback; (D) granting her father a life estate.

25. In a sale-leaseback transaction, the seller does all of the following **except**: (A) retains possession of the property being sold; (B) guarantees the mortgage payments; (C) receives an infusion of cash; (D) becomes a tenant.

Chapter #2 Review Questions - Answers

1. Ans-A A grant deed has been executed once it has been signed by the grantor.   Pg. 2-1

2. Ans-B Delivery and acceptance of a deed is presumed with recording.   Pg 2-1

3. Ans-C A problem with a warranty deed results in a claim against a seller who may lack the ability to pay. A claim against a title insurance company to enforce a title policy is far more likely to be enforceable.   Pg 2-3

4. Ans-D Anyone who signs a deed can be called a grantor.   Pg 2-3

5. Ans-B The death of a joint tenant who secured a loan with a trust deed, terminates the lender's lien against the property, unless the other joint tenant(s) co-signed on the loan.   Pg 2-3

6. Ans-C Concurrent ownership of real property by two or more parties, each of whom has an undivided interest (not necessarily equal) without right of survivorship, is described as tenancy in common.   Pg 2-4

7. Ans-D Separate property is the most commonly distributed according to the Statute of Succession.   Pg 2-4

8. Ans-A A title insurance policy insures title as of the date or transfer of title. The death of the policy holder (buyer) does not terminate the title insurance company's obligation to insure marketable title was present at the time of the transfer.   Pg 2-5

9. Ans-B An ALTA policy protects against damages resulting from encroachments over the property lines disclosed in a survey, a CLTA policy does not.   Pg 2-6

10. Ans-D "Metes" are measures of length, and "bounds" are measures of boundaries.   Pg 2-6

11. Ans-D A 36 mile square measures 36 miles by 36 miles and contains 36 townships.   Pg 2-7

12. Ans-B A square parcel of land containing 160 acres is one quarter of a section and measures 1/2 mile by 1/2 mile.   Pg 2-7

13. Ans-C Once all the conditions of escrow have been satisfied, the escrow officer becomes a separate agent for each party, whereas during the escrow, the escrow officer was a dual agent for both parties.   Pg 2-8

14. Ans-B When a broker or escrow is holding a client's money and the clients get into a dispute over the money, it is appropriate for the broker or escrow to file an interpleader action in court. The interpleader action asks the court to decide the dispute between the parties to a contract.   Pg 2-9

15. Ans-A The purchase price is a debit to the buyer on the closing statement.   Pg 2-10

16. Ans-B A property owner who carries the proper amount of fire insurance coverage will be indemnified in the event of loss and should neither gain nor lose.   Pg 2-10

17. Ans-C (1) The consideration is the selling price minus existing loans assumed by the buyer.
    (2) $90,750 divided by $500 = 121.5 taxable units;
    (3) The tax rate is $.55 for each $500 of consideration, plus $.55 for any fraction of $500. Therefore, 121.5 taxable units will be taxed at 122 taxable units.
    (4) 122 x $.55 = $67.10   Pg 2-111

18. Ans-A For property tax purposes, property is normally reassessed whenever the property is sold.   Pg 2-12

19. Ans-B A senior citizen who wishes to defer payment of property taxes must contact the State Controller.   Pg 2-12

20. Ans-D For federal income tax purposes, the $5,000 cost of the wall is added to their cost basis in the home as a capital improvement.   Pg 2-14

21. Ans-A The seller of one-to-four dwelling units subject to a Mello-Roos lien must make a good faith effort to obtain a disclosure notice concerning the special tax and give the notice to a prospective buyer.   Pg 2-13

22. Ans-D Benefits of the ownership of real estate under the Federal Income Tax law include depreciation, 1031 tax deferred exchanges, and installment sales.   Pg 2-14

23. Ans-A An improvement used for residential income property may be depreciated over a minimum of 27.5 years.   Pg 2-15

24. Ans-C In a sale-leaseback the owner sells the property to an investor. The investor then leases the property back to the prior owner. The prior owner stays in possession and becomes a tenant, holding a less-than-freehold estate.   Pg 2-16

25. Ans-B In a sale-leaseback, the seller retains possession of the property, receives an infusion of cash, becomes a tenant, but does not guarantee the mortgage payments.   Pg 2-16

Chapter 3

FINANCING REAL ESTATE

(Approximately 9% of Salesperson Exam)

I. **FINANCE DOCUMENTS** - a loan secured by real property usually consists of a promissory note and a trust deed.

  A. **Promissory Note** - a **negotiable instrument** which serves as the **evidence of the debt**. It is also called a "debt repayment" contract.

  *Note: A **holder in due course** is an innocent party who purchases a negotiable instrument without knowledge of any defects.*

  1. **Straight Note (term note)** - no principal payments are made during the term of the note. The entire principal is paid at maturity. **Straight notes generally carry higher interest rates** than amortized installment notes.

  2. **Fully Amortized Installment Note** - calls for regular periodic payment of both principal and interest to completely repay the loan. **Amortization tables** are used to determine the monthly payment. **Amortization** can be described as the **liquidation** of a financial obligation, such as a loan. In an amortized loan, as the loan gets older, the amount of the monthly payment applied to payment of principal goes up and the **amount applied to payment of interest goes down**.

  3. **Partially Amortized Note (Balloon Note)** - a partially amortized loan allows a borrower to have lower monthly payments during the life of the loan and pay a balloon payment at the end of the term of the loan. A **balloon payment** is any payment which is significantly larger than the other payments.

  B. **Mortgages and Trust Deeds** are the instruments used to secure the promissory note. "Security interest" is a term designating the interest of a creditor in the property of a debtor. A mortgage or trust deed creates a security interest in a borrower's property. **Mortgages and trust deeds are not negotiable instruments,** they are security devices.

Question #1 A loan secured by real property usually consists of: (A) a financing statement and trust deed; (B) a promissory note and a trust deed; (C) FHA or VA insurance; (D) a security agreement and financing statement.

Question #2 Amortization tables are used to: (A) determine the interest rate on a loan; (B) compute the APR; (C) compute the monthly payment; (D) determine the term of the loan.

Question #3 The liquidation of a financial obligation on an installment basis is known as: (A) conveyancing; (B) acceleration; (C) amortization; (D) conversion.

<u>**Answers:**</u> *#1-B; #2-C; #3-C*

1. **Parties**
   a. **Mortgage**
      (1) **Mortgagor (Borrower)** - signs the promissory note and mortgage.
      (2) **Mortgagee (Lender)** - holds the promissory note and mortgage during the life of the loan.
   b. **Trust Deed (deed of trust)** - A trust deed does not create an estate in property.
      (1) **Trustor** (Borrower) - **signs the promissory note** and the trust deed. The trust deed gives the trustee the right to foreclose **(naked legal title)** by way of a trustee sale. The trustor retains the actual legal title.
      (2) **Beneficiary** (Lender) - lends the money and holds the **promissory note and trust deed**. The consent of the beneficiary should be obtained for consolidation agreements, boundary line changes, and deed restriction agreements, because all of these may seriously impact the value of the property securing the debt. When the debt is paid in full, the **beneficiary signs a "Request for Full Reconveyance"** and sends it to the trustee.
      (3) **Trustee** (Agent for Beneficiary) - chosen by the beneficiary. The trust deed passes the **power of sale from the trustor to the trustee** by way of a trustee's sale (non-judicial foreclosure). Upon receipt of the "Request for Full Reconveyance" from the beneficiary, the trustee signs and records the **"Reconveyance Deed"** to return the power of sale to the trustor and show the trust deed has been paid in full.

Notes: 1. *Trust deeds and mortgages get recorded to secure the debt.*
2. *Trust deeds and mortgages differ as to parties, title and rights of redemption.*
3. *The trust deed is merely incidental to the debt.*

2. **Default On A Mortgage - usually requires a court foreclosure (judicial foreclosure).** After a court foreclosure sale on a mortgage, the mortgagor (borrower) has the ability to redeem the property by payment of the loan in full (**right of redemption**) for as long as one year from the date the property was sold. The mortgagor retains possession of the property until the right of redemption expires.

3. **Default On A Trust Deed** - a beneficiary may elect to foreclose by a court foreclosure. More often, the beneficiary elects to have the trustee foreclose through a trustee sale (non-judicial foreclosure). **The trustee sale is the quickest, easiest and most expedient method;** it takes approximately **four months to complete**.

Question #4   All the following are considered an estate in real property, **except:** (A) reversion; (B) deed of trust; (C) fee simple; (D) leasehold.

Question #5   When using a trust deed to purchase a home, the buyer borrowing the money is called the trustor. The trustor: (A) receives a promissory note for the amount that is borrowed; (B) receives a less than freehold estate; (C) signs a promissory note; (D) holds the trust deed which is used as security for the loan.

Question #6   Who has the right of possession of the property during the redemption period following the court foreclosure sale on a mortgage? (A) the person who purchased the property at the court foreclosure sale; (B) the trustor; (C) the mortgagee; (D) the mortgagor.

Answers: #4-B; #5-C; #6-D

   a. The trustee first records a **Notice of Default**. The trustee must wait for at least **three months** after recording the notice of default before she can advertise the trustee sale. The trustee sale must then be advertised (published) at least once a week for three weeks.
   b. The trustor has the **right to reinstate** the loan (bring it current) at any time up until **five days** before the trustee sale.
   c. The **trustor has no right of redemption** after the trustee sale.
   d. **Deficiency Judgment** - possible only if there is a court foreclosure on a non-purchase money loan and the fair market value is less than the loan amount (this rarely occurs).

Notes:
1. A purchase-money loan is:
   a. Any seller financing.
   b. Any loan created to purchase 1-4 owner-occupied residential units.
2. Foreclosure can be defined as a legal procedure whereby property used as security for a debt is sold to satisfy the debt in the event of default.
3. A court foreclosure on a trust deed may give the trustor a right of redemption.
4. When a lender takes a **deed-in-lieu of foreclosure,** the **lender becomes the owner** and is required to assume the junior liens. The **junior liens** remain against the property.

4. **Senior Lien (Senior Loan)** - the first loan against the property.

5. **Junior Lien (Junior Loan)** - any loan which is not first (such as a second trust deed, third trust deed, etc.). A **borrower's equity** in the property is the most important concern to a lender making a junior loan. The beneficiary of a junior loan benefits from recording a **Request for Notice of Default** so that she will be quickly notified if the borrower defaults on a prior loan.

6. **Late Charge** - lenders may not impose a **late charge** until a payment is **more than ten days late.**

7. **Balloon Payment** - is a final payment in an installment note that is substantially larger than the prior payments. A lender must notify a borrower when a balloon payment is due; **not less than 90 nor more than 150 days** before the balloon payment is due.

8. **Conflict** - any conflict between the terms of the promissory note and the terms of the trust deed will be **controlled by the terms of the promissory note**.

Question #7   When a lender in a trust deed takes a deed-in-lieu of foreclosure, who becomes the owner of the property? (A) vendor; (B) trustor; (C) beneficiary; (D) trustee.

Question #8   Broker Jane sold a home. The seller carried back a second trust deed. Broker Jane recorded a "Request for Notice of Default." Who normally benefits from a "Request for Notice of Default?" (A) the beneficiary in the second trust deed; (B) the trustor; (C) the trustee; (D) the mortgagor.

Question #9   Lenders may not impose a late charge in a payment due on a promissory note secured by a trust deed until the payment is: (A) 5 days late; (B) more than 7 calendar days late; (C) 10 days late; (D) more than 10 days late.

Answers: #7-C; #8-A; #9-D

9. **Hard Money Loan** - is a loan where the borrower receives cash using a new note secured by a trust deed or mortgage. There are limits on the commissions a loan broker may charge when negotiating small hard money loans. Commissions are limited on first trust deeds or mortgages of less than $30,000 and junior loans of less than $20,000. Examples: The maximum commission a loan broker may charge to negotiate an $8,000 hard money first trust deed, due in two years is 5% ($400). The maximum commission a loan broker may charge to negotiate a $4,000 hard money second trust deed, due in 3 years is 15% ($600).

10. **Negative Amortization** - when monthly loan payments are insufficient to pay the interest on a loan. **This results in the loan balance going up.**

11. **Graduated Payment Adjustable Mortgage (GPAM)** - has partially deferred payments of principal and interest at the start of the loan term. A GPAM involves negative amortization in the early years of the loan. After the first three to five years, the principal and interest payments usually increase substantially to pay the loan off during the remainder of the term.

12. **Shared Appreciation Mortgage (SAM)** - gives a lender the right to an agreed percentage of the appreciation in the market value of the property in exchange for an initial below-market interest rate. These loans are most desirable when prices of **homes are steadily appreciating in value.**

13. **Fictitious Trust Deed** - is a recorded trust deed or mortgage containing details which may be incorporated by reference and apply to later loan documents.

C. **Land Contracts** - (real property sales contract, land sale contract, installment sale contract, agreement to convey, agreement for purchase and sale, contract of sale, conditional sales contract, real property conditional installment sales contract) - a written contract where the **seller (vendor) becomes the lender**, allowing the buyer (vendee) to owe him all or part of the purchase price. The **seller (vendor) retains legal title to the property until the buyer (vendee) has met the contract conditions (usually payment of the debt in full).** Land contracts are not negotiable instruments.

Question #10 The maximum commission a loan broker may charge to negotiate an $8,000 hard money first trust deed, due in 2 years is: (A) $200; (B) $400; (C) $800; (D) $1,000.

Question #11 The maximum commission a loan broker may charge to negotiate a $4,000 hard money second trust deed, due in 3 years is: (A) $200; (B) $400; (C) $600; (D) $800.

Question #12 A shared appreciation mortgage (SAM) is most beneficial when: (A) prices of homes are steadily appreciating; (B) there is a tight money market; (C) financing is readily available; (D) prices of homes are declining.

Answers: *#10-B; #11-C; #12-A*

1. **Security Device** - a land contract may be described as a **security device** whereby a **seller (vendor)** becomes the lender to a **buyer (vendee)**. The **vendee and vendor** relationship is like a **trustor and beneficiary.** When a vendor in a land contract receives payments from a vendee, the vendor must first use the money to make payments due on any loans against the property. A vendor in a land contract may not use a vendee's impound money for any purpose other than paying the impounds without the consent of the payor.

Note: The vendee may be called the "payor."

2. **Title** - the vendor retains legal title until the debt is paid. The vendee gets possession of the property and becomes **an equitable owner holding equitable title.**

3. **Prepayment -** a vendee may prepay a contract for four or less residential units.

4. **Cal-Vet -** land contracts are used in the California Veterans Farm and Home Purchase Plan (Cal-Vet) financing with the **Department of Veterans Affairs** as vendor.

5. **Recording** - a vendee may record a land contract at the county recorder's office to give others constructive notice of his interest. If a land contract has been recorded, a quiet title action would be brought by the vendor to clear the title when the vendee refused to quitclaim his interest back to the vendor.

6. **Grant Deed** - when compared to a land contract of sale, it may be different with respect to the interest conveyed to the buyer, the signatures of the parties, and/or the designation of purchase price.

II. SOURCES OF FINANCING

A. **Primary Mortgage Market** - where loans are originated. It is made up of institutional and non-institutional lenders.

1. **Institutional Lenders** - receive most of their deposits from "household savings" (savings of individual depositors). Institutional lenders are **insurance companies, savings and loans (savings banks), and commercial banks.**

Question #13 In a land contract the buyer (vendee) gets: (A) possession; (B) a freehold estate; (C) An estate in fee; (D) all of the above.

Question #14 When a buyer has recently purchased a home with a valid land sale contract, what type of title does the buyer have? (A) sole title; (B) equitable title; (C) pending title; (D) legal title.

Question #15 When a vendee is buying a home with a land sale contract, what should he do to protect his interests? (A) get a standard title insurance policy; (B) record the land sale contract at the county recorder's office; (C) get a certificate of title; (D) get a bill of sale.

Answers: #13-A; #14-B; #15-B

  a. **Insurance Companies**
     (1) Loan correspondents (mortgage bankers) usually negotiate and service their loans.
     (2) Usually do not make construction loans.
     (3) Prefer large long term loans on existing commercial property (for example, a developer wanting a long term **$3,000,000 loan to purchase** and rehabilitate an existing **shopping center** would borrow the money from an insurance company).
  b. **Savings Banks (Savings and Loan Associations)**
     (1) The main source for home loans (1 - 4 family units).
     (2) As a result of **deregulation**, savings and loans can pay **any amount of interest** on money deposited with them.
     (3) Savings Banks have the greatest percentage of their assets in real estate loans.
  c. **Commercial Banks**
     (1) Prefer **short term loans**; therefore commercial banks are a primary source of construction financing.
     (2) **Federal Reserve Board** - regulates banks and the national money supply by:
        (a) Adjusting the **discount rate**. Raising the discount rate tightens the money market.
        (b) Changing **minimum cash reserve** requirements.
        (c) Buying or selling existing **government bonds** through the **Federal Open Market Committee**. Selling bonds tightens the money supply.

Notes:
1. A decrease in real estate sales and an increase in the use of second trust deeds indicates a tight money market.
2. Interest rates on real estate loans are primarily determined by demand and supply of money.
3. When interest rates on bonds increase, the supply of funds for real estate loans decreases.
4. When compared to real estate investments, some investors prefer stocks and bonds because they have greater liquidity.

 2. **Non-institutional Lenders**
    a. **Private Lenders (sellers, private investors, etc.)** - the major source of junior loans.

Question #16 Which of the following types of lenders would have the greatest percentage of, and the most funds invested in, real estate loans? (A) life insurance companies; (B) commercial banks; (C) savings banks; (D) mutual savings banks.

Question #17 Should a tight money policy be implemented by the Federal Reserve Board, the net effect would be an increase in: (A) the use of new first trust deed financing in real estate transactions; (B) the use of second trust deed financing in real estate transactions; (C) the volume of sales of single-family homes; (D) the supply of lendable funds for housing construction.

Question #18 Which lender is a major source for junior loans negotiated today? (A) insurance companies; (B) commercial banks; (C) Federal Land Bank; (D) private lenders.

Answers: #16-C; #17-B; #18-D

- b. **Mortgage Companies (Mortgage Bankers, Mortgage Loan Correspondents)**
    (1) Mortgage Companies are licensed by the Department of Real Estate as real estate brokers and/or by the Department of Corporations as Residential Mortgage Lenders (RML) or California Finance Lenders (CFL). Mortgage bankers generally originate conventional (including "subprime") loans.
    (2) Often lend their own money.
    (3) Negotiate loans which are readily saleable in the secondary mortgage market.
    (4) **Warehousing** - collecting loans prior to sale. Warehousing involves putting together mortgage portfolios.

B. **Secondary Mortgage Market** - **resale marketplace for loans**, where existing loans are bought and sold. **Liquidity and marketability are important** in the secondary mortgage market. The participants in the secondary mortgage market have increased the amount of housing credit available to the economy. The major participants in the secondary mortgage market are:

1. **Federal National Mortgage Association (FNMA, Fannie Mae)** - was created for the purpose of increasing the amount of housing credit available to the economy. It is **concerned primarily** with the development of the secondary mortgage market for conventional, FHA, and VA loans originated in the primary mortgage market.

2. **Government National Mortgage Association (Ginnie Mae)** - a federal agency within the Department of Housing and Urban Development (HUD).

3. **Federal Home Loan Mortgage Corporation (Freddie Mac)** - works with Fannie Mae and Ginnie Mae to increase the availability of mortgage money and maintain the secondary market for residential mortgages.

Question #19 The term "warehousing," as it is used in real estate financing would probably refer to: (A) Securities registered with the Corporations Commissioner; (B) a mortgage banker collecting loans prior to resale; (C) large storage buildings used to secure some real estate loans; (D) none of the above.

Question #20 Certain lenders consider the liquidity and marketability of loans to be of paramount importance when they issue mortgages secured by real property. The importance of liquidity and marketability of loans most closely refers to the: (A) activities of the secondary mortgage market; (B) make up of security offered by the FDIC; (C) subsequent resale of the homes used to secure the mortgages; (D) desirability of short term real estate loans over long term real estate loans.

Question #21 The primary purpose behind the creation of the Federal National Mortgage Association (FNMA) was: (A) providing funds to large home builders in or near urbanized areas; (B) lending money on FHA Title II loans when conventional lenders are unwilling to do so; (C) to increase the amount of money available to finance housing; (D) supervising public lending associations.

©2013 John Henderson

Answers: _#19-B; #20-A; #21-C_

III. GENERAL CONCEPTS AND DEFINITIONS

A. **Mortgage Loan** - a loan secured (collateralized) by real estate.

B. **Mortgage Yield** - the interest a lender receives from a mortgage (not the principal). Mortgage yield can be described as the **lender's effective interest return** from a loan.

C. **Demand Sources for Mortgage Money** (borrowers) - include construction, sales financing, and refinancing. The Federal National Mortgage Association is a supply source, not a demand source for mortgage money.

D. **Interim Loan (short term)** - finances construction. The terms "interim loan" and "construction loan" are **synonymous** (mean the same thing).

   1. **Maturity Date on a Construction Loan** - computed from the **date of the note**.

   2. **Interest on a Construction Loan** - computed from the date the loan proceeds are placed in escrow.

E. **Take-Out Loan (long term)** - received by a buyer to pay for new construction. The proceeds are used by the builder to pay off the interim (construction) loan.

F. **Standby Commitment** - any time a lender agrees to provide a loan, at a set interest rate, at some future date.

G. **Variable Interest Rate Loan** - interest rate can increase or decrease depending on money market conditions.

H. **Beneficiary Statement** - statement by a lender disclosing the current loan balance.

I. **Impound Account** - a trust account established to hold funds for future needs relating to a parcel of real estate. The impound account benefits both the beneficiary (lender) and the trustor (borrower). **"Impound" means to hold, reserve, or impress.** The monthly payments on a first trust deed with impounds typically includes principal and interest, taxes and insurance, but **not homeowner association fees.** When a lender receives the money from the borrower, the lender puts the money to cover taxes, insurance, and sometimes special improvement assessments in the impound account. The portion of the payment to cover **principal and interest payments is not impounded.**

Question #22 The term used by lenders, "mortgage yield," refers to: (A) the total amount the lender receives when a mortgage is paid off; (B) the effective interest return obtained from a first trust deed; (C) all of the money received by a lender after deducting closing costs and loan fees; (D) an increase in the value of a property which has a mortgage.

Question #23 All of the following are demand sources for mortgage money, **except:** (A) construction; (B) refinancing; (C) Federal National Mortgage Association; (D) sales financing.

Question #24 Lenders may require a reserve or impound account for some loans. Included within those accounts are borrowers' funds which are held to assure payment for all of the following recurring items, **except**: (A) monthly mortgage interest payments; (B) insurance premiums; (C) property taxes; (D) special improvement assessments.

Answers: #22-B; #23-C; #24-A

J. **Borrower's Credit History** - an indicator of the risk inherent in the loan. The **degree of risk** is usually considered by lenders to be the **most important factor** when making the decision whether or not to make a home loan. Most lenders use FICO (Fair, Isaac and Company) scores to determine a borrower's ability to repay the loan. The higher the score, the lower the risk to the lender.

K. **Loan-to-Value Ratio (LTV)** - the **percentage of the appraised value which a lender will lend** on a property. If a lender requires an 80/20 LTV, the lender will lend 80% of the lender's appraised value and require a 20% cash down payment.

   1. **Down Payment** - the lower the loan-to-value ratio, the higher the down payment (buyer's equity).

   2. **Security** - the loan-to-value ratio provides the **most security to the lender of a junior loan.** The borrower's equity represents the lender's basic protection for the loan.

   3. **Financing Costs** - a long term loan with a low down payment and a high loan-to-value ratio results in an increase in the total financing cost.

L. **Discount Points (Points)** - a form of prepaid interest demanded by the lender when a loan is negotiated. Each discount point costs one percent of the face amount of the loan. Lenders commonly charge points to increase effective yields, close the gap between fixed interest rates and market rates, and help defray the costs of the loan. **Remember**, there are no points in a Cal-Vet loan.

M. **Discounting a Note** - selling a note for less than the face amount or the current balance. When an investor buys a loan at a discount and later forecloses, the **lender forecloses for the current loan balance**, not the discounted amount. (For example, an owner carries back a $125,000 loan and then sells it to an investor for $123,500. The buyer immediately defaults. The investor would foreclose by way of trustee sale for the full $125,000.)

N. **Equity** - defined as either the difference between the value and the loan, or the owner's share of the total property value, or the initial down payment. The cash provided by a buyer as a down payment may be described as **"equity funds."** Real estate investments are commonly funded by a combination of debt (loan) and equity funds (down payment).

Question #25 Loan-to-value ratio may be defined as: (A) mortgage loans as a percent of capitalization rate; (B) mortgage loans as a percent of interest; (C) mortgage loans as a percent of appraised value; (D) mortgage loans as a percent of assessed value.

Question #26 Elizabeth purchased a home with a low down payment and a long term loan. This financing would most likely result in: (A) increasing the total financing cost; (B) decreasing the total financing cost; (C) having no effect on the total financing cost; (D) accelerating the amortization of the debt.

Question #27 Real estate investments are commonly funded by combining: (A) debt and equity funds; (B) liquid and non-liquid investments; (C) the supply and demand of investment capital; (D) guaranteed returns and speculative investments.

Answers: #25-C; #26-A; #27-A

O. **Methods of Taking Over an Existing Loan**

   1. **Subject To** - when a buyer takes property subject to an existing loan, the lender keeps the seller on the loan as the borrower. The seller is liable for a deficiency (the benefit is to the buyer). **If foreclosed, the buyer's loss is limited to his equity.**

   2. **Assumption** - when a buyer **assumes** a loan, the buyer becomes primarily liable. The **seller is relieved from primary liability** and is held secondarily liable.

   3. **Substitution of Liability** - when a lender agrees to a **"substitution of liability,"** the seller is relieved from all liability on the loan.

P. **Joint and Several Liability** - when there is more than one borrower (obligor) on a promissory note, the lender will include the term **"jointly and severally."**

Q. **Interest Rates**

   1. **Simple Interest** - charged on an unpaid principal amount and used on most home loans. The interest is calculated by the formula: **Interest = Principal x Rate x Time (I = PRT).**

   2. **Nominal Rate** - the interest rate named in the loan document.

   3. **Annual Percentage Rate (APR)** - a standardized method of calculating the interest rate under the Federal Truth-In-Lending Law (see Truth-In-Lending Law later in this chapter).

   4. **Effective Rate** - interest rate that is actually paid by the borrower for the use of the money.

R. **Pledge - a borrower gives up possession** of the item securing the debt (for example, an existing loan is given as security for a new loan). **Pledge is the opposite of hypothecate.**

S. **Inflation** - caused when there is more money available than there are goods for sale. The trend of economic inflation **benefits the trustor.**

Question #28 When lending money to two or more joint tenants using a single promissory note, the lender would be best advised to increase the security on the note by inserting which of the following phrases after the names of the joint tenants? (A) personally and corporately; (B) together as individuals; (C) individually and severally; (D) jointly and severally.

Question #29 What is the formula for determining simple interest? (A) I = RT; (B) I = PRT; (C) I = V/R; (D) none of the above.

Question #30 Roberto, the holder of a $100,000 first trust deed note, wants to borrow $30,000 to build a house. If he gives up possession of the first trust deed note as security for the $30,000 loan, the arrangement would be regarded as: (A) a chattel mortgage; (B) an illegal security subordination; (C) a subordinated trust deed; (D) a pledge.

Answers: #28-D; #29-B; #30-D

1. **Purchasing Power** - **if housing prices rise 20%**, the purchasing power of the **housing dollar goes down 16-2/3%** (16-2/3% = 1/6).

2. **Excellent Inflation Hedges** - include equity assets, ownership of real estate and an income producing property that will maintain its value.

3. **Appreciation** - a **trustor benefits from appreciation** in value due to inflation. Appreciation also protects a lender who made a no down payment loan without government backing.

T. **Deflation** - caused when there are more goods available than money to purchase them. During deflation, the general level of prices decrease and the value of money increases.

U. **Debt-Income Ratio** - used by lenders as a **loan qualifying tool.** Lenders in the prime mortgage market generally prefer that not more than **25% to 28%** of a real estate loan applicant's **gross income be spent for housing**.

V. **Loan Origination Fee -** the costs related to the origination of a loan are often passed on to the borrower as a loan origination fee.

Notes:
1. ***Leverage** is using **borrowed money** (financing) to the maximum extent possible.*
2. *A **hidden cost of home ownership** is the **loss of interest** on the owner's equity.*
3. *A **seller's market** exists when prices rise and there are more buyers than sellers. When a market turns from a buyer's market to a **seller's market, prices rise** because there is a shortage of properties available for sale.*
4. ***Unemployment rates** do **not directly effect mortgages** and interest rates.*
5. *Changes in **consumerism, land use controls, and the real estate industry,** all affect real estate in future years.*
6. ***Business Cycles** - business goes through the four cycles: depression, recession, expansion, and prosperity.*

Question #31 Lenders use a "debt-income ratio" as a: (A) loan qualifying tool; (B) government loan ratio; (C) method used in appraising property; (D) method of setting escrow fees.

Question #32 A woman purchased an apartment building with a small down payment and obtained the maximum loan available to finance the balance of the purchase price. One year later the property had appreciated 2%, she then sold the property making 20% on her original investment. This is a good example of: (A) assemblage; (B) escalation; (C) deflation; (D) leverage.

Question #33 A change in which of the following would have an effect on real estate in future years? (A) consumerism; (B) land use controls; (C) real estate industry; (D) all of the above.

Answers: #31-A; #32-D; #33-D

IV. GOVERNMENT LOAN PROGRAMS

A. **Federal Housing Administration (FHA)** - was created by the National Housing Act to enable buyers to purchase homes with a **small down payment**. The **unique feature of FHA** financing is that **FHA insures lenders** against loss. The seller usually pays the FHA loan fee.

1. **Loan Application - the borrower** applies directly to the **lender (mortgagee)** and not to the FHA for the loan.

2. **Down Payment** - the **down payment on FHA loans varies** with the **amount of the loan.**

3. **Interest Rates** - are determined by **mutual agreement between borrower and lender.** The Federal Reserve Board does not have authority to change interest rates on government insured mortgages, such as FHA.

4. **Points** - are charged by most lenders in connection with FHA insured loans to close the gap between market rates and fixed rates, increase the effective yield, and to obtain the market yield on the FHA loans.

5. **Loan Clauses - no alienation clause or prepayment penalty** is allowed.

6. **Mortgage Insurance Premium (MIP)** - required for FHA loans. It protects the lender in the event of default by borrower. It is paid by the borrower, either as a lump sum or amortized.

Notes:
1. *Private Mortgage Insurance (PMI) - a private program similar to FHA Mortgage Insurance Premium (MIP). Borrowers may obtain mortgage insurance through FHA or PMI.*
2. *The usual ceiling height in a home purchased with FHA financing is 8 feet.*

Question #34   Which of the following is a unique characteristic of the FHA loan program? (A) it is easy to qualify for; (B) it has a low loan-to-value ratio; (C) it requires a low down payment; (D) FHA insures the lender against loss.

Question #35   Who usually pays the FHA loan fee? (A) the borrower; (B) the seller; (C) the lender; (D) the lender in the secondary mortgage market.

Question #36   In which of the following programs will a borrower pay for insurance on a loan? (A) FHA or PMI; (B) Fannie Mae, Ginnie Mae, and or Freddie Mac approved loans; (C) VA loans; (D) only FHA loans.

Answers: #34-D; #35-B; #36-A

B. Veterans Administration (VA) Loan Program - financing may not exceed the value established by the Certificate of Reasonable Value (CRV) government appraisal. The CRV determines the amount of the down payment. Some VA loans require no down payment. A buyer would most likely be able to borrow 100% of the purchase price with no down payment in a VA loan.

Notes:
1. *The maximum loan amount in both the FHA and VA loan programs varies in different regions of the nation. Unlike most conventional loans, there is no prepayment penalty clause in FHA and VA loans.*
2. *If a veteran sells his home to a non-veteran buyer "subject to" his existing VA loan, he is personally liable for any loss suffered by the VA in the event of default by the buyer.*

C. California Veterans Farm and Home Purchase Plan (Cal-Vet) - a Cal-Vet loan may also be called a **DVA** (Department of Veterans Affairs) loan.

1. **Payments** - a veteran applies and makes payments to the **Department of Veterans Affairs** which holds the title.

2. **Land Contracts** - the state (Cal-Vet) purchases homes and farms and receives a grant deed from the seller. Cal-Vet then sells them to California veterans using land contracts (real property sales contract, installment sales contract, agreement to convey, agreement for purchase and sale, or contract of sale).

3. **Discount Points** - Cal-Vet loans do not charge discount points.

4. **Owner Occupied** - a veteran or a member of his immediate family must occupy property purchased with a Cal-Vet loan. FHA will loan on rental property, but VA and Cal-Vet will not.

Question #37 Martha offers to purchase Peter's property for $239,000. Martha, who is not a veteran, takes title subject to Peter's VA loan. What is the effect on liability? (A) Martha is primarily liable for the loan; (B) Peter and Martha are both liable for the loan; (C) Peter is liable for the loan; (D) neither Martha nor Peter is liable for the loan.

Question #38 When a buyer initially purchases a home with Cal-Vet financing, the buyer receives: (A) a bill of sale; (B) a contract of sale; (C) a trust deed; (D) a lease with an option to buy.

Question #39 The FHA will allow, but VA and Cal Vet will not allow, which of the following loans? (A) a loan for the purpose of buying farm equipment; (B) a loan for the purchase of farm or agricultural land; (C) a business opportunity; (D) loan on a home which is to be rented out.

Answers: #37-C; #38-B; #39-D

V. LOAN CLAUSES

A. **Acceleration Clause** - any clause in a loan which requires the loan to be **paid off** upon the happening of a certain event. An alienation clause is one example of an acceleration clause.

B. **Alienation (Due on Sale) Clause** - an alienation clause in a loan requires the borrower to pay off the loan when title is transferred. Alienate means "to transfer or convey." The opposite of alienation is acquisition.

C. **Subordination Clause** - a lender agrees to give up priority to later loans. Priority of a loan will be determined by the time of recording, unless there is a subordination clause in the loan. The subordination clause allows future loans to have priority. A subordination clause **benefits the trustor (borrower)**.

D. **Open-End Loan Clause (revolving line of credit)** - allows a borrower to re-borrow principal previously repaid. An open-end provision in a mortgage is most beneficial to a borrower who needs to re-borrow money previously paid to the lender without rewriting the loan documents.

E. **Prepayment Penalty Clause** - allows borrowers to prepay loans only if they pay the lender extra money. A prepayment penalty is not allowed on a loan against a borrower's residence after the loan is **five years old.** A prepayment penalty benefits the lender (beneficiary). A trustor making advance payments on his loan might have to pay a prepayment penalty. A lender might waive a prepayment penalty in a tight money market when there is a lack of funds.

F. **"Or More" Clause** - permits a borrower to prepay without penalty.

G. **Blanket Encumbrance (Blanket Loan)** - using more than one piece of land to secure a debt. A "release clause" allows some of the land to be released upon partial payment of the debt. The beneficiary of a blanket trust deed signs a **request for partial reconveyance** when part of the debt is paid. The trustee then signs and records a **partial reconveyance deed.**

Question #40 The opposite of "alienation" is which of the following? (A) accretion; (B) acquisition; (C) ad valorem; (D) amortization.

Question #41 A subordination clause placed in a trust deed: (A) permits the obligation to be paid off ahead of schedule; (B) prohibits the trustor from making an additional loan against the property before the entire loan is paid off; (C) allows for periodic renegotiations and adjustment in the terms of the obligation; (D) gives priority to liens subsequently recorded against the property.

Question #42 A clause in a real estate loan which permits the borrower to re-borrow additional funds, at a future date is called: (A) an adjustable mortgage; (B) a junior mortgage; (C) an open-end mortgage; (D) an extendible mortgage.

Answers: #40-B; #41-D; #42-C

Notes:
1. When a builder paid to have several lots released from beneath a blanket encumbrance, his percentage of equity in the remaining encumbered lots increased.
2. A property tax lien cannot be a blanket encumbrance.

VI. FINANCING AND CREDIT LAWS

A. **Truth-In-Lending Law (Regulation Z, Reg. Z)** - part of the Federal Consumer Credit Protection Act, designed to protect the borrower.

1. **Purpose** - to assure a meaningful disclosure of credit terms by the lender. The lender must disclose to the borrower **the Annual Percentage Rate (APR), which is the relative cost of credit expressed in percentage terms.** This standardized method of calculating the interest rate allows borrowers to make an intelligent comparison between different loans.

2. **Application of the Law** - applies to all real estate loans that are **not** for business purposes.

*Note: **Agricultural loans** are **not regulated** by the Truth-In-Lending Law (Reg. Z).*

3. **Disclosure Statement** - provides the borrower with the following:
   a. Name of the lender
   b. Finance charge
   c. Annual Percentage Rate (APR)

Note: The finance charge does not include appraisal fees and credit report fees.

4. **Advertising** - must disclose the specifics of all credit terms (if any credit terms are mentioned). If an **interest rate** is mentioned, the ad must disclose the **APR**. The APR may be mentioned without additional disclosures.

Question #43   Mr. Carson bought 10 acres of vacant land for $20,000 per acre, making a down payment of $20,000, and executing a straight note and blanket trust deed for the balance. A provision of the note states that when Mr. Carson made a principal payment of $20,000, the trustee would issue a partial reconveyance for one acre. Mr. Carson has paid a total of $40,000 of the principal on the note and now owns two acres free and clear. The percentage of his equity in the encumbered property: (A) has been eliminated; (B) remains unchanged; (C) has increased; (D) has decreased.

Question #44   The purpose of the Truth-in-Lending Law is to: (A) prevent usurious charges for credit; (B) limit the borrower's credit cost; (C) assure a meaningful disclosure of credit terms; (D) establish a maximum APR.

Question #45   When a lender runs an ad in the newspaper using only the APR: (A) the nominal interest rate must also be stated; (B) the total loan balance must be disclosed; (C) no additional disclosures need be made; (D) if the loan is for less than $20,000, only the finance charge must be added.

Answers: #43-C; #44-C; #45-C

5. **Non-purchase Money Loans (refinance loans)** on the borrower's residence include the right to rescind or cancel. The borrower has the right to rescind a loan agreement until **midnight of the third business day after the promissory note is signed,** unless the loan was used to finance the purchase of the borrower's residence.

6. **Purchase Money Loans** - created to purchase the borrower's personal residence carry **no right to rescind.**

B. **Real Estate Settlement Procedures Act (RESPA)**

1. **Intent** - to provide borrowers with fast and reliable information on the costs of completing a real estate transaction. One of the main purposes of RESPA is to provide a prospective borrower with an opportunity to shop for settlement services.

2. **Loans Covered** - loans on **four or less residential units** made by lenders whose deposits are insured by an agency of the federal government.

3. **Lender Requirements Under RESPA**
   a. Deliver to the borrower the HUD "Settlement Costs" information booklet and a good faith estimate of costs within **three business days** after the loan application is received.
   b. The lender cannot charge the borrower for preparing the Uniform Settlement Statement, which must be given to the borrower at or before settlement (close of escrow).

4. **Referral Fees (kickbacks)** - paid by those who provide settlement services are prohibited. All unearned fees are prohibited.

Question #46 The Truth-in-Lending Law allows borrowers a limited right of rescission for non-purchase money loans. The time which is allowed for rescission begins when the: (A) credit application is submitted to the lender; (B) lender gives loan approval; (C) loan is funded by the lender; (D) loan documents are signed by the borrower.

Question #47 To comply with RESPA, a lender must furnish a prospective borrower with an information booklet prepared by HUD no later than the third business day from which of the following dates? (A) the date the uniform settlement statement is delivered to the borrower; (B) the date the escrow on the sales transaction is opened; (C) the date the lender receives the borrower's loan application; (D) the date the borrower requests a copy of the booklet.

Question #48 When a lender is required to provide a Uniform Settlement Statement to the borrower, the maximum fee or charge that the lender may legally charge the borrower for preparation and submission of this required statement is: (A) $25.00; (B) 1/2% of the loan amount; (C) 1% of the loan amount; (D) nothing.

Answers: #46-D; #47-C; #48-D

C. **Mortgage Loan Disclosure Statement (Loan Broker Statement)** - must be given to the borrower **for every loan negotiated by a broker** within three days of receipt of a completed loan application, or before the borrower is obligated to take the loan (whichever is earlier).

D. **Exclusive Loan Listing** - taken by a broker is limited to a term of **not more than 45 days**.

E. **Equal Credit Opportunity** - the purpose of the Federal Equal Credit Opportunity Act (and supporting California state laws) is to prohibit and discourage discrimination in lending practices based upon age, sex, race, marital status, color, religion or national origin. All credit applicants must be considered in light of appropriate credit guidelines, and in the same manner. If a credit reporting agency refused to correct errors in a credit report, the consumer may seek actual damages plus attorney's fees and court costs, and punitive damages.

VII. ECONOMIC INDICATORS

A. **Consumer Price Index (CPI)** - a statistical measure of changes in the prices of goods and services over time. The CPI is a standard measure of inflation.

　　1. **Calculation** - when calculating the Consumer Price Index (CPI), housing expenses is one of the largest denominators because housing is one of the largest expenses for consumers.

　　2. **Rent Adjustment** - the Consumer Price Index (CPI) is commonly used in **commercial leases** as a way of adjusting the rent for inflation.

Note: Price indexes determine the purchasing power of the United States dollar.

B. **Gross Domestic Product (Gross National Product)** - the measure of goods and services produced by the nation during any one calendar year. When the GDP or GNP rises, personal income, home construction, and home sales also rise.

Question #49 Linda applied for a real estate loan. The loan application requested her to disclose her race and marital status. What can she do? (A) refuse to fill out that portion of the loan application; (B) sue the lender and the real estate broker; (C) nothing; (D) completely fill out the loan application if she wants to get the loan.

Question #50 Mr. and Mrs. Nasr were denied a home loan due to a very negative credit report. They obtained a copy of the report and found that the critical information contained in the report was false. They sent the credit reporting agency all the information necessary to disprove the false information and requested that the agency correct their records. If the credit reporting agency fails to correct the information in their files, the Nasrs could file a court action and seek: (A) actual damages; (B) attorney's fees, and court costs; (C) punitive damages; (D) any of the above.

Question #51 When calculating the Consumer Price Index (CPI), housing expenses is one of the largest denominators because: (A) CPI is based upon all consumer purchases; (B) more people buy homes than buy businesses; (C) housing impacts economy; (D) housing is one of the largest expenses for consumers.

Answers: #49-A; #50-D; #51-D

Chapter #3 Review Questions

This exam contains 27 questions. You have an average of 78 seconds per question on the Salesperson Exam. 27 questions x 78 seconds per question = 2106 seconds. Please give yourself 35 minutes to complete this practice exam, and take the exam in one sitting.

1. A person who purchased a note without knowledge of defects would be called a: (A) caveat emptor; (B) trustee; (C) endorser with recourse; (D) holder in due course.

2. All of the following are negotiable instruments, **except:** (A) an installment note; (B) a personal check; (C) a bank draft; (D) a trust deed.

3. The consent of the beneficiary in a trust deed should be obtained for: (A) consolidation agreements; (B) boundary line changes; (C) deed restriction agreements; (D) all of the above.

4. In a trust deed, the power of sale is given from: (A) trustor to beneficiary; (B) beneficiary to trustor; (C) beneficiary to trustee; (D) trustor to trustee.

5. In a real estate loan, when the required loan payments are insufficient to pay the interest due, the result is: (A) an increase in the amount applied to principal reduction payments; (B) a reduction in the term of the loan; (C) negative amortization; (D) an increase in the term of the loan.

6. A Graduated Payment Adjustable Mortgage (GPAM) provides for: (A) the loan to be renegotiated by mutual agreement of borrower and lender; (B) the loan to have several short term loans embedded within it; (C) the loan to be amortized; (D) the loan to start at a lower monthly payment of principal and interest during the first three to five years.

7. The type of real estate financing instrument which transfers equitable title to real property to the buyer, but retains legal title in the name of the seller, is called: (A) a mortgage; (B) a security agreement; (C) a real property conditional installment sales contract; (D) a conditional trust deed.

8. The sale of real property by a conditional installment sales contract gives the buyer (vendee): (A) the right of possession; (B) an estate of inheritance; (C) a freehold estate; (D) all of the above.

9. The primary source of funds for residential mortgages made by institutional lenders is: (A) household savings; (B) Federal Housing Administration; (C) Federal Deposit Insurance Corporation; (D) Federal Home Loan Band.

10. A home buyer who desires a small cash down payment, or a property owner who wishes to convert a portion of his equity into cash, may use a junior trust deed as security. The best source of junior loans is usually provided by: (A) savings and loan associations; (B) private lenders; (C) insurance companies; (D) banks.

11. The Federal National Mortgage Association (FNMA) is concerned primarily with the development of: (A) the secondary mortgage market for conventional, FHA and VA loans originated in the primary market; (B) the primary market for FHA and VA loans originated in the secondary market; (C) the primary market for conventional loans; (D) the secondary mortgage market for Cal Vet loans.

12. As used in real estate finance, the term "beneficiary statement," identifies a statement which: (A) designates the one who will receive a property in the event of a borrower's death; (B) the lender makes as to the current balance required to pay off a real estate loan; (C) the insurer makes, stating the amount that will be paid to the policyholder if the improvements are destroyed by fire; (D) the homeowner makes, listing the beneficial features of an assumable loan.

13. When making real estate loans, the lower the loan-to-value ratio, the higher the: (A) loan amount; (B) equity; (C) likelihood of a default; (D) appraised value.

14. In order to purchase a home for $300,000 a buyer borrowed $250,000 through the services of a loan broker. Each discount point charged on this loan will cost the borrower how much? (A) $250; (B) $300; (C) $2,500; (D) $3,000.

15. When Jack sells his home he wants to relieve himself of the primary liability for payment of the existing loan. He must find a buyer who is willing to: (A) sign a release agreement; (B) assume the trust deed and note liability; (C) take title subject to the existing trust deed and note; (D) execute a subordination agreement.

16. To hedge against the erosion of his money caused by inflation, a prudent investor would most likely invest in: (A) government bonds; (B) equity interests; (C) trust deeds and mortgages; (D) bank accounts.

17. What usually happens when the general level of prices decreases? (A) the value of money decreases; (B) commodity prices increase; (C) the value of money increases; (D) there is no change in the value of money.

18. The mortgage insurance paid on an FHA loan: (A) protects the borrower from a loss due to fire; (B) protects the lender in the event of the borrower's death; (C) protects that lender in the event of default by borrower; (D) Is paid for by the lender.

19. A buyer would most likely be able to borrow 100% of the purchase price with no down payment with which of the following types of financing? (A) VA; (B) FHA; (C) Cal Vet; (D) FNMA.

20. When real estate is purchased under the California Veterans Farm and Home Purchase Plan, payments are made to and legal title to the property is held by: (A) the trustee; (B) the California veteran; (C) the Veterans Administration; (D) the Department of Veterans Affairs.

21. A buyer wants to buy a home whereby she is to continue the payments of an existing amortized loan secured by a first trust deed. For her to assume the existing loan without penalty, the real estate agent should check to be sure the promissory note does not include: (A) an alienation clause; (B) a release clause; (C) a subordination clause; (D) a partial release clause.

22. If a classified ad is placed in a newspaper advertising a house for sale, and only the Annual Percentage Rate is stated: (A) the total finance charge must also be included; (B) the total number of payments must be included; (C) the amount of the down payment must be included; (D) additional disclosures are not required.

23. A first trust deed used to purchase a borrowers personal residence may be rescinded by the borrower: (A) until midnight of the third business day following the signing of the loan documents; (B) within 24 hours following the signing of the loan documents; (C) at any time prior to the funding of the loan; (D) there is no right to rescind the loan created to purchase the borrowers residence.

24. Some loans must comply with the RESPA (Real Estate Settlement Procedures Act). When the loan is secured by residential real property, and contains four or less residential units, the loan must comply with the RESPA regulations if the loan is made by: (A) the seller of the property who carries back a note secured by a purchase money first trust deed; (B) a private lender who loans her own money through a licensed real estate broker; (C) lenders whose deposits are insured by an agency of the federal government; (D) any of the above.

25. A home warranty company is offering referral fees to any real estate salesperson who refers a customer to them. These referral fees are: (A) illegal kickbacks and prohibited; (B) standard business practice in the real estate industry; (C) legal if the referral fee does not exceed $50; (D) legal if disclosed to everyone.

26. Which of the following is often used in a commercial lease to adjust the rent over time for inflation? (A) average commercial rental amounts in the area; (B) the Consumer Price Index (CPI); (C) latest economic short-term indicators; (D) the Standard and Poor's Index.

27. Which indicator would best define the purchasing power of the U.S. dollar? (A) interest rates; (B) gold standard; (C) discount rate; (D) price indexes.

Chapter #3 Review Questions - Answers

1. Ans-D A person who purchased a note without knowledge of defects is called a holder in due course.   Pg 3-1

2. Ans-D Mortgages and trust deeds are not negotiable instruments, they are classified as security devices.   Pg 3-1

3. Ans-D The consent of the beneficiary in a trust deed should be obtained for consolidation agreements, boundary line changes, and deed restriction agreements, because all of these may seriously impact the value of the property securing the debt.   Pg 3-2

4. Ans-D In a trust deed, the power of sale is given from the trustor to the trustee.   Pg 3-2

5. Ans-C In a real estate loan, when the required loan payments are insufficient to pay the interest due, the result is negative amortization; the loan balance goes up instead of down.   Pg 3-4

6. Ans-D A Graduated Payment Adjustable Mortgage (GPAM) provides for the loan to start at a lower monthly payment of principal and interest during the first five years.   Pg 3-4

7. Ans-C A real property conditional installment sales contract, is one of the many names for the land contract. The buyer (vendee) receives equitable title and the seller (vendor) retains legal title.   Pg 3-4

8. Ans-A The sale of real property by a conditional installment sales contract gives the buyer (vendee) the right of possession.   Pg 3-5

9. Ans-A The primary source of funds for residential mortgages made by institutional lenders is household savings.   Pg 3-5

10. Ans-B Private lenders are the major source for junior loans.   Pg 3-6

11. Ans-A The Federal National Mortgage Association (FNMA, Fannie Mae) is concerned primarily with the development of the secondary mortgage market for conventional, FHA and VA loans originated in the primary market;   Pg 3-7

12. Ans-B The term "beneficiary statement," is a statement which the lender makes as to the current balance required to pay off a real estate loan.   Pg 3-8

13. Ans-B The loan-to-value ratio is the percentage a lender will lend of the appraised value of the property securing the debt. The lower the loan-to-value ratio, the higher the equity (down payment).   Pg 3-9

14. Ans-C (1) Each discount point costs 1% of the loan amount.
    (2) $250,000 x 1% = $2,500   Pg 3-9

15. Ans-B When a buyer assumes a loan, the seller (original borrower on the loan) is relieved from primary liability.   Pg 3-10

16. Ans-B Equity interests (equity assets), such as real estate, are the best hedge against inflation.   Pg 3-11

17. Ans-C When the general level of prices decreases, the value of money increases.   Pg 3-11

18. Ans-C The mortgage insurance paid on an FHA loan protects that lender in the event of default by borrower.   Pg 3-12

19. Ans-A The VA is the best source for no down payment loans on the state exam questions.   Pg 3-13

20. Ans-D When real estate is purchased under the California Veterans Farm and Home Purchase Plan, payments are made to and legal title to the property is held by the Department of Veterans Affairs, not the Veterans Administration.   Pg 3-13

21. Ans-A The buyer cannot assume a loan with an alienation (due on sale) clause.   Pg 3-14

22. Ans-D If an ad discloses the Annual Percentage Rate (APR) additional disclosures of financing are not required.   Pg 3-15

23. Ans-D There is no right to rescind the loan created to purchase the borrowers residence.   Pg 3-16

24. Ans-C Lenders whose deposits are insured by an agency of the federal government must comply with RESPA when making loans secured by property containing four or less residential units.   Pg 3-16

25. Ans-A Referral fees from companies offering settlement services, such as an escrow company, title company, and/or home warranty company, are illegal.   Pg 3-16

26. Ans-B The Consumer Price Index (CPI) is often used in a commercial lease to adjust the rent over time for inflation.   Pg 3-17

27. Ans-D Price indexes determine the purchasing power of the United States dollar.   Pg 3-17

Chapter 4

PRACTICE OF REAL ESTATE AND DISCLOSURES

(Approximately 25% of Salesperson Exam)

I. **CALIFORNIA REAL ESTATE LAWS AND REGULATIONS** - **the basic purpose of real estate law is to prevent fraud**. Most of the laws which regulate the real estate industry are found in the **Business and Professions Code**. Real estate laws are passed under the authority of the police power of government.

   A. **Department of Real Estate (DRE)** - regulates the real estate industry.

   Note: Department of Real Estate is scheduled to become "**Bureau of Real Estate**" (BRE) sometime in 2013.

   1. **Real Estate Commissioner** - appointed by the governor to head the DRE. The Real Estate Commissioner has the right to **promulgate** regulations which control the actions of real estate licensees and have the force and effect of law. These regulations **are found in the California Code of Regulations**. Only the **Real Estate Commissioner** can issue, restrict, suspend, or revoke a real estate license (the courts cannot).

   Note: "Promulgate" means to publish or make laws known.

   2. **Criminal Prosecutions** - The District Attorney of the county in which the activity occurred would prosecute a non-licensed person who performed acts requiring a real estate license.

   3. **Commission Disputes** - settled by civil lawsuits. The DRE does not settle commission disputes.

   B. **Licenses** - any person who does **any real estate act for another, for compensation,** or expected compensation (regardless of form or time of payment), **must have a license**.

Question #1 The California Real Estate Commissioner has the authority to: (A) assess damages against real estate licensees who engage in fraudulent activities; (B) promulgate rules and regulations to promote the enforcement of the California real estate laws; (C) issue non-resident real estate licenses to states which prohibit their residents from holding California real estate licenses; (D) all of the above.

Question #2 Mr. Nguyen does not have a real estate license. He runs an investment firm, advertising and selling properties for his clients. Since these transactions require a real estate license, who will prosecute him for this criminal violation of the real estate law? (A) the local police; (B) the Real Estate Commissioner; (C) the State Attorney General; (D) the District Attorney of the county in which the activity occurred.

Question #3 The seller in a real estate transaction decided not to pay the commission to his real estate agent. Which of the following should the real estate agent do? (A) file a vendor's lien on the seller's property; (B) file a complaint with the real estate commissioner; (C) file an action in civil court; (D) all of the above.

Answers: #1-B; #2-D; #3-C

1. Real estate acts **requiring a license** include:
   a. Assisting buyers and sellers of real estate.
   b. Answering detailed inquiries about real estate and financing.
   c. **Property management - managing real property for the general public. A real estate license** is required to **manage real property.**

2. **Exceptions** - the following individuals do not need a license:
   a. **Principal** - the buyer or seller of real property acting for his own benefit, not through an agent.

Note: A principal buying or selling **eight or more loans in a calendar year** is required to have a license or handle these transactions through a licensee.

   b. **Attorney-in-fact** - any competent person may be designated to act for another by a duly executed and recorded "power of attorney." One person authorized to act on behalf of another may be called an attorney-in-fact. An attorney-in-fact may not deed the property to himself. A principal may terminate a power-of-attorney by revocation.
   c. **Trustee** - can conduct a trustee's sale on a trust deed without a real estate license.
   d. **Unlicensed assistant** - works in a real estate office but performs clerical duties only.
      (1) It is illegal for a real estate licensee to hire an unlicensed assistant to make telephone solicitation calls to solicit sellers, buyers, and/or borrowers.
      (2) An unlicensed assistant may not choose the structural pest control inspector in a transaction; the choice must be made by agreement of the buyer and the seller.
      (3) An unlicensed assistant working for a loan broker may not advise a borrower that he will probably fail to qualify for the loan.
      (4) A real estate broker may hire an unlicensed person for the purpose of creating advertising material, but the broker must read and approve all material before it is used.
   e. **Resident Property Manager** - without a real estate license, a manager may manage only the property where he or she resides. The owner of a **16 or more unit** residential property must live in the property or have a resident property manager.

C. **Brokers** - an individual broker's license entitles a person to conduct a brokerage business under his/her own name or, if so licensed, under a fictitious business name.

Question #4 Who is authorized to manage real property for the general public? (A) a Certified Property Manager; (B) a licensed real estate broker; (C) an affiliate member of the California Association of Realtors; (D) any responsible adult.

Question #5 Someone who has been granted a "power of attorney" may **not** do which of the following: (A) deed a property to himself; (B) pay himself a commission; (C) deed the property to another; (D) sign the name of his principal to legal documents.

Question #6 When a real estate broker hires an unlicensed person for the purpose of creating advertising material the broker must: (A) allow the unlicensed person to create the advertising material as he/she sees fit; (B) read and approve all material before it is used; (C) approve the material in writing before it is used; (D) create the material him/herself and only use the unlicensed person to fine tune the material.

Answers: *#4-B; #5-A; #6-B*

1. **Fictitious Business Name** - when a real estate broker decides to operate an office using a fictitious business name, before soliciting business under that fictitious business name the broker must:
   a. File a "Fictitious Business Name Statement" (also called a DBA) at the county recorder's office in the county where his office is located;
   b. Publish the fictitious business name in the newspaper as required by law;
   c. Have a broker's license issued by the Department of Real Estate after the name has been approved by the Real Estate Commissioner.

2. **Nicknames** - When a licensee is a natural person, the use of a nickname in place of his or her legal given name (first name) shall not require a fictitious business name statement, provided that where the nickname is used, the licensee also uses his or her surname (last name) as it appears on their real estate license, and includes their real estate license identification number.

3. **Agent Supervision** - a broker must exercise reasonable supervision over salespersons and non-licensees in his/her employment. A broker can designate a salesperson to manage an office and review contracts, as long as the salesperson has a minimum of two years of full time experience within the last five years working for any real estate broker. When a salesperson shows a home listed on the multiple listing service (MLS), the **salesperson is directly responsible to his/her employing broker**.

4. **Sharing Commission** - a broker can share her commission with an out-of-state broker, an unlicensed buyer, or a seller, as long as the broker discloses this to all parties.

5. **Employment Agreement** - the Real Estate Commissioner requires that every salesperson and every broker working for another broker have a written employment agreement with the employing broker. The agreement does not have to be approved by the Real Estate Commissioner. Both the employing broker and the employee licensee must keep a copy of this employment agreement for **three years** from the termination of employment. The employing broker does not need to have employment contracts with clerical employees and/or janitorial staff. However, everyone in the office (salespersons, clerical and janitorial staff) must be insured as employees under the **Workers Compensation Insurance Law.**

Question #7 A licensed real estate salesperson is directly responsible to the: (A) seller; (B) buyer; (C) employing broker; (D) none of the above.

Question #8 How long must a real estate salesperson keep a copy of his employment contract with a broker, after quitting the office? (A) one year; (B) two years; (C) three years; (D) four years.

Question #9 The broker of a real estate office should know that Workers' Compensation Insurance is required for: (A) only those employees paid more than minimum wage; (B) clerical personnel only; (C) employees over 21 years old only; (D) all employees of the broker.

Answers: *#7-C; #8-C; #9-D*

---

6. **Transfer of License** - a broker must notify the Commissioner upon transfer of a salesperson's license. If a salesperson is fired for a violation of real estate law, the broker must **immediately** (forthwith) send the Commissioner a **certified written statement of facts**.

7. **Change of Address** - a broker who changes his/her main office or branch office address must send a written notice to the Real Estate Commissioner no later than the **next business day** following the change. The office may be in the broker's home, if not prohibited by local ordinances.

8. **Termination of Employment** - upon termination of employment of the salesperson, a broker will return the license to the salesperson within **three business days.**

9. **Record Keeping** - the Business and Professions Code provides that a real estate broker will retain for **three years** copies of all listings, deposit receipts, canceled checks, trust records, and other documents executed by, or obtained by, the broker in connection with any transaction for which a real estate broker's license is required. The retention period will run either from the date of the closing of the transaction or, if the transaction is not consummated, from the date of the listing.

10. **Trust Ledger (Trust Journal)** - a broker must keep a true record of all trust funds that he, or any of his employees, touch. **"If you touch it, log it!"** For example, receipt of a buyer's earnest money deposit accompanying an offer must be logged in the trust ledger.

Question #10   When a real estate broker fires a real estate salesperson for a violation of the real estate law, the broker must: (A) notify the Real Estate Commissioner immediately by telephone; (B) notify the Real Estate Commissioner by certified written statement of facts within three days of the date of termination of the licensee; (C) do nothing, it is not the responsibility of the broker to inform the Real Estate Commissioner; (D) notify the Real Estate Commissioner forthwith by a certified written statement of facts.

Question #11   A broker is required by law to keep a copy of a deposit receipt for a minimum of three years from: (A) the date the deposit receipt was accepted by the seller; (B) the date of closing of the transaction; (C) the recording of the deed; (D) whichever date is earliest.

Question #12   A real estate broker must keep records of all money received by him and/or anyone working for him in a book called: (A) a profit and loss statement; (B) a closing record book; (C) a trust ledger; (D) a reconciliation book.

Answers: #10-D; #11-B; #12-C

11. **Trust Fund Account** - a separate checking account established by a broker to hold clients' money. The purpose of the broker trust account is to separate (segregate) clients' funds from the broker's. This separation avoids commingling and protects clients' funds from legal claims against the broker.

    a. A broker must place all funds received on behalf of principals in a trust account, neutral escrow depository, or into the hands of the principal who is entitled to them. This must be done no later than **three business days** following receipt of the funds by the broker or the broker's salesperson, unless there is a written instruction from the buyer to hold a check uncashed until acceptance or rejection of the offer. If a broker does not hold money beyond these limits, the broker is **not required to have a trust account**.

    b. A real estate broker may operate a property management company and a real estate sales office with his or her broker's license. The client trust funds from both activities may be placed in one trust account as long as a separate record for each trust fund deposit and disbursement is properly maintained by the broker. It is not necessary for a broker to maintain separate trust accounts for each activity. **However, if a broker owns an apartment building, the funds collected for his own building may not be put in the client trust account.**

    c. A broker may have **no more than $200** of his or her own money in the trust account.

    d. Any employee who is authorized by a broker may make withdrawals from the trust account. If an employee is not licensed, he must be fidelity bonded with a fidelity bond large enough to cover the maximum amount of trust funds to which the employee has access to at any given time.

    e. The broker must reconcile (balance) her trust account monthly.

    f. After a broker reconciles his client trust account, the broker's client liabilities should match the trust account balance.

    g. The broker's trust fund account must be in the name which appears on the broker's license, which is the broker's name or the fictitious business name used by the broker.

Question #13   How long may a real estate licensee hold a deposit check from the buyer before it is placed in trust account, escrow, or returned to the buyer? (A) one business day; (B) three business days; (C) before close of escrow; (D) a real estate licensee must immediately deposit the check in the broker's trust account.

Question #14   An unlicensed employee of the broker who is authorized in writing by the broker may make withdrawals from the broker's trust account provided the employee: (A) maintains no personal funds in the trust account; (B) is covered by a fidelity bond for at least the amount of the funds to which the employee has access to at any given time; (C) has committed to get a real estate license within the next 6 months; (D) has been employed by the broker for at least 2 out of the last 5 years.

Question #15   After a broker reconciles his client trust account, the broker's client liabilities should match the trust account: (A) overages; (B) shortages; (C) balance; (D) fidelity bond.

Answers: #13-B; #14-B; #15-C

12. **National Association of Realtors** - **"Realtor"** is the name used by members. A broker advertising himself as a Realtor who is not a member of the National Association of Realtors is acting both unethically and illegally and will be subject to discipline.

D. **Salespersons** - a salesperson may use his or her license only when the license is being held by a licensed real estate broker. The salesperson is either an employee or independent contractor of the broker.

   1. **Employee** - under **California Real Estate Law**, a salesperson is considered to be an employee of a broker.

   2. **Independent Contractor** - most real estate salespersons are considered to be independent contractors for income tax and social security tax purposes. Brokers report a salesperson's income as an independent contractor to the IRS with a 1099 form.

   3. **Compensation** - a salesperson may receive compensation for real estate acts from her employing broker only. It would be **illegal** for a salesperson working for a real estate broker to receive a referral fee or commission from a lender, loan broker, developer, or seller.

E. **Applying for a License** - when you pass the salesperson or broker exam, you have **one year** from the date of your exam to apply for the license.

Question #16   The real estate law views the salesperson employed by a real estate broker as: (A) an independent contractor; (B) a special agent; (C) a subagent; (D) an employee.

Question #17   The only person who can pay compensation to a real estate salesperson for real estate activities is: (A) the seller; (B) the buyer; (C) his or her employing broker; (D) the escrow company only when escrow closes.

Question #18   When an applicant passes the real estate exam, how much time does he/she have to apply for the license? (A) one year from the date of the exam; (B) one year from the date they received the results of the exam; (C) two years from the date of the exam; (D) two years from the date they received the results of the exam.

Answers: #16-D; #17-C; #18-A

F. **Real Estate Education, Research, and Recovery Account (REERRA)** - a portion of the real estate license fees are put into a client **recovery account** to protect the general public when they obtain uncollectible court judgments or arbitration awards against licensees.

   1. Recovery is limited to **$50,000 per transaction, $250,000 maximum per licensee.**

   2. **The licensee's license is suspended** until he or she reimburses the recovery account for claims paid, plus interest.

G. **Temporary License** - a 150-day temporary license may be issued to an otherwise qualified applicant who is on the state's list of child support obligors. The applicant will be advised that the license applied for cannot be issued unless a release is obtained from the district attorney's office during the 150-day temporary license period. If the applicant fails to submit an appropriate release from the district attorney's office to the DRE within the 150-day period, the licensee is suspended.

Note: The Department of Real Estate, Department of Corporations, and the Office of Real Estate Appraisers, check a license applicant's name against a list of late child support obligations.

H. **License Renewals** - after obtaining a real estate license, both real estate brokers and salespersons are required to renew their licenses every four years. All licensees must complete a series of continuing education courses covering **A**gency, **F**air Housing, **T**rust Fund Handling, **E**thics, and **R**isk Management **(AFTER)** in order to renew. The 45 clock hours of continuing education courses must include a **minimum of 18 hours of consumer protection courses**.

I. **Expired License**: when a real estate license expires, the licensee must immediately stop all activity which requires a license. Licensees must renew their licenses within a **two year grace period** if they wish to avoid taking the real estate exam again.

Question #19   Broker Wilson cheated clients in several real estate transactions and then disappeared. As a result of a lawsuit filed on one transaction a client was awarded a $25,000 judgment against Broker Wilson. What is the maximum amount that client will be able to recover from the Real Estate Education, Research, and Recovery Account (REERRA)? (A) $20,000; (B) $25,000; (C) $50,000; (D) $250,000

Question #20   What will the Department of Real Estate do if someone is attempting to renew a real estate license and his name appears on a list of persons (obligors) who have not complied with a court order to provide child support payments? (A) renew as a suspended license until paid; (B) renew as a temporary license, but the debt must be paid within 150 days; (C) renew for only one year, unless the licensee submits a letter from D.A. that the debt has been paid; (D) the license cannot be renewed until the debt is paid.

Question #21   When a real estate licensee is required to take 45 hours of continuing education courses to renew his/her license, included within the 45 hours of courses must be which of the following? (A) Agency, Ethics, Trust Fund Handling and Fair Housing; (B) Risk Management (C) 18 hours of consumer protection; (D) all of the above.

Answers: #19-B; #20-B; #21-D

II. ADVERTISING

A. Permissible Advertising

1. **Disclose Real Estate License Numbers** - both brokers and salespersons must disclose their real estate license numbers on all solicitation materials intended to be the first point of contact with consumers, and on real property purchase agreements when acting as agents in those transactions.

2. **Trust Deeds For Sale** - an ad offering **"Mega Buck" trust deeds for sale,** disclosing a specific yield **is legal, if the actual interest specified in the note and the discount** from the outstanding loan balance **are disclosed.**

3. **Gifts** - agents **may advertise** that they will give **gifts or prizes to buyers** if they reveal this to everyone. There is no financial limit on the size of the gift or prize. If a developer of a subdivision, such as a time-share, requires a buyer to attend a sales presentation to receive the gift or prize, this requirement must be revealed to the buyer.

4. **Secured Trust Deeds** - a licensee **may advertise "secured trust deeds"** as long as he or she discloses to what extent the trust deeds are secured.

B. Illegal Advertising

1. **Blind Advertising** - does not disclose that an agent is representing a seller. When advertising, a licensee must disclose that he is an agent. A real estate licensee may disclose his or her license status in newspaper advertisements when advertising listed property for sale by using the designation of either "Agt." or "Bro." **An ad placed in the newspaper by a real estate salesperson must also include the name of the broker.**

2. **Deceptive Advertising** - an ad that says, **"Move right in"** when the house needs major structural repair is considered illegal and deceptive advertising.

3. **Misleading Map** - in an ad for a subdivision is **false or misleading advertising.**

Question #22 A broker advertises the sale of "Mega-Buck Trust Deeds" in a newspaper. In the ad, the broker offers a specific yield arrived at by looking at the yield for the past year. This ad is: (A) not subject to regulation under the law; (B) legal only if the DRE has confirmed the yield; (C) legal if the ad also gives the actual interest rate specified in the note and the discount from the outstanding principal balance; (D) illegal according to the Truth-in-Lending Law.

Question #23 Upon going to work for a real estate broker, Janet, a licensed real estate salesperson, advertised in the newspaper that anyone who bought a property through her would receive a free microwave oven valued at $300. Her offer is: (A) legal, as long as full disclosure is made to all interested parties; (B) legal, provided that only a chance to win the microwave in a drawing is actually given the buyer; (C) illegal under all circumstances; (D) illegal, since the value of such a gift cannot exceed $200.

Question #24 A salesperson runs an ad in a newspaper. The ad must contain: (A) the name and address of the salesperson; (B) the name and address of the broker; (C) the name of broker and name of salesperson; (D) the name of the broker.

Answers: #22-C; #23-A; #24-D

4. **Puffing** - when a real estate licensee exaggerates the features of a property or the location in an ad by giving an opinion as part of the sales process such as, "This is a great house. This property is a wonderful buy." **Puffing is considered misrepresentation only if a reasonable person would rely upon the statement as fact, rather than an opinion.**

III. **ETHICS** - describes a set of values by which individuals guide their own behavior and relationship to others. "Ethics" also describes an agent's relationship with customers, other agents, and the general public. All licensees must adhere to the ethical and legal guidelines found in the Business and Professions Code. If a licensee is a member of the National Association of Realtors, the Real Estate Commissioner requires the licensee to obey the guidelines in the Realtor's Code of Ethics.

   A. **Pocket Listing** - the **unethical practice** by a real estate licensee of withholding a new listing from his Multiple Listing Service until he has had time to find a buyer himself.

   Note: There are several questions that describe improper actions performed by a real estate licensee, and ask if the action is "illegal" or merely "unethical." For exam purposes, assume that **any improper action by the real estate licensee is illegal.** If an agent crossed-out the portion of an offer after the buyer signed it, the agent's action would be **both unethical and unlawful.**

   B. **Options, Net Listings, and Guaranteed Sales** - are allowed in California as long as a full disclosure of the licensee's involvement in the transaction and the legal effect of such an agreement is explained to the person with whom the licensee is transacting business.

IV. **VIOLATIONS OF THE REAL ESTATE LAW** - by a licensee or non-licensee can result in a **$20,000 fine, six months in jail, and/or loss of the real estate license.** When the Real Estate Commissioner believes a licensee has violated real estate law and has decided to take action against the licensee, the Commissioner must first serve the licensee with an **accusation**.

Question #25 Which of the following is a correct statement about puffing? (A) puffing is always illegal; (B) puffing is unethical unless it is approved by the broker; (C) puffing is only an opinion of value of a specific property as of a given date; (D) puffing is considered misrepresentation if a reasonable person would consider it a statement of fact, rather than an opinion.

Question #26 The word "ethics," when used in a discussion of real estate agents, most nearly means: (A) trust and honesty; (B) the values that guide an agent's relationship with customers, other agents, and the general public; (C) knowledge of the law; (D) held in highest esteem by other agents.

Question #27 When an agent withholds a new listing from other agents and/or the MLS in order to attempt to sell the listing herself, it is considered unethical and described as: (A) commingling; (B) a pocket listing; (C) making a secret profit; (D) the fiduciary duty of the agent.

Answers: #25-D; #26-B; #27-B

Common violations of real estate law include:

A. **Misrepresentation** - failure to disclose material facts or lying (for example, when appraising an income producing property with the capitalization approach, an agent would be guilty of misrepresentation if he failed to include expenses such as vacancies, management and maintenance). The most common types of misrepresentation are innocent, negligent, and/or fraudulent.

B. **False Promise** - a false promise and a misrepresentation are not the same thing. A misrepresentation is a false statement of fact. A false promise is a false statement about what the promisor is going to do. A false promise is actual fraud. For example, if an agent promises a seller he will advertise the seller's home every week, but does not do so, it is actual fraud.

C. **Undisclosed Dual Agency** - acting as an agent for more than one party (principal) in a real estate transaction **without the knowledge and consent of both parties.** An agent who disclosed dual agency to only one of the parties will not be entitled to any commission.

D. **Commingling** - is when an agent mixes a principal's or client's money with the agent's own money (keeping a client's money in a broker's safe is commingling). When a licensee deposits a client's money into his personal or business account rather than into a trust account, it is commingling, a violation of the Business and Professions Code, and is grounds for suspension or revocation of a real estate license.

E. **Conversion** - stealing client's money.

F. **Secret Profit** - (see Chapter 6).

G. **Kickbacks (Referral Fees)** - paid to real estate licensees by escrow companies, structural pest control companies, title companies, and/or home warranty companies, are illegal.

Question #28   A real estate licensee misrepresented his relationship with a large real estate firm in order to impress a prospective buyer. The agent's action would be considered: (A) appropriate business practice; (B) legal, but unethical; (C) illegal; (D) legal only if a sale results from his relationship with the buyer.

Question #29   An agent promised his buyer a 7.5% loan, but at close of escrow pressured the buyer to accept an 8% loan. The buyer gave in to the agent's pressure and accepted the 8% loan. The agent's conduct was: (A) legal; (B) illegal; (C) usual; (D) unusual.

Question #30   Which of the following is commingling and also violates the law regulating trust funds? (A) a broker put the tenant's security deposit in his client trust account for tenant, and the broker owns the apartment building being managed; (B) a broker put a buyer's deposit in the broker's general account; (C) a broker put the tenant's security deposit in his client trust account and the broker's client owns the apartment building being managed; (D) a broker put the rent he collected in his client trust account and the broker's client owns the apartment building being managed.

Answers: #28-C; #29-B; #30-B

V. ADVANCE FEES

A. **Advance Fee Contracts** - When a broker wants to charge fees prior to providing services, the advance fee contracts and advertising materials must be submitted to the real estate commissioner for approval at least **10 calendar days before they are used.**

B. **Advertising** - when a broker receives an advance fee for publishing a special pamphlet advertising properties which he has not listed for sale, he must give an **accounting to the seller**, upon demand, for any funds he has collected for the advertising.

C. **No Guarantee** - an advance fee contract used in connection with a real estate transaction or when listing a business opportunity must include: a description of the services to be performed, the total amount of the advance fee to be charged to the client, and the date the fee is to be paid. An **advance fee contract may not include a guarantee** that the sale, lease, or exchange will be completed.

VI. SPECIAL RULES (related to trust deeds and land contracts)

A. **Recording** - any broker who **negotiates a loan** or the sale of real property involving a trust deed must have the **trust deed recorded before the funds are released from escrow**. If the lender gives written authorization for the release of funds before the trust deed is recorded, the broker must give the lender a written recommendation to record within **ten days**.

B. **Collecting Payments** - any broker who services a loan by collecting payments must be authorized by the lender in writing. The broker may retain the payments in his trust account for no more than **25 days** without written authorization from the lender.

Question 31 Advance fee contracts must be submitted for approval to the real estate commissioner: (A) at least five days before they are used; (B) at least ten days before they are used; (B) not less than five days after they are used; (D) not less than ten days after they are used.

Question #32 An advance fee contract used in connection with a real estate transaction or when listing a business opportunity must include all of the following, **except:** (A) a description of the services to be performed; (B) the total amount of the advance fee to be charged to the client; (C) a guarantee that the sale, lease, or exchange will be completed; (D) the date the fee is to be paid.

Question #33 When a real estate broker is collecting payments on a promissory note for a lender as part of a loan servicing agreement, the broker may retain the funds in his trust account for: (A) 10 days; (B) 14 days; (C) 25 days; (D) 60 days.

Answers: #31-B; #32-C; #33-C

C. **Promotional Note** - one of a series of notes that is **less than three years old**, secured by liens on parcels in a subdivision which is **regulated as a real property security. After three years**, the note ceases to be a **promotional note and is no longer regulated as a real property security. Remember, a 37 month old promotional note is not regulated as a real property security.**

VII. PROPERTY MANAGEMENT

A. **Compensation** - property managers should not be compensated with kickbacks and/or discounts on goods and supplies. Property managers usually receive a **flat fee plus a percentage of the gross income** over the term of the lease. The amount of compensation is set by mutual agreement between the owner and the property manager.

B. **New Buildings** - are easier to manage and have maintenance schedules that are simpler to establish because their appliances, fixtures, and machinery are new and have operating and maintenance manuals.

C. **Management Agreement** - the most essential document needed to establish the relationship between a property management company and the property owner is a **written property management agreement.**

D. **Owner Responsibility - an owner has the ultimate responsibility** for periodic inspections and maintenance of rental property. When leasing industrial space, the owner and/or property manager is required to make sure the property complies with all applicable building codes.

E. **Institute of Real Estate Management (IREM)** - is a national organization of individual property managers who have met exacting educational and experience requirements. Members are designated as **Certified Property Managers "CPM."**

Question 34   A promotional note will no longer be regulated as a real property security when the note is: (A) 17 months old; (B) 24 months old; (C) 30 months old; (D) 37 months old.

Question #35   It is ethical for real property managers to be compensated in all of the following ways, **except**: (A) by receiving a percentage of gross receipts; (B) by receiving a commission on new leases; (C) as payment for major repairs or alterations performed by the property manager; (D) the receipt of kickbacks or discounts on goods and supplies.

Question #36   A property management agreement usually arranges for payment of compensation as follows: (A) a salary plus a percentage of the net income; (B) flat fee plus a percentage of the gross income; (C) out-of-pocket expenses plus a percent of the gross income; (D) paid only on duties performed.

Answers: #34-D; #35-D; #36-B

VIII. MOBILEHOMES - a mobilehome is personal property until or unless the owner has completed the necessary steps to convert the mobilehome into real property.

   A. Converting Mobilehomes Into Real Property - an owner must do all of the following:

   1. Obtain a building permit;

   2. Attach the mobilehome to an approved foundation;

   3. Record a document reflecting that the mobilehome has been affixed to an approved foundation, and;

   4. Obtain a certificate of occupancy. A mobilehome installed on a foundation in compliance with the law is deemed real property and can be sold with a deed.

   B. Registered Mobilehomes - A real estate license does not allow an agent to sell new mobilehomes, but a real estate licensee may handle the sale of used mobilehomes. A mobilehome is considered "used" once it has been sold to a buyer and **registered** with the Department of Housing and Community Development. **Remember, a real estate licensee may sell a mobilehome once it has been registered.**

   C. Advertising Mobilehomes - an ad offering mobilehomes for sale that says, **"No Down Payment,"** is illegal and deceptive advertising when in fact, a down payment is required, and the buyer is advised to borrow the down payment from a second lender. A real estate licensee must withdraw any advertisement of a mobilehome for sale, lease, or exchange **within 48 hours** after the real estate licensee's receipt of notice that the mobilehome is no longer available for sale, lease, or exchange.

   D. Transfer Document - the document used to transfer and/or encumber a registered mobilehome is a certificate of title (certificate of ownership).

   E. Notification of Sale - when a real estate broker sells a registered mobilehome, the broker must give written notice of the transfer to the Department of Housing and Community Development no later than **ten calendar days** after the sale.

Question #37 Mr. Longing purchased a new mobilehome from a dealer two months ago. It is now located in a mobilehome park. Broker Smith took a listing to sell it. Which of the following is true? (A) Broker Smith cannot sell it, because the land is not being sold with it; (B) Broker Smith cannot sell it, because it has not been registered with the Department of Housing and Community Development for a period of more than one year; (C) Broker Smith can arrange a sale of the mobilehome and a sublease of the land; (D) Broker Smith cannot handle the sale of a mobilehome unless it is new.

Question #38 If a mobilehome which is not attached to a permanent foundation is sold, the document which would be used to transfer title is: (A) a grant deed; (B) a certificate of title; (C) a contract of sale; (D) a mobilehome deed.

Question #39 When a real estate licensee handles the sale of a registered mobilehome, the agent must give written notice to the Department of Housing and Community Development within how many days? (A) three calendar days; (B) five business days; (C) ten calendar days; (D) ten business days.

Answers: #37-C; #38-B; #39-C

IX. **BUSINESS OPPORTUNITIES** involve the sale or lease of both the inventory and good will of an existing business enterprise or opportunity. Business opportunities are **classified as personal property.** The **document used to transfer title** is a **bill of sale**, not a deed.

   A. **Sales Tax** - when purchasing a business, the buyer (transferee) should request a **"certificate of clearance" from the State Board of Equalization** during escrow. The certificate of clearance is a receipt proving the seller has remitted the sales tax. This receipt protects the buyer of a business from successor's liability for unpaid taxes.

   B. **Franchise** - the buyer of a franchise is buying the **right to conduct business under the seller's (franchisor's) marketing plan.** The Franchise Investment Law is designed primarily to **protect the prospective franchisees** when considering the purchase of a franchise. Franchisors would normally raise money from loans, stock sales and franchise fees.

   C. **Escrow** - must be used in the sale of a business including a liquor license.

X. **FAIR HOUSING LAWS**

   A. **Federal Law**

      1. **U.S. Supreme Court case - decided in 1968,** upheld anti-discrimination laws on the basis of the Thirteenth Amendment to the U.S. Constitution. The Thirteenth Amendment is the basis of fair housing laws throughout the United States.

Question #40   The buyer of a business opportunity should get a clearance from which of the following agencies in order to avoid "successor's liability?" (A) Secretary of State's Office; (B) State Board of Equalization; (C) Alcoholic Beverage Control Board; (D) Department of Real Estate.

Question #41   Bob agreed to purchase a business from Joe. Under the terms of their agreement, Bob will have the right to offer, and distribute, goods or services under Joe's marketing plan. This agreement between Bob and Joe may be best described as: (A) a franchise agreement; (B) a property securities transaction; (C) a business opportunity agreement; (D) a personal securities investment.

Question #42   In what year did the U.S. Supreme Court uphold anti-discrimination laws related to fair housing and upon which amendment to the United States Constitution did they base their decision? (A) 1968 and the Fifth Amendment; (B) 1988 and the First Amendment; (C) 1968 and the Thirteenth Amendment; (D) 1868 and the First Amendment.

Answers: #40-B; #41-A; #42-C

2. **Title VIII of the Civil Rights Act of 1968** (Federal Fair Housing Act, Federal Open Housing Law) - prohibits discrimination in housing transactions.
   a. **Complaints** must be filed with the **Department of Housing and Urban Development (HUD)** within **one year** of the discrimination.
   b. The Civil Rights Act of 1968 allows a person who is discriminated against to bring a private civil action in state or federal court.
   c. The **Federal Open Housing Law is enforced by the U.S. Attorney General** when a conspiracy exists to resist the law.
   d. An ad which included the phrase "retiree's dream home" violates HUD advertising guidelines.

B. **California State Law**

1. **Fair Employment and Housing Act (Rumford Act)** - prohibits discrimination in supplying **housing accommodations** based on race, color, religion, sex, marital status, national origin, ancestry, age, familial status, or disability.

*Note: "Housing accommodations" as defined in the law is improved or unimproved real property used or intended to be used as a residence by the owner and which consists of **not more than four dwelling units**.*

   a. **The Department of Fair Employment and Housing is the state agency created under this act** which is responsible for enforcing fair housing laws on the state level. Victims have **one year** after the discrimination occurs to file a complaint.
   b. If the Fair Employment and Housing Act is violated:
      (1) The owner must complete the rental or sale, or
      (2) The complainant is entitled to the next available unit, and
      (3) The owner may be held liable for civil damages, and
      (4) The owner may be liable for up to $1,000 in punitive damages.
   c. The Fair Employment and Housing Act applies to all housing accommodations but does not apply to renting or leasing to a roomer or boarder in a single-family house, provided that no more than one roomer or boarder lives in the household.

Question #43 Under Federal Fair Housing Law (Title VIII of the Civil Rights Act of 1968), persons who are the victim of discrimination in housing are permitted to file: (A) a complaint with HUD; (B) a lawsuit in state or local courts; (C) a lawsuit in federal courts; (D) any of the above.

Question #44 The enforcement of anti-discrimination law in housing accommodations in California, on the basis of race, religion, color, sex, national origin, or ancestry, is the responsibility of the: (A) Department of Fair Employment and Housing; (B) Real Estate Commissioner; (C) Division of Fair Housing; (D) Department of Corporations.

Question #45 "Housing accommodations" as defined in the Fair Employment and Housing Act is improved or unimproved real property used or intended to be used as a residence by the owner and which consists of not more than: (A) one dwelling unit; (B) three dwelling units; (C) four dwelling units; (D) ten dwelling units.

Answers: #43-D; #44-A; #45-C

2. **Housing Financial Discrimination Act (Holden Act)** - makes discrimination in lending practices illegal.
   a. Prohibits **Redlining** - charging higher interest rates or not lending in certain neighborhoods based upon suspect characteristics, such as race, color, age, national origin.
   b. Prohibits lending institutions from charging an extra annual fee (per annum) on loans to non-English speaking borrowers.

3. **Unruh Civil Rights Act** - a California state law prohibiting discrimination by businesses.

C. **General Fair Housing Information**

1. **Suspect Classifications** - discrimination in housing transactions based upon race, religion, color, marital status, national origin or sex, of the buyer, seller, landlord, tenant, and/or neighborhood, is unenforceable, contrary to public policy, and illegal.

2. **Steering** - showing minority buyers homes that are only in segregated areas violates fair housing laws (for example, an agent might avoid showing homes to an Hispanic buyer in areas where no Hispanics live).

3. **Non-Disclosure** - the race, color, sex, national origin, or religion, of a buyer or tenant is not a material fact and should not be disclosed by an agent to his principal, even if asked.

4. **Marital Status** - it is a violation of fair housing law for a landlord to discriminate against single tenants. It is even illegal for a landlord to make, or cause to be made, any written or oral inquiry concerning the marital status of a prospective tenant.

5. **Misquoting Prices** - quoting a higher price to minorities and a lower price to others causes both a seller and his agent to be liable for damages in a lawsuit.

Question #46 A savings bank charges a 1/8% higher interest rate on loans to non-English speaking borrowers. This fee is: (A) permitted if the fee is included in the finance charge required to be disclosed under the Federal Truth in Lending Law; (B) in violation of the Holden Act; (C) not in violation of the Housing Financial Discrimination Act; (D) prohibited by the statute of frauds.

Question #47 Discrimination in housing transactions based upon race, religion, color, marital status, national origin or sex of the buyer, seller, landlord, tenant and or neighborhood, is; (A) unenforceable; (B) contrary to public policy; (C) illegal; (D) all of the above.

Question #48 The owner of a 10 unit apartment building ran the following classified ad in the newspaper: "Charming two bedroom apartment unit for rent. Married couples preferred." Is this a violation of fair housing laws? (A) no, because he used the word "preferred" instead of "only;" (B) no, because there are no fair housing restrictions on advertising rental units; (C) yes, this ad would indicate illegal discrimination, based upon marital status; (D) no, because he has advertised like this in the past and has had no complaints so far.

Answers: #46-B; #47-D; #48-C

6. **Deed Restrictions** - a **racial deed restriction is unconstitutional** and unenforceable, but the **sale is valid.** Racial deed restrictions may be removed by court order.

7. **Panic Selling (panic peddling, blockbusting)** - occurs when agents attempt to persuade neighbors to sell by telling them that members of another ethnic group are moving into the neighborhood. This is a violation of both state and federal law.

8. **Innocent Buyer** - an **innocent buyer** of a home is **not guilty of discrimination** when the seller and real estate agent conspired to discriminate by refusing to sell to a minority buyer.

9. **Hiring** - a real estate broker is subject to discipline by the Real Estate Commissioner and is in violation of fair housing laws if he practices steering, blockbusting and/or hires salespersons from only one ethnic group.

10. **Refusing to Show a Home** - an **agent is not guilty of discrimination** if she refuses to show a home to a minority buyer when the **seller is away and has instructed the agent that the home is not available for showing to anybody** until he has returned.

11. **Americans With Disabilities Act (ADA)** - the law which requires **equal access to public buildings for disabled** (handicapped) persons.

XI. MANDATED DISCLOSURES

A. **Transfer Disclosure Law** - a seller must provide a buyer with a **transfer disclosure statement (TDS)** which discloses the condition of the property to the buyer. The seller must make a reasonable inspection of the property before completing the TDS. The TDS includes both the condition of the improvements and the condition of the land.

1. **TDS Required** - a seller must give a TDS to the buyer of **four or less residential units, even when selling the property "as is."** A TDS is also required when an owner sells his home without using an agent as a "For Sale By Owner."

Question #49 A real estate agent working in an Hispanic neighborhood informed the residents they should move out because Asians were moving into the area. All of the following are correct statements, **except:** (A) this conduct is panic selling; (B) this conduct is blockbusting; (C) this conduct is legal, but unethical; (D) this conduct is illegal.

Question #50 The law which mandates equal access to public buildings for all handicapped persons is known as: (A) the Fair Business Access Act of 2003; (B) the Handicapped Americans Act; (C) the Unruh Act; (D) the Americans with Disabilities Act.

Question #51 When a seller sells his home "as is," which of the following is true? (A) seller must still give the buyer a real estate transfer disclosure statement; (B) the sales agreement should warn that the buyer should beware; (C) "as is" means that nothing is warranted by the seller; (D) seller is relieved from the legal obligation to give the buyer a real estate transfer disclosure statement.

Answers: #49-C; #50-D; #51-A

2. **TDS Not Required** - for husband-wife transfers, probate sales, foreclosure sales, bankruptcies, REO's, and when one co-owner sells to another co-owner.

3. **Role of the Real Estate Agent**
   a. The seller must make a reasonable inspection before completing the disclosure statement. The real estate licensee **may not fill out a TDS** for the seller.
   b. The TDS should be prepared when the listing is taken and a copy kept in the listing broker's office. If seller refuses to fill out the TDS truthfully at the time of the listing, the **agent should not accept the listing**.
   c. The listing and selling agents must also inspect the property and add any additional disclosures regarding conditions within their knowledge.
   d. If a seller refuses to give a TDS to a buyer, the agent should give the buyer a written statement informing the buyer that he is entitled to a TDS and the seller has refused to provide it.
   e. The broker who procured the offer is responsible for delivering the TDS to the buyer. The TDS should be delivered to the buyer as soon as practicable before transfer of title.

4. **Rights of Buyer**
   a. A buyer has **two years** to sue a real estate licensee for failure to disclose known defects in the TDS.
   b. If the TDS or amended TDS is delivered after the execution of an offer, the buyer has **three days** after delivery in person, or **five days** after delivery by mail, to terminate the offer in writing.

5. **Environmental Hazards** - a TDS must include environmental hazards of which the seller is aware (like lead-based paint, asbestos, radon gas, etc.). If the seller or the seller's agent gives the buyer the "Environmental Hazards" pamphlet, neither the seller nor agent is required to say more about environmental hazards (assuming no awareness of such a problem).

Question #52 A real estate licensee inspected a home for sale and discovered some problems in the property. How long does the buyer have to sue for the failure of the licensee to disclose problems in the TDS? (A) 1 year; (B) 2 years; (C) 3 years; (D) 5 years.

Question #53 A real estate broker, acting as the agent for a seller, handed the buyer an amendment to the TDS. The buyer has the right to: (A) terminate the sale within three days; (B) sue for criminal and civil damages; (C) do nothing, because he is still obligated to proceed with the transaction; (D) terminate the sale within five days and bring a criminal action against the broker.

Question #54 A statement that discloses the presence of various environmental hazards includes disclosures for which of the following substances? (A) asbestos; (B) lead based paint; (C) radon gas; (D) all of the above.

Answers: #52-B; #53-A; #54-D

6. **Easton v. Strassburger** - a California court decision which led to the creation of the Transfer Disclosure law. In the case, the real estate agent was deemed responsible not only for what was known or accessible only to the agent or his or her principal, but also for what the agent should have known, following a reasonably competent and diligent inspection of the property. The agent was required to disclose all facts materially affecting the value or desirability of the property.

B. **Natural Hazard Zone Disclosure Statement** - must be given to a buyer who is entitled to the TDS. Additionally, the seller must make these disclosures when selling any property in one or more of the following areas:

1. **Special Flood Hazard Area** - designated by the Federal Emergency Management Agency.

2. **Area of Potential Flooding** - shown on a map as an area which would be inundated if a dam failed.

3. **Very High Fire Hazard Severity Zone** - shown on a map designated as a very high fire hazard zone.

4. **Wildland Area** - contains substantial forest fire risks and hazards.

5. **Earthquake Fault Zone** - area over earthquake faults.

6. **Seismic Hazard Zone** - area in which an earthquake may cause strong ground shaking, soil liquefaction, or landslides.

Note: There is no such things as a "Severe Weather Hazard Zone."

Question #55 The court case of Easton v. Strassburger expanded which of the following real estate procedures? (A) disclosures of economic obsolescence; (B) selling properties "as is;" (C) disclosure of all known material facts regarding the physical condition of the property; (D) advising buyers of their right to have their own inspections.

Question #56 A seller (or agent for the seller) must give the buyer a "Natural Hazard Disclosure Statement" if the property is within which of the following areas? (A) Special Flood Hazard Area; (B) Very High Fire Hazard Severity Zone; (C) Earthquake Fault Zone; (D) all of the above.

Question #57 The Natural Hazard Disclosure Law requires disclosures be made to buyers of properties in all of the following areas, **except**: (A) Very High Fire Hazard Severity Zone; (B) Earthquake Fault Zone; (C) Severe Weather Hazard Zone; (D) Area of Potential Flooding.

Answers: #55-C; #56-D; #57-C

C. **Earthquake Safety Guides** - The Seismic Safety Commission has developed a "Homeowner's Guide to Earthquake Safety" and a "Commercial Property Owner's Guide to Earthquake Safety." Delivery of the Earthquake Safety Guide(s) is required in the following transactions:

1. **Homeowner's Guide** - must be given to the buyer of any real property improved with a residential dwelling **built prior to January 1, 1960** and consisting of one-to-four units, any of which are of conventional light-frame construction.

2. **Commercial Property Owner's Guide** - must be given to the buyer of any masonry building with wood frame floors or roofs **built before January 1, 1975** (if residential property, both guides are given; if commercial property, only the Commercial Guide is given).

3. **Guides Include** - maps and information on geologic and seismic hazard conditions for all areas of the state, explanations of the related structural and nonstructural hazards, and recommendations for mitigating the hazards of an earthquake. The **State Geologist** delineates earthquake fault zones around traces of potentially active earthquake faults on official maps of seismic activity areas. Earthquake fault zones are usually about **1/4 mile wide** on the official maps.

4. **Limits on Disclosure** - if a buyer receives a copy of the Homeowner's Guide (or, if applicable, the Commercial Property Owner's Guide) neither the seller nor the broker are required to provide additional information regarding geologic and seismic hazards, the one exception being that sellers and brokers must disclose that a property is in an earthquake fault zone.

5. **Exemptions** - certain exemptions apply to the obligation to deliver the booklet when transferring either a dwelling of one-to-four units or a reinforced masonry building. These exemptions are essentially the same as those that apply to delivery of the Real Estate Transfer Disclosure Statement.

D. **Lead-based Paint Disclosure** - the buyer of "target housing" (pre-1978 housing) must be given an EPA pamphlet entitled "Protect Your Family From Lead In your Home" prior to entering into a contract to purchase the home. If the pamphlet is given after the contract is formed, the buyer has the right to cancel the contract. Additionally, the seller and/or agent who violates this disclosure law may be subject to civil and/or criminal penalties.

Note: Target housing **does not include** pre-1978 housing which is designated for the **elderly or handicapped** unless children reside there or are expected to reside there.

Question #58 A seller is required to deliver the Homeowner's Guide to Earthquake Safety to the buyer of any one-to-four unit residential properties built prior to: (A) 1952; (B) 1960; (C) 1969; (D) 1975.

Question #59 The seller is required to deliver the Homeowner's and/or the Commercial Guide to Earthquake Safety to the buyer of most masonry buildings with wood frame floors or roofs built prior to: (A) 1975; (B) 1980; (C) 1985; (D) 2000.

Question #60 Which of the following would be considered a "target house" under the lead based paint disclosure law? (A) home built for the elderly in 1976; (B) single family residence built in 1975; (C) home built for handicapped in 1970; (D) single family residence built in 1980.

Answers: #58-B; #59-A; #60-B

Chapter #4 Review Questions

This exam contains 28 questions. You have an average of 78 seconds per question on the Salesperson Exam. 28 questions x 78 seconds per question = 2184 seconds. Please give yourself 36 minutes to complete this practice exam, and take the exam in one sitting.

1. What is the basic purpose of the real estate law in California? (A) raise revenue for the California's general fund; (B) provide more jobs for California's workforce; (C) keep track of all real estate transactions; (D) prevent fraud.

2. Broker Bob's real estate license was revoked because he violated the California Real Estate Law. What California code did he violate? (A) Real Estate Code; (B) Business and Professions Code; (C) Code of Civil Procedure; (D) California Commercial Code.

3. Jose is an unlicensed employee of a real estate broker. He was hired to hand out door hanger fliers in the neighborhood near the office and to make solicitation telephone calls to potential sellers and buyers. This is: (A) unlawful for the broker; (B) unethical for Jose; (C) normal and appropriate behavior; (D) unlawful for both the broker and the unlicensed assistant.

4. When a real estate broker decides to operate an office using a fictitious business name, before soliciting business under that fictitious business name the broker must: (A) file the name at the county recorder's office in the county where his office is located; (B) publish the fictitious business name in the newspaper as required by law; (C) have a broker's license issued by the Department of Real Estate after the name has been approved by the Real Estate Commissioner; (D) do all of the above.

5. Which of the following contracts or documents does **not** require approval by the Department of Real Estate prior to use? (A) an advance fee contract; (B) a mortgage loan disclosure statement; (C) a real property security disclosure statement; (D) an employment agreement between broker and salesperson.

6. A licensee must keep a record of contracts and commissions received for three years from what date? (A) date of the offer; (B) close of escrow; (C) date of receipt of the commission check; (D) date the commission check cleared the bank.

7. Which of the following is true regarding the broker's trust account? (A) a real estate broker must have a trust account; (B) a real estate broker must maintain a minimum balance of $100 in the account; (C) a real estate broker must maintain a minimum balance of $200 in the account; (D) a real estate broker is not required to maintain a trust account.

8. How frequently must the real estate broker reconcile his trust account? (A) daily; (B) weekly; (C) monthly; (D) annually.

9. An agent licensed as a salesperson is considered an independent contractor of the broker for the purpose of: (A) no broker supervision or interference by the broker; (B) broker taking liability for the salesperson's errors; (C) paying income taxes and social security taxes and unemployment insurance; (D) eligibility for worker's compensation insurance coverage.

10. What type of background check does the Real Estate Commissioner, Corporations Commissioner and the Office of Real Estate Appraisers use on applicants for their licenses? (A) financial statements; (B) real estate holding; (C) credit rating; (D) late child support obligations.

11. When a real estate agent lets her license expire how long is the grace period for her to renew the license without being required to retake the state exam? (A) 1 year; (B) 2 years; (C) 3 years; (D) there is no grace period, if you let your license expire you must retake the state exam.

12. A licensee may advertise secured trust deeds if he discloses which of the following? (A) the extent to which the trust deeds are secured; (B) the property addresses of the trust deeds; (C) the lenders' names; (D) his securities dealer's license number.

13. As to ethics, the best guidelines to determine whether an action is ethical will be found in which of the following? (A) the "Realtor's Golden Rule;" (B) the Business and Professions Code; (C) the conduct of other real estate agents in your office; (D) what is in the best interest of the real estate licensee.

14. Which of the following actions by real estate licensee is **not** considered ethical conduct? (A) all parties in a real estate transaction are to be treated fairly; (B) disputes between brokers should be settled by arbitration rather than court hearings; (C) complete records of all real estate transactions being maintained by licensees; (D) approval by a broker of pocket listings taken by salespersons in his employ.

15. Real estate brokers are prohibited from commingling their funds with the funds of their clients. Commingle means the opposite of: (A) trust account; (B) mingle; (C) escrow; (D) segregate.

16. An advance fee collected by a mortgage broker to pay for the processing of the loan is: (A) illegal under RESPA; (B) legal, if it is a flat fee; (C) legal, if under $200; (D) legal, only if the advance fee agreement has been approved by the DRE and the money is held in the broker's trust account until used.

17. A real estate broker who is employed as a resident property manager is entitled to a commission which is: (A) set at 10% of gross receipts; (B) limited to no more than 10% of gross receipts; (C) limited by law; (D) any amount agreed to by the parties.

18. Wayne owns a 50 unit apartment building. John, a licensed real estate broker has been hired by Wayne to manage the building. Joan lives in the building and has been designated as the resident property manager. Who has the ultimate responsibility for inspection and maintenance of the apartment building? (A) Joan; (B) Wayne; (C) John; (D) the Real Estate Commissioner.

19. The document used to transfer title to a business opportunity (personal property) is which of the following? (A) a trust deed; (B) a chattel mortgage; (C) a bill of sale; (D) a security agreement.

20. Which of the following phrases in an ad would violate HUD guidelines for advertising? (A) good neighborhood; (B) retiree's dream home; (C) wedding chapel on site; (D) seeking female roommate.

21. Under the Federal Fair Housing Law (Title VIII of the Civil Rights Act of 1968), persons complaining of discrimination in housing are permitted to enforce their rights by bringing which of the following actions? (A) a civil action filed in federal court; (B) a civil action in state or local court; (C) a complaint filed with HUD; (D) any of the above.

22. Listing a home at an inflated asking price for minority prospects to pay, but accepting a lower price from non-minority prospects: (A) is a violation of the federal Fair Housing Laws by the seller only; (B) could cause the listing agent and the seller to be liable for money damages in a Fair Housing suit; (C) is not a violation of the Fair Housing Law because the property is still available to minority prospects; (D) is illegal only if an a government backed loan is being used to purchase the property.

23. When a deed includes the racial identity of the parties, it can be rewritten under which of the following circumstances: (A) it was created prior to 1978; (B) the title company says it is okay to rewrite it; (C) it is offensive or discriminatory; (D) by court order.

24. A seller must give a TDS to the buyer in which of the following real estate transactions? (A) sale of a vacant lot; (B) sale of a commercial building; (C) sale of a triplex residential building; (D) all of the above.

25. If a potential seller refuses to disclose slide problems when filling out a real estate transfer disclosure statement, the real estate broker should: (A) accept the listing and obey the principal's direction not to disclose the slide problem; (B) not accept the listing, (C) tell the seller it will be "okay," if he sells without an agent; (D) accept the listing and verbally disclose the slide problem to the buyer.

26. In what California court case did the court rule that the seller and agent must disclose all facts materially affecting the value or desirability of the property to the buyer? (A) Easton v. Westwick; (B) Easton v. Strassburger; (C) Marburry v. Madison; (D) Jones v. Mayer.

27. When a potentially active earthquake fault zone is located near a home, buyers must be given special earthquake disclosures. The earthquake faults are designated on maps available to the public. Typically how wide are the earthquake fault zones on these maps? (A) ¼ mile; (B) ½ mile; (C) ¾ miles; (D) 1 mile.

28. A family recently purchased a home built in 1972. The buyers did not receive the EPA pamphlet "Protect Your Family From Lead in Your Home." Which of the following is true? (A) the buyers can cancel the transaction; (B) there is no problem if the family has no children below the age of 6 years old; (C) if the buyers are given a certificate stating there is no lead based paint in the home, it is all right; (D) the buyers are still obligated to purchase the home.

Chapter #4 Review Questions - Answers

1. Ans-D The basic purpose of real estate law is to prevent fraud. Pg 4-1

2. Ans-B Most California Real Estate Law is found in the California's Business and Professions Code. Pg 4-1

3. Ans-D It is a violation of the law by the broker to hire an unlicensed person to perform real estate acts, and it is a violation of the law by the unlicensed person to perform those acts.   Pg 4-2

4. Ans-D Before soliciting business a fictitious business name the broker must: file the name at the county recorder's office in the county where his office is located, publish the fictitious business name in the newspaper as required by law, and have a broker's license issued by the Department of Real Estate after the name has been approved by the Real Estate Commissioner.   Pg 4-3

5. Ans-D The employment agreement between broker and salesperson does not require approval by the Department of Real Estate.   Pg 4-3

6. Ans-B Generally, real estate licensees must keep copies of all documents for three years from the date of the listing or close of escrow, whichever occurred last.   Pg 4-4

7. Ans-D A real estate broker is not required to maintain a trust account.   Pg 4-5

8. Ans-C A broker must reconcile his trust account monthly.   Pg 4-5

9. Ans-C An agent licensed as a salesperson is considered an independent contractor of the broker for the purpose of paying income taxes and social security taxes and unemployment insurance.   Pg 4-6

10. Ans-D The Real Estate Commissioner, Corporations Commissioner and the Office of Real Estate Appraisers check all applicants for licensees against a list of late child support obligations.   Pg 4-7

11. Ans-B When a real estate agent lets his or her license expire there is a two year grace period for him/her to renew the license without being required to retake the state exam.   Pg 4-7

12. Ans-A A licensee may advertise "secured trust deeds" as long as he or she discloses to what extent the trust deeds are secured.   Pg 4-8

13. Ans-B The best guidelines to determine whether an action is ethical will be found in the Business and Professions Code.   Pg 4-9

14. Ans-D A pocket listing is considered to be the unethical practice of withholding a new listing from the multiple listing service until the agent has had time to find a buyer himself.   Pg 4-9

15. Ans-D Commingle means the opposite of segregate.   Pg 4-10

16. Ans-D Advance fee contracts must be approved by the Department of Real Estate and the money held in the broker's trust account until used.   Pg 4-11

17. Ans-D The amount of commission paid a property manager is not set by law. It is established by mutual agreement between the owner and the property manager.   Pg 4-12

18. Ans-B The owner has the ultimate responsibility for inspection and maintenance of an apartment building.   Pg 4-12

19. Ans-C The document used to transfer title to a business opportunity (personal property) is a bill of sale.   Pg 4-14

20. Ans-B "Retiree's dream home" violates HUD guidelines for advertising.   Pg 4-15

21. Ans-D Under the Federal Fair Housing Law (Title VIII of the Civil Rights Act of 1968), persons complaining of discrimination in housing are permitted to enforce their rights by bringing a civil action filed in federal court, a civil action in state or local court, or a complaint filed with HUD.   Pg 4-15

22. Ans-B To require minorities to pay higher prices than other people is discrimination under both federal and state law and subjects the licensees involved to liability for money damages.   Pg 4-15

23. Ans-D When a deed includes the racial identity of the parties, it can be rewritten by court order.   Pg 4-16

24. Ans-C The seller must give a TDS to the buyer in the sale or lease for more than one year of four or less residential units. A triplex is a three unit residential building and the seller must give the buyer a TDS.   Pg 4-17

25. Ans-B If a seller refuses to truthfully disclose defects when filling out a real estate transfer disclosure statement, the real estate broker should refuse to take the listing.   Pg 4-18

26. Ans-B Easton v. Strassburger ruled that the seller and agent must disclose to the buyer all facts materially affecting the value or desirability of the property. This case led to the creation of the Transfer Disclosure law.   Pg 4-19

27. Ans-A The earthquake faults zones are 1/4 mile wide on maps available to the public.   Pg 4-20

28. Ans-A If the buyers do not receive the EPA pamphlet "Protect Your Family From Lead in Your Home" when buying a home built prior to 1978, the buyers can cancel the transaction.   Pg 4-20

Notes:

Chapter 5

CONTRACTS

(Approximately 12% of Salesperson Exam)

I. **CONTRACTS** - California's Civil Code states, "A contract is an agreement to do or not to do a certain thing."

   A. **Contract Terminology**

   1. **Unilateral Contract** - a contract in which a promise is given by one party to persuade the other party to do some action **(a promise for an act)**. The second party is not bound to act, but if he does act, the first party must keep his promise **(such as option contracts or open listings).**

   2. **Bilateral Contract** - a contract in which the promise of one party is given in exchange for the promise of the other party **(a promise for a promise)**. The parties are bound to perform. These promises are often the basis for a contract **(for example, exclusive listings and deposit receipts).**

   3. **Executory Contract** - a contract in which something remains to be done by one or both parties.

   4. **Executed Contract** - a contract in which both parties have completely performed their duties.

   5. **Express Contract** - a contract expressed in **words, either oral or written.**

   6. **Voidable Contract** - a contract which is valid and enforceable on its face, but because of some defect, one or more of the parties may reject (void) it. **A voidable contract is valid until it is voided** (rescinded) by the injured party.

   7. **Void Contract** - not a contract, it lacks legal effect. A void contract lacks one or more of the four essential elements required by law to make a contract.

Question #1 An employment contract between the seller of a home and a broker, whereby the seller agrees to pay the broker a commission if she produces a "ready, willing, and able" buyer and in return, the broker agrees to use due diligence in procuring the buyer, is called: (A) a unilateral executory contract; (B) a unilateral executed contract; (C) a bilateral executory contract; (D) a bilateral executed contract.

Question #2 Joe, a licensed real estate broker, has just written up an exclusive listing on Fred's home. At this time, Joe's listing may be described as: (A) a bilateral contract; (B) an executory contract; (C) an express contract; (D) all of the above.

Question #3 A contract which is voidable remains binding upon the buyer and seller until the contract is: (A) invalidated; (B) rescinded; (C) discovered; (D) qualified.

Answers: #1-C; #2-D; #3-B

8. **Valid Contract** - a contract that is binding and enforceable. It has all **four of the essential elements** required by law.

9. **Contract Date** - the date the contract is formed. The contract (deposit receipt) is formed when the final acceptance is communicated to the offeror.

B. Four Essential Elements of Contracts

1. **Capable Parties** - everyone is capable of contracting (including aliens), except:
   a. Minors - persons under the age of 18. A **minor may not enter into a contract** to hold title to real property, unless he is emancipated. A real estate contract (listing or purchase agreement) entered into by a minor is void. Most other non-real estate contracts are voidable by the minor.

   Notes: 1. Married minors and veterans who are minors are considered emancipated and can enter into contracts. A divorced 17 year old is considered an emancipated minor.
   2. Convicts in prison may not enter into most contracts. A convict may not enter into a contract to purchase real property.

   b. Mentally incompetent individuals - once the court rules that an individual is mentally incompetent, he or she loses the right to enter into a contract.

2. **Mutual Consent** - for a contract to be valid, there must be mutual consent or assent to the terms. In real estate contracts, **mutual consent is created by three steps:**
   a. Step 1 - an **offer** by one party.
   b. Step 2 - **acceptance** by the other party. The acceptance must be absolute and unqualified (a mirror image of the offer); if it modifies the terms of the offer in any material way, it becomes a counter-offer.
   c. Step 3 - the acceptance must be **communicated to the offeror**. A seller's acceptance of an offer has been communicated to the buyer as soon as the buyer receives a fax from the seller confirming the acceptance.

Question #4 The contract date of a deposit receipt is the date in that: (A) the earnest money was received; (B) the contract has been prepared by the agent; (C) buyer signed the contract; (D) final acceptance was properly communicated back to the offeror.

Question #5 Broker Jones represented a young man in the sale of his home. Broker Jones did not considered the age of the young man when he listed and sold the home. After the grant deed had been signed and delivered into escrow, the title company discovered the young man who signed the deed was not yet 18 years old and was not emancipated. The grant deed would be: (A) illegal; (B) void; (C) binding; (D) valid.

Question #6 John made an offer which the seller accepted; however, the seller changed a term of the offer as he made his acceptance. This can be described as a: (A) purchase contract; (B) counter-offer; (C) addendum; (D) amendment.

Answers: *#4-D; #5-B; #6-B*

Notes: Mutual Consent can be prevented by:
1. **Fraud** - contract is usually voidable. The buyer or seller must have relied upon a misrepresentation in order to claim fraud.
2. **Mistake** - a contract entered into as the result of a mistake is void or voidable.
3. **Duress** - a contract entered into under duress is voidable by the injured party. For example: A contract entered into by a tenant under threat of eviction by the owner is voidable by the tenant.

3. **Lawful Object** - a contract must be legal in formation and operation. Both its consideration and its object must be lawful. A contract entered into for an **illegal purpose is void.**

4. **Consideration** - every executory contract requires sufficient consideration. Consideration is anything of value; it does not have to be money, it can be a benefit conferred or a promise. **In a bilateral contract, the promises are often the consideration.** The words "adequate, valuable, good or sufficient" in a contract refer to consideration. **Valuable consideration** in a contract consists of: services to be provided by one or both parties, whatever the parties consider to be of value, and/or money.

Note: **"Performance" is not an essential element** to form a contract.

C. **Statute of Frauds** - determines which contracts must be in writing to be enforceable. The following contracts **must be in writing to be enforceable:**

1. **Not Performed Within One Year** - a contract which by its terms is not to be performed within one year of its making.

2. **Lease for More Than One Year** - a contract leasing real property for more than one year.

3. **Listing** - a listing to sell real property.

4. **Selling Real Property** - a contract selling real property.

5. **Another's Debt** - an agreement to **pay the debt of another.**

Question #7 A contract entered into under duress would be: (A) voidable; (B) valid; (C) void; (D) illusory.

Question #8 All of the following contracts are voidable **except** a contract entered into: (A) under undue influence; (B) for an illegal purpose; (C) under duress; (D) as the result of fraud.

Question #9 The words "adequate, valuable, good or sufficient" in a contract refer to: (A) mutual consent; (B) performance; (C) consideration; (D) compensation.

Answers: #7-A; #8-B; #9-C

Notes: 1. Some oral real estate contracts are enforceable, such as:
   a. A lease of real property for **one year or less.**
   b. A listing contract to sell personal property (a business opportunity).
   c. **An agreement between brokers to share a commission.**
2. A seller may sue a broker who fails to keep an oral promise.

D. Performance of Contracts

1. **Assignment** - contracts are assignable unless they call for some personal quality of the promisor, or unless they expressly or implicitly negate the right to assign (for example, a listing cannot be assigned because it is a personal service contract).

2. **Novation** - the agreement of the parties to substitute a new contract for an existing one with the intent to replace the original contract (for example, a **broker might be replaced in a listing by way of novation**).

3. **Tender** - an unconditional offer of money or performance according to the terms of a contract.

4. **Waiver** - a unilateral act and its legal consequences. A waiver in a contract occurs when one party agrees to give up a right voluntarily.

5. **Rescission (Annulment)** - the revocation or repealing of a contract by mutual consent by parties to the contract, or for cause by either party to the contract. When a buyer backs out of a contract to buy a home and the seller exercises his right of rescission, the seller must return the deposit to the buyer. Additionally, the seller can sue the buyer and attempt to sell the property to someone else in order to limit the damages.

Question #10 According to the Statute of Frauds, all of the following contracts are required to be in writing to be enforceable, **except**: (A) a listing to sell real property; (B) a contract selling real property; (C) an agreement between real estate brokers to share a commission; (D) none of the above.

Question #11 What is it called when one party is substituted for another party in a contract? (A) waiver; (B) rescission; (C) redaction; (D) novation.

Question #12 The meaning of the word "waiver," as it is applicable to a real estate transaction most nearly means: (A) a unilateral act and its legal consequences; (B) the justifiable reliance by one party upon the intentional act or omission of another; (C) tender; (D) estoppel.

Answers: #10-C; #11-D; #12-A

6. **Addendum** - additional documents attached to and made part of a contract.

7. **Amendment** - a change to an existing contract by mutual agreement of the parties.

8. **Interpretation** - when there is a conflict between portions of a contract which are handwritten information and preprinted clauses in a contract, the handwritten information takes precedence over the preprinted clauses.

E. **Remedies for Breach of Contract**

1. **Sue for Specific Performance** - used only when dollar damages will not provide an adequate remedy for buyer. **In the opinion of the law, all real property is unique,** therefore dollar damages will not "make the buyer whole" when a seller wrongfully backs out of a contract to sell real property. When suing for specific performance, **the court will order a seller to sign the deed** if the buyer can prove the monetary consideration was **sufficient relative to the value** of the property.

*Note: A **broker may not sue a buyer or a seller for specific performance** of a real estate contract; instead, the broker sues for money damages.*

2. **Sue for Damages**
    a. **Liquidated Damages Clause** - a clause in a contract fixing the amount of damages should one of the parties default.
    b. The standard residential **deposit receipt** contains a **liquidated damages clause,** "... in event of default by buyer, seller shall retain as liquidated damages, **3% of the purchase price or the amount of the deposit, whichever is less.**"
    c. When a buyer defaults, the **liquidated damages** are usually **divided equally** between the **seller and the listing agent**.

Question #13   In a legal dispute when there is a conflict between the preprinted clauses and the handwritten information in a contract, which will control? (A) preprinted clauses take precedence over handwritten information; (B) the handwritten information takes precedence over the preprinted clauses; (C) the preprinted clauses and handwritten information are considered equally; (D) handwritten information is illegal on preprinted contracts.

Question #14   In real estate contracts, the consideration must be sufficient relative to value in order to win a lawsuit seeking: (A) a lis pendens; (B) specific performance; (C) an attachment; (D) damages.

Question #15   When the facts of a lawsuit suggest that an award of money damages would not provide an adequate remedy for breach of contract, the person bringing the suit may seek specific performance. Which of the following people will **not** get a specific performance judgment from the court? (A) a real estate broker in his capacity as agent for the principal; (B) a buyer who is purchasing a home; (C) an attorney-in-fact acting for a buyer who resides in another state; (D) the buyer of vacant land.

Answers: *#13-B; #14-B; #15-A*

II. LISTING AGREEMENTS
- a listing is an **employment contract** between a principal (usually the seller) and an agent (the broker) employing the agent to do certain things for the principal. A **bona fide listing** to sell real property must contain capable parties, mutual consent, lawful object, consideration, and be in writing. In the listing contract the "terms of sale" should include the exact terms the seller is willing to accept. The **listing belongs to the broker**, not the salesperson who took the listing. A listing is a two party contract, between broker and the seller. If the **broker for a real estate office dies, all listings in the office are cancelled.** The new broker has to re-list the old listings.

A. Types of Listings

1. **Open Listing (Non-Exclusive Listing)** - a contract given by an owner authorizing a broker to act as his agent. The broker must be the "procuring cause" (responsible for the consummation of the transaction) to be entitled to a commission.

2. **Exclusive Agency Listing** - a contract in which a seller agrees to pay a commission to the listing agent if his property sells through the listing agent or any other agent, but the seller retains the right to sell directly to a buyer and pay no commission. A seller who gives an **exclusive agency listing** to one broker, and **an open listing to a second broker** would be **liable for two commissions** if the second broker sold the property.

3. **Exclusive Authorization and Right to Sell Listing** - a contract in which a seller agrees to sell through the listing broker only. If his property is sold by anyone during the term of the listing (listing broker, another broker, the seller, or any other source), the listing broker has the right to the commission.

Question #16   When a salesperson takes a listing, the listing is the property of: (A) the salesperson who took the listing; (B) the broker who employs the salesperson; (C) both the employing broker and the listing salesperson; (D) the multiple listing service.

Question #17   Broker John has an open listing on a home. One day he shows the home to Buyer Bud. Buyer Bud says he does not like the home and leaves. One week later Buyer Bud goes to Broker Joan. Broker Joan has an open listing on the exact same home and shows it to Buyer Bud. This time Buyer Bud says he loves the home. He has Broker Joan write and present an offer, which is accepted by the seller. Who is entitled to the commission? (A) Broker John; (B) Broker Joan; (C) Broker John and Broker Joan must split the commission; (D) none of the above.

Question#18   With regard to the practice of real estate, which of the following statements is correct? (A) a real estate agent's commission is limited by law in all transactions; (B) a broker may never collect a commission if a sale is consummated after a listing has expired; (C) an agreement to divide commissions between cooperating brokers must be in writing to be enforceable; (D) in an exclusive agency listing, a seller may sell directly to a buyer without being liable for a commission.

Answers: *#16-B; #17-B; #18-D*

Notes: 1. **Net Listing** - *a listing where the agent's commission consists of any money that is left over after the seller receives a fixed amount.* **For example,** *if an agent agrees to take a $300,000 net listing, the seller receives the first $300,000 and the agent gets the rest as his commission. If the seller accepts a $340,000 offer, the seller receives $300,000 and the agent receives $40,000. If the seller accepts an offer of $300,000 or less,* **the agent receives no commission.** *A net listing requires an agent to disclose the selling price and the amount of his commission to the seller when presenting an offer.*

2. **Exclusive Authorization and Right to Locate Property** *(Buyer Listing) - a contract in which a buyer agrees to buy through the buyer's agent only. A buyer's agent under this listing may act as a single agent for the buyer only, or act as a dual agent for buyer and seller (with the knowledge and consent of both parties). An exclusive buyer's agent may also represent other buyers.*

B. **General Listing Information**

1. **Property Description** - a listing does not need a legal description as long as it adequately describes the property listed for sale. A street address is adequate as long as the seller does not own any other property with the same street address.

2. **Due Diligence** - when a broker takes an exclusive listing, she is obligated to advertise the property and use due diligence to procure a buyer.

3. **Typical Listing - authorizes the broker to accept a deposit** as the seller's agent. If the broker is not authorized to receive a deposit, but receives one anyway, he is treated as the buyer's agent for that one act.

4. **Broker Protection Clause (Broker Safety Clause) - a clause in a listing** which allows a broker to receive a commission if a buyer he introduced to the property buys the property after the listing has expired.

Question #19 In which of the following listings would the agent who was the procuring cause of a successful offer possibly earn no commission? (A) open listing; (B) exclusive agency listing; (C) exclusive right to sell listing; (D) net listing.

Question #20 An exclusive right to locate property listing with a buyer is: (A) a single agency representing the buyer only; (B) a dual agency for both buyer and seller, even without the consent of the parties; (C) a single agency to the buyer, but could become a dual agency representing both buyer and seller with the knowledge and consent of both parties; (D) not allowed.

Question #21 A real estate broker has the right to be paid a commission when a property sells during the listing period. What is the name of the clause in many listings which allows the broker to earn a commission when the property sells after the listing has expired? (A) broker's safety clause; (B) exculpatory clause; (C) subordination clause; (D) none of the above.

Answers: *#19-D; #20-C; #21-A*

5. **Hold Harmless Clause** - a clause in a listing contract designed to protect an agent from liability for false information given by the seller about the condition of the property.

6. **Commission** - may be in the form of **cash, a check, an assignment of a promissory note, and/or anything of value.** A seller may turn down an offer which fails to meet the exact terms of the listing without liability to the buyer and without liability for the commission.

7. **Termination Date** - any **exclusive listing** must have a definite termination date. The termination date may be any length of time; the length is determined by mutual agreement between the seller and the listing agent. An agent may use an **open listing** without a termination date.

8. **Cancellation of Listing** - The owner can cancel an exclusive listing at any time, but may be liable for the payment of damages under the agreement.

Note: An agent should check the bylaws or the charter of a non-profit unincorporated association to see who has the authority to sell the property before taking a listing.

III. **Residential Purchase Agreement (RPA, Deposit Receipt)** - contract used to write an offer, the contract to sell real property. It is called a deposit receipt because the buyer usually gives the agent a deposit of money accompanying the offer and receives a copy of the offer as a receipt for the deposit. The deposit may be in the form of cash, check, promissory note, and/or almost anything of value agreeable to the parties. The agent should inform the seller about what type of deposit accompanies the offer, prior to the seller's acceptance of the offer.

   A. **Contingencies** - an offer with contingencies is enforceable. If a contingency fails, the buyer is not obligated to perform. Agents should always advise their clients of the advantages and disadvantages of removing the contingency and let the client decide. When discussing a contingency in a contract with a buyer or seller, the real estate agent should be sure to explain the duration of the contingency, the nature of the contingency and the method of removal of the contingency.

Question #22 The purpose of a "hold harmless" clause in a listing contract is to protect the agent from liability for: (A) any and all lawsuits resulting from the transaction; (B) misrepresentations made by the agent to a potential buyer; (C) false information given by the seller concerning the condition of the property; (D) damages as a result of the buyer misrepresenting his qualifications to get the loan.

Question #23 What are the minimum and maximum lengths of time for which a real estate agent may have an exclusive authorization and right to sell listing on real property? (A) 1 day and 90 days; (B) 1 week and 45 days; (C) 1 month and 6 months; (D) the listing may be for any length of time, determined by mutual agreement of seller and listing agent.

Question #24 A real estate licensee may do any of the following **except**: (A) claim compensation on a loan he arranged, but did not negotiate; (B) claim compensation on an open listing without a definite termination date; (C) sell his own property and claim a commission expense on taxes: (D) claim compensation on an exclusive listing without a definite termination date.

Answers: #22-C; #23-D; #24-D

- B. **Termination** - each of the following terminates an offer:

    1. **Revocation** - a buyer (offeror) may revoke his offer prior to communication of its acceptance for any reason. A buyer may not revoke his offer after the seller (offeree) has properly posted acceptance of the offer. When a buyer withdraws an offer he must receive his deposit back.

    2. **Rejection** - of the offer by the seller, or a counter-offer by the seller automatically terminates the original offer.

    3. **Death of Buyer** - death prior to communication of acceptance terminates the offer.

    4. **Expiration** - of time limit given in the offer for acceptance terminates the offer.

- C. **Time is of the essence clause - found in the residential purchase agreement;** it refers to the entire contract.

- D. **General Information About Residential Purchase Agreements**

    1. **Title Vesting** - when a married couple elects to take title as **husband and wife,** they have taken title in **community property.** If a real estate licensee advised buyers about how to take title when preparing a residential purchase agreement (deposit receipt), she may be giving tax advice, legal advice, and/or possibly providing a basis for a claim of discrimination.

    2. **Home Inspection** - if a buyer properly notifies the seller of a problem resulting from a home inspection during escrow, and the **seller quickly fixes** the problem, the buyer is bound by the contract. **The buyer must pay** for repairs if his property inspector damages the seller's property.

    3. **Arbitration Clause** - if the parties did not initial the arbitration clause and the buyer wishes to rescind the contract and get his deposit back, his remedy is to **file a court action.**

- E. **Multiple Offers** - a listing agent who receives **multiple offers on one property must present all of them at the same time** to the seller and let the seller decide which one to accept.

Question #25 A prospective buyer may withdraw her offer at any time before the seller's acceptance of her offer has been communicated to her: (A) unless the offer states that the offer is irrevocable; (B) provided the offer is not supported by a deposit; (C) only if the offeree has made a counter-offer; (D) for any reason.

Question #26 The "time is of the essence" clause in the residential purchase agreement refers to which of the following? (A) offer will expire if not accepted within ____ days of presentation; (B) offer is contingent upon ____; (C) deposit must be delivered into escrow within ____ days of acceptance; (D) the entire contract.

Question #27 Broker Hernandez had just received a full price offer on her listing. As the broker was leaving her office to present the offer, another broker handed her a second offer for $1,000 less than the listed price but which contained a larger down payment and better terms. What should broker Hernandez do? (A) tell the other broker the listing has already sold; (B) present both offers to the seller at the same time; (C) present both offers to the seller in the order received; (D) approach the first offeror and seek a higher offer on behalf of Hernandez's client.

Answers: #25-D; #26-D; #27-B

F. **Hold Deposit** - the deposit receipt gives the broker the authority to hold a buyer's deposit for **three business days**, or until the offer is accepted. If a seller requests the deposit after an offer has been accepted, the broker must obtain the written consent of the buyer before releasing the check to the seller.

IV. **OPTIONS** - an option is a contract to keep an offer to lease or sell real property open for a set period. During the term of the option, the seller agrees **not to revoke his offer** to sell. An option must be supported by actual monetary consideration (for example, in a lease-option, payment of rent can be the consideration for the option). An option contract totally restricts the optionor because it effectively clouds title to the property until the option has expired. An option does not necessarily require a separate sales contract.

  A. **Obligation** - the optionee has **no obligation to buy.**

  B. **Title** - the option does not give the optionee a legal interest in the title to the property encumbered by the option.

  C. **Right To Use** - the option does not give the optionee any right to use the land.

  D. **Option Listing (Listing with Option to Buy)** - an agent who has an option to buy a property which she also has listed for sale has a conflict of interest. In order to exercise the option to buy, the **agent must reveal to seller (in writing) any offers on the property and the amount of her profit.** Additionally, to exercise her option, the **agent must obtain the written consent of the seller.**

Question #28 What gives a broker the authority to hold a buyer's deposit for three business days, or until the offer is accepted? (A) the deposit receipt; (B) the listing; (C) the transfer disclosure statement; (D) the agency disclosure.

Question #29 A broker has an oral listing to sell real property. The broker presented an offer, which the seller accepted. The seller then requested that the broker give him the buyer's deposit check. The broker must: (A) first deposit the check into the broker's trust account; (B) deposit the check with a neutral escrow within three business days; (C) obtain the written consent of the buyer before releasing the check to the seller; (D) return the check to the buyer within three business days.

Question #30 What is the name of the agreement whereby the agent has the right to represent the seller in the sale of the property or purchase the property himself? (A) open listing; (B) option listing; (C) exclusive agency listing; (D) exclusive right to sell listing.

Answers: #28-A; #29-C; #30-B

V. MISCELLANEOUS REAL ESTATE PRACTICE

A. **Desk Cost** - A broker's **desk cost** is calculated by dividing the total operating expenses of the office, including salaries, rent, insurance, etc., by the number of salespersons.

B. **Company Dollar** - the **company dollar** is calculated by subtracting commissions paid to salespersons from the gross income of the brokerage.

C. **Negotiation of Commissions** - real estate commissions are negotiable. If a group of real estate brokers tried to set **fixed commission rates,** it would violate **anti-trust laws**. A listing on one-to-four residential units must contain the disclosure that commissions are negotiable.

Question #31 To be competitive, yet profitable in business, a real estate broker needs to be concerned with "desk cost." Which of the following most nearly represents the correct way to calculate "desk cost?' (A) add the total cost of all the furniture for each salesperson; (B) calculate the gross annual profit for the firm, less the expenses, divided by the number of salespersons; (C) divide the annual gross commission earned by the number of desks; (D) divide the total operating expenses of the office, including salaries, rent, insurance, etc. by the number of salespersons.

Question #32 A company dollar can be defined as: (A) the money required to establish the office; (B) the money left over after expenses; (C) the money left over after all commissions are subtracted from gross income; (D) the money the company sends to support the office.

Question #33 Which listing must contain this statement, "the amount of our rate of commission is not fixed by law. It is set by each broker individually and may be negotiable between the seller and broker." (A) a listing on a 50 unit apartment building; (B) a listing on a commercial building; (C) a listing on a building used for manufacturing; (D) a listing on one-to-four residential units.

Answers: #31-D; #32-C; #33-D

Chapter #5 Review Questions

This exam contains 16 questions. You have an average of 78 seconds per question on the Salesperson Exam. 16 questions x 78 seconds per question = 1248 seconds. Please give yourself 20 minutes to complete this practice exam, and take the exam in one sitting.

1. When two parties attempt to form a contract, but fail to include one or more of the four essential elements of contracts, this attempted contract is properly called: (A) an enforceable contract; (B) a void contract; (C) an express contract; (D) a unilateral contract.

2. None of the following persons may lawfully enter into a valid contract to purchase real property **except:** (A) unemancipated minors; (B) minors who are wards of the court; (C) convicts in prison; (D) aliens.

3. Broker Smith presented a written offer to Seller Burns from buyer Taylor. The offer stated that upon acceptance buyer Taylor would deposit $15,000 in escrow. Seller Burns made some amendments by innerlining changes, but did not change the amount of deposit. Buyer Taylor agreed to all the changes and changed the amount of the deposit to $1,000. Broker Smith should be aware that: (A) Buyer Taylor has created a counter-offer because of the changed deposit; (B) Broker Smith must get Seller Burns' acceptance of the counter-offer; (C) no contract has yet been formed; (D) all of the above are true.

4. Which of the following is **not** an essential element in the formation of a contract? (A) offer; (B) acceptance; (C) capable parties; (D) performance.

5. Which of the following are necessary for a real property conditional sales contract to be valid? (A) consideration, offer and acceptance, mutuality, competent parties, and legally sufficient writing; (B) consideration, offer and acceptance, expressed time element and price; (C) lawful object, competent parties, offer and acceptance, and legally sufficient writing; (D) consideration, offer and acceptance, lawful object, competent parties, and legally sufficient writing.

6. An offer of performance in connection with a contract is called: (A) a conditional offer; (B) a tender; (C) a covenant; (D) a license.

7. The clause in a real estate deposit receipt that sets forth a definite amount of damages to be paid to the seller in the event of a breach of contract by the buyer, and which requires both buyer and seller's initials to be placed in the designated places on that contract is known as: (A) caveat emptor clause; (B) buyer beware clause; (C) seller's damages clause; (D) liquidated damages.

8. Who are the parties to a listing contract? (A) broker and seller; (B) broker, seller and salesperson who took the listing; (C) broker, seller, salesperson who took the listing, and multiple listing service; (D) broker, seller, salesperson who took the listing, multiple listing service, butcher, baker and candlestick maker.

9. Under which of the following listings must the seller pay a commission, even though he finds the buyer himself? (A) non-exclusive listing; (B) exclusive agency listing; (C) exclusive right to sell listing; (D) open listing.

10. What gives a broker the authority to receive a deposit for a seller as the seller's agent? (A) the deposit receipt; (B) the listing; (C) the transfer disclosure statement; (D) the agency disclosure.

11. A broker is trying to list real estate owned by a non-profit unincorporated association. To be sure that the proper party signs the listing, he should: (A) ask the lending institution that lent the money to build the church; (B) ask two past officers of the association; (C) check the bylaws or the charter to see who has the authority to sell the property; (D) examine the minutes of the last Board of Director's meeting.

12. Each of the following will terminate an offer to buy real estate, **except:** (A) the offeror revokes offer after offeree has properly posted acceptance of the offer; (B) the offeree fails to accept the offer within the time limit specified in the offer by the offeror; (C) the offeree makes a counteroffer to the offeror; (D) the offeror dies or is declared legally incompetent prior to offeree's acceptance.

13. Broker Bob wrote up an offer to buy real property for Buyer Don. Before Broker Bob could inform Buyer Don that his offer had been accepted, Buyer Don died of a heart attack. Under these circumstances there is: (A) a binding contract on the heirs of Buyer Don; (B) a binding contract because, the death of the buyer does not terminate an offer; (C) no contract; (D) a binding contract, only if Broker Don places a copy of the signed contract in the deceased buyer's hand prior to the funeral.

14. In which of the following contracts does one of the parties agree not to revoke an offer? (A) lease; (B) option; (C) open listing; (D) deposit receipt.

15. Broker Hernandez took a listing from owner, Mr. Nguyen. Mr. Nguyen also gave Broker Hernandez the option to purchase this commercially zoned land within 30 days. On the 27th day of the option period, Broker Hernandez decided to purchase the land. Broker Hernandez must do which of the following before purchasing this property which he has also listed for sale? (A) furnish owner with any material information Broker Hernandez has in his possession concerning the property; (B) disclose to Mr. Nguyen any outstanding offers on the property; (C) obtain written consent of Mr. Nguyen approving the amount of profit or anticipated profit if any is to be realized; (D) do all of the above.

16. When a group of competing local brokers get together and agree on setting commissions based upon a minimum commission schedule, this is considered: (A) a violation of anti-trust law; (B) appropriate business cooperation; (C) good consumer protection; (D) allowed, if approved by their local realty MLS.

Chapter #5 Review Questions - Answers

1. Ans-B When parties attempt to form a contract, but fail to include one or more of the four essential elements of contracts; this attempted contract is properly called a void contract.
Pg 5-1

2. Ans-D Aliens may lawfully enter into a valid contract.   Pg 5-2

3. Ans-D The acceptance must be unqualified to have mutual consent to the contract. When buyer Taylor changed the amount of the deposit, buyer Taylor was making a counter-offer to seller Burns. There is no contract until Seller Burns accepts this counter-offer.   Pg 5-2

4. Ans-D The four essential elements of contracts are: capable parties, mutual consent, lawful object and consideration, not performance.   Pg 5-2, 5-3

5. Ans-D Real estate contracts typically require: consideration, offer and acceptance, lawful object, competent parties, and legally sufficient writing.   Pgs 5-2, 5-3

6. Ans-B A tender is an offer of performance as part of a contract.   Pg 5-4

7. Ans-D The liquidated damages clause in the deposit receipt fixes the amount of damages to be received by the seller upon default of the buyer.   Pg 5-5

8. Ans-A The listing belongs to the broker, not the salesperson. A listing is a two party contract, between broker and the seller.   Pg 5-6

9 Ans-C In the exclusive right to sell listing the seller must pay a commission, even if the seller finds the buyer himself.   Pg 5-6

10. Ans-B The listing gives a broker the authority to receive a deposit for a seller as the seller's agent.   Pg 5-7

11. Ans-C A broker is trying to list real estate owned by a non-profit unincorporated association should check the bylaws or the charter to see who has the authority to sell the property.   Pg 5-8

12. Ans-A When the offeree posted his acceptance of the offer, he accepted the offer. The offeror cannot revoke an offer after the offeree has properly given his acceptance.   Pg 5-9

13. Ans-C There is no contract, because the death of the buyer revoked the offer prior to the communication of seller's acceptance to the buyer.   Pg 5-9

14. Ans-B During the term of the option, the seller agrees not to revoke his offer to sell.   Pg 5-10

15. Ans-D Before an agent with an option listing can exercise the option he must:
(1) disclose the existence of any other offers;
(2) disclose all material information, including the full amount of his commission and;
(3) obtain the written consent of the seller.   Pg 5-10

16. Ans-A If a group of real estate brokers tried to set fixed commission rates, it violates anti-trust laws.   Pg 5-11

Chapter 6

LAWS OF AGENCY

(Approximately 17% of Salesperson Exam)

I. **AGENCY LAW AND DEFINITIONS** - an agent is a person authorized to represent a principal in business dealings with other parties.

   A. **Nature of Agency Relationships** - there are **three common agency relationships in real estate sales**: an agent for the seller only, an agent for the buyer only, or a dual agent for both the seller and the buyer. There is no need to pay consideration to create an agency relationship.

   B. **Agent and Subagent** - in describing the relationship between a **seller and a salesperson employed by the listing broker,** the salesperson is considered an **agent of the seller, not a subagent of the seller.**

      1. **Subagent** - a subagent is an agent who is appointed by the seller's agent to perform some or all of the seller's agent duties.

      2. **Principal and Subagent** - if a principal authorizes the appointment of a subagent, the principal is responsible for the acts of his or her subagent.

   Note: *When a seller's agent appoints a subagent with the seller's approval, the subagent represents the seller in a like manner as the original seller's agent. The original seller's agent is not responsible to buyers for the wrongful acts of the subagent. If the seller's agent appoints a subagent without the seller's approval, the seller's agent is liable for the acts of the other agent (the subagent), the seller is not liable.*

      3. **Fiduciary Duty of a Subagent** - a real estate broker acting as a subagent for the seller has a fiduciary duty to the seller, but no fiduciary duty to the agent who appointed him as a subagent.

Question #1 In describing the relationship between a seller and a salesperson employed by the listing broker, the salesperson is considered: (A) an agent of the seller; (B) a subagent of the seller; (C) an employee of the seller; (D) an independent contractor, employed by the seller.

Question #2 A real estate broker who has been appointed as a subagent for a seller, with the seller's approval, has which of the following duties? (A) a fiduciary duty equally to both the buyer and the seller; (B) a fiduciary duty to the seller only; (C) a fiduciary duty to the seller and the broker who appointed him as the subagent; (D) a duty to be honest and fair to the seller and a fiduciary duty to the broker who appointed him as the subagent.

Question #3 When a real estate broker has been authorized by another real estate broker to act as a subagent for a seller and the seller has approved the appointment of the subagent, the subagent is primarily responsible to: (A) the broker who appointed him; (B) the seller; (C) both the broker and seller equally; (D) neither the broker nor the seller.

Answers: #1-A; #2-B; #3-B

C. Dual and Single Agent

1. **Dual Agent** - represents both the seller and the buyer in one transaction.

2. **Single Agent** - a single agent is the opposite of a dual agent. A single agency broker is more **client-oriented;** he represents a buyer only or a seller only, not both at the same time.

D. General Agent and Special Agent

1. **General Agent** - an agent authorized by a principal to perform acts associated with an ongoing business for the principal. The essential feature of a general agency is the continuity of service (for example, a property manager for a large apartment complex).

2. **Special Agent** - an agent who is authorized by a principal to perform a particular act or transaction, without the continuity of service of a general agent. A real estate broker is usually employed as a special agent by a seller to find a buyer for a particular property.

II. CREATION OF AGENCY AND AGENCY AGREEMENTS - agency may be created by express agreement, implied agreement, ratification, or estoppel.

A. **Express Agreement -** the agreement is created by words, either oral or written.

B. **Implied Agreement** - the agreement is created by acts and conduct, rather than words.

C. **Ratification** - the principal approves the agency after it has been performed.

D. **Estoppel** - a legal and equitable doctrine under which a person is barred from asserting or denying a fact because of the person's previous acts or words.

Notes: 1. An "estoppel certificate" is a statement by a tenant confirming the terms of the lease and that the tenant has no claims against the landlord.
2. Under limited circumstances, an agency may be created by necessity or emergency.
3. "Subornation" means doing something by lie, trickery, or deceit. An agency relationship may not be created by subornation.

Question #4   When a real estate broker is employed to represent a seller in the sale of a property, the broker is usually employed to act as: (A) a limited agent; (B) a privileged agent; (C) a general agent; (D) a special agent.

Question #5   The agency of a real estate broker may be established by: (A) express agreement; (B) implied agreement; (C) ratification or estoppel; (D) any of the above.

Question #6   The term "estoppel" describes: (A) an architectural element; (B) a plumbing fixture; (C) a document confirming the terms of a lease and that tenant has no claims against the landlord; (D) a trade fixture.

Answers: #4-D; #5-D; #6-C

III. SCOPE OF AUTHORITY - an agent has authority which the principal **actually, expressly**, or **ostensibly** (apparently) confers upon him.

   A. **Actual Authority** - the authority a principal intentionally confers upon an agent, or by want of ordinary care, allows an agent to believe that he or she possesses.

   B. **Express Authority** (Specific Authority) - created by an express agreement between the parties (a contract) which precisely delineates the activities the agent is authorized to undertake.

   C. **Ostensible Authority** (Implied Authority, Ostensible Agency) - may result from the conduct of the parties. If a broker provided agency services for both a buyer and a seller without the proper disclosures (because he was unaware that both the buyer and the seller considered him their agent), he became an ostensible agent.

IV. RESPONSIBILITIES OF AGENT TO SELLER/BUYER AS PRINCIPAL

   A. **Fiduciary Duty** - an agency relationship creates a **fiduciary duty**. A fiduciary owes a **duty of utmost care, integrity, trust, and loyalty** to the principal they represent. A fiduciary must place the best interest of his principal above the interest of all others, even his own.

   B. **Relationship** - the fiduciary (agency) relationship between a **broker and principal** is similar to the relationship between a **trustee and beneficiary** in a trust deed. The broker representing the principal does not become an attorney-in-fact for the principal.

   C. **Confidentiality** - Confidential or privileged information (personal financial information) obtained by an agent about his or her principal must be kept confidential forever. The obligation of an agent to keep this information confidential never ends.

   D. **Responsibilities - a principal is responsible for an agent's actions.** However, **the seller is not liable** for misrepresentations made by a selling agent (a buyer's broker in a transaction involving two agents) because in that situation, the buyer is the principal of the selling agent, not the seller.

Question #7 A broker provided agency services for both a buyer and a seller without the proper disclosures because he was unaware that both the buyer and the seller considered him to be their agent. Consequently, the broker was involved in which of the following: (A) voidable agency; (B) accidental agency; (C) ostensible agency; (D) deniable agency.

Question #8 The fiduciary relationship between an agent and the principal is comparable to the relationship between: (A) trustor and beneficiary; (B) mortgagor and mortgagee; (C) trustor and trustee; (D) trustee and beneficiary.

Question #9 The relationship of a broker representing a principal when dealing with a third party in selling, buying, or exchanging property is defined as all of the following **except**: (A) a fiduciary relationship; (B) an agency relationship; (C) an attorney-in-fact relationship; (D) broker/client relationship.

Answers: #7-C; #8-D; #9-C

E. Agent - Principal Relationship

1. **Duties of the agent**
   a. Disclose **all material facts** to the principal. If a listing agent discovers during escrow that a buyer (represented by his own agent) recently purchased many similar properties for a far greater price, he should disclose this information to the seller and let the seller decide what action to take.
   b. A real estate agent must present all offers unless:
      (1) Patently (obviously) frivolous, or
      (2) The principal has told him not to present further offers, or certain types of offers, or
      (3) The property has already sold and escrow has closed.
   c. An **agent must obey the principal's lawful instructions**. If the agent does not obey, he is **liable for damages.**

2. **Agent's rights**
   a. **Compensation** - the agent must do one of two things:
      (1) Find a buyer ready, willing, and able to purchase on the exact terms of the listing, or
      (2) Secure a binding contract between the buyer and the seller.
   b. An agent who secures a binding contract, or procures a perfect offer, is entitled to a commission, even if the seller cannot or will not sell.
   c. An **agent must be licensed at the time of sale and have a written employment contract** to enforce the listing and collect a commission.

Note: *If a **seller wants to pay a commission** to a broker under an **oral listing**, it is permissible for the real estate broker to accept the commission.*

Question #10 Agents must present offers to the seller until: (A) opening of escrow; (B) buyer has qualified for the loan; (C) documents were already drawn; (D) close of escrow.

Question #11 If a real estate broker fails to obey all lawful instructions given by his principal, the broker could be: (A) subjected to fine and/or imprisonment under the law; (B) prohibited by a court from working as a real estate broker; (C) liable in damages for any injuries suffered by the principal as a result; (D) all of the above.

Question 12 A seller entered into an oral listing agreement to sell real property with the broker, without a subsequent written verification. The payment of a commission to the broker under these circumstances would be: (A) permissible if the seller elects to do so; (B) a violation of the regulations of the Real Estate Commissioner; (C) regarded as contrary to public policy; (D) a violation of criminal law.

Answers: #10-D; #11-C; #12-A

F. **Agent's Liability to Third Parties (typically buyers)**

1. **Silence - failure to disclose material facts** (usually latent defects - for example, an agent may fail to reveal that a house is built on a septic tank or has a leaky roof). An **"as is" clause** in a deposit receipt **does not eliminate the duty to disclose material facts**. A **salesperson** who is working as **an agent for a seller** has the **responsibility to treat the buyer fairly and honestly and cannot withhold material information. For example:** When an agent discovers many homes in the subdivision have been "red tagged" because of septic tank failures, the agent should immediately disclose the problem to potential buyers.

2. **Lawsuits** - a buyer sues and collects from the seller. The seller, in turn, sues and collects from the agent (if the seller was unaware of the agent's fraud). In actual practice, the buyer who is the victim of misrepresentation sues both the broker and the seller (an example is, a situation in which a broker misrepresents the income produced by an apartment building).

3. **Limits on Authority** - if an agent acts in excess of his authority or misrepresents a property, he is liable to both the principal and the third party.

4. **Changing Terms** - a real estate agent may **never** change the terms of a buyer's offer without the buyer's approval.

5. **Misrepresentation by Agent** - an agent who intentionally misrepresents a property to a buyer may be subject to tort liability in a civil action, criminal action, and/or discipline by the Real Estate Commissioner. Additionally, the seller may be subjected to a rescission of the contract and a civil suit for damages because of the fraud.

Note: **Tort** - a negligent or intentional wrongful act arising from breach of duty.

Question 13 When dealing with the general public, which of the following may a broker **not** do? (A) delegate duties; (B) refuse to take a listing; (C) remain silent regarding material facts known only to him; (D) all of the above.

Question #14 Both the seller and broker were sued by the buyer because the broker failed to disclose the leaky roof to the buyer. The broker knew of the problem but forgot to disclose it to the buyer. The probable result of the lawsuit would be: (A) buyer was not entitled to recover from either the broker or the seller; (B) buyer recovered from the broker, but not the seller; (C) buyer recovered from the seller, but not the broker; (D) buyer would be successful in the suit against both seller and broker and the seller would be successful in the suit against the broker.

Question #15 When a broker, while acting as an agent for the seller in a sale of real property, misrepresents the property to a buyer, the broker may cause the seller to be subjected to: (A) rescission of the contract by the buyer; (B) a court action for damages by the buyer; (C) tort liability for damages; (D) any of the above.

Answers: #13-C; #14-D; #15-D

6. **Misrepresentation by Seller** - when a broker relies on **false information from the seller** and the buyer rescinds, the broker is entitled to a full commission and indemnity from legal action by the buyer.

V. **DISCLOSURE OF AGENCY** - California's Agency Disclosure law requires agents to disclose the common agency relationships in transactions concerning the sale or a lease for more than one year, of **four or less residential units**. The agency disclosure form required by this law sets forth disclosure obligations and describes certain duties a licensee owes to a principal in a real property transaction.

A. **Agency Relationships** - under California real estate law there are three common agency relationships in most real estate sales: an agent for a seller only, an agent for a buyer only, or a dual agent for both a buyer and a seller.

Note: A buyer's agency is a real estate brokerage which represents buyers only, and not sellers.

B. **Three Required Steps of Agency Disclosure**

1. **Disclose** - give the seller or the buyer the required agency disclosure form.
   a. Listing Agent - the listing agent must deliver an agency disclosure form to the seller as soon as practical and before entering into a listing agreement.
   b. Selling Agent - the selling broker must deliver the form to the buyer as soon as practical and before the buyer signs the offer to buy. The selling broker must provide the form to the seller as soon as practical and before presenting the offer.

2. **Elect** - choose the agency relationship for the transaction.
   a. Listing Agent - as soon as practical, a listing agent must disclose to the seller whether the listing agent is acting exclusively as the seller's agent, or as a dual agent representing both the seller and the buyer.
   b. Selling Agent - as soon as practical, a selling agent must disclose to the buyer and seller whether the agent is acting exclusively as the buyer's agent, exclusively as the seller's agent, or as a dual agent representing both the buyer and the seller.

Question #16 A broker made a sale to a buyer based on false information provided by the seller. The broker acted in good faith and had reasonably relied on the false information. Thereafter, the buyer rescinded the contract because of the fraud. Under these circumstances, the broker is normally entitled to: (A) only a reimbursement for out-of-pocket expenses; (B) a full commission and indemnity for any liability caused by legal action by the defrauded buyer against the broker; (C) one-half of the money deposited by the buyer in escrow; (D) no commission because an agent is responsible for the principal's action.

Question #17 The agency disclosure form must be given to the parties in which of the following transactions? (A) sale of a theater; (B) sale of an office building; (C) sale of vacant land; (D) sale of a residential triplex.

Question #18 Which of the following is true concerning a buyer agency? (A) it is illegal in California; (B) the agent represents buyers only; (C) the agent represents mostly buyers, but some sellers; (D) the agent must charge an advance fee to the buyer.

Answers: #16-B; #17-D; #18-B

3. **Confirm** - the disclosed agency relationships must be confirmed in writing, either in the purchase agreement or in separate writings executed or acknowledged by the seller, the buyer, and the agent(s), prior to or coincident with, the execution of the contract.
    a. If an agent properly discloses dual agency and obtains consent to represent both parties, he may collect a commission from each of them.
    b. If **an agent does not properly disclose a dual agency** to all parties, he may:
        (1) Be disciplined,
        (2) Provide grounds for either party to rescind,
        (3) Not receive any commission.

C. **In-House Sale** - describes a transaction in which both the buyer and the seller are represented by licensees working for one broker. In an in-house sale the licensee working with the buyer **may not be an agent for the buyer only**, because the brokerage already has an agency relationship with the seller. The only legal agency relationships in an in-house sale are "agent for seller" or "dual agent." Dual agency is most often used in in-house sales.

VI. DISCLOSURE OF ACTING AS PRINCIPAL OR OTHER INTEREST

A. **Relatives** - an agent must reveal if a **buyer is related** to him.

B. **Licensee as Principal** - whenever he is a principal in a real estate transaction, an agent must disclose to a buyer and/or seller that he has a license.

C. **Secret Profit** - an agent may not make any undisclosed profit in a real estate transaction. An agent in a real estate sales transaction who received a commission from the lender in the transaction must reveal the commission to both the buyer and seller.

Note: A **buyer who is not licensed may make a secret profit** without violating the law. An unlicensed buyer may buy a piece of real estate without telling the seller he already has someone ready to immediately buy the property from him at a large profit.

Question #19 Which of the following is **not** a required step for a licensee under the current agency disclosure law? (A) representation; (B) election; (C) confirmation; (D) disclosure.

Question #20 When a real estate agent acts as a dual agent for both the buyer and seller in a 1031 exchange, and does not disclose his dual agency to both parties, he may: (A) provide grounds for either party to rescind the purchase agreement; (B) be prevented from receiving any commission; (C) be disciplined by the Real Estate Commissioner; (D) all of the above.

Question #21 All of the following statements are true concerning an in-house sale, **except**: (A) the listing broker can buy the property himself; (B) the listing broker can act as an agent for the seller only; (C) the listing broker can act as an agent for the buyer only; (D) the listing broker can act as a dual agent for the seller and the buyer.

Answers: #19-A; #20-D; #21-C

VII. TERMINATION OF AGENCY - agency may be terminated by any of the following:

A. **Death or Incapacity** - of the agent (broker) or principal (seller or buyer).

B. **Mutual Consent** - of the agent and principal.

C. **Destruction** - of the subject matter of the agency.

D. **Expiration** - of the time given in an exclusive listing terminates the agency.

E. **Agent May Renounce** - the agency, but he will be liable for damages.

F. **Principal May Revoke** - the agency, but he will be liable for damages.

G. **Completion of Purpose** - for which the agency was established (close of escrow).

Note: An agency relationship may be created by **but not terminated by estoppel.**

Question #22 All of the following will terminate an agency relationship, **except**: (A) the death of the agent or the seller; (B) the mutual consent of agent and seller; (C) the destruction of the subject property; (D) estoppel.

Answers: *#22-D*

Chapter #6 Review Questions

This exam contains 11 questions. You have an average of 78 seconds per question on the Salesperson Exam. 11 questions x 78 seconds per question = 858 seconds. Please give yourself 14 minutes to complete this practice exam, and take the exam in one sitting.

1. Which of the following is a common agency relationship under California law? (A) agent for seller; (B) agent for buyer; (C) dual agent; (D) all of the above.

2. Why do some clients prefer "single agency" representation? (A) a "single agency" broker may have one of his salespersons become the agent for the seller and have another salesperson in his office become the agent for the buyer; (B) the "single agency" broker provides better service because he represents both the seller and buyer in the same transaction: (C) in a "single agency" transaction, the seller cannot choose his own broker or represent himself; (D) the "single agency" broker is more client oriented.

3. When a real estate licensee acts as an agent for a principal without authority or color of authority and the acts are later approved by the principal, an agency relationship was created by: (A) implication; (B) ratification; (C) express authorization; (D) estoppel.

4. An agency relationship may **not** be created by: (A) subornation; (B) oral agreement; (C) ratification; (D) necessity or emergency.

5. When a real estate broker becomes an agent for a seller or a buyer in a real estate transaction, what type of relationship has been established? (A) a gratuitous relationship; (B) a fiduciary relationship; (C) an independent contractor relationship; (D) a subcontractor relationship.

6. When a broker obtains confidential financial information about his principal during a real estate transaction, that information must be kept confidential for how long? (A) only until close of escrow; (B) 30 days after close of escrow; (C) three years after closing of the transaction; (D) forever.

7. When you, as a real estate agent, know that the seller will not accept an offer from the buyer, you should not do which of the following: (A) write new terms on the back of the offer and go back to the buyer for approval; (B) present the offer to the seller anyway; (C) upon rejection of the offer by the seller, induce the seller to make a counter-offer; (D) change the buyer's offer to what you believe the seller will accept, initial the changes, and then present the offer to the seller.

8. The selling agent, Jones, prepared an offer for a buyer of a home. At the very latest, when should agent Jones give the buyer the Agency Disclosure form? (A) as soon as he meets the buyer; (B) before showing the buyer the house; (C) before preparing the offer for the buyer; (D) at opening of escrow.

9. A real estate agent handling the sale of four or less residential units must elect his or her agency relationship to all the parties: (A) as soon as practical; (B) as soon as an offer has been accepted; (C) at the close of escrow; (D) whenever asked by either party.

10. A seller accepted an offer presented by a real estate broker. During escrow, the seller discovered that the buyer was the brother of the broker. This relationship was not disclosed in the offer. The seller can: (A) do nothing because the property sold for the full asking price; (B) cancel the transaction, but be liable for the full commission; (C) cancel the transaction without liability for the commission; (D) none of the above.

11. A lender paid a 3% commission to an agent in a real estate transaction. This must be revealed to: (A) the buyer only; (B) the seller only; (C) both the buyer and seller; (D) neither the buyer nor seller.

Chapter #6 Review Questions - Answers

1. Ans-D   The three common agency relationships under California law are: agent for seller, agent for buyer, and dual agent.   Pg 6-1

2. Ans-D   Some clients prefer "single agency" representation because the "single agency" broker can be more client oriented.   Pg 6-2

3. Ans-B   When a real estate licensee acts as an agent for a principal without authority or color of authority and the acts are later approved by the principal, the agency relationship was created by ratification.   Pg 6-2

4. Ans-A   "Subornation" means doing something by lie, trickery, or deceit. An agency relationship may not be created by subornation.   Pg 6-2

5. Ans-B   When a real estate broker becomes an agent for the seller or buyer in a real estate transaction, a fiduciary relationship has been established.   Pg 6-3

6. Ans-D   Confidential or privileged information (personal financial information) obtained by an agent about his or her principal must be kept confidential forever.   Pg 6-3

7. Ans-D   A real estate agent may never change the terms of a buyer's offer without the buyer's approval.   Pg 6-5

8. Ans-C   An agent must give a buyer the Agency Disclosure form before the buyer signs the offer to buy.   Pg 6-6

9. Ans-A   A real estate agent handling the sale of four or less residential units must elect his or her agency relationship to all the parties as soon as practical.   Pg 6-6

10. Ans-C   The broker must disclose to the seller that the buyer is related to him. The broker's failure to disclose the family relationship gives the seller the right to cancel the transaction without liability for the commission.   Pg 6-7

11. Ans-C   Compensation paid to a real estate agent by a lender must be disclosed to all parties to the transaction.   Pg 6-7

Chapter 7

VALUATION AND MARKET ANALYSIS
(APPRAISAL)

(Approximately 14% of Salesperson Exam)

I. **Appraisal** - an opinion of the value of a specific property on a **given date** to indicate the market conditions influencing the value of the property at a particular point in time. It is valid only for that date.

   A. **First Step** - the first step is to **define the problem.**

   B. **Final Step** - after the appraiser has collected all the data and applied different appraisal approaches, the **next (or final) step is to reconcile (correlate)** the values found in the different approaches.

   C. **Marketability and Acceptability - are important** in determining the appraised value of residential property. The property tax assessment of value is unimportant in determining the appraised value. The ultimate test of functional utility is marketability.

   D. **Appraisal Dates**

      1. **Date of Value** - the date of the inspection of the property.

      2. **Date of the Appraisal** - the date of the final writing or delivery of the appraisal report.

   Note: An appraiser is most interested in the "date the price was agreed upon."

II. **APPRAISAL REPORTS** - there are three basic styles of written appraisal reports:

   A. **Letter Form Report** - the least formal appraisal report. It can be a simple letter to the client summarizing the information.

   B. **Form Report** (Summary Report, Uniform Residential Appraisal Report) - a **checklist** form, with fill-in spaces, used primarily by appraisers for lending institutions. The "form report" is the most commonly used appraisal report.

   C. **Narrative Report** - the most comprehensive and complete analysis. It includes all information found by the appraiser as well as the reasoning and computations for the value conclusion. The narrative report has headings such as: Introduction, Site and Improvement Analysis, Supporting Data, and Opinion of Value.

Question #1 After the appraiser has collected all the data and applied the appropriate appraisal method(s), what is the next step in the appraisal process? (A) simply average out the value estimates; (B) reconcile or correlate the values found in the different approaches; (C) assign appropriate value to individual estimates and average the total number; (D) give an opinion of value.

Question #2 When an appraiser uses the market data approach to appraisal, she would be most interested in the date: (A) the price was agreed upon; (B) escrow was opened; (C) recording occurred; (D) escrow closed.

Question #3 Which type of appraisal report has the following headings: Introduction, Site and Improvement Analysis, Supporting Data, Opinion of Value? (A) letter report; (B) form report; (C) narrative report; (D) oral report.

Answers: #1-B; #2-A; #3-C

Notes:
1. Reports **do not usually** include information about a **buyer's financial condition.**
2. The "Statement of Purpose" in a narrative appraisal report includes the "type of value being estimated" (such as current market value or replacement value of the improvements).
3. An appraiser may appraise property for a corporation in which she owns stock if she discloses her stock ownership in her appraisal report.
4. A **certified general real estate appraiser's** license is required to appraise a non-residential property valued over $250,000 (example: a shopping center valued at $500,000).
5. A property inspector is not authorized to prepare an appraisal report.

III. PRINCIPLES OF VALUATION

A. Principle of Substitution (Comparison, Market Data) - the value of a property is usually determined by the cost of acquiring an equally desirable substitute property because no prudent person would pay more for a property than others are willing to pay. This principle is used in all appraisal techniques and is the **basis of the market data approach**, also known as the **comparison** or **substitution** approach.

B. Principle of Highest and Best Use - the best use of a parcel of land which will produce the **greatest net rate of return** over a given period of time. Determining the highest and best use is one of the first things an appraiser does when appraising vacant land. When appraisers use highest and best use principle on a **parcel with an existing structure of little value**, the appraiser **subtracts the demolition cost** of the structure from the value of the land. When appraising **vacant land,** the **primary purpose of a site analysis** is to determine the highest and best use. When the highest and best use is expected to change, the current use is called the **interim use.**

C. Principle of Conformity - holds that maximum value is found when land uses are compatible and have a reasonable degree of architectural harmony. Zoning ordinances are often used to help set conformity standards in a neighborhood.

Question #4   What appraisal license is required to appraise a strip mall valued at $500,000? (A) certified general real estate appraiser; (B) certified residential real estate license; (C) residential license; (D) trainee license.

Question #5   When the highest and best use of a property is expected to change, the current use is called: (A) the temporary use; (B) the interim use; (C) the transitional use; (D) the possible use.

Question #6   When homes in an area represent the highest and best use of the land and are similar in architectural design, this would best exemplify which of the following principles of appraisal? (A) change; (B) conformity; (C) contribution; (D) progression and regression.

Answers: #4-A; #5-B; #6-B

D. **Principle of Contribution** - when appraising a component or portion of income property, the appraiser considers its contribution to the net return (for example, if an owner of a 40-unit apartment building is considering installing a swimming pool, the owner needs to know how much, or what percentage, the investment will contribute to his net return). A **remodeling and modernization** program emphasizes the **net effect on income.**

E. **Principle of Regression** - the value of a **more expensive home is pulled down** when lesser quality (substandard) homes are built nearby. Building a large number of average priced homes in an area which previously had mostly high priced homes tends to destabilize values.

IV. **BASIC VALUATION DEFINITIONS**

A. **Value (worth)** - defined by appraisers as follows:

1. **Relationship** between the thing desired and the purchaser.

2. **Power** of one commodity to attract other commodities in exchange.

3. **Present worth** of future benefits arising from ownership of the property.

B. **Market Value (objective value)** - based on the concept of a "willing buyer" and a "willing seller." It is the most probable price the property should bring on the open market within a reasonable length of time. "Market value" is most nearly synonymous with **"market price."**

C. **Utility Value (subjective value)** - value as the property is used by the owner.

Question #7 An owner of a 40-unit apartment house is considering installing a swimming pool. He seeks a professional opinion from an appraiser. The appraiser would base his opinion upon which principle of appraisal? (A) contribution; (B) regression; (C) substitution; (D) integration.

Question #8 The value of the best property in a neighborhood is adversely affected by a substandard property nearby. This can be described as the principle of: (A) balance; (B) regression; (C) contribution; (D) progression.

Question #9 Market value is the price a willing buyer will pay and a willing seller will accept with both being fully informed, and the property being exposed to the market for a reasonable period of time. Market value is best expressed as: (A) present value of future income; (B) cost to reproduce improvements new; (C) value of a property is in the eye of the beholder; (D) objective value.

Answers: _#7-A; #8-B; #9-D_

    D. Improved Value of Land - the current market value of the land and improvements combined.

Notes:
1. Market value has very little relationship to original cost.
2. **Unearned Increment** - when property gains value due to inflation or an increase in population.
3. The **greatest stability in value** is found when there is a reasonable degree of conformity of style and design in a residential neighborhood.
4. Changes in financing terms will effect the **price, but not the value** of the property.
5. Real estate has inherent value when it represents the maximum utility of available resources.

V. ESSENTIAL ELEMENTS OF VALUE (**D U S T**)

    A. Demand - desire in the marketplace.

    B. Utility - ability of the property to satisfy a need or desire.

    C. Scarcity - availability in the marketplace.

    D. Transferability - to be marketable, the property must be transferable as to use or title.

Note: Cost, appreciation, and expectation **are not** essential elements of value.

VI. FOUR GREAT FORCES INFLUENCING VALUE

    A. Social Ideals and Standards

    B. Economic Influences

    C. Environmental and Physical Characteristics

    D. Governmental or Political Influences

Notes:
1. "Private restrictions" is not one of the four great forces influencing value.
2. An appraiser would have **little concern with the economy** when appraising a **medical building**.

Question #10 The "improved value" of land is: (A) the current market value of the land and improvements combined; (B) the present value of income to be received from the use of the land in the future; (C) the replacement cost of the improvements minus the depreciation; (D) the difference between the contract rent and the economic rent.

Question #11 When comparing the value of property and the price of property, changes in financing terms will affect: (A) value only; (B) price, not value; (C) only properties that have been sold; (D) both value and prices.

Question #12 All of the following are essential elements of value, **except**: (A) utility; (B) expectation; (C) scarcity; (D) transferability.

Answers: #10-A; #11-B; #12-B

VII. ADDITIONAL FACTORS INFLUENCING VALUE

A. **Exposure** - in commercial properties, merchants like properties on the south and west sides of the street, and on the southwest corner of intersections. **The north and east sides of the street are less desirable.**

B. **Topography** - the contour of the surface of the land. Some limited irregularity in contour is best for residential property (like gentle rolling hills).

C. **Orientation** - placement of a building on its lot in relation to exposure to sun, prevailing wind, traffic, and privacy from the street.

D. **Cost** - past expenditures of money to acquire the property. The cost equals the value of the improvements when the improvements are new and the improvements represent the highest and best use of the property.

E. **Price (market price)** - what the buyer really pays for the property. Conditions of sale may effect the price of the property (such as good financing, forced sale, or high pressure salesmanship).

F. **Plottage** - an added **increase in value** when **two or more lots are joined together**, above and beyond the value of the individual lots.

G. **Effective Age** - the apparent age of the improvement as opposed to its actual age (for example, a property which is 20 years old but has been superbly maintained may have an effective age of 9 years).

VIII. METHODS OF ESTIMATING VALUE

A. **Market Data Approach (Comparison Approach, Comparative Approach, or Substitution Method)** - sales of similar properties in the area are studied to form an opinion of value. Based upon the **principle of substitution**, the market data approach is the oldest, quickest, easiest to learn, and it is very adaptable. It is commonly used by agents and appraisers to appraise residences and vacant land. The market data approach is also used to **appraise amenity properties.**

Question #13 When developers select land for a residential subdivision they consider topography. Many developers believe that: (A) subdivisions which are built on rolling hills are less attractive aesthetically than those located on flat land; (B) some limited irregularity in topography is generally desirable for residential subdivisions; (C) flat land is more aesthetically desirable than rolling hills; (D) none of the above.

Question #14 The position of a building on a lot in relationship to exposure to the rays of the sun, prevailing wind, view, privacy from the street, etc., is known as: (A) elevation; (B) plottage; (C) orientation; (D) assemblage.

Question #15 The market data approach to appraisal is based upon which of the following? (A) principle of regression; (B) principle of anticipation; (C) principle of contribution; (D) principle of substitution.

Answers: #13-B; #14-C; #15-D

1. **Unit of Comparison** - when appraising a **single family home,** it is the entire property.

2. **Features** - when a comparable property has a feature not found in the subject property, the appraiser adjusts the comparable property to the characteristics of the subject property. The adjustment is made by subtracting the value of the feature from the sale price of the comparable. Appraisers find that adjusting for differences is the most difficult step in the process, but it is necessary because two properties are rarely identical in every way.

3. **Inactive Market** - the market data approach is not very effective in an inactive (slow moving) market and in times of **rapidly changing economic conditions.**

Note: When a residential neighborhood is comprised of mostly **owner occupied residential** properties, it tends to **stabilize values**. Increasing the population density and home sale turnover rate tends to destabilize a residential neighborhood.

B. **Cost Approach (Replacement Approach)** - used when other approaches are not appropriate, (such as **specific purpose buildings** or new subdivision homes). The cost approach is the least appropriate for appraising older buildings, because depreciation becomes difficult to calculate as the building gets older. The cost approach usually sets an upper limit on value. The cost approach has four steps:

1. **Step 1 - estimate the value of the land.** Land is usually appraised by **market data, comparative, or substitution methods.** It is most important to have a separate appraisal of the land and the improvements in the cost approach to appraisal. The units of comparison for land include:
   a. **Frontage - the distance a property adjoins a street or thoroughfare.**
   b. **Front Foot Value -** the deeper the lot, the greater the front foot value.
   c. **Cost Per Square Foot or Cost Per Acre -** the most common unit of comparison for appraising land.

2. **Step 2 - estimate replacement costs of improvements (as if new).**
   a. **Square Foot Method -** appraisers use exterior dimensions and compare the cost to build a similar quality improvement.

Question #16   In the market data approach to appraisal, any differences between the comparables and the subject property are handled in which of the following ways? (A) subject property is adjusted to the standards set by the comparables; (B) the subject property values are averaged to form a price range; (C) the comparables are adjusted to a market average; (D) the comparables are adjusted to the characteristics of the subject property.

Question #17   When a residential neighborhood is comprised mostly of owner occupied residential properties it tends to: (A) stabilize values; (B) attract commercial shopping centers to the neighborhood; (C) deteriorate faster than areas with many rental properties; (D) lower property values.

Question #18   The best appraisal method used by an appraiser to establish the value of a "specific purpose property" would be which of the following: (A) the market data approach; (B) the cost approach; (C) the capitalization or income approach; (D) the gross multiplier approach.

Answers: #16-D; #17-A; #18-B

b. **Cubic Foot Method** - used in multistory structures when the height between floors varies. Replacement cost of a warehouse would be calculated by cost per cubic foot.

c. Both **square foot** and **cubic foot** are **comparison or comparative methods**. Comparative methods are the easiest methods for estimating replacement cost.

d. **Quantity Survey Method** - an estimate of all labor and materials is compiled for each component of the building. This method is the **most detailed and accurate method of estimating cost of new improvements.**

e. **Unit-in-Place Cost Method** - adds the cost of the individual units as installed. It is also time consuming and **seldom used**.

Note: The **replacement cost** of an improvement is the cost to build a comparable structure. The **reproduction cost** of an improvement is the cost to build an exact duplicate. The **reproduction cost is usually higher than the replacement cost.**

3. **Step 3 - subtract accrued depreciation from the replacement cost of improvements.**
   a. **Depreciation is loss in value from any cause.** Depreciation accrues over time. Accrued depreciation is the most difficult to measure accurately. Unlike an accountant concerned with artificial tax depreciation, an appraiser looks for any actual loss in value.
   b. **Causes of depreciation** - depreciation may be the result of **obsolescence or physical deterioration.**
      (1) **Obsolescence**
         (a) **External (economic or social) obsolescence** is caused by **external events** (events occurring outside property lines). **Economic obsolescence is most difficult to correct.** Examples of economic obsolescence include:
            1) Nonconforming improvements near the property;
            2) Governmental restrictions (taxes, zoning, etc.);
            3) Social or economic changes;
            4) A poor sewer system in the area

Question #19 The fastest and easiest method of estimating the replacement cost of improvements is the:
(A) reproduction cost; (B) unit-in-place cost method; (C) quantity survey method; (D) comparative method.

Question #20 What type of depreciation is most difficult to correct? (A) internal obsolescence; (B) economic obsolescence; (C) physical obsolescence; (D) wear and tear.

Question #21 A developer wanted to subdivide land into residential lots. The city planning commission decided to increase the front yard setback requirement by 10 feet. The resulting loss in buildable space caused a loss in value of the lots. This loss in value was the result of: (A) physical obsolescence; (B) functional obsolescence; (C) economic obsolescence; (D) physical deterioration.

Answers: #19-D; #20-B; #21-C

- 5) Changes in supply and demand;
- 6) Airport noise;
- 7) An oversupply of like properties in the neighborhood;
- 8) Nearby nuisances - for example, an appraiser may lower his opinion of value as a result of noxious fumes coming from the property next door. This is economic obsolescence, not functional obsolescence.

(b) **Internal (functional) obsolescence** is caused by events occurring **within the property lines and observable during an inspection** by an appraiser, such as:

1) Poor design of improvements. When two adjacent homes cost the same to build but one is worth substantially less than the other, the difference in value would be functional obsolescence.
2) Outdated facilities (like an old kitchen, an outdated heating system, or a one-car garage).
3) Changes in construction styles.

(2) **Physical deterioration** is caused by events occurring within the property lines such as:

(a) Wear and tear (loss from wear and tear is **not obsolescence**).
(b) Deferred maintenance.

Note: **Obsolescence**, *not physical deterioration,* **is the major cause of depreciation.**

(3) **Definitions:**
(a) **Curable Depreciation** - economically and physically possible to correct.
(b) **Incurable Depreciation** - either too expensive or physically impossible to correct.
(c) **Economic Life** is the period of time in which an income property generates income in excess of its expenses. The income justifies the existence of the building. **The economic life is normally shorter than the physical life**, hence more buildings are torn down than fall down.

4. **Step 4 - add the value of the land to the depreciated value of the improvements.**

Question #22 The flight pattern at a nearby airport was changed so that planes pass directly over a residential neighborhood. The resulting loss in value to these properties was the result of: (A) economic obsolescence; (B) physical deterioration; (C) functional obsolescence; (D) physical obsolescence.

Question #23 Which of the following would be an example of functional obsolescence? (A) new zoning laws; (B) incompatible land use in the neighborhood; (C) a deteriorated driveway; (D) a one-car garage.

Question #24 All of the following factors contribute to obsolescence, **except**: (A) wear and tear from years of use; (B) obsolete equipment; (C) changes in locational demand; (D) misplaced improvements in the neighborhood.

Answers: #22-A; #23-D; #24-A

C. Capitalization (Income) Approach - establishes the **present worth of future benefits** which may be obtained from an income-producing property (apartments, shopping centers, commercial buildings, restaurants). It determines the **value** of an asset by dividing the **annual net income by** a desired **rate of return called capitalization rate or cap rate**. Capitalization is a mathematical process used to **convert income into value.**

1. **Steps to Determine Value**
   a. Determine **annual net income (net operating income).**
   b. Select the appropriate **cap rate.** Selecting the appropriate cap rate is the most difficult step in the capitalization approach to appraisal. The three methods of calculating cap rate are - Market **C**omparison, **B**and of Investment, and **S**ummation **(C.B.S.).**
   c. **Divide** the **annual net income** by the **cap rate** to find the value of the property.

2. **Annual Net Income (Net Operating Income)** is determined by the following formula:
   a. Estimate the potential **gross income** the property is capable of producing (**Market Rent, Economic Rent, Scheduled Gross Income**) - this is the rent the property would bring in the open market at the date of appraisal. It is also defined as the rent received for comparable space in the current economic marketplace.
   b. **Subtract Vacancies** (actual vacancies or vacancy factor and collection losses) to find the **Effective Gross Income (Adjusted Gross Income).**
   c. **Subtract Expenses (t i m m u r)** - property **t**axes and **i**nsurance (**fixed operating expenses**), **m**anagement (**there is always a management expense**), **m**aintenance, **u**tilities, and **r**eserves for replacements, to find the **annual net income.**

Notes:
1. Loan expenses (principal and interest), personal income taxes and depreciation are not considered in establishing the annual net income.
2. Property tax is the largest fixed operating expense.
3. Rental Schedules - are usually established by market comparison.

Question #25 Determining the appropriate capitalization rate is the most difficult step in the capitalization approach to appraisal. In order to calculate capitalization rate, the appraiser can utilize which of the following methods: (A) market comparison; (B) band of investment; (C) summation; (D) any of the above.

Question #26 In the capitalization approach to appraisal, which of the following expenses is subtracted from the scheduled gross income to arrive at the effective gross income? (A) taxes; (B) vacancies; (C) loan payments; (D) depreciation of improvements.

Question #27 In the capitalization approach, which of the following expenses is **not** deducted from gross income to determine annual net income? (A) electricity; (B) cost of capital; (C) cost of management; (D) replacement reserves.

Answers: #25-D; #26-B; #27-B

3. **Capitalization Rate** - the rate of return demanded by an investor before he will part with his money. The foundation of all cap rates is set by conservative interest rates (banks, bonds, etc.). Risk is another factor in determining capitalization rate. The greater the risk, the higher the capitalization rate demanded by investors (for example, leasing a building for a post office involves little risk of vacancy and results in a lower capitalization rate). **Capitalization rates** consider the **quantity, quality, and durability of the rent.**
   a. When **interest rates increase, capitalization rates increase**.
   b. If **capitalization rates increase**, the **value of the property decreases**.
   c. If net income remains unchanged, but **interest rates increase**, the **owner's equity decreases**.
   d. The capitalization rate includes a "return on the investment" (interest) and a "return of the investment" (depreciation of improvements). Capitalization rate does not include federal taxes.

D. **Gross Multiplier (Rent Multiplier, Gross Rent Multiplier, GRM)** - **converts income into value in one step.** It is not usually used by appraisers because it is not as accurate as the capitalization approach.

   1. **Gross Multiplier Formula** - appraisers divide **the sale price of comparable properties** by their **gross monthly or gross annual income**.

   2. **Separate Site Analysis** - least important when appraising with gross multiplier.

IX. APPRAISAL AND CONSTRUCTION TERMS

Acre: **43,560** square feet = **4,840 sq. yds.** = about **209 feet by 209 feet, if square.**

Alquist-Priolo Act: discloses the location of **earthquake fault lines** on maps for all counties in California.

Question #28 Two similar buildings are leased on a long term basis, one for a post office and the other for a hardware store. Using the capitalization approach to appraise the properties, the post office would demand: (A) a lower capitalization rate; (B) the same capitalization rate as the hardware store; (C) a higher capitalization rate; (D) the two capitalization rates could not be compared because the properties involve different uses.

Question #29 In the appraisal of an income-producing property, to arrive at a capitalization rate, no provision should be made for which of the following: (A) depreciation; (B) federal taxes; (C) return of the investment; (D) return on the investment.

Question #30 Which of the following best describes an acre? (A) 4,350 sq. ft.; (B) 4,840 sq. yds.; (C) 43,500 sq. ft.; (D) 50,000 sq. ft.

Answers: #28-A; #29-B; #30-B

Backfill: dirt used to fill excavations or brace foundations.

Bearing Wall: a wall supporting any vertical load in addition to its own weight. A bearing wall is normally left in place during remodeling. Bearing walls can be constructed at any angle to doorways. Bearing walls are considered real property.

Benchmark: a monument used by a surveyor to establish the elevation at a particular point on land.

Board Foot: a unit of measurement of lumber that is one foot wide, one foot long, one inch thick; any combination of 144 cubic inches.

BTU (British Thermal Unit): a measurement of heat used in rating the capacity of heating systems.

Commercial Acre (Buildable Acre): 43,560 sq. ft. minus the space taken by streets, alleys, sidewalks, parkways, etc.

Compaction: compressing fill dirt to bear the weight of a building. If a building's foundation is cracked, and the doors and windows do not close properly, a **report on the soil stability is obtained from a registered civil engineer**.

Conduit: a metal pipe in which electrical wiring is installed. An electrician installs the conduit in a construction project.

Contractors' License: Under the Contractors' State License Law, every person who performs the work of a contractor in this state must be licensed by the Contractors' State License Board. Licensing exemptions include minor work not exceeding $500, and an owner's own work, unless the owner intends to offer the property for sale within one year of completion.

Corrective Maintenance: repairing broken equipment in an income producing property.

Dangerous Gases: Structures may contain dangerous gases, such as Carbon monoxide, radon and or formaldehyde. **Carbon dioxide is not usually considered a dangerous gas.**

Question #31 A developer ordered several truckloads of soil to be used in a new housing project for backfill. The most probable use of this backfill will be: (A) as topsoil for landscaping and beautification purposes; (B) to fill in the old septic tank; (C) to fill in excavations or to brace around foundation walls; (D) to supplement the results of the percolation test.

Question #32 When building a home, which of the following workers normally install the conduit? (A) roofers; (B) plumbers; (C) electricians; (D) carpenters.

Question #33 Each of the following is a dangerous gas which may be present in a home, **except**: (A) carbon monoxide; (B) radon; (C) carbon dioxide; (D) formaldehyde.

Answers: #31-C; #32-C; #33-C

Deciduous: plants that lose their leaves in the autumn and winter. It is not a type of soil.

Drywall Construction: uses gypsum, fiberboard, and plywood, but not plaster.

Elevation Sheet: drawings which show the front and side views of homes in a subdivision as they will appear when finished.

Energy Efficiency Ratio (EER): measures the efficiency of appliances (such as air conditioners). The higher the ratio, the more efficient the unit.

Flashing: sheet metal used to protect a building from seepage of water (like the valley of a roof).

Footing: the spreading concrete base or bottom of a foundation wall. The size and dimensions of footings relate to the foundation of the building.

Foundation Plan: shows the location, size and dimensions of the footings, concrete piers and details of the subfloor area.

Front Footage: measurement of property on its street line; it is used for sale or valuation purposes.

Hip Roof: a roof which slopes or inclines on all four sides.

HVAC: refers to the Heating, Ventilation, Air Conditioning system in a commercial lease.

Insulation: the "R" value ("R" rating) measures insulation's resistance to heat. The "R" value of the insulation must be disclosed to the buyer of a home in a new subdivision. The higher the "R" value, the greater the insulation. Wall insulation is adequate if the inside of an exterior wall is about the same temperature as other interior walls.

Joist: one of a series of parallel beams used to support the ceiling and floors. **It is a parallel.**

Kiosk: a free-standing information booth in a mall.

Question #34 An elevation sheet for a new subdivision shows which of the following? (A) topography of the land, including slope, elevation of grading of the site; (B) interior views of the homes as they will appear when finished; (C) drawings of the front and side views of the homes as they will appear when finished; (D) aerial views of the homes as they will appear when finished.

Question #35 In home construction, a "footing" refers to: (A) a masonry beam found under the floorboard; (B) a steel girder to which the floorboards are affixed; (C) the spreading part at the base of a foundation wall or pier; (D) a slab of concrete upon which asphalt is usually laid.

Question #36 A real estate broker would look at which of the following in order to find the location, size and dimensions of the footings, concrete piers and details of the subfloor area? (A) floor plan; (B) plot plan; (C) elevation plan; (D) foundation plan.

Answers: *#34-C; #35-C; #36-D*

Old Electrical Wiring: does not necessarily make a home a **substandard home.** If the wiring was properly installed and met code requirements at the time the house was built, the house is not substandard simply because the wiring does not meet current code requirements.

Percolating Water: underground water which does not flow in a defined channel. Percolating water seeps through the soil.

Percolation Test: a soil analysis that determines how quickly water will seep through soil (such as for sewage purposes). A percolation test would be done before a septic tank is installed.

Plot Plan (Plot Map): shows the location of improvements on a lot.

Potable Water: water which is suitable for drinking.

Ridgeboard: the highest structural point in a frame house.

Setback: the distance a building must be set back from the street or the side and back boundary lines. It effects the dimensions for building purposes only.

Side Yard Setback: the distance a building must be set back from the side line of a lot.

Sill (Mudsill): the lowest part of a frame house that rests on the foundation.

Soleplate: a board on which walls and partition studs rest.

Strip Commercial Development: a single line of store buildings constructed along a major transportation route.

Question #37   Water that is suitable for drinking and is not contaminated is said to be: (A) potable water; (B) privy water; (C) alluvium water; (D) avulsion liquid.

Question #38   Water seeping up from the ground from an indeterminable source would be described as: (A) riparian water; (B) littoral water; (C) percolating water; (D) appropriation water.

Question #39   A commercial development that has a single line of store buildings constructed along a major transportation route is described as: (A) a cluster development site; (B) a strip commercial development; (C) a neighborhood shopping center; (D) a street commercial zone development.

Answers: #37- A; #38-C; #39-B

Termite Report: filed with the Structural Pest Control Board where copies are kept for two years. Copies of the report can be obtained by anyone. A copy must be given to both the seller and buyer. The Structural Pest Control Board will issue reports showing the presence of "wood destroying organisms." If a Structural Pest Control report is requested by the buyer, the seller or agent must give a copy of the report to the buyer as soon as practical. Subterranean termites are the most destructive kind.

Toxic Waste Report: should be requested from the Environmental Protection Agency (EPA) if a property is next to an abandoned gas station.

Turnkey Project: one that is ready for occupancy, a tenant can move in immediately.

Water Table: the depth at which water is found.

Question #40 What state agency would a consumer contact in order to obtain a written report disclosing the presence of wood destroying organisms? (A) Department of Real Estate; (B) Department of Corporations; (C) Structural Pest Control Board; (D) Department of Housing and Community Development.

Question #41 An appraiser is appraising a home, and notices an abandoned gas station next door. The appraiser should recommend which of the following? (A) a soils report by a civil engineer; (B) a toxic waste report from the EPA; (C) a rezoning of the property; (D) a structural pest control report.

Question #42 Which of the following would best describe a turnkey project? (A) a subdivision located in a remote area; (B) a subdivision whose design has been approved by the local planning commission; (C) a construction project that is ready for occupancy; (D) an interior lot located in the middle of a subdivision.

Answers: #40-C; #41-B; #42-C

Chapter #7 Review Questions
This exam contains 20 questions. You have an average of 78 seconds per question on the Salesperson Exam. 20 questions x 78 seconds per question = 1560 seconds. Please give yourself 26 minutes to complete this practice exam, and take the exam in one sitting.

1. The ultimate test of functional utility is: (A) maintenance costs; (B) design; (C) utility costs; (D) marketability.

2. Which of the following appraisal reports would be (is) the most comprehensive and complete? (A) narrative report; (B) abbreviated report; (C) letter form report; (D) short form report.

3. When may an appraiser appraise a property owned by a corporation in which he is a shareholder? (A) never; (B) only when the lender is that corporation; (C) when he discloses his ownership of shares in the appraisal report; (D) only when the action is approved by the board of directors.

4. The market data approach to appraisal is based upon: (A) the principle of change; (B) the principle of substitution; (C) the principle of conformity; (D) the principle of highest and best use.

5. When an appraiser determines market value, he would be least concerned with: (A) prudent value in exchange for a prudent price; (B) original cost; (C) objective value; (D) an open market.

6. Each of the following is one of the special forces influencing value, **except**: (A) social ideals and standards; (B) economic influences; (C) private restrictions; (D) political or government regulations.

7. When a developer purchases two or more contiguous lots, thus placing them under common ownership for the purpose of increasing the value per lot, it is known as: (A) co-ownership; (B) cooperative ownership; (C) plottage; (D) disassemblage.

8. When using the market data approach to appraise a single-family residence, the unit of comparison is: (A) square foot; (B) cubic foot; (C) capitalization rate; (D) the entire property.

9. The method which is most commonly used by appraisers to value land or sites is: (A) the residual method; (B) the developmental method; (C) the unit-in-place survey method; (D) the comparative method.

10. When an appraiser compares "reproduction cost" and "replacement cost," "replacement cost" it would best be described as: (A) the cost to replace a building with some other building which would then be able to use the land to its highest and best use; (B) the original cost to build the building; (C) the present cost to build an exact replica of the building; (D) the present cost to build a comparable building having the same utility as the building it would replace.

11. All of the following would be considered economic obsolescence, **except**: (A) community businesses closing; (B) An old kitchen; (C) Incompatible zoning laws; (D) A new sewage treatment plant next to the property.

12. An appraiser would use which of the following approaches in appraising a shopping center? (A) comparison approach; (B) capitalization (income) approach; (C) replacement cost approach; (D) market data approach.

7-15 ©2013 John Henderson

13. Which of the following should be considered an expense item when arriving at a net operating income for a 50-unit apartment building: (A) income tax; (B) depreciation; (C) salary for a part-time gardener; (D) addition of a clubhouse.

14. When appraising income property with the capitalization approach, which of the following items is **not** a component of net operating income? (A) personal income taxes; (B) potential gross rental income; (C) vacancies; (D) operating expenses.

15. When a real estate appraiser is using a gross multiplier to determine property value, the appraiser calculates the appropriate gross multiplier by: (A) dividing the sale price by the net monthly income; (B) multiplying the annual gross income by the appropriate capitalization rate; (C) dividing the sales price by the gross monthly income; (D) dividing the sale price of comparable properties by the appropriate capitalization rate.

16. How long is each side of a square which contains one acre? (A) 209 ft.; (B) 100 sq. yds.; (C) 4,840 sq. ft.; (D) 43,560 sq. ft.

17. During the site inspection of a home, an appraiser finds that the inside of an exterior wall of a building is about the same temperature as the other interior walls. What does this tell the appraiser? (A) the heater is doing a great job; (B) the wall insulation is adequate; (C) heat is leaking out through the exterior walls; (D) the heating duct system is inadequate.

18. Parallel wooden members used to support ceilings and floors are called: (A) sole plates; (B) joists; (C) headers; (D) studs.

19. When real estate is sold, if requested, a copy of the structural pest control report must be given to: (A) the buyer, as soon as practical; (B) the title insurance company; (C) the broker; (D) the escrow company.

20. Who must receive a copy of the structural pest control report? (A) buyer; (B) seller; (C) agent; (D) both buyer and seller.

Chapter #7 Review Questions - Answers

1. Ans-D   The ultimate test of functional utility is marketability.   Pg 7-1

2. Ans-A   The narrative report is the most comprehensive and complete.   Pg 7-1

3. Ans-C   An appraiser may appraise a property which is owned by a corporation in which he is a shareholder if he discloses his ownership of shares in the appraisal report.   Pg 7-2

4. Ans-B   The market data approach to appraisal is based upon the principle of substitution.   Pg 7-2

5. Ans-B   Original cost has little impact upon market value.   Pg 7-4

6. Ans-C   "Private restrictions" is not one of the special forces influencing value.   Pg 7-4

7. Ans-C   Plottage is an added increase in value when two or more lots are joined together, above and beyond the value of the individual lots.   Pg 7-5

8. Ans-D   The unit of comparison when using the market data approach to appraise a single-family residence is the entire property.   Pg 7-6

9. Ans-D The method which is most commonly used by appraisers to value land or sites is the comparative method.   Pg 7-6

10. Ans-D The present cost to build a comparable building having the same utility as the building it would replace is a very good definition of replacement cost.   Pg 7-7

11. Ans-B Economic or social obsolescence results from events occurring outside the property lines, such as the choices in A, C, and D. An old kitchen is considered functional obsolescence.   Pg 7-8

12. Ans-B An appraiser would use the capitalization or income approach to appraise a shopping center.   Pg 7-9

13. Ans-C The salary for a gardener should be considered an expense item when arriving at a net operating income for an apartment building.   Pg 7-9

14. Ans-A When appraising income property with the capitalization approach, personal income tax is not a component of net operating income.   Pg 7-9

15. Ans-C When a real estate appraiser is using a gross multiplier to determine property value, the appraiser calculates the appropriate gross multiplier by dividing the sale price by the gross monthly or annual income.   Pg 7-10

16. Ans-A Each side of a square which contains one acre is about 209 ft long. **Warning:** this same question on one copy of the exam may offer as a best answer 208 ft. instead of 209 ft. The real measurement is 208.71 ft. per side.

17. Ans-B When the appraiser finds that the inside of an exterior wall of a building is about the same temperature as the other interior walls, it tells the appraiser that the wall insulation is adequate.   Pg 7-12

18. Ans-B Joists are parallel beams used to support ceilings and floors.   Pg 7-12

19. Ans-A When requested by the buyer, a copy of the structural pest control report must be given to the buyer as soon as practical.   Pg 7-14

20. Ans-D Both buyer and seller must receive a copy of the structural pest control report (termite report).   Pg 7-14

Notes:

SECTION II.

MATH WORKBOOK

COPYRIGHT 2013
JOHN HENDERSON
ALL RIGHTS RESERVED

All rights reserved. No portion of this publication may be reproduced, transmitted, transcribed, stored in a retrieval system, or transmitted into any language in any form by any means without the written consent of John Henderson.

Published in USA by
The Real Estate Centre

Remember! You can skip every math problem and still pass the exam.

MATH
(Approximately 0 to 4 math questions on the typical Salesperson Exam)

There has been a remarkable decline in the number of math questions asked on the Salesperson Exam. The range is currently about 0-4 math questions on most Salesperson Exams. Please remember - **This is Not a Guarantee**. The Department of Real Estate can add math questions to the exam at any time.

I. CALCULATORS - You may no longer bring your own calculator to the state exam. The Department of Real Estate will provide you with a basic calculator to use.

II. CIRCLE DIAGRAM Rules

1. Percentage always goes in box "**C**."

2. Little number in "**A**," big number in "**B**," where "**C**" is less than 100%.

3. Little number in "**B**," big number in "**A**," where "**C**" is more than 100%.

4. The "**A**" number always gets divided by the other number.

5. Always annualize the figures.

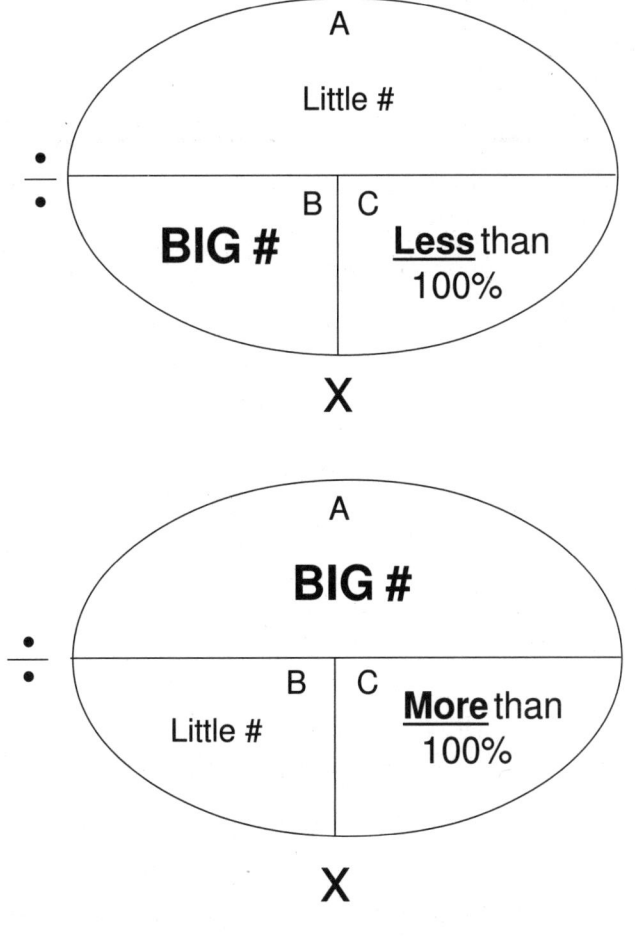

MWB-1 ©2013 John Henderson

CAPITALIZATION APPRAISAL PROBLEMS

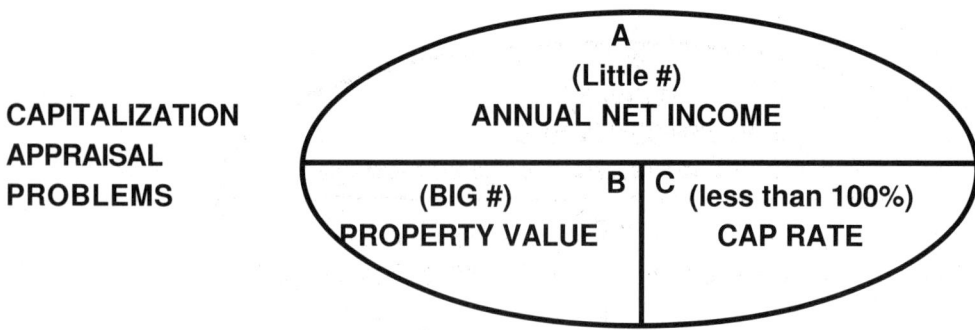

1. The net income of an apartment building went down $400 per month when a freeway was built nearby. If investors demand a 12% capitalization rate for this area, how much has the property lost in value?
   A. $3,333
   B. $20,000
   C. $36,000
   D. $40,000

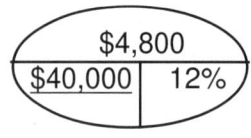

   ANS. 1   D
   (1) $400 x 12 = $4,800.
   (2) $4,800 divided by 12% = $40,000.

2. Leonard, an intelligent real estate investor, wants to purchase a 40-unit apartment building that has an annual net income of $174,000. How much would he be willing to pay for the building, if he uses a 8% capitalization rate?
   A. $1,400,000
   B. $1,650,000
   C. $1,985,000
   D. $2,175,000

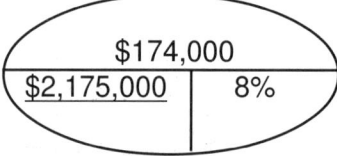

   ANS. 2   D
   (1) $174,000 divided by 8% = $2,175,000.

3. A small income property generates a monthly gross income of $1,000. Over the last five years it has been vacant for three months. The annual expenses are $3,000. If an appraiser applied a 12% capitalization rate to this property, what would be the value?
   A. $58,000
   B. $65,000
   C. $70,000
   D. $90,000

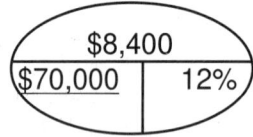

   ANS. 3   C
   (1) $1,000 x 12 = $12,000 annual gross income.
   (2) 12 months x 5 years = 60 months.
   (3) 3 months vacancies divided by 60 months = .05 = 5% vacancy factor.
   (4) $12,000 Annual gross income x 5% vacancy factor = $600 annual vacancy loss.
   (5) $12,000 - $600 = $11,400 adjusted gross income.
   (6) $11,400 adjusted gross income - $3,000 annual expenses = $8,400 annual net income.
   (7) $8,400 divided by 12% = $70,000.

INVESTMENT PROBLEMS

```
         A
      (Little #)
  INCOME/PROFIT/YIELD
(Do not include return of original money)
─────────────────────────────
   (Big #)        B│C  (less than 100%)
AMOUNT INVESTED       RATE OF RETURN
```

1. How much would an investor need to invest in order to earn $75 per month from an investment which offers a 5% rate of return?
   A. $4,000
   B. $9,000
   C. $12,000
   D. $18,000

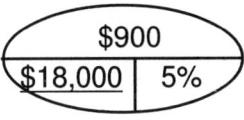

   ANS. 1   D
   (1) $75 x 12 = $900 per year
   (2) $900 divided by 5% = $18,000

2. Joyce purchased a home for $125,000. She received a loan from the bank for 88% of the purchase price, payable at $1,549 per month including 12% interest. She then sold the home for $139,750 before she even made the first payment on the loan. What was her equity at the time of the sale?
   A. $12,000
   B. $14,750
   C. $29,750
   D. $125,000

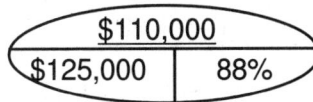

   ANS. 2   C
   (1) $125,000 x 88% = $110,000 loan amount
   (2) $139,750 - $110,000 loan = $29,750 equity

3. An investor purchases a $5,000 straight note for $4,500, which is due in one year. The note bears an interest rate of 6%. What percent rate of return will the investor make, when the loan is paid-off at the end of one year?
   A. 6%
   B. 12%
   C. 17.8%
   D. 20%

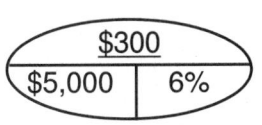 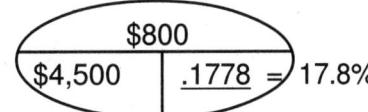

   ANS. 3   C
   (1) $5,000 X 6% interest = $300
   (2) $5,000 - $4,500 = $500 profit as a result of the discount
   (3) $300 interest + $500 profit = $800 made by the investor
   (4) $800 (made) divided by $4,500 (invested) = 17.8%

FINANCE PROBLEMS

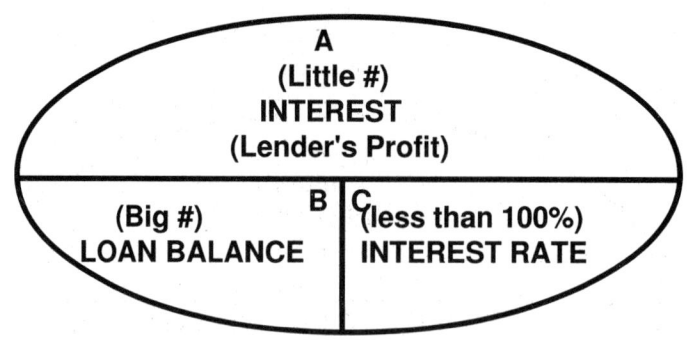

1. Mary borrowed $26,500 using a straight note, for a term of 20 years at an interest rate of 15% per annum. How much interest would she pay during the term of the note?
   A. $26,500
   B. $79,500
   C. $95,000
   D. None of the above

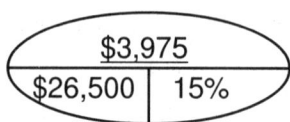

   ANS. 1 B
   (1) $26,500 x 15% = $3,975 interest per year.
   (2) $3,975 x 20 years = $79,500

2. William is the beneficiary on a 10 year straight note. The annual interest rate is 8.4%. If in 5 years he has received $5,460 in interest, what is the principal amount of the loan?
   A. $5,460
   B. $11,050
   C. $13,000
   D. $65,000

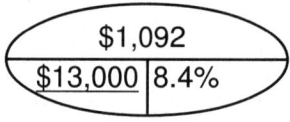

   ANS. 2 C
   (1) $5,460 divided by 5 years = $1,092 interest per year.
   (2) $1,092 divided by 8.4% = $13,000 principal.

3. John borrowed $20,000 from a bank to purchase a small piece of real estate. He paid 4 points to get the loan. The loan contained a 2% prepayment penalty, based upon the original loan amount. His monthly payment was $163.00, including interest of 8% per year. Five years later, John sold this real estate and paid-off the loan. If the loan had an average loan balance of $18,500, during the five years John owned the property, what was the bank's gross profit on this loan?
   A. $7,000
   B. $7,248
   C. $8,600
   D. $9,999

   ANS. 3 C
   (1) $20,000 x 4% = $800 points
   (2) $20,000 x 2% = $400 prepayment penalty
   (3) $18,500 x 8% = $1,480 interest per year
   (4) $1,480 x 5 years = $7,400
   (5) $800 + $400 + $7,400 = $8,600 gross profit by bank.

COMMISSION PROBLEMS

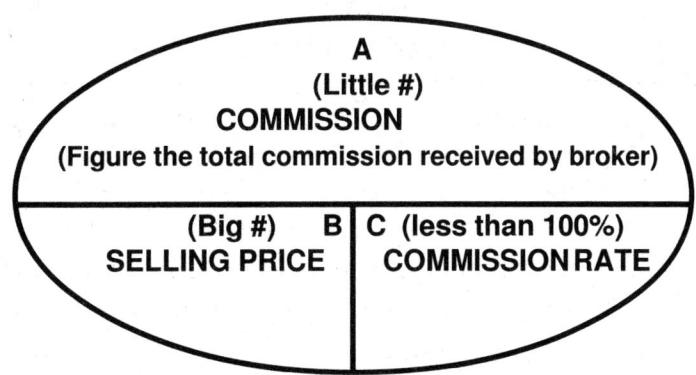

1. Broker Bob and Broker Bill agreed to divide a 4-1/2% commission equally on the sale of a home, which sold for $162,500. Mary, the listing salesperson, works for Broker Bob on a 50-50 commission split. Mary would receive approximately how much commission as a result of the sale?
   A. $1,828
   B. $2,828
   C. $3,656
   D. $7,312

	$7,312.50	
	$162,500	4.5%

   ANS. 1 A
   (1) $162,500 x 4 1/2% = $7,312.50 total commission.
   (2) $7,312.50 divided by 2 = $3,656.25 commission to Broker Bob's office.
   (3) $3,656.25 divided by 2 = $1,828.13 commission to Mary.

2. Sam, a salesperson working for Broker Martha, received a 45% share of a 6% commission. His share came to $8,100. What was the selling price of the property?
   A. $100,000
   B. $150,000
   C. $250,000
   D. $300,000

   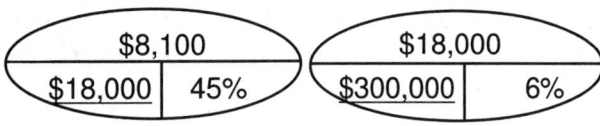

   ANS. 2 D
   (1) $8,100 Commission divided by 45% share = $18,000 total commission.
   (2) $18,000 divided by 6% = $300,000 selling price.

SELLING PRICE PROBLEMS

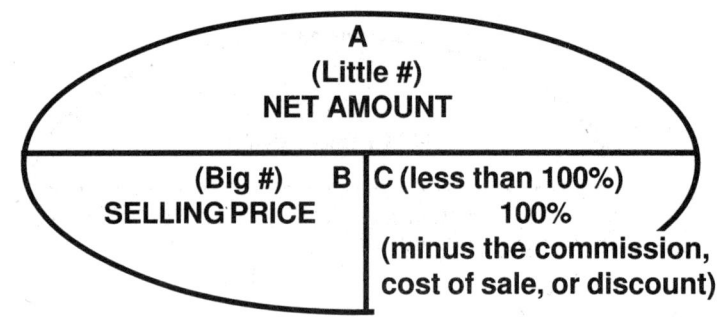

1. Mark sold his home and carried back a $37,400 second trust deed. He immediately sold the loan at a discount to an investor and received $24,310. What was the rate of discount?
   A. 25%
   B. 30%
   C. 35%
   D. None of the above

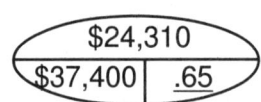

   ANS. 1 C
   (1) $24,310 divided by $37,400 = .65 = 65%
   (2) 100% - 65% = 35% discount

2. A bank charged the borrower 4 points for making a loan. The bank then sold the loan immediately to an investor at a discount of 3-1/2 percent and received $34,790. What was the original loan amount?
   A. $35,750
   B. $36,052
   C. $36,350
   D. $37,987

   ANS. 2 B
   (1) $34,790 divided by 96.5% = $36,051.81
   (2) "B" is the best answer.
        Note: *The 4 points have nothing to do with answering this question.*

3. Ron sold his home which had no loans against it. He received a settlement check from escrow for the amount of $91,740 after paying escrow fees of $1,291.80 plus a 6% real estate broker's commission. What was the selling price?
   A. $92,000
   B. $96,857
   C. $97,995
   D. $98,970

   ANS. 3 D
   (1) $91,740 + $1,291.80 = $93,031.80 net amount after paying commission
   (2) $93,031.80 divided by 94% = $98,970 selling price.

COST PROBLEMS

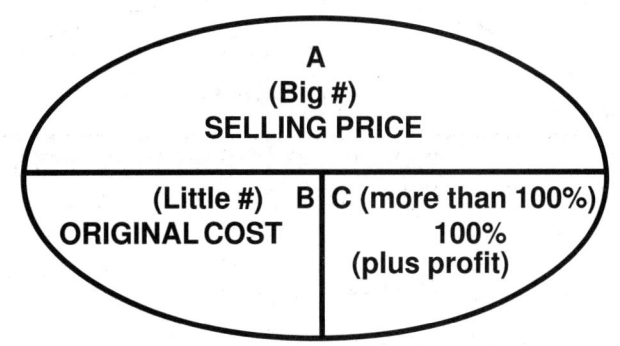

1. Linda sold a home for $250,000. She made a 20% profit. What did the home cost?
A. $183,333
B. $200,000
C. $208,333.33
D. $272,500

ANS. 1   C

(1) $250,000 divided by 120% = $208,333.33

2. Mr. Gray sold an apartment building for $137,000. This was 10% more than what he paid for it. His original cost was approximately:
A. $124,545
B. $128,000
C. $139,000
D. There is insufficient information to arrive at an answer

ANS. 2   A

(1) $137,000 divided by 110% = 124,545.45

3. Mr. Jackson sold a vacant lot for $72,000. He broke even, after paying the expenses of the sale. The expenses of the sale represented 12% of his original cost of the lot. What was his original cost of the lot?
A. $78,000
B. $68,528
C. $64,286
D. $61,927

ANS. 3   C

(1) $72,000 divided by 112% = $64,285.71 cost
(2) "C" is the best answer

AREA PROBLEMS

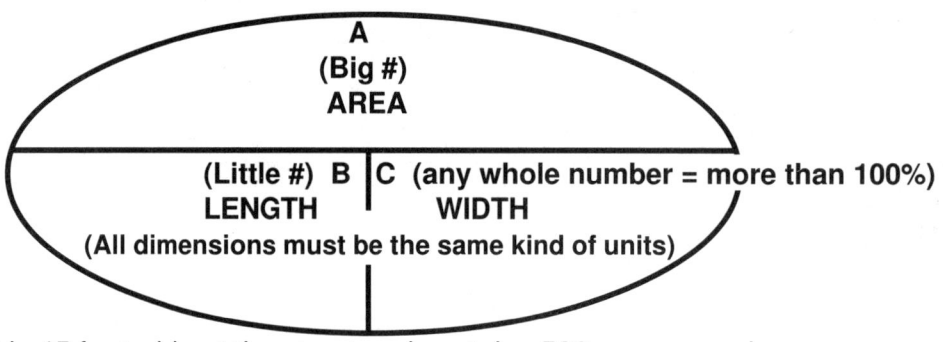

A
(Big #)
AREA

(Little #) B | C (any whole number = more than 100%)
LENGTH | WIDTH
(All dimensions must be the same kind of units)

1. A rectangular lot is 45 feet wide at the street and contains 520 square yards. How deep is the lot?
A. 80 ft.
B. 104 ft.
C. 112 ft.
D. 120 ft.

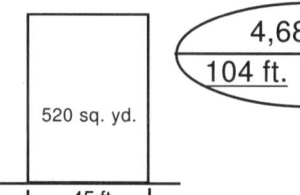

ANS. 1 B
(1) There are 9 sq. ft. in a sq. yd.
(2) 520 sq. yd. x 9 = 4,680 sq. ft.
(3) 4,680 sq. ft. divided by 45 ft. = 104 ft deep.

2. A parcel of land 220 feet wide and 330 feet deep contains approximately how many acres?
A. .75 acres
B. 1-1/3 acres
C. 1-1/2 acres
D. 1-2/3 acres

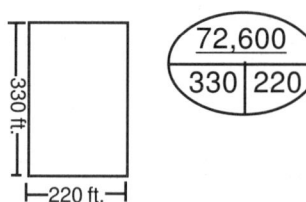

ANS. 2 D
(1) 330 ft. x 220 ft. = 72,600 sq. ft.
(2) An acre contains 43,560 square feet.
(3) 72,600 sq. ft. divided by 43,560 sq. ft. = 1.666 = 1-2/3 acres

3. Debbi owns a parcel of land which contains exactly one acre. She divides this parcel into 4 equally sized lots. If her lots form a rectangle which is 240 feet deep, approximately how wide is each of the 4 lots?
A. 45 feet
B. 55 feet
C. 60 feet
D. 80 feet

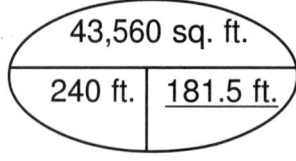 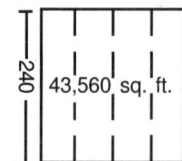

ANS. 3 A
(1) An acre = 43,560 sq. ft.
(2) 43,560 divided by 240 ft = 181.5 feet (width of combined lots)
(3) 181.5 feet divided by 4 lots = 45.375 feet wide.
(4) "A" is the best answer.

BALLOON PAYMENT PROBLEMS

Balloon Payment - is a final payment on an installment note that is substantially larger than the prior payments.

1. Which loan will require a balloon payment?
   (A.) $22,500 with interest at 14.25% per year payable $320 a month for 10 years; the total interest is $19,827;
   (B) $40,000 with interest at 10% per year payable $429.85 a month for 15 years; the total interest is $37,373;
   (C) $100,000 with interest at 9.5% per year payable $840.86 a month for 30 years; the total interest is $202,709;
   (D) none of the above.

   Ans. A (1) $320 x 12 x 10 = $38,400 total payments;
   (2) $38,400 - 19,827.60 interest = $18,572.40 has been paid on principal reduction;
   (3) $22,500 - $18,572.40 = $3,927.60 balloon payment.

2. A $100,000 straight note payable interest only at 7%, is due in 15 years. What will be the amount of the balloon payment at the end of the term of the loan?
   (A) $583;
   (B) $99,417;
   (C) $100,000;
   (D) $100,583

   ANS. D (1) $100,000 x 7% = $7,000
   (2) $7,000 divided by 12 months = $583.33
   (3) The final payment is $100,583.33 = $100,000 (loan balance) + $583.33 the final monthly interest payment.

Notes:

SECTION III.

FINAL BRIEFING

COPYRIGHT 2013
JOHN HENDERSON
ALL RIGHTS RESERVED

All rights reserved. No portion of this publication may be reproduced, transmitted, transcribed, stored in a retrieval system, or transmitted into any language in any form by any means without the written consent of John Henderson.

Published in the USA by
The Real Estate Centre

Don't forget to
RTDQ

All your efforts will be wasted if you don't

Read

The

Darn

Question

(and all four answers!)

HOW TO STUDY FOR THE STATE EXAM

Confirm Your Test Date and Location

DRE Internet site: www.dre.ca.gov
DRE Phone: (877) 373-4542

What To Study

1. **Download** the Update from our website, www.RealEstateCentre.biz. The state exam can change at any time so it's important to keep current with the updates. Keep the Update available when studying the Salesperson Prep Outline and take note of any new information.

2. **Read** the Salesperson Prep Outline. Answer the questions at the bottom of each page. Grade yourself. Immediately, go back to each page and figure out why you answered any of the questions incorrectly. When you get to the end of a chapter, answer the **Chapter Review Questions**, as you would take the actual state exam. Grade yourself only after you have completed the entire exam. Go back into the chapter and figure out why you answered any questions incorrectly. Read Page FB-4 this **Final Briefing** at least two times and practice my test taking techniques when answering any of the questions in this book. Practice answering some of the questions in the Math Workbook, but remember: You can miss all the math questions and still pass the state exam

> **Note:** *A clinical study proved* **chewing gum while studying** *increased both long and short term memory. I know it sounds silly, but give it a try. Eating about eight almonds per day also allegedly increases memory.*

3. Once you've studied the front half of the book, begin taking the **Practice Exams** in the back half of the book. Each time you take a **Practice Exam**, try to simulate the real exam. Give yourself 3 hours and 15 minutes to answer 150 questions. Do not write your answers directly on the questions. After you complete each exam, grade yourself and try to determine why you had problems with the questions you missed. Then, take the test again answering only those questions you missed on the first try. **Repeat this process** until you're **able to answer 90% (or better) of all the questions in this book, based upon understanding, not memorization.**

4. **Your goal** is to **master all of the course material**. You can be confident that you've mastered the material when you know the Course Outline and you're **able to answer 90% (or better) of all the questions in this book, based upon understanding, not memorization.**

5. If you **run out of time** to master this book, divide your time as follows – spend **50%** of your available study time on the Update, Salesperson Prep Outline, Math Workbook, Final Briefing, and Glossary. Spend the remaining **50%** of your available study time on **all the questions found in the book.**

What Not To Study

It's best not study any other material until you have **mastered the material in this book**. If you've mastered 90% of our course materials, you are well prepared to pass the state exam. If you want to study additional material, go ahead, but you might benefit even more from a short break.

HOW TO PASS THE STATE EXAM

The Final 24 Hours Before Your Exam

1. Take a day off from work.

2. **Review** the Update, Salesperson Prep Outline, Math Workbook, Final Briefing, and Glossary

3. Take at least one **complete practice exam** of 150 questions, using the test taking technique described on Page FB-4. Grade yourself. If you get a score of 90% or better, you are ready to pass the state exam. If you score between 85% and 89%, it could go either way. Luck will be a real factor when you take your test. If you score below 85% correct, you are not ready to pass the state exam, and I recommend you consider rescheduling your test. You can usually reschedule your exam online up until the day before your exam. You can even decide at the last minute not to go to the exam and reschedule over the internet. There is no penalty for failing to show up for an exam.

4. **Take a break** during your study day to get some exercise. Studies show that light exercise clears your mind, improves your thinking, and raises your performance on exams.

5. Print driving directions to the exam (found on the DRE website: www.dre.ca.gov).

6. Get a good night's sleep.

7. Have a healthy and nutritious breakfast the morning of your exam – a healthy breakfast can improve your test results.

8. Leave early for your exam. Give yourself extra time for the drive. If you find yourself running late, stay calm, drive carefully and consider rescheduling your exam.

What You Should Bring To The Exam

1. The **letter from the state** which tells you exactly where and when you are taking the exam. This is your admission letter to the test. Read the letter carefully, and be on time. **Remember** to bring the driving directions you printed from the DRE website.

2. Photo ID (Driver's License, Passport, California ID Card).

3. Wear comfortable lightweight clothing. Bring a jacket since the room may be cold.

4. A watch – timing on the exam is critical.

5. Bring $50.00 for gas, parking, food and drink.

6. Bring the print-out of the driving directions to the exam.

What You Should NOT Bring To The Exam

The following items are not permitted in the examination room: pencils, erasers, purses, backpacks, briefcases, suitcases, food, drink, study materials, portable computers, PDAs (personal digital assistants), or calculators. Furthermore, cell phone use is prohibited during the examination. **Do not bring cell phones to the exam room.**

Note: All exam sites, **except Sacramento** currently administer the exam at computer workstations, but this may change. Sacramento examinees should check with the DRE to confirm if the exam will be given on paper or computer. If your exam is given on paper, our **Update** will have special instructions for students taking the exam in Sacramento.

The Exam Environment

The electronic exam sites usually open the doors to the testing room about 30 minutes before the scheduled starting time for the exam. When you check-in with the proctor, you will be given a mouse with a number on it. That number tells you which desk you are assigned to. You are also given a basic calculator, a scratch tablet (small dry erase marking board about the size of a clipboard), a dry erase pen and a little tiny eraser.

When you get to your desk, turn on the computer. The monitor is built into the desk, but it can be tilted to decrease the light reflection. Read the instructions on the monitor. You decide when you are ready to start the test. If you arrive early, you can start the test before the official start time, but you will not receive extra time to complete the test, as the exam times itself out automatically. If you arrive late, you will be able to take the exam, but you will have less time to complete your exam, as it will time out at the official end time. **Don't be late!**

One Minute Before You Start The Exam
Visualize Success

Before you start your exam take a deep breath, and slowly exhale as you silently count to ten. During this time, visualize opening the envelope with the results of your exam. In this visualization you will see the words, "Congratulations you have passed the real estate exam."

Start The Exam
Take Control Of Time

Before you read question #1, prepare a timeline on your scratch tablet. You have 3 hours and 15 minutes to complete the Salespersons Exam. Set up a timeline on your scratch tablet to guide through your exam in 3 hours.

Question #1	Start
Question #37	45 min.
Question #75	1 hr. 30 min.
Question #113	2 hr. 15 min.
Question #150	3 hr.
	+15 extra minutes

You have now divided the exam into quarterly segments. When you get to question #37 you are about one quarter of the way through the 150 questions on the exam. Stop and look at your watch. If you are now 45 minutes into the exam, congratulations, you are right on schedule. If it is earlier don't worry, but don't go too fast. If you get to question number 37 and it is 55 minutes into the exam, WARNING, YOU ARE GOING TOO SLOWLY! At that pace, you will fail the exam because you risk running out of time. You have spotted a fatal error, **BUT YOU HAVE TIME TO FIX THE PROBLEM** because the schedule you are using is a 3 hour schedule. You really have 3 hours and 15 minutes for the exam. You now know you must speed up your rate. Check yourself at questions # 37, 75, 113, and 150 and **you will never run out of time on your exam.**

It is OK to skip questions when you go through the questions. The left-hand side of your computer screen shows you any questions you skipped. This makes it easier than ever to skip questions you are unsure of as you go through the test the first time and come back to them later.

Go Through The Exam Four Times

You are now ready to start answering questions.

First time through the exam, skip (leave blank) any question you cannot answer in one minute or less without guessing. After one time through the exam, stop for a moment. Count the number of questions you skipped. You may find that you've skipped between 20 to 40 questions, but you have quickly built a solid foundation of correct answers. Check the timer on your computer monitor to see how much time you have left. Divide the number of minutes left by the number of questions skipped. You started the exam with 78 seconds per question, but because you answered many questions quickly, you should now have two or even three minutes left for each of the questions you skipped.

Second time through the exam, go back and try to answer the questions you skipped. Remember, if you are not sure of the answer after two minutes or less, leave the answer blank and move on.

Third time through the exam, you are ready to start guessing. When guessing, remember these guidelines:

1. Long answers are correct more frequently than short answers.
2. Positively stated answers are correct more frequently than negatively stated answers.
3. Eliminate any answer which contains words like only, always, every, or never.
4. Eliminate any choice which contains an unfamiliar term.
5. Never guess choice "D" when it reads "None of the above." "None of the above" is rarely a correct answer.
6. On questions related to regulatory issues, chose the answer that best prevents fraud (regulatory questions include those related to regulating the actions of a developer, lender, or licensee).
7. When guessing, keep in mind that "D" is often the correct answer when it reads "All of the above."

Fourth time through the exam, proofread. When you proofread, look for **three things**:

Math, Clerical, and Perceptual errors.

1. When looking for **math errors**, double check your calculations.
2. When looking for **clerical errors**, reread as many questions and answers as possible to make sure you marked the correct answer for each question.
3. The most difficult error to spot is a **perceptual error**. You've made a perceptual error when you find that you misread a question when you first answered it. On this second reading you have an opportunity to discover the error and correct it. However, don't change answers on a hunch.

Use the entire 3 hours and 15 minutes of the exam. It is a mistake to leave your seat more than thirty seconds before you run out of time.

When you have followed these guidelines and completed the exam,

Congratulations!
You just passed the state exam.

SECTION IV.

GLOSSARY OF TERMS AND NUMBERS FOR THE STATE EXAM

COPYRIGHT 2013
JOHN HENDERSON
ALL RIGHTS RESERVED

All rights reserved. No portion of this publication may be reproduced, transmitted, transcribed, stored in a retrieval system, or transmitted into any language in any form by any means without the written consent of John Henderson.

Published in USA by
The Real Estate Centre

Vocabulary
Vocabulary
Vocabulary
Vocabulary Vocabulary Vocabulary
Vocabulary Vocabulary
Vocabulary
Vocabulary Vocabulary
Vocabulary

Vocabulary

It's the key to passing your exam!

Glossary of Exam Terms

ABSTRACT OF TITLE - a written summary of the chain of title.

ACCELERATION CLAUSE - any clause in a loan requiring the loan be paid off upon the occurrence of a certain event. An alienation clause is an example of an acceleration clause.

ACCESSION - the acquisition of property by its being added to other property.

ACCRETION - the process of gradual or imperceptible additions to land bordering a river or stream.

ACKNOWLEDGMENT - the declaration before a notary by a person who executed a document stating that he did in fact sign the document. A deed must be acknowledged to be recorded. Once acknowledged, it is accepted as prima facie evidence in court.

ACRE - 43,560 square feet, or 4,840 square yards, or about 209 feet by 209 feet (if square).

ACTUAL AUTHORITY - the authority that a principal actually confers on the agent.

ACTUAL GAIN (profit) - for income tax purposes, it is determined by subtracting the adjusted cost basis from the exchange value of a property.

ACTUAL NOTICE - when a person actually knows something, such as when an agent knows someone has taken possession of a property.

AD VALOREM (according to value) - a property tax is an ad valorem tax.

ADJUSTED COST BASIS - for income tax purposes, it is the cost basis plus capital improvements, plus existing assessment liens assumed by the buyer, minus depreciation, minus gain(s) deferred from prior transactions.

ADJUSTED SELLING PRICE - for income tax purposes, it is the selling price minus the expenses of the sale.

ADVERSE POSSESSION - acquiring title by five years of exclusive, notorious, and open possession of a property (contrary to the best interests of the true owner) under a claim of right or color of title. When property is acquired by adverse possession, a quiet title action would be used to perfect title.

AGENCY - an agent is a person authorized to represent a principal in business dealings with other parties. Paying consideration is not required to create an agency relationship.

AGENCY DISCLOSURE LAW - as of January 1, 1988, the California Agency Disclosure Law requires agents to disclose agency relationships as soon as their relationship with a buyer or seller becomes more than casual. This applies to transactions concerning the sale, or a lease (for more than one year), of four or less residential units. The three steps to agency disclosure are disclose, elect, and confirm.

ALIENATE - to sell, transfer or convey. Both real and personal property may be alienated.

ALIENATION (DUE ON SALE) CLAUSE - an alienation clause in a loan requires the borrower to pay off the loan when title is transferred. The opposite of alienation is acquisition.

ALL INCLUSIVE TRUST DEED (AITD, wrap around trust deed, hold harmless trust deed, overriding trust deed) - a junior lien which is subordinate to, yet includes, the liens to which it is subordinated. AITD's are commonly used with land contracts.

ALLUVION (Alluvium) - the soil deposited by accretion.

ALQUIST-PRIOLO ACT - requires the disclosure of earthquake fault lines on a map.

AMENITY PROPERTY - a home. Amenity properties are appraised by the Market Data Approach.

AMERICANS WITH DISABILITIES ACT (ADA) - the federal law which requires equal access to public buildings for handicapped persons.

AMORTIZATION - the liquidation of a financial obligation, such as a loan.

AMORTIZATION TABLES - used to determine monthly payments.

AMORTIZED INSTALLMENT NOTE - a promissory note which calls for periodic payments of both principal and interest.

ANGLES - a change in geographic direction is often referred to by using an angle expressed in degrees, minutes and seconds; it is often described as "so many degrees from the North or South points of the compass."

ANNUAL NET INCOME - used in the Capitalization Approach to appraisal and determined by this formula: Gross Income - Vacancies - Expenses = Annual Net Income.

ANNUAL PERCENTAGE RATE (APR) - the relative cost of credit expressed in percentage terms and disclosed under the Truth-In-Lending Law (also called Reg. Z).

APPRAISAL - an opinion of the value of a specific property on a given date; it is valid for that date only.

APPROPRIATION - occurs when the government gives permission to a non-riparian owner to take water from a public waterway.

APPURTENANCES - things used with the land for its benefit. Appurtenances are real property.

APPURTENANT EASEMENT - benefits the land of a dominant tenement. The buyer of the dominant tenement automatically receives the appurtenant easement.

ARBITRATION CLAUSE - a clause in a contract in which the parties agree to arbitrate a dispute rather than go to court.

ASSESSMENT LIEN - a lien which is recorded by a local government when a property owner fails to pay for street improvement within 30 days of receipt of the bill.

ASSESSMENT ROLL - establishes the tax base. Property is assessed every year at 100% of its taxable value (100% of fair market value or 100% of full cash value). If sold, property is reassessed during the year.

ASSIGNMENT - a contract is usually assignable. Leases can be assigned; when a lease holder assigns a lease, the person who acquires the lease (the assignee) becomes the tenant. Listings cannot be assigned because a listing is a personal service contract calling for the personal performance of the broker.

ASSUMED ASSESSMENT LIEN - a preexisting assessment lien which is assumed (taken over) by a buyer of real property.

ASSUMPTION - when a buyer assumes a loan, he or she becomes primarily liable. The seller is still liable, but is in a secondary position.

ATTACHMENT LIEN (WRIT OF ATTACHMENT) - property is held by court order as security for a possible judgment in a pending lawsuit. An attachment lien is valid for three years.

ATTORNEY-IN-FACT - acting for another with a duly executed and recorded power of attorney.

AVULSION - sudden violent tearing away of land by water.

BACKFILL - dirt used to fill in excavations or brace a foundation.

BALLOON NOTE - partially amortized.

BALLOON PAYMENT - any payment which is significantly larger than the other payments.

BANKER'S YEAR - based on a 30 day month and 360 day year, used for proration and loan calculations.

BEARING WALL - a wall supporting any vertical load in addition to its own weight. It is normally left in place during remodeling and can be constructed at any angle to doorways. Bearing walls are real property.

BENEFICIARY - the lender in a trust deed. A beneficiary holds the promissory note and trust deed during the life of the loan.

BENEFICIARY STATEMENT - statement by a lender disclosing the current loan balance.

BILATERAL CONTRACT - a contract in which the promise of one party is given in exchange for the promise of the other party (a promise for a promise). Both parties are bound to perform. These promises are often the basis for a contract (for example, exclusive listings, deposit receipts).

BLANKET ENCUMBRANCE - a real estate loan which covers (blankets or secures) more than one parcel of land; it is commonly used when building new homes.

BLIND ADVERTISING - does not disclose that an agent is representing the seller. When advertising, a licensee must disclose that he is an agent. Additionally, the ad must name the broker.

BOARD FOOT - a unit of measurement of lumber which is one foot wide, one foot long, and one inch thick (any combination of 144 cubic inches).

BONDS - loan instruments.

BONA FIDE - in good faith, without fraud or deceit, genuine. A bona fide land contract or listing has all the elements required by law.

BOOT - cash, other "unlike" property, or "mortgage relief" used to balance the equities of the properties in a 1031 tax deferred exchange.

BORROWER'S CREDIT HISTORY - provides the lender with information used to determine the risk inherent in the loan.

BROKER - a person employed for a fee by another to perform a real estate act requiring a license. A broker is the employer of salespersons.

BTU (British Thermal Unit) - a measurement of heat used in rating the capacity of heating systems.

BUILDING RESIDUAL TECHNIQUE - an appraiser uses the building residual technique when the value of a building is an unknown factor. The technique determines how the building contributes to the value of the entire property.

BUSINESS AND PROFESSIONS CODE - a set of California laws regulating business, such as the real estate industry.

BUSINESS OPPORTUNITIES - are personal property. The document used to transfer title to personal property is a bill of sale, not a deed.

CALIFORNIA VETERANS FARM AND HOME PURCHASE PLAN (Cal-Vet) - the state purchases homes and sells them to California veterans using land contracts.

CAPABLE PARTIES - everyone is capable of contracting, except minors and those who are mentally incompetent. It is one of the four essential elements of a contract.

CAPITAL IMPROVEMENT - investment of money in physical improvements of a property (for example, adding a wall, remodeling, or upgrading a heating system). It is not deductible as an expense, but is added to the cost basis and depreciated over the life of the improvements.

CAPITALIZATION (INCOME) APPROACH - establishes the current value of future benefits which may be obtained from an income producing property (apartments, commercial buildings, restaurants, etc.). The value of an asset is determined by dividing the annual net income by a desired rate of return called the capitalization rate ($V = I/R$).

CAPITALIZATION RATE - the rate of interest which is considered a reasonable return on an investment. The greater the risk, the higher the capitalization rate demanded by an investor. Capitalization rates consider the quantity, quality, and durability of the rent. The three methods of calculating capitalization rate are (C.B.S.) Market Comparison, Band of Investment, and Summation.

CC&R's - covenants, conditions, and restrictions usually placed in a "declaration of restrictions" which restricts land use in a subdivision.

CERTIFICATE OF CLEARANCE - receipt from the State Board of Equalization showing that the seller of a business opportunity has paid all sales taxes.

CERTIFICATE OF REASONABLE VALUE (CRV) - government appraisal for a VA loan. The Certificate of Reasonable Value determines the amount of the down payment. Some VA loans do not require a down payment.

CHAIN OF TITLE - the record of prior transfers and encumbrances affecting the title of a parcel. It is usually searched by a title company employee.

CLOUD ON TITLE - items effecting title which may prevent transfer. For example, if a woman purchased a home prior to marriage, but sold it during the marriage and signed her married name on the grant deed, it would create a cloud on title.

COLOR OF TITLE - that which appears to be good title but isn't.

COMMERCIAL ACRE (Buildable Acre) - 43,560 sq. ft. minus the space taken by streets, alleys, and sidewalks.

COMMERCIAL AREA - a single line of store buildings along a major route, also known as a strip commercial development or a strip center.

COMMINGLING - occurs when an agent mixes a principal's or client's money with the agent's own money.

COMMUNITY APARTMENT PROJECT - a subdivision in which an owner sells apartment units to the tenants, with the tenants owning the parking area, halls, walks, etc., in common.

COMMUNITY PROPERTY - each spouse owns 50%. Community property is assumed when title says "husband and wife." Community property is also assumed whenever a husband and wife buy property, unless they specifically take title as joint tenants or tenants in common.

COMMUNITY PROPERTY LAW - comes from the Treaty of Guadalupe Hidalgo between the United States and Mexico.

COMMUNITY REDEVELOPMENT AGENCY (CRA) - funded through the issuance of tax allocation bonds and secured by anticipated property tax revenues.

COMPACTION - compressing fill dirt to bear the weight of a building. A report on soil stability should be obtained from a registered civil engineer if a building's foundation is cracked, and the doors and windows do not close properly.

COMPANY DOLLAR - calculated by subtracting commissions paid to sales agents from the gross income of the brokerage.

COMPENSATING BALANCE - a provision in a loan requiring the borrower to keep a certain amount of money on deposit with the lender in return for the loan.

COMPLETION OF ESCROW - occurs when all terms of the escrow instructions have been met.

CONCURRENT ESTATES - ownership by two or more persons, with title held jointly and severally.

CONDITION PRECEDENT - something which must happen or be performed before an estate is vested in the grantee.

CONDITION SUBSEQUENT - something which will cause an estate to be lost should a certain event happens.

CONDUIT - a metal pipe in which electrical wiring is installed.

CONSIDERATION (Documentary Transfer Tax) - the selling price minus any existing loans assumed by the buyer.

CONSIDERATION (contract law) - consideration may be anything of value; it does not have to be money. It is one of the four essential elements of a contract.

CONSTRUCTIVE EVICTION - any disturbance of a tenant's use or possession of a leased premises which is caused by the landlord. The property must be rendered wholly or substantially unsuitable for the use for which it was leased.

CONSTRUCTIVE (LEGAL) NOTICE - events which by law put people on notice. Recording a document gives constructive notice. The act of taking possession of land, while holding an unrecorded deed, gives constructive notice.

CONSUMER PRICE INDEX (CPI) - a statistical measure of changes in the prices of goods and services over time.

CONTRACT DATE - the date the contract was formed. A contract is formed when the final acceptance is communicated to the offeror.

CONVENTIONAL LOAN - loans made by lenders without governmental guarantees.

CONVERSION - stealing client's money.

COOPERATIVE APARTMENT (stock cooperative, co-op, stock co-op) - an apartment building, owned by a corporation, in which tenancy in an apartment unit is obtained by purchase of shares of the stock of the corporation. The owner of the shares (a tenant or lessee) is entitled to occupy a specific apartment in the building.

CORPORATE SEAL - a corporate seal on a deed implies that the person signing the deed is authorized to sign for the corporation.

COST APPROACH - used by an appraiser when other approaches are inappropriate (special purpose buildings, new subdivision homes). The cost approach is the least appropriate for appraising older buildings because as a building gets older, depreciation becomes difficult to calculate.

COST BASIS - for tax purposes, it is the purchase price.

COVENANT - an agreement or promise to do or not do a particular thing, such as an agreement to build a house of a particular architectural style or to use (or not use) property in a certain way.

CPI (Consumer Price Index) - measures the cost of living.

CRAWL SPACE - the distance between the ground and the first floor of a building. Most building codes require that crawl spaces must be at least 18 inches high.

CREDIT (in Escrow Closing Statement) - prepaid taxes appear as a credit to the seller in the escrow closing statement. A credit increases the account balance.

CUBIC FOOT METHOD - used to determine the replacement cost of improvements in multistory structures when the height between floors vary (for example, the replacement cost of a warehouse would be calculated by cost per cubic foot).

CURABLE DEPRECIATION - economically and physically possible to correct.

DATE OF THE APPRAISAL - the date of the final writing or delivery of an appraisal report.

DATE OF VALUE - the date a property is inspected is generally used as the date of value.

DBA (Doing Business As) - the fictitious business statement filed by a broker. It must be approved by the Real Estate Commissioner. A DBA is good for five years.

DEBIT - the selling price appears as a debit on the buyer's closing statement. A debit decreases the account balance.

DEBT-INCOME RATIO - used by lenders as a loan qualifying tool.

DECIDUOUS - plants that lose their leaves in autumn and winter. It is not a type of soil.

DEED - the written instrument which, when properly executed, delivered, and accepted, conveys title to real property from one person (the grantor) to another (the grantee). Deeds are indexed by the names of the parties (grantor and grantee).

DEED-IN-LIEU OF FORECLOSURE - a borrower voluntarily deeds property back to a lender to stop foreclosure. Junior liens against the property remain in place.

DEFAULT ON A MORTGAGE - usually requires court foreclosure. After a court foreclosure sale on a mortgage, the mortgagor (borrower) can redeem the property by paying the loan in full (statutory right of redemption). The mortgagor retains possession of the property until the right of redemption expires.

DEFICIENCY JUDGMENT - is possible only when there is a court foreclosure on a non-purchase money loan and the fair market value is less than the loan amount (this rarely occurs).

DEFLATION - prices decrease. A decrease in prices causes an increase in the value of money.

DEMAND SOURCES - construction, sales financing, and refinancing are all demand sources of borrowers for mortgage money.

DEPARTMENT OF HOUSING AND URBAN DEVELOPMENT (HUD) - a federal agency overseeing the nation's housing.

DEPARTMENT OF REAL ESTATE (DRE) - the state agency which regulates the real estate industry.

DEPOSIT RECEIPT - the contract used to write an offer, the contract selling real property.

DEPRECIATION (appraisal) - any loss in value. Depreciation accrues over time. Accrued depreciation is the most difficult kind to measure accurately. Unlike taxation, for appraisal purposes land can and does depreciate.

DEPRECIATION (taxation) - allowed on improved income, trade, or business property. It is based on the cost of improvements. For taxation purposes, land never depreciates.

DESK COST - calculated by dividing the operating expenses of the office by the number of agents.

DISCOUNT POINTS - prepaid interest demanded by lender when a loan is negotiated. Each discount point costs one percent of the face amount of the loan.

DISCOUNT RATE - the interest rate charged by the Federal Reserve Board when banks borrow money from it. Raising the discount rate tightens the money market.

DISCOUNTING A NOTE - selling a note for less than the face amount or the current balance. When an investor buys a loan at a discount and later forecloses, the lender forecloses for the current loan balance, not the discounted amount.

DOCUMENTARY TRANSFER TAX - collected when a deed is recorded. The tax is based on consideration (selling price minus any existing loans assumed by the buyer).

DOMINANT TENEMENT - the land that gets the benefit of an easement.

DOWNZONING - changing zoning from high density use to a lower density use, such as changing from commercial C-1 zoning to residential R-1, or from R-3 to R-1.

DRYWALL - panels made of gypsum.

DUAL AGENCY - acting as an agent for more than one party (principal) in a real estate transaction. Dual agency is illegal unless the agent has obtained the knowledge and consent of both parties.

DUE DILIGENCE - occurs when an agent promises to search for a buyer in an exclusive listing. It includes an obligation to advertise the property.

EASEMENT - the right to enter or use another person's land within definable limits; it may be created for any length of time and is irrevocable during the time limit specified. All easements are real property.

EASEMENT IN GROSS - benefits a person or corporation (such as a utility easement for power lines).

EASTON V. STRASSBURGER - the court case that held that a seller and his or her agent must disclose to a buyer all facts materially affecting the value or desirability of the property. This decision led to the passage of the Seller Transfer Disclosure law.

ECONOMIC LIFE - the period of time in which an income property generates income in excess of its expenses. The economic life of a property is usually shorter than its physical life.

EFFECTIVE AGE - the apparent age of an improvement as opposed to its actual age (for example, a property which is 20 years old, but has been superbly maintained, may have an effective age of 9 years).

EFFECTIVE GROSS INCOME (Adjusted Gross Income) - used to appraise income property, it is the income left over after vacancies are subtracted from gross income, but before expenses are subtracted (used in the Capitalization Approach).

EFFECTIVE RATE - the interest rate that is actually paid by the borrower for the use of the money.

ELEVATION SHEET - shows the front and side views of homes in a subdivision.

EMANCIPATED - married minors and veterans who are minors are considered emancipated and can enter into contracts.

EMINENT DOMAIN - occurs when the government takes property, also called condemnation. It is the power of government to take private property for public use; fair market value is paid for property taken under eminent domain. Eminent domain is not part of police power or zoning.

ENCROACHMENT - wrongful placement of an improvement on the property of another, a type of trespass. An owner is allowed three years in which to sue a neighbor to have the encroachment removed.

ENCUMBRANCES - burdens on property, including money burdens (liens, such as trust deeds, mortgages, taxes, judgments, etc.) and non-money burdens (zoning, easements, deed restrictions, etc.).

ENERGY EFFICIENT RATIO (EER) - measures the efficiency of appliances, such as air conditioners. The higher the ratio, the more efficient the unit.

EQUAL DIGNITIES RULE - when a contract is required to be in writing, the authority of an agent to enter into a contract for his principal must also be in writing.

EQUITY - the difference between the value and the loan on a property, the owner's share of the total value of the property, or the initial down payment.

EROSION - the gradual wearing away of land by natural forces. It results in the loss of title.

ESCHEAT - occurs when a person dies, leaving no heirs and no will, and the state gets his or her property. Land may never be acquired by escheat.

ESCROW - the deposit of instruments and/or funds with a neutral third party who has been instructed to carry out the provisions of an agreement or contract. The purpose of escrow is to make sure that the conditions of transfer are met prior to closing.

ESCROW CLOSING STATEMENT - a detailed accounting of all money received and distributed at close of escrow.

ESCROW INSTRUCTIONS - are not usually notarized or recorded.

ESTATE AT SUFFERANCE - created when a lessee stays in possession of the premises after the proper time.

ESTATE AT WILL - a lessee can stay as long as both the lessor and the lessee mutually agree.

ESTATE FOR YEARS (lease) - any lease creates an estate for years. An estate for years must have a termination date.

ESTATE IN REVERSION - held by the original grantor if a property is to revert to him.

ESTATE OF PERIODIC TENANCY (month-to-month) - rental agreement that continues from period to period.

ESTATES (what is owned) - ownership rights and interests.

ESTOPPEL - a legal and equitable doctrine under which a person is barred from asserting or denying a fact because of the person's previous acts or words.

ET AL - and others.

ET UX - and wife.

EXCLUSIVE AGENCY LISTING - a contract in which a seller agrees to pay a commission to a listing agent if a property is sold by any agent; the seller also retains the right to sell directly to a buyer and pay no commission.

EXCLUSIVE AUTHORIZATION AND RIGHT TO SELL LISTING - a contract in which an owner agrees to sell through the listing broker only. If property is sold by anyone (the listing broker, another broker, the owner, or any other source) during the term of the listing, the listing broker is entitled to a commission.

EXCLUSIVE LOAN LISTING - a contract employing a broker to find a loan for a borrower. It may not exceed a term of more than 45 days.

EXECUTED - when escrow instructions are "executed" by both buyer and seller, they are signed. When escrow instructions are "executed" by an escrow agent, they have been fulfilled. When an escrow officer records a deed, he or she is executing escrow instructions.

EXECUTED CONTRACT - a contract in which both parties have completely performed their duties.

EXECUTION SALE - occurs when property is sold under a "writ of execution" to satisfy a judgment.

EXECUTIVE SALE - there is no such thing as an executive sale. This is used in a trick question.

EXECUTORY CONTRACT - a contract in which something remains to be done by one or both parties.

EXPOSURE - merchants prefer properties on the south and west sides of the street, and the southwest corner of intersections. The north and east sides are less desirable.

EXPRESS CONTRACT - a contract expressed in words, either oral or written.

EXTENDED COVERAGE POLICY - a title insurance policy that includes a survey and protects against unrecorded events.

EXTERNAL (ECONOMIC OR SOCIAL) OBSOLESCENCE - caused by external events occurring outside property lines.

FAIR EMPLOYMENT AND HOUSING ACT (Rumford Act) - prohibits discrimination in supplying housing accommodations based on race, color, religion, sex, marital status, national origin, ancestry, age, familial status or disability.

FALSE PROMISE - a false statement about what a promisor is going to do. A false promise and a misrepresentation are not the same thing. A misrepresentation is a false statement of fact.

FEDERAL HOME LOAN MORTGAGE CORPORATION (FHLMC, Freddie Mac) - a major participant in the secondary mortgage market.

FEDERAL HOUSING ADMINISTRATION (FHA) - created by the National Housing Act to encourage home ownership. FHA loans enable buyers to purchase homes with a small down payment, while insuring lenders against loss.

FEDERAL LAND BANK SYSTEM - the best source for farm loans and loans on large tracts of land.

FEDERAL NATIONAL MORTGAGE ASSOCIATION (FNMA, Title 3, Fannie Mae) - a major participant in the secondary mortgage market. Formerly a government agency, it is now a corporation with stock traded on the New York Stock Exchange.

FEDERAL RESERVE BOARD - regulates banks and influences the money supply of the economy.

FEE SIMPLE ABSOLUTE - the greatest estate one can have in real property.

FEE SIMPLE DEFEASIBLE - conditions or limits on the use of the property.

FEE SIMPLE ESTATE (of inheritance, perpetual estate, estate in fee) - an estate which is indefinite in duration and can be sold or inherited.

FICTITIOUS TRUST DEED OR MORTGAGE - a recorded trust deed or mortgage containing details which apply to later loan documents.

FIDUCIARY RELATIONSHIP - a relationship of trust and good faith. The relationship is similar to a trustee and a beneficiary; however, a trustor does not necessarily have a fiduciary relationship with a beneficiary.

FINAL PUBLIC REPORT - issued by the Commissioner when all his requirements for a subdivision have been met. It is valid for five years unless there is a material change.

FIXED EXPENSES - property taxes and insurance.

FIXTURES - objects attached to the land. Fixtures may become real property.

FLASHING - sheet metal used to protect a building from seepage of water, such as in the valley of a roof.

FOOTING - the concrete base or bottom of a foundation wall.

FORECASTING - occurs when an appraiser projects or estimates the annual expenses for an income producing property in a reconstructed operating statement.

FOREIGN INVESTMENT IN REAL PROPERTY TAX ACT (FIRPTA) - requires that a buyer of real property must withhold and send to the Internal Revenue Service (IRS) 10% of the gross sales price if the seller of the real property is a foreign person.

FOUNDATION PLAN - shows the location of the footings and piers under a house.

FRAUD - a misrepresentation which usually makes a contract voidable. The buyer or seller must have relied upon the misrepresentation to claim fraud.

FREEHOLD ESTATE - an estate of indeterminable duration.

FRIVOLOUS OFFER - an offer which no rational person would accept.

FRONT FOOT VALUE - the deeper the lot, the greater the front foot value.

FRONT FOOTAGE - the measurement of property on its street line, used for sale or valuation purposes.

FRONTAGE - the distance a property adjoins a street or thoroughfare.

FRUCTUS INDUSTRIALES - crops which must be planted annually.

FUNDING OF THE BUYER'S LOAN - occurs when escrow notifies lender to release funds for the loan.

GABLE ROOF - a pitched roof, sloping on two sides.

GOVERNMENT BONDS - government loan instruments. When the Federal Reserve Board sells existing government bonds through the Federal Open Market Committee, it tightens the money supply.

GOVERNMENT NATIONAL MORTGAGE ASSOCIATION (GNMA, Ginnie Mae) - major participant in the secondary mortgage market. It is a federal agency within the Department of Housing and Urban Development (HUD).

GRANDFATHER CLAUSE - allows an owner to continue to use structures which do not conform with new zoning laws.

GRANT DEED - the most commonly used deed, containing two implied warranties: (1) the grantor has not conveyed title to any other person, and (2) the estate is free from undisclosed encumbrances. These facts are warranted by the grant deed and not covered by title insurance.

GROSS LEASE - the lessor pays expenses (a fixed amount).

GROSS MULTIPLIER (rent multiplier, gross rent multiplier) - found by dividing the sale price of comparable properties by their gross monthly or gross annual incomes.

GROSS NATIONAL PRODUCT (now called the Gross Domestic Product) - the measure of goods and services produced by the nation during any one calendar year.

GUARANTEED NOTE - a seller or agent guarantees the yield or return; it is classified as a real property security.

HARD MONEY LOAN - a cash loan in which the borrower receives cash using a new note secured by a trust deed (for example, a home equity loan). The commissions, costs, and expenses to negotiate hard money first trust deeds of less than $30,000, and hard money junior loans of less than $20,000, are limited by law.

HIP ROOF - a roof sloping on all four sides.

HOLDER IN DUE COURSE - an innocent party who purchases a negotiable instrument without knowledge of any defects.

HOMESTEAD EXEMPTION - a method of protecting a limited amount of equity in a personal residence from subsequent unsecured creditors. A homestead must be recorded, and may be recorded by either spouse without the knowledge or consent of the other. A homestead is not an encumbrance.

HOUSING ACCOMMODATIONS - improved or unimproved real property used or intended to be used as a residence by the owner; it consists of no more than four dwelling units.

HOUSING FINANCIAL DISCRIMINATION ACT (Holden Act) - California state law making discrimination in lending practices illegal.

HVAC - the Heating, Ventilation, Air Conditioning system in a commercial lease.

HYPOTHECATE - the borrower retains possession of the item securing the debt (for example, a trust deed, mortgage, or the pink slip for a car loan).

IMPOUND ACCOUNT - a trust account established to hold funds for future needs relating to a parcel of real estate. Impound means to hold, reserve, or impress.

INCOME, TRADE OR BUSINESS PROPERTY - property which produces income to the owner.

INCURABLE DEPRECIATION - either too expensive or physically impossible to correct.

INFLATION - caused when there is more money available than there are goods for sale.

IN-HOUSE SALE - a transaction in which both the buyer and the seller are represented by agents working for one broker. When a brokerage has a property listed for sale, no agent in the brokerage may be the agent for the buyer only, because the brokerage has an agency relationship with the seller.

INJUNCTION - a court order restricting a party from doing an act (such as violating private restrictions). A court order saying "Stop that!"

INSTITUTIONAL LENDERS (insurance companies, savings and loans, and commercial banks) - they receive most of their deposits from "household savings" of individual depositors.

INSULATION - the "R value" measures the insulation's resistance to heat. The higher the R value, the greater the insulation. Wall insulation is considered adequate if the inside of an exterior wall is about the same temperature as interior walls.

INTERIM LOAN (short-term) - finances construction. The terms "interim loan" and "construction loan" are synonymous (they mean the same thing).

INTERIM USE - the current use, when the highest and best use is expected to change.

INTERNAL (FUNCTIONAL) OBSOLESCENCE - caused by events occurring within the property lines and observable during an inspection by an appraiser.

INTERPLEADER ACTION - escrow would file an interpleader action in court to settle a dispute between a buyer and seller over the deposit.

INTESTATE SUCCESSION - occurs when a person dies without a will, but with heirs.

INVERSE CONDEMNATION - occurs when a private party forces government to purchase, (for example, as a result of freeway or airport noise). It is the opposite of eminent domain.

INVESTMENT PROPERTY - vacant land held for an investment. When it is sold, losses can be deducted. Investment property cannot be depreciated.

JOINT AND SEVERAL LIABILITY - when there is more than one obligator (borrower) on a promissory note, the lender will include the terms "jointly and severally."

JOINT TENANCY - created when two or more persons take title as joint tenants. Four unities are required for joint tenancy (T-TIP) –Time, Title, Interest, Possession.

JOIST - one of a series of parallel beams used to support the ceiling and floors. It is a parallel.

JONES VS. MAYER - the U.S. Supreme Court case (decided in 1968) which upheld anti-discrimination laws on the basis of the Thirteenth Amendment to the U.S. Constitution.

JUDGMENT LIEN - when an abstract of judgment is recorded, it creates a court ordered general, involuntary lien upon all real property of the debtor located in the county of recordation. A judgment lien is valid for ten years and enforced by way of an execution sale. The court orders the sale of property to satisfy a judgment with a writ of execution.

JUNIOR LOAN - any loan which is not first (for example, a second trust deed, or third trust deed, etc.).

KICKBACKS - any type of compensation from escrow companies, termite companies and title companies given to a licensee for referring business. Kickbacks are illegal.

KIOSK - a free-standing information booth in a mall.

LACHES - an unfair delay in asserting legal rights which will not be excused by the court.

LAND CONTRACT (real property sales contract, installment sales contract, agreement to convey, agreement for purchase and sale, or land contract of sale) - a written contract where the seller (vendor) agrees to transfer title to real property (give a grant deed) to the buyer (vendee) after the buyer has met the contract conditions.

LAND RESIDUAL METHOD - an appraiser uses the land residual method when the unknown factor is the value of the land.

LAWFUL OBJECT - a contract must be legal in formation and operation. Both its consideration and its object must be lawful.

LENDER'S (ALTA) POLICY - includes a survey and provides the lender with extended coverage protection.

LESS-THAN-FREEHOLD ESTATE (leasehold estate or chattel real) - personal property, not real property. It is the legal interest in real property held by a tenant who is leasing or renting.

LESSEE - tenant.

LESSOR - landlord.

LEVERAGE - using borrowed money (financing) to the maximum extent possible.

LICENSE - the personal and nonassignable right to do a particular act (or acts) on the land of another.

LIENS - money encumbrances placed against a property either voluntarily (with the owner's consent) or involuntarily (without the owner's consent). A lien is a "charge" against real property.

LIFE ESTATE - a freehold estate, limited to the duration of someone's life.

LIFE TENANT - holder of the life estate.

LIKE FOR LIKE PROPERTIES - in a 1031 tax deferred exchange it is "income, trade, business, or investment properties."

LIQUIDATED DAMAGES CLAUSE - a clause in a contract fixing the amount of damages in case one of the parties defaults.

LIQUIDITY - describes how quickly an investment can be converted into cash.

LIQUIDITY OF A BUSINESS - measured by subtracting current liabilities from current assets.

LIS PENDENS - notice of pending litigation concerning title or possession of real property.

LISTING - an employment contract between a principal (usually the seller) and an agent (broker) employing the agent to do certain things for the principal.

LISTING WITH OPTION TO BUY - an agent who has an option to buy a property which he has also listed for sale has a conflict of interest. To exercise his option to buy, the agent must reveal to the seller (in writing) any offers on the property and the amount of his profit. Additionally, to exercise his option, the agent must obtain the written consent of the seller.

LITTORAL RIGHTS - refer to non-moving water (a pond, lake, ocean).

LOAN TO VALUE RATIO (LTV) - the percentage of the appraised value which a lender will lend on a property. If a lender requires a 80/20 LTV, the lender will lend 80% of the lender's appraised value and require a 20% cash down payment.

LOCK-IN CLAUSE - a borrower is prohibited from paying off a loan in advance.

MARGINAL TAX RATE - the tax rate on the next dollar earned.

MARKETABILITY - the most important test of functional utility.

MARKET RENT (economic rent, scheduled gross income) - the rent a property would bring in the open market on the date of appraisal. It represents the potential gross income the property can produce.

MARKET DATA APPROACH (Comparison, Comparative or Substitution Method) - sales of similar properties in the area are studied to form an opinion of value. The market data approach is the oldest, quickest, and easiest to learn approach. It is very adaptable and commonly used to appraise of residences and land. The market data approach is also used to appraise amenity properties.

MARKET VALUE (objective value) - based on a "willing buyer" and "willing seller" concept. It is the most likely price the property should bring on the open market within a reasonable length of time.

MATERIAL FACTS - facts which are likely to influence or persuade a party to enter into a contract.

MECHANIC'S LIENS - liens recorded by persons who have performed work or furnished materials for the improvement of real property, for which they were not paid. They must be verified and recorded.

METES AND BOUNDS - a legal description of land created by a survey. Metes and bounds describes boundaries but does not measure land or buildings.

MINIMUM CASH RESERVE - the Federal Reserve Board requires banks to keep a small percentage of money deposited in their vaults as a reserve to meet cash requirements of depositors. Raising the minimum cash reserve requirement tightens the money market.

MISREPRESENTATION - failure to disclose material facts, lying.

MISTAKE - contract is void or voidable.

MORTGAGE - a document used to secure payment of a promissory note; it is seldom used in California. Mortgages are not negotiable instruments.

MORTGAGE LOAN - a loan secured (collateralized) by real estate.

MORTGAGE LOAN DISCLOSURE STATEMENT (Loan Broker Statement) - provides a borrower with detailed information about a loan, including all costs and expenses that will be charged to the borrower. This statement must be given to the borrower when signed, for every loan negotiated by a broker.

MORTGAGE YIELD - the interest (not the principal) which a lender receives from a mortgage.

MORTGAGEE - the lender in a mortgage.

MORTGAGOR - the borrower in a mortgage.

MUTUAL CONSENT - for a contract to be valid, there must be mutual consent or assent to the terms. In real estate contracts, mutual consent is created by three steps: (1) offer, (2) acceptance, (3) communication of acceptance back to offeror.

MUTUAL MORTGAGE INSURANCE - required for FHA loans. It protects the lender in case of foreclosure and is paid by the borrower, either as a lump sum or amortized.

NEGATIVE AMORTIZATION - occurs when monthly loan payments are insufficient to pay the interest and/or principal payments necessary to pay off the loan. As a result, the loan balance increases.

NEGATIVE DECLARATION - under the Environmental Quality Act, a negative declaration indicates that a subdivision does not harm the environment.

NEGOTIABLE INSTRUMENT - a written document which is freely transferrable, like money (such as personal checks, bank drafts and promissory notes). Mortgages, trust deeds and land contracts are not negotiable instruments.

NET LEASE - a lessee pays expenses such as taxes, insurance, and maintenance.

NET LISTING - any listing where an agent receives all money over a set selling price as his commission, rather than a percentage of the selling price.

NOMINAL RATE - the interest rate named in the loan document.

NONCONFORMING USE - a preexisting, ongoing use of a property in a manner which is now prohibited by a change in zoning laws.

NOTICE OF NONRESPONSIBILITY - recorded by the owner if someone else (such as a tenant or vendee in a land contract) has work done on the owner's property. The notice must be recorded within ten days of obtaining knowledge of the improvement.

NOVATION - the agreement of parties to substitute a new contract for an existing one with the intent to replace the original contract. A broker might be replaced in a listing by way of novation.

OBSERVED CONDITION METHOD - for appraisal purposes, it involves considering functional obsolescence, economic obsolescence, and physical deterioration.

OBSOLESCENCE - the major cause of depreciation for appraisal purposes. Obsolescence is a cause of depreciation, not a method of calculating depreciation.

OPEN END LOAN (revolving line of credit) - allows borrower to re-borrow principal previously paid back.

OPEN LISTING (Nonexclusive Listing) - a contract given by an owner authorizing a broker to act as his agent. The broker must be the procuring cause (responsible for the consummation of the transaction) to be entitled to a commission.

OPTION - a contract to keep an offer to lease or sell real property open for a set period. The optionor agrees not to revoke his offer to sell during that period of time.

OR MORE CLAUSE - permits borrower to pre-pay without penalty.

ORIENTATION - placement of a building on a lot in relation to exposure to sun, prevailing wind, traffic, and privacy from the street.

OSTENSIBLE AUTHORITY - apparent authority.

OWC (Owner Will Carry) - when a seller carries back a trust deed from a buyer, the seller is the beneficiary and the buyer is the trustor. It creates a specific voluntary lien against the property.

PANIC SELLING (or blockbusting) - when agents attempt to persuade home owners to sell by telling them that members of another ethnic group are moving into the neighborhood. It violates both state and federal law.

PARAMOUNT TITLE - title which is superior or foremost to all others.

PASS-THROUGH SECURITIES - the Government National Mortgage Association (Ginnie Mae) guarantees the principal and interest payments on mortgages in pass-through securities. A mortgage company would buy pass-through securities in times of changing financial conditions.

PERCENTAGE LEASE - a lease in which the lessee pays rent based on a percentage of the gross receipts of the lessee's business.

PERCOLATING WATER - underground water which does not flow in a defined channel.

PERCOLATION TEST - a soil analysis that determines how quickly water will seep through soil (such as for sewage purposes). A percolation test would be conducted before a septic tank is installed.

PERPETUITY - an interest in real estate which may last for an unlimited period of time, such as an estate in perpetuity or easement in perpetuity.

PERSONAL RESIDENCE - the primary residence of a taxpayer.

PHYSICAL DETERIORATION - caused by events occurring within property lines. It is a cause of depreciation for appraisal purposes.

PLEDGE - an existing loan, given as security for a new loan.

PLOT PLAN (Plot Map) - shows the location of improvements on a lot.

PLOTTAGE - joining two or more lots together for an added increase in value; the increased value is above and beyond the value of the individual lots added together.

POCKET LISTING - a listing which is hidden from other agents.

POLICE POWER (government regulation of property) - the right of government to pass and enforce laws for the order, safety, health, morals, and general welfare of the public (such as rent control, planning and zoning laws, building and subdivision laws). It is not part of eminent domain law.

POTABLE - water that is suitable for drinking.

PRELIMINARY TITLE REPORT - prepared before title insurance policy is issued and shows most recorded documents that have an effect on title.

PREPAYMENT PENALTY CLAUSE - allows borrowers to prepay a loan only if extra money is paid to the lender. A prepayment penalty is not allowed on a loan against a borrower's residence after the loan is five years old.

PRESCRIPTION - an easement may be acquired by five years of open, notorious, continuous, hostile use, under a claim of right or color of title. Confrontation with the owner is not required, and the property taxes need not be paid. An easement by prescription terminates after five years of non-use.

PRICE (market price) - what the buyer pays for a property. Conditions of the sale may effect the price (for example, good financing, a forced sale, or high-pressure salesmanship).

PRICE INDEXES - determine the purchasing power of the United States dollar.

PRIMARY MORTGAGE MARKET - where institutional and non-institutional lenders originate loans.

PRINCIPAL - either the owner or the buyer of a property. If a principal employs an agent, the principal is responsible for the agent's actions.

PRINCIPLE OF CHANGE - property values change constantly. A typical neighborhood goes through three phases of change: integration, equilibrium, and disintegration.

PRINCIPLE OF CONTRIBUTION - when appraising a component or portion of income property, the appraiser considers its contribution to the net return.

PRINCIPLE OF HIGHEST AND BEST USE - the best use of a parcel of land, the use which will most likely produce the greatest net rate of return over a given period of time.

PRINCIPLE OF REGRESSION - the value of expensive homes is lowered when homes of lesser quality (substandard) are built nearby.

PRINCIPLE OF SUBSTITUTION (used in all appraisal techniques) - the maximum value of a property is determined by the cost of acquiring an equally desirable substitute property. It is the basis of the market data approach and is also known as the comparison or substitution approach.

PRIORITY - refers to who gets paid first when a property is foreclosed. Assessment liens have priority over all private liens, such as trust deeds or mechanic's liens. Mechanic's liens have priority as of the day work began or materials were first furnished. They do not have priority over for government liens.

PRIVATE MORTGAGE INSURANCE (PMI) - a private program similar to FHA Mutual Mortgage Insurance.

PRIVATE RESTRICTIONS - created by the grantor or developer either in a deed or by written agreement (CC & R's). They do not include zoning laws or liens.

PROGRESSIVE TAX - the federal income tax is a progressive tax. The higher your income, the higher percentage of tax you must pay.

PROMISSORY NOTE - a negotiable instrument which serves as evidence of a debt. It is also called a debt repayment contract.

PROMOTIONAL NOTE - one of a series of notes that is less than three years old and is secured by liens on parcels in a subdivision. After three years, the note ceases to be a promotional note and is no longer regulated as a real property security.

PROMULGATE - to publish or make laws known. The Real Estate Commissioner has the right to promulgate regulations which control the actions of real estate licensees and have the force and effect of law.

PROPERTY RESIDUAL TECHNIQUE (the simplest method) - land and improvements are valued as a single unit. The property's total net income is divided by one "overall" capitalization rate.

PRORATION - the division of expenses such as taxes, insurance, interest on an assumed loan, and rent at the close of escrow. Most proration problems can be answered in two steps: (1) establish who is going to pay, and (2) calculate the amount using a 30-day month and a 360-day year (banker's year).

PUBLIC RESTROOMS - where you will go as soon as you complete your exam (it's a long test)!

PUBLIC RESTRICTIONS - laws passed by government to regulate the use of property, most commonly zoning laws.

PUFFING - occurs when, in an ad, a broker exaggerates features of the property or location by giving his or her opinion as part of the sales process. Examples include, "This is a great house." "This property is a wonderful buy." Puffing is considered to be misrepresentation only if a reasonable person would rely upon the statement as a fact, rather than as an opinion.

PURCHASE-MONEY LOAN - any seller financing or loan created to purchase one-to-four owner-occupied residential units.

QUANTITY SURVEY METHOD - a detailed estimate of all labor and materials is compiled for each component of the building. It is accurate, but time consuming, and is seldom used (except by builders).

QUIET TITLE ACTION - a court suit to perfect title, usually by removing a cloud on title. A quiet title action would be used to clear title under a forfeited recorded contract (land contract).

QUITCLAIM DEED - usually used to quiet title or to clear a cloud on title. It contains no warranties and merely conveys the rights of the grantor (if there are any).

RATIFICATION - approval by principal of an agent's actions after the fact.

REAL ESTATE COMMISSIONER - the head of the DRE. He or she issues regulations which have the effect of law and appear in the California Code of Regulations.

REAL ESTATE SETTLEMENT PROCEDURES ACT (RESPA) - provides purchasers with fast and reliable information on the costs of completing a real estate transaction for buyers of one-to-four residential units with a federally regulated loan.

REAL PROPERTY SECURITIES - historically, these transactions are likely to involve fraud. In order to prevent fraud, special rules apply when selling real property securities.

REALTIST - a member of the National Association of Real Estate Brokers, historically composed primarily of African-American Real Estate Brokers.

REALTOR - a member of the National Association of Realtors.

RECONSTRUCTED OPERATING STATEMENT - an estimate of income and expenses (including management costs). It is used in the capitalization approach to appraisal. Management is the most often overlooked expense, but there is always a management expense.

RECORDED TRACT MAP OR LOT AND BLOCK SYSTEM - when land is subdivided, a tract map showing the location of parcels is recorded. A legal description of a piece of property can be created by reference to this map.

RECOVERY ACCOUNT - a portion of real estate license fees is put into an account to protect the general public when a judgment or arbitration award against a licensee is uncollectable. Recovery is limited to $20,000 per transaction, $100,000 maximum per licensee.

RECURRING COSTS - when mentioned in a closing statement, they include impounds.

REDEMPTION - a right to buy back your property after a court ordered sale.

RECONVEYANCE DEED - signed and recorded by a trustee to remove a trust deed when a loan is paid in full.

REDLINING - charging higher interest rates or not lending in certain neighborhoods based upon "suspect characteristics," such as race, color, creed, age, national origin, etc.

REHABILITATION - restoration of property to a former or improved condition without changing the basic plan or design.

RELEASE CLAUSE - allows a portion of land to be released upon partial payment of the debt. When part of the debt is paid, the beneficiary of a blanket trust deed signs a Request for Partial Reconveyance. The trustee then signs and records a Partial Reconveyance Deed.

RELICTION - an increase of land by the permanent withdrawal of a sea or river.

RENEGOTIABLE RATE MORTGAGE - can adjust by no more than 5% over the life of the loan.

REO (Real Estate Owned) - foreclosed property which now is owned by the lender.

REPLACEMENT COST (of an improvement) - the cost to build a comparable structure.

REPRODUCTION COST (of an improvement) - the cost to build an exact duplicate of the structure. Reproduction cost is usually higher than replacement cost.

REQUEST FOR FULL RECONVEYANCE - signed by a beneficiary and sent to a trustee when a loan is paid in full. The trustee then signs and records a Reconveyance Deed to clear the lien from public records.

REQUEST FOR NOTICE OF DEFAULT - recorded by the beneficiary of a junior loan to insure that the beneficiary will be notified if the borrower defaults on a prior loan.

RESCISSION OF THE CONTRACT - when a party to a contract backs out and returns anything received under the contract.

RESERVES FOR REPLACEMENT - typically a monthly allocation to provide money for replacement of carpets, appliances, etc. for income property.

RESIDENT PROPERTY MANAGER - may only manage the property where he or she resides without having a real estate license. The owner of a residential property with 16 or more units must live in the property or have a resident property manager.

RESTRICTIONS - restrict the free use of the land by an owner.

RETURN OF THE INVESTMENT - depreciation of improvements.

RETURN ON THE INVESTMENT - interest or profit.

RIDGEBOARD - the highest structural point in a frame house.

RIGHT OF REDEMPTION - after a judicial foreclosure, the borrower has the right to buy the property back from whoever purchased it. There is no right of redemption after a trustee sale.

RIGHT OF SURVIVORSHIP - the most important characteristic of joint tenancy. If one joint tenant dies, the surviving joint tenant(s) receives the decedent's interest automatically and avoids probate. A joint tenant may do anything except will their tenancy.

RIPARIAN RIGHTS - refer to moving water (stream, river, watercourse).

RUMFORD ACT (Fair Employment and Housing Act) - California state law which forbids discrimination in housing transactions. Complaints are submitted to the California Department of Fair Employment and Housing which also enforces fair housing laws on the state level. Victims have one year to file a complaint.

SALE-LEASEBACK - occurs when a seller (holder of a freehold estate) becomes a tenant (holder of a less-than-freehold estate). It allows a seller to deduct future rent payments as a business expense.

SALESPERSON - an employee or independent contractor of a broker. A salesperson may receive compensation for real estate acts only from an employing broker. It is illegal for a salesperson working for a broker to receive a referral fee or commission from a lender, loan broker, developer, or seller.

SCHEMATICS - preliminary architectural drawings, such as site plans and elevations.

SECONDARY MORTGAGE MARKET - a resale marketplace for loans; it is where existing loans are bought and sold.

SECRET PROFIT - an agent may not make an undisclosed profit in a real estate transaction.

SECTION - the legal description of a square parcel of land measuring 1 mile by 1 mile (5,280 feet by 5,280 feet). It contains 640 acres.

SECURED TRUST DEEDS - an agent may advertise "secured trust deeds" as long as he or she discloses the extent to which the trust deeds are secured.

SELLER TRANSFER DISCLOSURE STATEMENT (TDS) - a seller (transferor) must provide a buyer of one-to-four residential units with a standard form which discloses the condition of the property. The form includes both the condition of the improvements and the condition of the land. This statement is not required for husband-wife transfers, probate sales, foreclosure sales, bankruptcies, and REO's.

SELLER'S MARKET - exists when prices rise and there are more buyers than sellers.

SERVIENT TENEMENT - the land that is crossed by an easement and is encumbered (burdened) by the easement.

SETBACK - the distance a building must be set back from the street, the side, and the back boundary lines. It effects the property's dimensions for building purposes only.

SEVERALTY - separate ownership, ownership by one person or corporation, sole ownership.

SEVERANCE - describes the act of removing something attached to the land and, by doing so, changing its status from real property to personal property.

SERVITUDE - is a burden on land which transfers automatically when the land is sold.

SHEATHING - plywood panels placed beneath roof tiles to prevent water seepage.

SHORT RATE - a refund received by a seller when a home is sold and the homeowner's insurance is cancelled. The short rate refund is less than the credit the seller would receive if the buyer were to take over the existing homeowner's insurance policy.

SIDE YARD SETBACK - the distance a building must be set back from the side line of the lot.

SILL (Mudsill) - the lowest part of a frame house. It rests on the foundation.

SIMPLE INTEREST - charged on an unpaid principal amount and used on most home loans. Interest is calculated by the formula: Interest = Principal x Rate x Time (I = PRT).

SOLDIERS AND SAILORS CIVIL RELIEF ACT - limits foreclosure.

SOLEPLATE - a board on which walls and partition studs rest.

SPECIFIC PERFORMANCE - a law suit to force a party to a contract to perform the act they promised to perform. It is used only when dollar damages do not provide an adequate remedy. When a seller wrongfully backs out of a contract to sell real property, it is the opinion of the law that "all real property is unique" and therefore dollar damages will not make the buyer "whole." When suing for specific performance, the court will order a seller to sign the deed, if the buyer can prove the monetary consideration was sufficient relative to the value of the property.

SQUARE FOOT METHOD - appraisers use exterior dimensions and compare the cost to build an improvement of similar quality. It costs less per square foot will be less to build a two story structure than a one story structure with the same square footage.

STANDARD COVERAGE (CLTA) POLICY - the most commonly purchased title policy. It covers matters of record, lack of capacity, forgery, and defective delivery of a deed. It does not include a site inspection or survey.

STANDBY COMMITMENT - anytime a lender agrees to provide a loan at a set interest rate and at some future date.

STATUTE OF FRAUDS - determines which contracts must be in writing to be enforceable.

STATUTE OF LIMITATIONS - determines how long an individual can wait to sue.

STEERING - showing homes only in segregated areas to minority buyers violates fair housing laws (for example, an agent avoids showing homes to Hispanic buyers in areas where no Hispanics live).

STOCK IN A MUTUAL WATER COMPANY - appurtenant to the land. It is considered real property. This stock provides access to water at reasonable rates to the land owner.

STRAIGHT LINE DEPRECIATION - under current tax law, annual depreciation is calculated by dividing the value of improvements by the depreciable life (27.5 or 39 years).

STRAIGHT NOTE (term note) - all of the principal is paid at maturity. The interest may be paid during the term of the note or at maturity. Straight notes generally carry higher interest rates than amortized installment notes.

SUBAGENT - an agent appointed by a seller's agent to perform some or all of the seller's agent duties. If the principal has authorized the agent to appoint a subagent, the principal is responsible for the acts of the subagent.

SUBCHAPTER-S CORPORATION (S-Corporation) - gains and losses pass directly to the shareholders.

SUBDIVIDED LANDS LAW - designed to prevent fraud. It is regulated by the Commissioner.

SUBDIVISION MAP ACT - grants cities and counties control over the design (physical improvements) of a subdivision (such as streets and sewers).

SUBJECT TO - when a buyer takes property subject to an existing loan, the lender will keep the seller on the loan as the borrower. The seller is liable for any deficiency, and the buyer's loss is limited to his equity if there is a foreclosure (the benefit is to the buyer).

SUBLEASE - an original lessee gives up a portion of his overall interest in the leasehold. A sublease transfers possession of the real property, but not ownership. The original lessee is liable for the rent.

SUBORDINATION CLAUSE - a clause in which a lender agrees to give up priority to later loans. A subordination clause benefits the trustor (borrower).

SUBSTANDARD LOAN - a loan likely to go into default.

SUBSTITUTION OF LIABILITY - when a lender agrees to a substitution of liability, the seller is relieved from any liability on the loan.

SUFFICIENT CONSIDERATION - anything of value; it does not have to be money; it can be a benefit conferred or a promise. In a bilateral contract, the promises are often the consideration. Every executory contract requires consideration.

SURRENDER - lessor and lessee mutually agree to terminate the lease.

SYNDICATIONS - invest in real estate and sometimes make real estate loans. They are sometimes formed as corporations which have limited liability and may hold title to both real and personal property.

TAKE-OUT LOAN (long-term) - received by a buyer to pay for new construction. The proceeds are used by a builder to pay off an interim (construction) loan.

TAX DEFERRED EXCHANGE (1031 Exchange) - when property is exchanged, taxes may be deferred. The properties exchanged must be "like for like" properties. They must be any combination of income, trade or business, or investment properties.

TAX SHELTER - an investment, such as real estate, which allows an investor to defer payment of taxes on current income to a later year.

TAXABLE (RECOGNIZED) GAIN - the smaller of the actual gain or the boot. Taxable gain is taxed in the year of the exchange.

TENANCY - a mode or method of holding title to property.

TENANCY IN COMMON - may be the title vesting when two or more persons own an undivided interest in a property. It only requires one unity (unity of possession).

TENDER - an unconditional offer of money or performance according to the terms of a contract.

TERMITE INSPECTION - should be made before the property is listed for sale.

TERMITE REPORT - filed with the Structural Pest Control Board. Copies are retained for two years and can be obtained by anyone. A copy must be given to the owner.

TIGHT MONEY MARKET - will cause a decrease in real estate sales and will increase the use of second trust deeds.

TITLE PLANT - the records maintained by a title insurance company of recorded documents effecting real estate.

TITLE POLICY - an insurance policy insuring a policy holder (grantee) and any heirs that a marketable title was received (reasonably free from doubt in law).

TITLE VESTINGS - how property is owned, also called tenancy.

TITLE VIII OF THE CIVIL RIGHTS ACT OF 1968 (also known as the Federal Fair Housing Act or Federal Open Housing Law) - prohibits discrimination in housing transactions.

TOPOGRAPHY - limited irregularity in contour is best for residential property.

TORT - a negligent or intentional wrongful act arising from breach of duty.

TOXIC WASTE REPORT - recommended if a property is next to an abandoned gas station.

TRADE FIXTURE - a fixture attached to real property as part of the tenant's trade or business. A trade fixture is the personal property of a business tenant.

TRUST DEED - the instrument used in California to secure payment of a promissory note. Trust deeds are not negotiable instruments.

TRUST FUND ACCOUNT - a separate checking account used to hold clients' money.

TRUSTEE (agent for the beneficiary) - an agent chosen by the beneficiary. A trust deed conveys the power to sell a property by way of a trustee's sale (nonjudicial foreclosure) from the trustor to the trustee. This right to sell the property by a nonjudicial foreclosure is called "bare title." The trustee reconveys the bare title when the debt is paid in full.

TRUSTOR - the borrower in a trust deed. A trustor signs the promissory note and trust deed, which gives trustee the right to foreclose by way of a trustee sale. The trustor retains legal title.

TRUTH-IN-LENDING LAW (Regulation Z) - part of the Federal Consumer Credit Protection Act to protect borrowers and assure a meaningful disclosure of credit terms.

TURNKEY PROJECT - one that is ready for occupancy; a tenant can move in immediately.

U.S. GOVERNMENT RECTANGULAR SURVEY SYSTEM - describes very large pieces of land (desert land, ranches and farms). Land is referred to in terms of Townships and Sections.

UNEARNED INCREMENT - occurs when property gains value due to either inflation or an increase in population.

UNILATERAL CONTRACT - a contract in which a promise is given by one party to persuade another party to do some action (a promise for an act). The second party is not bound to act, but if he does act, the first party must keep his promise (for example, option contracts and open listings).

UNIT-IN-PLACE COST METHOD - adds together the cost of individual structural components of a building. It is time consuming and seldom used.

UNLAWFUL DETAINER ACTION - a lawsuit to evict a lessee. It is brought by an offended lessor.

UNRUH CIVIL RIGHTS ACT - prohibits discrimination by businesses.

USURY - the conscious charging by a private lender of more than the maximum amount of interest allowed by law. The interest on a loan negotiated by a real estate broker is exempt from the usury law limits.

UTILITY VALUE (Subjective Value) - the value of the property based on its use by the owner.

VALID CONTRACT - a contract that is binding and enforceable. It has the four essential elements required by law: mutual consent, capable parties, lawful object, and consideration.

VALUE (Worth) - the relationship between the thing desired and the purchaser, the power of one commodity to attract other commodities in exchange. It is also defined as the present worth of future benefits arising from ownership of property.

VENDEE - the buyer in a land contract becomes an equitable owner holding equitable title (the right to use and possess).

VENDOR - the seller in a land contract, the vendor holds legal title.

VETERAN'S ADMINISTRATION (VA, GI) - government financing program to provide real estate loans for veterans.

VOID CONTRACT - not a contract. It lacks legal effect.

VOIDABLE CONTRACT - a contract which is valid and enforceable on its face, but because of some deficiency, one or more of the parties may reject (void) it. A voidable contract is valid until it is voided (rescinded).

WAIVER - a unilateral act and its legal consequences.

WAREHOUSING - collecting loans prior to sale. It involves putting together mortgage portfolios.

WARRANTY DEED - no longer in use. In California it has been replaced by title insurance.

WATER TABLE - the depth at which water is found.

ZONING - the government division of land into districts according to use.

Most Commonly Tested Numbers

Times / Dates:

3 Days - after delivery of TDS in person to buyer, for buyer to terminate his offer in writing.

3 Business Days - after loan documents signed, Truth-in-lending right to rescind.

5 Days - after delivery of TDS by mailing to buyer, for buyer to terminate his offer in writing.

1 Week - after closing, the broker/escrow must record trust deed.

10 Days - to post and record a Notice of Nonresponsibility.

10 Days - for a broker to recommend a lender record a trust deed.

10 Calendar Days - for agent to report sale of registered mobilehome to the Department of Housing and Community Development.

21 Days - landlord must return security deposit to tenant.

25 Days - a broker must remove earned fees in excess of $200 from his trust account.

Monthly - a broker must reconcile his/her client trust account monthly.

Property Tax Year - July 1-June 30.

1 Year or less - oral lease of real property.

1 Year - from the date you took the exam to apply for your real estate license after you pass the exam.

1 Year - to file a Rumford Act complaint with the Department of Fair Employment and Housing.

More than 1 Year - lease of real property must be in writing.

2 Years - grace period to renew your real estate license after it expires.

2 Years - to sue an agent for failure to disclose defects in the TDS.

3 Years - keep all real estate documents.

3 Years - to sue a neighbor to have an encroachment removed.

3 Years - for overages in a trust account to be turned over to the Controller's office.

37 Months - promotional note is no longer a real property security.

4 years - must renew sales and broker licenses.

5 Years - possession required to take title by adverse possession.

5 Years - usage to create an easement by prescription.

5 Years - non-use terminates an easement created by prescription.

5 Years - DBA expires.

27.5 Years - minimum depreciation period for residential income property (apartment buildings).

39 Years - minimum depreciation period for non-residential income property (commercial buildings).

1968 - Jones v. Mayer, established the 13th Amendment as a basis for Fair Housing Laws.

<u>Measurements</u>

1 Square Yard = 9 square feet.

7.5 Feet - minimum ceiling height (FHA).

8 Feet - usual ceiling height (FHA).

25 Feet = approximate width of an easement which is 1 mile long and covers 3 acres.

1 Acre = 43,560 square feet = 4,840 square yards, (209' by 209' if in shape of square).

160 Acres = 1/4 of a section, measuring 1/2 mile by 1/2 mile.

1 Mile = 5,280 feet long.

1 Mile Square = 1 section = 640 acres.

6 Mile Square = 1 township = 36 sections = 36 square miles (1/2 township=18 square miles).

36 Mile Square = 36 townships

SECTION V.

SALESPERSON PRACTICE EXAMS

COPYRIGHT 2013
JOHN HENDERSON
ALL RIGHTS RESERVED

All rights reserved. No portion of this publication may be reproduced, transmitted, transcribed, stored in a retrieval system, or transmitted into any language in any form by any means without the written consent of John Henderson.

Published in USA by
The Real Estate Centre

NEED A LITTLE EXTRA HELP?

Try our online interactive practice tests.

These easy to use practice tests will give you the edge you need to pass your licensing exam. Subscribe and receive TWO MONTHS of unlimited access, inlcuding:

1000+ questions - this is a convenient way to familiarize yourself with test questions in this book, and to do so in a format that's similar to the one used by the DRE.

Two study modes - learning and exam simulation mode. Our exam simulation mode is as close as it gets to your real exam.

Updated questions - questions are updated regularly to reflect changes in the exam.

Use anywhere, anytime - no download or installation required. Once you're a registered user, you can access the tests from any computer, anywhere, anytime.

For more information, and to subscribe, go to
www.RealEstateCentre.biz

Sales Practice Exam #1

1. As used in real estate practices, the land of a riparian owner borders on: (A) a river; (B) a stream; (C) a watercourse; (D) any of the above.

2. When making new real estate loans, lenders often charge the borrower a fee for expenses incurred for things such as document preparation and related work. The fee charged is usually a percentage of the face amount of the loan, and is referred to on the borrower's closing statement as a: (A) prepayment penalty; (B) mortgage loan disclosure fee; (C) loan origination fee; (D) loan discount fee.

3. Who signs the promissory note and mortgage? (A) mortgagor; (B) mortgagee; (C) lender; (D) beneficiary.

4. All property is either real property or personal property. Which of the following would normally be considered real property? (A) natural growing vegetation; (B) trade fixtures; (C) lumber in a lumber yard; (D) crops which have been sold prior to harvest.

5. Buyer Baker bought a farm. At the time of the purchase, the seller Sampson was growing corn on the north 40 acres of the farm. Sampson intended to harvest the corn before the close of escrow, but never got around to it. No mention was made of the corn in the sales agreement and/or escrow instructions. Escrow has now closed, Buyer Baker is in possession and it is time to harvest the corn. Who gets to harvest the corn? (A) the buyer would have the right to harvest the corn because he always intended to do so; (B) the buyer would get to harvest the corn because it goes with the land and is considered real property. (C) the buyer would get to harvest the corn because of his equity in the corn; (D) the seller would get to harvest the corn because the corn is his personal property and was not mentioned in the sales agreement.

6. Which of the following is an example of a freehold estate? (A) the interest created by a trust deed; (B) an estate at will; (C) a life estate; (D) a leasehold estate.

7. The impairment of desirability and usefulness in real estate brought about by economic changes in the community is known as: (A) over-improvement; (B) obsolescence; (C) economic life; (D) private restrictions.

8. Gross leases are most often used with: (A) residential property; (B) retail space; (C) office space; (D) shopping malls.

9. When a tenant voluntarily moves out of his apartment with the intention never to return, it would be described as: (A) abandonment; (B) notice to quit; (C) eviction; (D) adverse possession.

10. Usually, the holder of a life estate based on the holder's own life may do any of the following, **except**: (A) lease the property to someone; (B) borrow against the property; (C) devise the property to his relative; (D) sell the property to someone.

11. Which of the following represents an example of police power? (A) a condemnation action on property for construction of a freeway; (B) CC&Rs placed in a deed by a developer; (C) enforcement of contracts by equitable civil proceedings in court; (D) zoning laws which restrict and limit the use of land.

12. A contractor obtained a construction loan, and the loan funds are to be released in a series of progress payments. Most lenders disburse the last payment when the: (A) building is completed; (B) notice of completion is filed; (C) buyer approves the construction; (D) period to file a mechanic's lien has expired.

13. Each of the following elements must be established to obtain an easement by prescription, **except**: (A) use of the property which is hostile and adverse to the true owner; (B) existence of a claim of right or color of title; (C) open and notorious use which is continuous and uninterrupted for a period of 5 years; (D) a confrontation with the true owner.

14. Private restrictions on the use of land may be created by: (A) private land use controls; (B) written agreement; (C) a developer's general plan restrictions for a subdivision; (D) all of the above.

15. Government land use, planning and zoning laws are important examples of: (A) exercise of eminent domain; (B) use of police power; (C) deed restrictions; (D) escheatment.

16. Generally when the government forces the sale of private land for public use, it is governed by due process of law and is accomplished through: (A) exercise of the police power; (B) eminent domain; (C) estate in reversion; (D) escheat.

17. "Depression", "recession", "expansion", and "prosperity" represent the four phases of: (A) the investment cycle; (B) the secondary mortgage market cycle; (C) the business cycle; (D) the real estate cycle.

18. When a real estate broker is acting as a subagent for the seller, her fiduciary duty is owed by and primary responsibility is to: (A) the buyer only; (B) the seller only; (C) the buyer and seller equally; (D) neither the buyer or seller.

19. Which of the following laws exert the greatest control over the California housing and construction industries? (A) Uniform Building Code, National Electrical Code, Uniform Plumbing Code; (B) State Housing Law, local building codes and the Contractor's License Law; (C) Subdivision Map Act, local building codes, city's master plan; (D) eminent domain, zoning ordinances, State Housing Law.

20. When there is a conflict between different building codes, which code has precedence? (A) local building codes; (B) state building codes; (C) the Uniform Building Code; (D) whichever code sets the highest standards for construction and safety.

21. A tenant leased a building from an owner. The owner then sells the building to a new owner. The tenant's financial situation changed after the building was sold. Which of the following is true? (A) the new owner can make the lessee pay-off the lease; (B) the change in lessee's financial situation is none of the new owner's business; (C) the new owner can increase the security deposit required from the tenant; (D) the new owner can raise the rent.

22. A home was sold and the escrow closed October 1, 2009. How would the property taxes for the 2009-2013 tax year typically be prorated between the seller and the buyer? (A) the seller pays for the entire year; (B) the buyer pays for the entire year; (C) the property taxes are divided equally between the buyer and the seller; (D) the seller would pay for the first three months of the property tax year (July, August, and September) by proration in escrow. The buyer would pay for the remainder of the tax year plus supplemental taxes based upon the reassessment that was triggered by the sale.

23. When you, as a real estate agent, know that a seller will not accept an offer from a buyer, you should **not** do which of the following: (A) write new terms on the back of the offer and go back to the buyer for approval; (B) present the offer to the seller anyway; (C) upon rejection of the offer by the seller, induce the seller to make a counter-offer; (D) change the buyer's offer to what you believe the seller will accept, initial the changes, and then present the offer to the seller..

24. A home sold for $200,000. The buyer assumed an existing loan against the property for $160,000. The documentary transfer tax for this county is $.55 per $500 of consideration. The transfer tax is: (A) $11; (B) $22; (C) $33; (D) $44.

25. Puffing is when an agent: (A) convinces the seller to pay a greater commission than is typical for the area; (B) convinces an appraiser to report a greater appraised value to the lender; (C) convinces the seller during his listing presentation that the he is well connected in the neighborhood; (D) exaggerates the features or condition of the property.

26. Joe owned a grocery store and wanted to raise some money. He decided to sell his land and building to an investor and leased it back to himself in order to continue running his grocery store. Which of the following would be a tax benefit to Joe? (A) all capital gains for Joe are deferred; (B) Joe has a new tax base for his future depreciation of the building; (C) Joe's rent payments to the investor will be fully deductible for income tax purposes as a business expense; (D) none of the above.

27. The roof of a rectangular building with sides that rise at inclined planes on all four sides is called a: (A) gable roof; (B) hip roof; (C) mansard roof; (D) baroque roof.

28. Which of the following best describes an "open-end" loan? (A) one in which personal property is held for added collateral; (B) a soft-money loan; (C) one in which additional financing could be obtained without rewriting the contract; (D) one under which many parcels of land are included under one trust deed.

29. Which of the following is an appraiser's primary concern in the appraisal of a residential subdivision? (A) square foot area of each home; (B) marketability and acceptability; (C) functional utility; (D) the adjoining neighborhood.

30. When determining the value of a property, which of the following dates is the most important to an appraiser? (A) the date the contract was signed; (B) the date the loan was funded; (C) the date the transaction was recorded; (D) the date the escrow closed.

31. Valuations of single-family dwellings are usually based on: (A) gross multiplier of annual income; (B) asking prices of comparable houses; (C) sales prices of comparable properties; (D) the assessed values of comparable homes.

32. To estimate the value of a parcel of vacant land, the appraiser concentrated only on the cost to the buyer of acquiring a comparable, substitute parcel of land. This approach is most similar to which of the following appraisal methods? (A) cost; (B) income; (C) gross multiplier; (D) market data.

33. When land is valued by its highest and best use, and there is a building on the land that has little or no value, the appraiser should: (A) ignore the building in his valuation; (B) add the salvage value of the building to his valuation; (C) deduct the demolition cost of the building from his highest and best use opinion of value; (D) establish a value by means of the cost approach to appraisal, instead of the highest and best use.

34. The primary purpose of a site analysis by an appraiser is to determine the: (A) applicable zoning laws; (B) highest and best use; (C) soil condition; (D) available amenities.

35. In real estate appraisal, "market value" is based primarily upon which of the following? (A) the asking price on the listing; (B) the reproduction cost of the property; (C) whatever a buyer is willing to pay; (D) the willing buyer and willing seller concept.

36. When attempting to determine current market value, real estate appraisers are least concerned with: (A) objective value; (B) value in exchange; (C) original cost; (D) an open marketplace.

37. When real estate increases in value because of an increase in population and/or inflation, this would be classified as: (A) social valuation; (B) economic obsolescence; (C) an unearned increment; (D) effective value.

38. Each of the following is an essential element of value, **except**: (A) demand; (B) appreciation; (C) scarcity; (D) utility.

39 The primary purpose of RESPA (Real Estate Settlement Procedure Act) is to: (A) set standards for home improvement procedures; (B) control which lenders may process real estate loan applications; (C) require lenders to make special disclosures without cost to the borrower, for loans involving the sale or transfer of four or less residential dwellings; (D) regulate non-federally related mortgage loans.

40. The placement of a building on a lot and its relationship to the surrounding environment is described as: (A) exposure; (B) elevation sheet; (C) plottage; (D) orientation.

41. A lender must notify a borrower when a balloon payment is due: (A) 28 days or earlier prior to the due date; (B) 30 to 90 days prior to the due date; (C) 90 to 150 days prior to the due date; (D) 6 months or earlier prior to the due date.

42. The most common method used by an appraiser in the appraisal of an amenity property would be: (A) gross multiplier; (B) capitalization approach; (C) market comparison; (D) cost approach.

43. When an appraiser analyzes rent using the income approach, she will base her appraisal on which of the following characteristics of the income? (A) quantity; (B) quality; (C) durability; (D) all of the above.

44. When would the cost approach to appraisal be least appropriate? (A) new homes in a sub-division; (B) middle-aged property; (C) old buildings; (D) multifamily property.

45. The unit of comparison when appraising land is: (A) frontage; (B) front foot value; (C) cost per square foot or cost per acre (D) any of the above.

46. Valuable consideration in a contract consists of: (A) services to be provided by one or both parties; (B) whatever the parties consider to be of value; (C) one dollar or more; (D) any of the above.

47. A bank purchased a loan for a 4% discount and then sold it for $96,500 which was a 3.5% discount off the face amount of the note. What was the face amount of the note? (A) $85,000; (B) $96,000; (C) $100,000; (D) none of the above.

48. When an appraiser determines a "loss in value from any cause," he is determining: (A) economic obsolescence; (B) depreciation; (C) principle of contribution; (D) adverse possession.

49. When real property suffers an impairment in value due to economic changes it is described as: (A) incurable physical restriction; (B) obsolescence; (C) over-improvement; (D) social deterioration.

50. A real estate appraiser reduced his opinion of the value of a home because the local sewer system was in poor condition and in need of repair. This loss in value would be classified as: (A) physical obsolescence; (B) functional obsolescence; (C) physical deterioration; (D) economic obsolescence.

51. Economic or social obsolescence could result from each of the following, **except**: (A) new zoning laws; (B) a city's leading industry moving out; (C) misplacement of improvements; (D) an outdated heating system.

52. Under California state law, the maximum fine which may be imposed by the Real Estate Commissioner on a person falsely claiming to be a real estate licensee is: (A) $2,000; (B) $5,000; (C) $20,000; (D) $50,000.

53. The process of calculating the present worth of a property on the basis of its capacity to continue to produce an income stream is called: (A) depreciation; (B) capitalization; (C) market data; (D) recapture.

54. The capitalization approach to appraisal is a process whereby an appraiser: (A) converts annual net income into capitalized value; (B) determines accrued depreciation; (C) establishes cost of capital investment; (D) finds value based upon gross income.

55. Interest rates on real estate loans are primarily determined by which of the following? (A) national defense policies; (B) demand and supply of money; (C) the relative value of the U.S. dollar on the international money market; (D) status of federally-insured loans.

56. When using the capitalization approach to appraisal, which of the items listed below would an appraiser subtract from scheduled gross income to arrive at annual net income? (A) cost of loans against the property; (B) allowance for rent loss and vacancies; (C) federal income tax; (D) reserve for appreciation of buildings.

57. The Alquist-Priolo Special Studies Act discloses the location of earthquake fault lines on maps for properties located: (A) only within five miles of an active fault line; (B) located in designated California counties; (C) all counties in California; (D) only in designated special study zones.

58. Lenders in the "prime" mortgage market generally prefer that not more than what percent of an applicant's gross income be spent for housing. (A) 20%; (B) 21% to 24%; (C) 25% to 28%; (D) 33%.

59. In home construction, the parallel wooden beams used to support ceiling loads and floors are called: (A) rafters; (B) studs; (C) headers; (D) joists.

60. Which of the following is conveyed incident and appurtenant to the land? (A) natural rights; (B) easements and restrictions; (C) servitudes; (D) all of the above.

61. A loan which calls for regular periodic payment of both principal and interest to completely repay the loan is called a: (A) straight loan; (B) balloon payment loan; (C) fully amortized loan; (D) variable rate mortgage loan.

62. A real estate broker was helping his brother find a home. The broker, representing his brother, negotiated a lease with an option to buy from an owner/seller of a home. The real estate broker must disclose that he is the brother of the tenant/optionee to: (A) the owner/seller of the home; (B) the seller's broker or agent; (C) the multiple listing service; (D) nobody.

63. When a loan is fully amortized by equal monthly payments of principal and interest, the amount applied to principal reduction: (A) remains constant throughout the term of the loan; (B) decreases while the interest payment increases as the loan gets older; (C) increases while the amount applied to interest payment decreases as the loan gets older; (D) increases by a constant amount.

64. When the debt has been paid in full, the trustee will record what legal instrument to remove the lien of a trust deed from the public record? (A) satisfaction of payment; (B) complete release statement; (C) deed of reconveyance; (D) redemption certificate.

65. The item that would appear as a debit on the buyer's closing statement is: (A) the purchase price; (B) prepaid rents; (C) prepaid property taxes; (D) none of the above.

66. In a real property sales contract, the seller who is also acting as the lender is usually referred to as the: (A) trustor; (B) trustee; (C) vendor; (D) vendee.

67. In a real estate transaction where the seller uses a land contract instead of a trust deed, the land contract may be described as: (A) identical to a mortgage; (B) a security device; (C) just like an option; (D) a third party instrument.

68. According to California law, all of the following could be created as blanket encumbrances, **except**; (A) trust deeds; (B) real property taxes; (C) mortgages; (D) mechanics liens.

69. A grant deed, when compared to a land contract of sale, may be different with respect to: (A) the interest conveyed to the buyer; (B) the signatures of the parties; (C) the designation of purchase price; (D) all of the above.

70. Promissory notes often include an "or more" clause. An "or more" clause would: (A) allow the borrower to make accelerated payments if he wishes; (B) indicate that the note has several borrowers; (C) provide the lender with the choice of raising the interest at will; (D) allow the borrower to borrow additional money on the same promissory note and trust deed.

71. A charge imposed on property is called : (A) an encumbrance; (B) a quitclaim; (C) a lien; (D) a covenant not to impose encumbrances.

72. The effect of a tight money policy implemented by the Federal Reserve Board would have a net effect of increasing: (A) sales volume of single family homes; (B) the supply of funds available for making real estate loans; (C) the use of new first trust deed financing in real estate transactions; (D) the use of second trust deeds in creating real estate transactions.

73. Henry is a tenant with a 5-year lease on a ranch belonging to Jack. Fred is the owner of an adjacent piece of land. One day, Fred asked Henry to grant him an easement to cross the ranch land. Henry grants Fred an easement in writing, granting Fred permission to cross the land. Is the easement valid under these circumstances? (A) no, because a tenant cannot grant a easement. An easement may only be granted by the owner of the property; (B) yes, but the easement may not extend beyond the term of the Henry's lease; (C) no, unless the lease has been duly recorded; (D) yes, subject to the ratification of the easement by Jack.

74. All of the following directly affect the movement of mortgage rates, **except**: (A) demand for funds; (B) rate of unemployment; (C) rate of inflation; (D) changes in money supply.

75. When four people own property as joint tenants: (A) they may hold unequal interests in the property; (B) there is still only one title to the whole property; (C) if one of the owners dies, her heirs become tenants in common with the surviving co-owners as tenants in common; (D) each owner has a separate legal title to his undivided interest in the property.

76. When analyzing a real estate loan application, a lender would correlate characteristics of the borrower, the loan, and the property securing the debt to make: (A) a real property appraisal; B) a loan commitment; (C) a credit rating for the borrower; (D) a statement of liability.

77. In which of the following ways is the FHA loan program different from conventional lending: (A) FHA makes loans only to veterans; (B) FHA is a mortgage insurer rather than a mortgage originator; (C) FHA interest rates are always lower than conventional interest rates by 2%; (D) FHA's maximum loan is limited to 75% of the appraised value.

78. When an eligible veteran purchases a home under the Cal-Vet program, the seller executes a grant deed in favor of: (A) the veteran; (B) the California Department of Veterans Affairs; (C) the veteran who then executes a grant deed in favor of the California Department of Veteran Affairs until the debt is paid in full; (D) the bank that made the Cal-Vet loan.

79. Under the Federal Truth-in-Lending Law, two of the most critical facts which must be disclosed to buyers or borrowers are: (A) term of the loan and discount rate; (B) finance charge and annual percentage rate; (C) discount points and advertising expense; (D) credit report fee and appraisal fee.

80. The Real Estate Settlement Procedures Act (RESPA) prohibits all of the following activities, **except**: (A) unearned fees; (B) seller requiring the use of a specific title insurer; (C) kickbacks paid to licensees by providers of settlement services; (D) buyer requiring a specific lender.

81. The formula to calculate net operating income of an apartment building is: (A) gross income minus loan expenses and income taxes; (B) gross rent multiplier minus vacancies and operating expenses; (C) gross income minus operating expenses and depreciation; (D) scheduled gross income minus vacancies and collection losses, minus operating expenses.

82. An agreement by a lender to make a long term loan on real estate at some future date, upon the borrower's request, is known as: (A) an interim loan commitment; (B) a standby loan commitment; (C) a backup loan commitment; (D) a staged incremental loan commitment.

83. A lender may require an impound account for some real estate loans. Who benefits from this impound account? (A) the beneficiary only; (B) the trustee only; (C) the trustor only; (D) the beneficiary and the trustor.

84. An interest in real property may be taken by either prescription or by adverse possession. The interest taken by prescription is: (A) the right to use land which belongs to another person; (B) a possessory interest; (C) an equitable title; (D) a private grant.

85. A quitclaim deed conveys only the present right, title and interest of: (A) the grantee; (B) the servient tenant; (C) the grantor; (D) the lessee.

86. Title to real property is transferred with a deed. A valid deed must contain all of the following, **except**: (A) signature of a competent grantor; (B) a granting clause; (C) an adequate description of the property; (D) the acknowledgment of the grantor's signature.

87. A valid deed can be: (A) transferred from grantee to grantee; (B) assigned to a beneficiary to hypothecate real property; (C) signed by a witnessed mark; (D) reassigned to another grantor.

88. A person holding title to real property in severalty would have: (A) title with several other owners; (B) an estate for years; (C) title with his or her spouse; (D) sole ownership.

89. A joint tenancy in real property can legally be created with the execution of a deed by: (A) a husband and wife to themselves as joint tenants; (B) existing joint tenants to themselves and others as joint tenants; (C) existing tenants in common to themselves as joint tenants; (D) any of the above ways.

90. Which of the following factors will the lender usually consider to be most important when making the decision whether or not to make a home loan? (A) the availability of mortgage loan funds; (B) the general economic outlook of the nation; (C) federal and state and local laws; (D) the degree of risk.

91. The "standard coverage" title insurance policy on real property insures the policy holder against loss occasioned by: (A) unrecorded liens or encumbrances; (B) a forgery in the chain of recorded title; (C) rights of parties in possession of the property; (D) governmental action, such as zoning.

92. Which of the following is **not** covered by the standard coverage (CLTA) title insurance policy? (A) lawsuits challenging marketable title at the date of the transfer; (B) matters of record; (C) rights of parties in possession; (D) transfers by an incompetent grantor.

93. Escrow instructions are commonly executed by: (A) buyers; (B) sellers; (C) third parties; (D) all of the above.

94. Which of the following would most likely result in the termination of a real estate sales escrow? (A) revocation of the escrow instructions by the broker for the buyer; (B) the mutual consent of the buyer and the seller; (C) the cancellation of the escrow by the seller; (D) the death of the seller.

95. During escrow, if a dispute should arise between the buyer and seller preventing the close of escrow, the escrow holder may legally: (A) arbitrate the dispute as a neutral party; (B) cancel the escrow and return all documents and monies to the respective parties; (C) file an interpleader action in court; (D) do none of the above.

96. According to the Seller Transfer Disclosure law, the real estate licensee: (A) must inspect all the common areas in a condominium subdivision; (B) must inspect the inaccessible areas and report her findings to the buyer and the seller; (C) has a responsibility to visually inspect the property and reveal pertinent information which the seller has failed to disclose; (D) must pay for the termite inspection.

97. Broker Bob has just taken an exclusive right to sell listing to sell a home. This brand new listing may be described as: (A) an implied, bilateral, executed, employment contract; (B) an express, unilateral, executed, employment contract; (C) an oral, unilateral, executory, employment contract; (D) an express, bilateral, executory, employment contract.

98. The term "express contract" describes a contract which is expressed: (A) only orally; (B) only in writing; (C) in words, either oral or written; (D) none of the above.

99. A contract based on an unlawful consideration is: (A) valid, until voided; (B) void; (C) legal; (D) enforceable, if in writing.

100. Which of the following agreements is required to be in writing in order to be enforceable? (A) a partnership agreement; (B) an agreement by a buyer to assume an existing real estate loan; (C) a lease of real property for one year; (D) a listing to sell a personal property mobilehome.

101. Mr. Baker sold his country home to Mr. Jones, but reserved a life estate and remained in possession of the property. Later, Mr. Baker sold the life estate to Mrs. Connor and surrendered possession of the property. Mr. Jones then demanded immediate possession of the property. Based on these facts, which of the following is most correct? (A) Mr. Baker is liable for damages to Mr. Jones; (B) Mrs. Connor should seek return of her purchase price; (C) Mrs. Connor may remain in possession; (D) Mr. Jones is entitled to possession.

102. Broker John took a 60 day exclusive agency listing to sell a property that was owned by Jones. After 30 days, Broker John had not sold the property, so Jones sent him a letter by certified mail canceling the listing. One week later Jones listed the property with Broker Bob using an open listing. Two weeks later, Broker Bob sold the property under the open listing. In this situation how will the commission be handled? (A) Broker Bob is the only agent to get a commission; (B) Jones had no legal ability to cancel the listing with Broker John, therefore Broker John gets a commission and Broker Bob gets nothing; (C) one commission will be split equally between Broker John and Broker Bob; (D) seller Jones will be held liable for two full commissions.

103. An exclusive listing contract is: (A) an employment contract; (B) a bilateral contract; (C) a promise for a promise; (D) all of the above.

104. When a broker takes an exclusive authorization and right to locate property listing with a buyer, the broker is authorized to: (A) act as the exclusive agent for that buyer only and agrees to work with no other buyers during the term of the listing; (B) incur expenses which the buyer is obligated to reimburse; (C) represent other buyers at the same time; (D) to receive a commission from the buyer regardless of whether or not he finds a property.

105. Any exclusive listing must contain: (A) a minimum five percent commission; (B) a definite termination date; (C) a unilateral agreement to perform; (D) an authorization to accept a deposit.

106. A "safety clause" is usually found in which of the following contracts: (A) deposit receipt; (B) lease; (C) listing; (D) option.

107. When a real estate broker arranges a loan originated by a federally related lender, the broker must provide the borrower with the federal RESPA booklet and disclosures when the loan is secured by a first trust deed and the proceeds are used for financing: (A) the purchase of a personal residence by a family who owns three or more similar units; (B) the purchase of one individual unit in a complex of six residential units on the same block; (C) the purchase of a single family dwelling by an individual buyer; (D) all of the above.

108. If a contingency in a contract fails, which of the following is true? (A) buyer is obligated to perform as per the terms of the contract; (B) buyer is not obligated to perform; (C) buyer must perform or is in breach of contract; (D) buyer must pay damages to the seller.

109. If a real estate licensee advised buyers about how to take title when preparing a deposit receipt, she may be: (A) giving tax advice; (B) giving legal advice; (C) providing a basis for a possible claim of discrimination; (D) all of the above.

110. A buyer selected an expert to inspect the septic tank of the home he was about to purchase. The inspector damaged the home's sprinkler system during the inspection. Who is liable for the cost of repairing the sprinkler system? (A) the seller will be liable; (B) the seller will be liable only if defects in the septic tank were found; (C) buyer will be liable for the damages, regardless of what was found during the inspection; (D) buyer will be liable for the damages, only if no defects were found.

111. The effective date of a residential purchase agreement is the date that: (A) the deposit was received by the buyer's agent; (B) the contract was drafted; (C) the buyer signed the contract; (D) the seller's acceptance was properly communicated to the buyer.

112. When a buyer buys a home "subject to" the seller's existing loan on the property: (A) both the buyer and seller will then be equally liable for the debt; (B) the seller is completely relieved from liability on the loan; (C) the buyer assumes all liability for the loan; (D) the buyer will not be personally liable for the loan and the seller remains the borrower of record.

113. All of the following statements regarding options are true, **except**: (A) the option binds the optionee to perform; (B) some valuable consideration must pass from optionee to optionor; (C) in the lease/option, the provisions of the terms of the lease is sufficient consideration to support the option; (D) an option does not give the optionee the right to use the land.

114. A real estate licensee generally acts as: (A) an ostensible agent; (B) a fiduciary; (C) a subcontractor for the seller; (D) a dual agent.

115. The position of trust assumed by the real estate broker as an agent for the seller or buyer is described legally as: (A) a fiduciary relationship; (B) a gratuitous relationship; (C) an independent contractor relationship; (D) a subcontractor relationship.

116. When representing a principal under a written listing agreement, what type of authority may an agent have? (A) actual authority; (B) specific authority; (C) ostensible authority; (D) all of the above.

117. A seller of real property is bound by the acts and representations of all of the following, **except**: (A) listing broker; (B) buyer's broker; (C) subagents; (D) listing broker's sales agents.

118. "Alienable" title means that the title: (A) Is encumbered; (B) Can be conveyed; (C) Cannot be conveyed; (D) Cannot be legally encumbered.

119. The most essential element to create an enforceable broker-principal relationship concerning a transfer of interest in real property is: (A) a written offer from a ready, willing and able buyer; (B) the written authority from the seller for the broker to accept a deposit; (C) a written employment contract; (D) an agreement setting the commission.

120. On January 2nd, a buyer called a real estate agent to find out if the buyer's offer had been accepted. The agent informed the buyer that the seller was out of town and would not be back until January 14th, after which she would make a decision as to whether the buyer's offer would be accepted. Under these circumstances, which of the following is true? (A) the buyer can exercise the liquidated damages provision on the contract; (B) the buyer can exercise the arbitration clause in the contract; (C) if the buyer decides not to wait for the seller to return, the buyer can rescind the offer and secure the return of the full amount of the deposit; (D) the buyer must wait until the seller returns.

121. When an existing contract is replaced by an new contract, it is called: (A) assignment; (B) rescission; (C) novation; (D) rehabilitation.

122. The maximum commission which can be charged by a real estate broker in the sale of residential income property is: (A) limited by California real estate law; (B) negotiable between the principal and broker; (C) limited to no more than 9 percent of the total sales price; (D) set by local custom.

123 The normal relationship between an escrow officer and the principals in a real estate transaction is that of: (A) an independent contractor; (B) a neutral agent; (C) an employee; (D) an advocate for both the buyer and seller.

124. The buyer of a business, in order to avoid "successor's liability" for unpaid sales tax, should require the seller to provide escrow with a "certificate of clearance" issued from what agency? (A) Internal Revenue Service; (B) State Board of Equalization; (C) Secretary of State; (D) Alcoholic Beverage Control Board.

125. Which of the following is an appropriate termination date for an exclusive right to sell listing of residential real property? (A) 3 days after notice of rescission by either the seller or the listing broker; (B) 60 days after a buyer approves the home inspection; (C) 90 days after a buyer has submitted the loan application; (D) 90 days after the listing is signed.

126. A farmer deeded his farm to his sons, Able, Baker, and Charley as joint tenants. Shortly thereafter, Baker sold his interest to William. Able died and willed his interest to Sally. Ownership of the property would be: (A) William and Charley as joint tenants; (B) Charley and William as tenants in common, Charley holding 2/3 interest, William 1/3 interest; (C) William and Sally as joint tenants; (D) Sally, William and Charley as tenants in common, each with a 1/3 interest.

127. Under no circumstances may a real estate broker: (A) receive commissions from both the buyer and the seller; (B) appoint a subagent to perform some of his duties; (C) misrepresent material facts; (D) sell property he has listed to one of his relatives.

128. A lender required a borrower to pay two points to get a $52,000 loan. How much did the two points cost the borrower? (A) $130; (B) $260; (C) $520; (D) none of the above.

129. Private restrictions on land may be created: (A) by deed only; (B) by deed or zoning ordinance; (C) by deed or written agreement; (D) by deed, written agreement, or zoning ordinance.

130. Seller Jane was represented by Agent Able. Able convinced Jane to accept an offer by verbally promising her he would find the "great replacement home" for her before the close of escrow. Assuming Agent Able was unable to find an acceptable replacement home for Jane, which of the following is most correct? (A) Jane has no legal recourse against the agent, because the promise was oral; (B) Jane can get out of the obligation to sell her home without liability; (C) Jane can bring a criminal action through the Department of Real Estate; (D) Jane can recover damages in a civil lawsuit against Agent Able resulting from a false promise.

131. Which of the following describes the practice of single agency? (A) the single agency broker is client oriented; (B) the single agency broker represents both the seller and buyer in the same transaction; (C) in a single agency transaction, the buyer cannot choose his own broker or represent himself; (D) in a single agency transaction, the agent serves two principals.

132. A real estate broker showed a property to a prospective buyer which was not currently listed for sale and without the seller's knowledge or consent. The broker then wrote up and presented an offer to the seller. In this situation, the broker acted: (A) unethically; (B) illegally; (C) as a single agent; (D) as a dual agent.

133. A "blind ad" placed in a newspaper by a licensed real estate salesperson does not properly: (A) identify the asking price of the property; (B) identify the broker; (C) identify the address of the property; (D) identify the seller.

134. Which of the following is an encumbrance? (A) a freehold estate; (B) fee simple absolute; (C) a recorded homestead; (D) an estate for years.

135. The document used to encumber a personal property mobilehome is a: (A) trust deed; (B) mobilehome deed; (C) promissory note; (D) certificate of title.

136. A real estate broker must retain copies of all listings, deposit receipts, canceled checks, loan documents, and trust records for: (A) one year; (B) two years; (C) three years; (D) four years.

137. Elizabeth, a licensed California real estate broker, received a referral of a buyer from an out-of-state broker. Elizabeth sold this buyer a home and wants to split the commission with the out-of-state broker. Under the California Real Estate Law: (A) Elizabeth may split the commission with a broker of another state; (B) Elizabeth cannot divide a commission with a broker of another state; (C) Elizabeth can pay a commission to a broker of another state only if that broker is also licensed in California; (D) none of the above.

138. The employment agreement between a broker and a salesperson must be retained: (A) by the broker for 3 years from the date of the execution of the contract: (B) by the salesperson for 3 years from the date of the execution of the contract; (C) by the broker for 3 years from the date of the termination of the salesperson's employment; (D) by both broker and salesperson for 3 years from the date of the termination of the salesperson's employment.

139. Which of the following is the most important reason for a broker to maintain a client trust fund account in addition to his regular business account? (A) to provide a means of control over the destiny of transactions being negotiated; (B) it is easier from an accounting point of view; (C) the bank is responsible for any loss to the trust fund account resulting from embezzlement; (D) the consequence which could occur should legal action be taken against the broker.

140. When a broker receives an advance fee for publishing a special pamphlet advertising properties which he has not listed for sale, he must: (A) give an accounting to the seller upon demand for any funds he has collected for the advertising; (B) hold the money until the property is sold; (C) only spend his advance fee before putting the left over money in his client trust account; (D) return all the money if the property is not sold.

141. When a real estate licensee negotiates a loan secured by real property, he must deliver the mortgage loan disclosure statement to the borrower: (A) within 2 days of the time the borrower signs it; (B) within three days of receipt of a completed loan application or before the borrower is obligated to take the loan, whichever is earlier; (C) within 36 hours of the time the borrower signs it; (D) before escrow closes.

142. A real estate broker negotiated a hard money loan secured by a second trust deed. As used in this context, "hard money" means: (A) a loan for no more than four years; (B) a cash loan; (C) a junior loan; (D) a loan obtained in a tight money market.

143. The oldest, easiest to learn, most adaptable, and quickest method of appraising residences and land, is which of the following: (A) the cost approach; (B) the capitalization approach; (C) the income approach; (D) the market data approach.

144. The purpose of the Federal Fair Housing Law is: (A) to eliminate discrimination throughout the United States; (B) to prohibit discrimination in housing transactions; (C) specifically to eliminate the practice of redlining by lenders; (D) none of the above.

145. A real estate licensee who shows minority buyers homes located in segregated neighborhoods only is guilty of: (A) steering; (B) redlining; (C) blockbusting; (D) panic buying.

146. Some real estate loans provide that the interest rate may be increased or decreased depending on money market conditions. This type of loan is called: (A) an interim loan; (B) a variable interest rate loan; (C) a loan secured by a land contract; (D) a fluctuating market condition adjustable loan.

147. A real estate broker would be subject to discipline by the Real Estate Commissioner and in violation of fair housing laws if he did which of the following? (A) steering; (B) blockbusting; (C) hired salespersons from only one specific ethnic group; (D) all of the above.

148. If an income property is valued at $300,000 using a 6% capitalization rate, how much would an investor pay for the property if he demanded a 8% capitalization rate? (A) $225,000; (B) $255,000; (C) $300,000; (D) $500,000.

149. Ted borrowed $2,500 and gave the lender a four year straight note. In 8 months he had paid $150 interest. What was the interest rate on the note? (A) 7%; (B) 8%; (C) 9%; (D) 10%.

150. Which of the following loans will require a balloon payment? (A) $22,500 with interest at 14.25% per year, payable $320 a month for 10 years; the total interest is $19,827.60; (B) $40,000 with interest at 10% per year, payable $429.85 a month for 15 years; the total interest is $37,373; (C) $100,000 with interest at 9.5% per year, payable $840.86 a month for 30 years; the total interest is $202,709; (D) none of the above.

Answers to Salesperson Practice Exam #1

1. D   A riparian owner owns land bordering on moving water, such as a river, stream and/or watercourse.

2. C   The fee charged by lenders for expenses incurred for things such as document preparation and related work is called the loan origination fee.

3. A   The mortgagor (borrower) signs the promissory note and mortgage.

4. A   Vegetation is real property.

5. D   The seller would get to harvest the corn because the corn is his personal property and was not mentioned in the sales agreement.

6. C A life estate is a freehold estate which is limited to someone's life.

7. B The impairment of desirability and usefulness in real estate brought about by economic changes in the community is known as obsolescence.

8. A Residential property is normally leased on a gross lease, with the tenant paying a fixed amount each month.

9. A When a tenant voluntarily moves out of his apartment with the intention to never return, it would be described as abandonment.

10. C The holder of a life estate based on the holder's own life may not devise (leave by will) the property to anyone.

11. D Zoning laws which restrict and limit the use of land are a common example of police power.

12. D Most lenders wait until the period to file a mechanic's lien has expired before disbursing the final loan proceeds to the builder.

13. D No confrontation with the true owner is necessary to obtain an easement by prescription.

14. D Private restrictions are created by private land use controls, written agreements and by a developer's general plan.

15. B Government land use, planning and zoning laws are all examples of police power.

16. B Eminent domain is the right of government to take private property for public use, with payment of fair compensation.

17. C "Depression", "recession", "expansion", and "prosperity" represent the four phases of the business cycle.

18. B A broker who is the subagent for the seller owes a fiduciary duty to the seller only.

19. B State Housing Law, local building codes and the Contractor's License Law exert the greatest control over the housing and construction industries in California.

20. D The code which sets the highest standards for construction and safety is the code the builder must follow. Remember "The most restrictive restriction restricts you!"

21. B The sale of a property does not usually terminate a lease. The new owner of the property has no more rights than the prior owner

22. D Property taxes are usually prorated based upon the months each party occupied the property. Escrow closed October 1, 2009, therefore the seller would pay for the first three months of the property tax year (July, August, and September) by proration in escrow. The buyer would pay for the remainder of the tax year plus supplemental taxes based upon the reassessment that was triggered by the sale.

23. D The agent may never change the terms of an offer without the buyer's consent.

24. D The documentary transfer tax is based upon consideration.
    (1) $200,000 - $160,000 = $40,000 consideration
    (2) $40,000 divided by $500 = 80 taxable units
    (3) 80 X .55=$44.00

25. D Puffing is when an agent exaggerates the features or condition of the property.

26. C Joe's rent payments to the investor will be fully deductible for income tax purposes as a business expense.

27. B A hip roof slopes or inclines on all four side..

28. C An "open-end" loan allows the borrower to re-borrow money previously paid back to the lender without rewriting the contract.

29. B Marketability and acceptability are the primary concern when appraising residential property.

30. A The date the contract was signed by the buyer and the seller would normally be the date on which a "willing buyer" and a "willing seller" mutually agreed upon the sale price (value) of that property.

31. C Valuations of single-family dwellings are usually based on sales prices of comparable properties.

32. D The appraiser uses the cost of acquiring a comparable, substitute parcel of land in the market data approach to appraisal.

33. C When appraisers use highest and best use on a parcel with an existing structure of little value, the appraiser subtracts the demolition cost of the structure from the value of the land.

34. B The primary purpose of a site analysis by an appraiser is to determine the highest and best use of the land.

35. D Market value is primarily based upon the willing buyer and willing seller concept.

36. C The market value of real property is least affected by the original cost.

37. C "Unearned Increment" describes when property gains in value due to inflation or an increase in population.

38. B Appreciation is not one of the essential elements of value.

39. C The primary purpose of RESPA (Real Estate Settlement Procedures Act) is to require federally regulated lenders to make special disclosures, without cost to the borrower, for loans involving the sale or transfer of four or less residential dwellings.

40. D The position of a building on land in its relationship to exposure to the sun, privacy from the street, prevailing winds, views, etc., is called orientation.

41. C A lender must notify a borrower when a balloon payment is due; not less than 90 nor more than 150 days prior to the due date.

42. C An amenity property is a home and is appraised by the market data approach (also called market comparison).

43. D When an appraiser analyzes rent using the income approach, she will base her appraisal on the characteristics of the quantity, quality and durability of the income.

44. C The cost approach is least appropriate for appraising old buildings because depreciation becomes difficult to calculate as the building gets older.

45. D   Frontage, front foot value, and cost per square foot or cost per acre are all appropriate units of comparison when appraising land.

46. D   Valuable consideration in a contract may consist of services to be provided by one or both parties, whatever the parties consider to be of value, and/or one dollar or more.

47. C   (1) 100% - 3.5% discount = 96.5%;
        (2) $96,500 divided by 96.5% = $100,000

48. B   In appraisal, loss in value from any cause is a definition of depreciation.

49. B   A loss or impairment in value due to economic changes would be described as economic obsolescence (social obsolescence).

50. D   The loss in value due to the poor sewer system is an external cause and is considered economic obsolescence.

51. D   An outdated heating system would result in functional obsolescence.

52. C   The maximum fine which may be imposed by the Real Estate Commissioner on a person falsely claiming to be a real estate licensee is $20,000.

53. B   The process of calculating the present worth of a property on the basis of its capacity to continue to produce an income stream is called: capitalization.

54. A   The capitalization approach to appraisal converts annual net income into capitalized value.

55. B   Interest rates on real estate loans are primarily determined by the demand and supply of money..

56. B   The appraiser subtracts allowance for rent loss and vacancies when calculating annual net income in the capitalization approach to appraisal.

57. C   The Alquist-Priolo Special Studies Act applies to all counties in California.

58. C   Lenders in the "prime" mortgage market generally prefer that not more than 25% to 28% of an applicant's gross income be spent for housing.

59. D   The parallel wooden beams used to support ceiling loads and floors are called joists.

60. D   Natural rights, easements and restrictions, and servitudes are all conveyed incident and appurtenant to the land.

61. C   A fully amortized loan calls for regular periodic payment of both principal and interest to completely repay the loan.

62. A   The broker must disclose any special relationship with the buyer/tenant/optionee when representing his brother in negotiations with a seller/ landlord/optionor.

63. C   The amount applied to principal reduction increases while the amount applied to interest payment decreases as the loan gets older.

64. C   When the debt has been paid in full, the trustee will record a deed of reconveyance (also called a reconveyance deed) to remove the lien of a trust deed from the public record.

65. A The purchase price is a debit on the buyers closing statement.

66. C The seller in a land contract is called the vendor.

67. B In a real estate transaction where the seller uses a land contract instead of a trust deed, the land contract may be described as a security device.

68. B A real property tax lien must specifically attach to one particular parcel. If one person owns several parcels of real property with overdue property taxes, the government will record a real property tax lien separately against each parcel.

69. D A grant deed, when compared to a land contract of sale, may be different with respect to the interest conveyed to the buyer; the signatures of the parties and the designation of purchase price.

70. A The "or more" clause permits the borrower prepay the loan without penalty.

71. C A lien can be described as a charge on property.

72. D In a tight money market, there is a shortage of funds for real estate loans and high interest rates. Many buyer turn to short term second trust deeds, often carried back by the seller at attractive terms.

73. B A tenant may grant an easement, but only for the term of the lease.

74. B The rate of unemployment does not directly affect the movement of mortgage rates.

75. B When several people own property as joint tenants, there is still only one title to the whole property.

76. B A lender would correlate characteristics of the borrower, the loan, and the property securing the debt to make a loan commitment.

77. B FHA insures loans for lenders.

78. B In the Cal-Vet program, the seller deeds the property to the California Department of Veteran Affairs. The California Department of Veterans Affairs then deeds the property to the veteran when the debt is paid in full.

79. B The most important part of the disclosure statement under the Federal Truth-in-Lending Law is the disclosure of the finance charge and the annual percentage rate (APR).

80. D The Real Estate Settlement Procedures Act (RESPA) allows the buyer to require the use of a specific lender in the transaction. RESPA specifically prohibits the other choices.

81. D The formula to calculate net operating income of an apartment building is scheduled gross income minus vacancies and collection losses, minus operating expenses.

82. B An agreement by a lender to make a long term loan on real estate at some future date, upon the borrower's request is known as a standby loan commitment.

83. D An impound account works to the benefit of the beneficiary (lender) and the trustor (borrower).

84. A The interest taken by prescription (an easement) is the right to use land which belongs to another person.

85. C A quitclaim deed conveys only the present right, title and interest of the person signing the quitclaim deed (grantor).

86. D A deed does not have to be acknowledged to be a valid deed.

87. C A grantor who does not know how to sign her name can "sign" the deed with a mark (X) in the presence of a witness.

88. D Ownership in severalty describes ownership by one person, an individual. The ownership has been severed from anyone else.

89. D A joint tenancy in real property can legally be created with the execution of a deed by a husband and wife to themselves as joint tenants, existing joint tenants to themselves and others as joint tenants or existing tenants in common to themselves as joint tenants.

90. D Lenders usually consider the degree of risk to be the most important factor when making the decision whether or not to make a home loan.

91. B The "standard coverage" title insurance policy (CLTA policy) protects against matters of record, such as a forgery in the chain of recorded title.

92. C The standard coverage (CLTA) title insurance policy does not protect against rights of parties in possession.

93. D Buyers, sellers, and third parties, execute escrow instructions.

94. B Escrow can be terminated by the mutual consent of both the buyer and seller.

95. C Escrow may file an interpleader action in court to settle an unresolved dispute between the buyer and the seller.

96. C According to the Seller Transfer Disclosure law, the real estate licensee has a esponsibility to visually inspect the property and reveal pertinent information which the seller has failed to disclose.

97. D This exclusive right to sell listing would be described as an express (in words), bilateral (promise for a promise), executory (something remains to be done), employment contract (employing the broker to represent the seller in the future sale of the property).

98. C An "express contract" is expressed in words, either oral or written.

99. B A contract based on an unlawful consideration is void.

100. B An agreement to pay the debt of another must be in writing to be enforceable.

101. C Baker, as owner of a life estate, had the right to transfer the interest to Mr. Connor. In this case, Mrs. Connor would remain in possession as long as the designated person, Mr. Jones, remained alive.

102. D The seller will have to pay two full commissions, one to Broker Bob as the procuring cause of the successful offer under an open listing, and one to Broker John, because the property sold during the term of his 60 day exclusive agency listing.

103. D An exclusive listing is a employment contract which is bilateral because it contains a promise for a promise, therefore, "all of the above" is the best answer.

104. C The broker in an exclusive authorization and right to locate property (buyer's listing) is authorized to represent other buyers.

105.	B	Any exclusive listing must contain a definite termination date.
106.	C	The "safety clause" is found in the listing.
107.	D	The borrower must receive the federal RESPA booklet and disclosures when the loan is secured by a first trust deed and the proceeds are used for financing the purchase of a personal residence by a family who owns three or more similar units, or the purchase of one individual unit in a complex of six residential units on the same block or the purchase of a single family dwelling by an individual buyer.
108.	B	If a contingency in a contract fails, the buyer is not obligated to perform.
109.	D	A real estate licensee should never advise buyers how to take title. A licensee who advises buyers how to take title may be subject to claims of giving tax advice, legal advice and discrimination.
110.	C	When the buyer hires an inspector, he is liable for any damages caused by his inspector.
111.	D	The effective date of the residential purchase agreement would be the date the seller's acceptance was communicated to the buyer.
112.	D	When a buyer takes property "subject to" an existing loan, the lender will keep the seller on the loan as the borrower. The seller would be liable for a deficiency (the benefit is to the buyer). The buyer's loss is limited to his equity if foreclosed.
113.	A	The option binds the optionor, not the optionee.
114.	B	Real estate licensees act as a fiduciary for the principal.
115.	A	The position of trust assumed by the real estate broker as an agent for the seller or buyer is described legally as a fiduciary relationship.
116.	D	An agent has authority which the principal actually, specifically or ostensibly (apparently) confers upon him.
117.	B	A seller of real property is not bound by the acts and representations of the buyer's broker. A buyer's broker is the agent of the buyer, not the seller.
118.	B	"Alienate" is to transfer title to property.
119.	C	A written employment contract is the most essential element to create an enforceable broker-principal relationship.
120.	C	If the buyer decides not to wait for the seller to return, the buyer can rescind the offer and secure the return of the full amount of the deposit.
121.	C	Novation is when the parties mutually agree to replace an existing contract with a new contract.
122.	B	The amount of commission in most real estate transactions is not set by local custom nor limited by law. The commission is set by negotiation between principal and broker.
123.	B	The normal relationship between an escrow officer and the principals in a real estate transaction is that of a neutral agent.

124. B The State Board of Equalization issues a certificate of clearance (clearance receipt) to show that the seller of a business opportunity has paid all sales taxes which were due.

125. D Any exclusive listing must contain a definite termination date. Only choice "D" establishes a definite termination date.

126. B Charley and William as tenants in common, Charley holding a 2/3 interest and William holding a 1/3 interest.

127. C A real estate broker is never allowed to misrepresent material facts. He may do the other choices.

128. D Each point costs 1% of the loan amount. Two points (2%) times $52,000 = $1,040. "None of the above" is the best answer.

129. C Private restrictions may be created by deed or written agreement. They cannot be created by zoning. Zoning is a form of public restriction.

130. D Seller can recover damages in a civil lawsuit against Agent Able resulting from a false promise.

131. A A single agency broker represents a buyer only or a seller only, not both. Therefore, a single agency broker can be more client orientated. The single agency broker is client-oriented.

132. C The broker was acting as a single agent, representing the buyer only in the transaction.

133. B A "blind ad" does not identify the broker.

134. D An estate for years is a lease. A lease effects and burdens the title to property.

135. D The document used to transfer and/or encumber a personal property mobilehome is a certificate of title.

136. C Under current law, all real estate documents must be retained by the real estate broker for three years.

137. A A California real estate broker can share her commission with an out-of-state broker.

138. D The employment agreement between the broker and a salesperson must be retained by both broker and salesperson for 3 years from the date of the termination of the salesperson's employment.

139. D Putting the clients funds in a client trust account, protects that money from creditors who may bring legal actions against the broker.

140. A When a broker receives an advance fee for publishing a special pamphlet advertising properties which he has not listed for sale, he must give an accounting to the seller upon demand for any funds he has collected for the advertising.

141. B When a real estate licensee negotiates a loan secured by real property, he must deliver the mortgage loan disclosure statement to the borrower within three days of receipt of a completed loan application or before the borrower is obligated to take the loan, whichever is earlier.

142. B   A "hard money loan" is a cash loan where the borrower receives cash using a new note secured by a trust deed.

143. D   The market data approach is the easiest to learn, most adaptable, and quickest method. It is the direct application of the principal of substitution. It is also called comparison or substitution.

144. B   The purpose of the Federal Fair Housing Law is to prohibit discrimination in housing transactions.

145. A   Showing minority buyers homes that are in segregated areas only violates fair housing laws and is called steering.

146. B   A loan which provides that the interest rate may be increased or decreased depending on money market conditions is called a variable interest rate loan.

147. D   A real estate broker would be subject to discipline by the Real Estate Commissioner and in violation of fair housing laws if he practiced steering, blockbusting and/or hired salespersons from only one specific ethnic group.

148. A   (1) $300,000 x 6% = $18,000 annual net income
         (2) $18,000 divided by 8% = $225,000

149. C   (1) 8 months = 2/3 of a year
         (2) $150 divided by 2 = $75 interest in 1/3 of a year
         (3) $75 x 3 = $225 interest per year
         (4) $225 divided by $2,500 = 9%

150. A   (1) $320 x 12 x 10 = $38,400 total payments
         (2) $38,400 - 19,827.60 interest = $18,572.40 has been paid on principal reduction
         (3) $22,500 - $18,572.50 = $3,927.50 balloon payment.

Salesperson Practice Exam #2

1. The most expedient thing for the beneficiary to do when a trustor goes into default on a trust deed is to institute: (A) an execution sale; (B) a trustee's sale; (C) a sheriff's sale; (D) judicial foreclosure.

2. When a lender agrees to make a construction loan to a builder at some future date, at an agreed upon interest rate, to be used for the future development of a parcel, such an agreement would best be termed: (A) an obligatory commitment; (B) an interim commitment: (C) a back up commitment: (D) a standby commitment.

3. On an FHA loan, the interest rate is set by: (A) FHA; (B) the lender; (C) agreement between the buyer and the lender; (D) the Federal Reserve Board.

4. A charge imposed on real property is called a: (A) an encumbrance; (B) a quitclaim; (C) a lien; (D) a covenant not to impose encumbrances.

5. Two vacant lots sold for a total of $17,940. Five years before, the owner purchased them for $15,600. If the following expenses were incurred during the period of ownership, how much did the owner gain or lose on the sale? EXPENSES: Interest loss 6% annually on original cost; annual weed burning $50 annually for both lots; miscellaneous expenses $10 annually for both lots; real property taxes $225 per year for each lot. (A) lost $4,890; (B) lost $2,240; (C) gained $4,890; (D) gained $2,240.

6. The difference between real and personal property is that real property: (A) may be held by two or more people as joint tenants; (B) is immovable; (C) is subject to depreciation; (D) is capable of being willed.

7. Mineral rights in land are: (A) automatically transferred; (B) not leased; (C) kept by the original owner; (D) conveyed apart from the surrounding land.

8. The ownership rights and interest in real property are called: (A) executory contracts; (B) estates or fees; (C) land sales contract; (D) liens.

9. Which is not an appropriate characteristic of a fee simple estate? (A) it is always free of encumbrances; (B) it is of indefinite duration; (C) it is transferable with or without consideration; (D) it is transferable by will or intestacy.

10. The degree, quality, nature, and extent of interest a person has in the property defines an estate in real property. An estate: (A) is never held in perpetuity; (B) can be held with another estate in the same property; (C) can only be created by a deed; (D) must always be received by a grant.

11. Henry, the holder of a $90,000 promissory note secured by a first trust deed, desires to borrow $60,000 to build a house. If the note is used as security for that loan, the agreement would be regarded as: (A) a subordinated first trust deed; (B) a pledge agreement; (C) a chattel mortgage; (D) an illegal real property security agreement.

12. A fee simple may be described as: (A) a title without limitations; (B) an estate for years; (C) a life estate; (D) the greatest interest one may hold in land.

13. A person bought a parcel of land measuring 110 yards by 220 yards. How many acres are in this parcel? (A) 2.5 acres; (B) 5 acres; (C) 10 acres; (D) 20 acres.

14. An estate of inheritance is: (A) fee simple determinable; (B) estate at sufferance; (C) estate in fee; (D) probate estate.

15. Personal property can be: (A) alienated; (B) hypothecated; (C) changed into real property; (D) all of the above.

16. A grant deed that allows someone to retain property as long as alcohol is not consumed on the property creates a: (A) fee simple absolute; (B) estate in forfeiture; (C) fee simple defeasible; (D) less than a freehold estate.

17. Bunky purchased a property for 20% less than the listed price and later sold the property for the original listed price. What percentage profit did he make? (A) 20%; (B) 25%; (C) 35%; (D) 45%.

18. All of the following are real property, **except**: (A) unextracted crude oil; (B) leasehold estates in residential real property; (C) an uncultivated grove of trees; (D) easements appurtenant.

19. In a lease whose duration is greater than one year, what is not required? (A) writing; (B) signatures from both the lessor and the lessee; (C) termination date; (D) amount of rent and the method of payment.

20. A transfer of possession of real property, but not ownership is called: (A) a mortgage; (B) a sublease; (C) a security agreement; (D) an easement.

21. The words "time, title, interest, and possession" are most closely related to which of the following? (A) ownership in severalty; (B) survivorship; (C) tenancy in common; (D) adverse possession.

22. If a property with a $2,400 gross monthly income sold at an annual GRM of 10.72, what did the property sell for? (A) $250,650; (B) $280,000; (C) $295,640; (D) 308,736.

23. When a married person dies intestate, his separate property is divided: (A) all to the spouse and nothing to the surviving children; (B) one-third to the spouse, two-thirds to the surviving children; (C) equally between surviving spouse and the surviving children; (D) none of the above.

24. The correct method for a landlord to evict a delinquent tenant is by: (A) giving him three days notice; (B) giving him thirty days notice; (C) calling the police; (D) bringing a court action.

25. The right of "quiet enjoyment and possession" means the landlord must protect the tenant from: (A) all nuisance; (B) possession without disturbance from someone claiming paramount title; (C) all encumbrances; (D) none of the above.

26. Which of these notices is important for a mechanic's lien? (A) notice of non-responsibility; (B) notice of cessation; (C) notice of completion; (D) all of the above.

27. When the Real Estate Commissioner intends to rescind his approval of a subdivision: (A) he issues an injunction; (B) he issues a desist and refrain order; (C) he revokes the developer's license; (D) none of the above.

28. Which of the following is considered to be both personal and revocable? (A) encroachment; (B) easement; (C) license; (D) option contract.

29. A lien that covers all real property of the debtor in the county where it is recorded is called: (A) a lis pendens; (B) a general lien; (C) a specific lien; (D) none of the above.

30. The verification and recordation of the document is required to create a valid: (A) notice of default; (B) trust deed; (C) judgment attaching real property; (D) mechanic's lien.

31. The time period when a lis pendens is effective is: (A) before the trial is held; (B) until the lawsuit is dismissed; (C) until the final judgment is rendered; (D) in any of the above situations.

32. In construction lending, the lender will usually release the final payment to the building contractor when the: (A) owner has recorded the notice of completion; (B) lien period has expired; (C) job has been completed; (D) mechanic's lien has been recorded.

33. In a new subdivision, who is responsible for assuring completion of paved streets, utilities, and curbs? (A) the developer; (B) the city; (C) the county; (D) the federal government.

34. A man divided an acre of land into four lots. He then sold the lots for $10,000 each. If his cost basis on each lot was $2,000, what was his total gain on the sale of the lots? (A) $8,000; (B) $10,000; (C) $32,000; (D) 40,000.

35. A court order to sell property after the final judgment in a lawsuit has been rendered is: (A) a foreclosure; (B) a deficiency judgment; (C) a writ of execution; (D) an attachment.

36. The term "et ux" means: (A) and others; (B) and utterances to be made later; (C) and wife; (D) none of the above.

37. A major difference between an easement and a license is that a license is: (A) assignable; (B) of indefinite duration; (C) written; (D) revocable.

38. What percentage profit would an investor make if he purchased two lots for $18,000 each, then divided them into three lots and sold them for $15,000 each? (A) 5%; (B) 21%; (C) 15%; (D) 25%.

39. Individuals do not normally have: (A) ability to sever property; (B) riparian rights; (C) power of eminent domain; (D) reliction rights.

40. The primary purpose of a master plan is to show the location of: (A) commercial, industrial, residential districts; (B) public streets; (C) seismic safety zones; (D) all of the above.

41. Ron owns a single family home which rents for $600 per month. A home across the street rents for $690 per month and recently sold for $78,000. If Ron applied the same gross rent multiplier to his home as was used on the home across the street, what would be the value of Ron's home? (A) $50,000; (B) $67,800; (C) $69,565; (D) $70,909.

42. A condominium is similar to an apartment in that: (A) the owner of the condominium and the tenant of the apartment each have an estate in real property; (B) the person in each unit has a fee interest; (C) the local tax assessor must assess each property separately; (D) none of the above.

43. Under federal income tax law, an individual may not deduct a loss on a sale of a home, unless: (A) the loss is greater than 20%; (B) the home is also used for business; (C) it was her primary personal residence; (D) it was bought as an investment and rented out.

44. All of the following are used to determine the gain or loss on the sale of real property for income tax purposes, **except**: (A) the miscellaneous costs of sale; (B) the brokerage commission; (C) the purchase price; (D) the mortgage payment.

45. Buyer buys a property from Mr. Valdez. Mr. Valdez agrees to take back a note secured by a trust deed to satisfy a portion of the purchase price. The trust deed would be: (A) a general lien; (B) a specific lien; (C) an involuntary lien; (D) an equitable lien.

46. Which is least satisfactory in providing a legal description? (A) the escrow instructions; (B) a standard title insurance policy; (C) a recorded grant deed; (D) a property tax bill for real property.

47. The purpose of the Equal Credit Opportunity Act is to: (A) standardize the methods for obtaining credit; (B) regulate the total amount of credit given to the borrower; (C) discourage discrimination in lending based on age, sex, race, marital status, color, religion or national origin; (D) all of the above.

48. Don sold his primary personal residence for $138,000. Two weeks later, he purchased and moved into a replacement residence, which he purchased for $136,870. The adjusted cost basis of his first residence was $120,000. For federal income tax purposes, he now has: (A) a basis of $138,000 and no taxable gain; (B) a basis of $120,000 and a taxable gain of $1,130; (C) a basis of $136,870 and a taxable gain of $1,130; (D) none of the above.

49. A house sells for $150,000. The buyer assumed an existing loan against the property for $130,000. The documentary transfer tax for this county is $.55 per $500 of consideration. The transfer tax is: (A) $11; (B) $22; (C) $33; (D) $44.

50. When commercial real estate is purchased today, the minimum period of time over which the owner can depreciate the improvements is: (A) 15 years; (B) 27.5 years; (C) 30 years; (D) 39 years.

51. What contributes most to the maintenance of value in a well planned community? (A) conformity to proper land use objectives; (B) prevention of major street construction; (C) nonconforming improvements; (D) improper orientation.

52. In the situation where no prudent person would pay more for a piece of land than others, which of the following principles would be best applied: (A) balance; (B) conformity; (C) intervention; (D) substitution.

53. In the definition of "highest and best use," one would likely find the phrase: (A) net return; (B) gross income; (C) depreciation; (D) integration.

54. The relationship between "effective" and "nominal" interest is that: (A) effective interest is what the buyer pays; nominal interest is what is named in the loan application; (B) effective interest is what the buyer pays, nominal interest is what is named in the advertising; (C) effective interest is what the buyer pays, nominal interest is what is specified in the note. (D) there is no difference.

55. What is the definition of value to an appraiser? (A) relationship of desirous persons and things desired; (B) ability of one commodity to command other commodities; (C) present worth of future benefits arising out of ownership of property; (D) all of the above.

56. How many parcels of land, each measuring 50' by 100', could be created from an acre of land? (A) 1; (B) 4; (C) 7; (D) 8.

57. A joint tenancy may be created by: (A) joint tenants, deeding their property to themselves, and another person, as joint tenants; (B) tenants in common, deeding their property to themselves as joint tenants; (C) husband and wife, deeding their property to themselves as joint tenants; (D) all of the above.

58. Under the principle of substitution, one assumes that one property may be substituted for another in terms of: (A) income; (B) use; (C) structural design; (D) any of the above.

59. An attorney-in-fact is which of the following: (A) a lawyer acting as the administrator of an estate; (B) a principal who has been given implied powers of agency; (C) an agent performing a dual agency; (D) a legally competent person who has been given a power of attorney.

60. If a broker wants to operate his business under the fictitious name of ABC Realty, he must do which of the following before conducting business under that name? (A) file the fictitious business name with city where he has the main branch of his brokerage; (B) publish the fictitious business name in any newspaper of general circulation; (C) register the fictitious business name with the DRE; (D) obtain a license from the DRE under the fictitious business name.

61. A licensee must make an adjustment between the comparable and the subject property because: (A) property eventually must increase in value; (B) property depreciates; (C) two properties are rarely similar concerning everything; (D) property eventually decreases in value.

62. An agent advertises that she will give a $1,000 credit in escrow to any seller who lists with her and that she will pay one-half of her commission to any buyer who purchases a property through her. This type of advertising is: (A) Illegal as it is a restraint of trade; (B) prohibited under RESPA; (C) legal, since the amount offered is less than $5,000; (D) legal if the disclosure is made to all parties to the transaction.

63. An appraiser determines an estimate of value based upon what date: (A) the date the purchase contract is signed; (B) the date escrow was opened; (C) the date the loan was funded; (D) the date the deed is recorded.

64. A landlord and tenant mutually agreed to terminate a 2-year lease before the two year term had expired. The tenant moved out and the landlord took possession of the premises. This is called: (A) surrender; (B) abandonment; (C) release; (D) accord and satisfaction.

65. An appraiser will seriously consider all of the following in arriving at an opinion of value, **except**: (A) property identification; (B) definition of value; (C) highest and best use; (D) assessed value.

66. A bona fide listing to sell real property must contain: (A) consideration, mutual consent, competent parties, and writing; (B) consideration, mutual consent, capable parties expressed time element and price; (C) capable parties, mutual consent, lawful object, consideration, and be in writing; (D) consideration, price, lawful object, competent parties, and legally sufficient writing.

67. Which of the following is an example of economic obsolescence? (A) a leaky roof; (B) no parking; (C) an oversupply of like properties in the neighborhood; (D) a severely deteriorated bearing wall.

68. When would the cost approach to appraisal be most appropriately used? (A) new property; (B) middle-aged property; (C) old property; (D) multi-family property.

69. Which of the following items may be short rated in escrow? (A) real estate taxes; (B) interest; (C) title insurance; (D) fire insurance.

70. When two or more contiguous parcels owned by one person have an increased value above the value of the individual lots, this is called: (A) value increase; (B) dual ownership; (C) plottage; (D) severalty ownership.

71. "Depreciation" as used in the cost approach to appraisal may be defined as: (A) a realized recapture of accrued income; (B) a loss in value from any cause; (C) wear and tear on the improvements; (D) a loss in the value of the land.

72. A $5,000 loan is sold to an investor for $4,500. It is a straight note, due and payable at the end of one year. It bears a 6% interest rate. What percentage return on the principal dollar invested will be made by the investor? (A) 6.6%; (B) 11%; (C) 17.8%; (D) 25%.

73. Which type of title policy insures against all risks to title? (A) American Land Title Association policy (B) extended coverage policy; (C) standard coverage policy; (D) no title policy covers all risks.

74. When the value of real property increased because of an increase in population, this could be classified as: (A) economic valuation; (B) economic obsolescence; (C) unearned increment; (D) none of the above.

75. A residential property is 15 years old, and has an average projected physical life of 40 years. This particular property has been superbly maintained and appears as if it were just 5 years old. This represents the concept of: (A) effective age; (B) physical age; (C) actual age; (D) progressive age.

76. Under an exclusive agency listing, broker David diligently advertised and marketed a $650,000 home owned by Mr. Marquez. Before the listing expired, Mr. Marquez found his own buyer and sold the home directly to the buyer without using broker David or any other agent. Mr. Marquez refused to pay broker David any commission. Broker David is entitled to: (A) no commission; (B) half of the commission; (C) reimbursement for all expenses incurred in advertising the home; (D) a full commission.

77. When a building earns sufficient income to justify its continued operation, this is called: (A) earning life; (B) productive life; (C) economic life; (D) none of the above.

78. The right or power to sell property in the event of default under the terms of the trust deed are given by: (A) trustee to trustor; (B) buyer to beneficiary; (C) buyer to seller; (D) trustor to trustee.

79. Tom is a homeowner who has failed to make payments on a trust deed for two months. The trustee has recorded a notice of default. What does Tom have? (A) right of redemption; (B) right of reinstatement; (C) loan moratorium rights; (D) a problem, he has lost his opportunity to stop foreclosure.

80. Usually home loans in real estate finance are calculated based on: (A) discounted interest; (B) compounded interest; (C) simple interest; (D) straight interest.

81. The Franchise Investment Law is designed primarily to protect the: (A) franchisees and/or subfranchisors who have an exclusive geographic territory; (B) prospective franchisees when considering the purchase of a franchise; (C) investors in franchisor corporations with a net worth of less than $5,000,000; (D) none of the above.

82. What does "encumbered" mean? (A) the degree, quantity, nature, and extent of interest one has in property; (B) the use of property by the debtor; (C) any action taken relative to the property; (D) anything that affects or limits or burdens the title to property.

83. The loan which allows the terms of an interest rate to increase or decrease over time is called: (A) a secured loan; (B) an interim loan; (C) a fixed rate loan; (D) a variable interest rate loan.

84. An appraiser's primary concern when analyzing real property is: (A) marketability and acceptability; (B) functionality; (C) supply and demand; (D) none of the above.

85. The monetary tools used by the Federal Reserve Board to control the money supply would include all of the following, **except**: (A) raising and lowering the discount rates to the member banks; (B) adjusting the minimum reserve requirements for banks; (C) expanding open market operations by buying and selling U.S. government bonds; (D) changing interest rates on government insured mortgages.

86. When using a purchase money trust deed, the trustor: (A) receives a promissory note for the amount borrowed; (B) lends money to the beneficiary; (C) signs the promissory note and trust deed and gives it to the beneficiary; (D) only signs the trust deed.

87. Anyone who sells a second trust deed for less than its value is: (A) leveraging an investment; (B) liquidating a piece of real property; (C) discounting a note; (D) subordinating a debt.

88. Bob purchased an existing loan from a lender for $13,500. At the time he purchased the loan it had just been created and had a loan balance of $15,000. The borrower never made a payment on the loan, and Bob decided to foreclose. What is the maximum amount Bob can foreclose for? (A) $13,500; (B) An investor who purchased an existing loan has no right to foreclose; (C) $13,500 minus the trustee fee; (D) $15,000.

89. A note payable for "interest only," is called a: (A) straight note; (B) amortized installment note; (C) nonnegotiable note; (D) adjustable rate note.

90. A buyer gave a salesperson a $1,000 personal note to act as the earnest money deposit in an offer to buy a home. The salesperson: (A) should not tell the seller what form of earnest money deposit accompanies the offer; (B) should inform the seller that the earnest money deposit is a personal note, prior to the seller's acceptance of the offer; (C) should not have accepted a personal note as an earnest money deposit; (D) should refuse to present the offer until the buyer replaces the $1,000 personal note with cash.

91. The person who loans money secured by a trust deed on a parcel of real property is called a: (A) trustor; (B) trustee; (C) mortgagor; (D) beneficiary.

92. In a court foreclosure sale on a trust deed: (A) the procedure is the same as a trustee sale; (B) the trustor has a redemption period; (C) a court foreclosure is illegal in California; (D) the procedure for a court foreclosure is usually faster than for a trustee sale.

93. A grant deed is deemed by law to be executed when it is: (A) signed by the grantor; (B) accepted by the grantee; (C) delivered to escrow; (D) recorded.

94. When a lender accepts a deed in lieu of foreclosure, the lender: (A) must also have the power of sale; (B) must take ownership of the property free and clear of all liens; (C) must go to court and get a deficiency judgment: (D) assumes junior loans.

95. What provides the most important protection for a lender on a junior trust deed? (A) the borrower's income; (B) the borrower's credit rating; (C) the borrower's equity in the property; (D) none of the above.

96. Sam listed a home for sale with Broker Bud for $350,000. Prospective buyer Danny submitted an offer at a purchase price of $320,000, offer to expire within three days. The next day, Sam issued a counter-offer changing only the sales price to $330,000. When Danny did not respond within the three-day period, Sam signed an acceptance of Danny's $320,000 offer and instructed Broker Bud to deliver it to Danny. Upon receipt of signed acceptance, Danny told Broker Bud he had decided not to purchase the property. Based on the foregoing, there is: (A) an enforceable contract; (B) an invalid contract; (C) a void contract; (D) no contract.

97. For a seller to relieve herself of primary liability when allowing the buyer to "take over" her existing loan, she must find a buyer who will: (A) assume the trust deed and note; (B) sign a release agreement; (C) buy the property "subject to" the existing loan; (D) the seller is never relieved from primary liability.

98. A broker took an exclusive loan listing to negotiate a loan of $3,000 for a borrower. The listing was for 90 days. Under these circumstances, the listing would be: (A) A valid, enforceable loan listing; (B) All right because loans below $6,000 are not regulated; (C) Illegal for the broker to take an exclusive listing for that period of time; (D) Illegal unless the broker was also a real property security dealer.

99. A clause in a trust deed that declares the total unpaid balance due and payable upon default is called: (A) a forfeiture clause; (B) an escalator clause; (C) a elevator clause; (D) none of the above.

100. Jack Russell, a real estate broker, who is not a Realtor, uses a sign which says "Realtor" at his office located in his home. He pays a 17 year-old high school student $10 for each listing the student brings into the office. He keeps his client's money in his safe at home. Which of the following is not a violation of the real estate law? (A) hiring an unlicensed person to solicit listings; (B) improper sign, using the term "Realtor" when he is not a member of the National Association of Realtors; (C) improper office location; (D) commingling the client's money with his own money in the home safe.

101. In order to create a valid joint tenancy, there is a requirement for: (A) the clause "with right of survivorship;" (B) a husband and wife relationship; (C) equal ownership interests; (D) all of the above.

102. One joint tenant may dispose of his interest by all of the following, **except**: (A) will; (B) sale; (C) gift; (D) lease.

103. Unlike a joint tenancy, the tenancy in common requires only one unity, the unity of: (A) time; (B) title; (C) interest; (D) possession.

104. When four people own one piece of real estate in joint tenancy, they: (A) do not have equal shares; (B) have one title; (C) allow their heirs to obtain their shares by will; (D) each have co-ownership with separate title.

105. How many eight acre parcels would fit in a section of land? (A) 40 parcels; (B) 80 parcels; (C) 160 parcels; (D) 640 parcels.

106. Ann acquires title as a single female. Ann subsequently marries. Ann then sells the property, signing her married name to the grant deed. This: (A) is immaterial; (B) creates a cloud on the title; (C) is automatically cured after 90 days; (D) this has no impact, because this was her separate property.

107. Under the California Environmental Quality Act, if a city or county agency determines that a proposed project has no significant effect on the environment and that a full environmental impact report is not required, the public agency will issue a: (A) declaration of approval; (B) positive declaration; (C) negative declaration; (D) declaration of support.

108. Implied covenants are not normally included in a: (A) grant deed; (B) quitclaim deed; (C) warranty deed; (D) all deeds include implied warranties.

109. All of the following statements about transfer of title to personal property are correct, **except**: (A) title to personal property usually passes by delivery of possession: (B) the condition of title to personal property may generally be determined by looking at the public records with the same accuracy as with real property; (C) a written document may be used in connection with the transfer of personal property, may not be required by law for a valid transfer; (D) personal property is usually regarded as located at the domicile of the owner, regardless of the actual location, and is governed by the laws of the owner's domicile.

110. The acknowledgment of a deed can be taken by: (A) the person granting the deed; (B) a notary who is also the mortgagee; (C) an employee of a corporation buying property; (D) the grantor only.

111. When a judgment has been recorded, it provides: (A) voidable notice; (B) constructive notice; (C) actual notice; (D) contingent notice.

112. The main purpose of a deed is to: (A) identify grantor and grantee; (B) provide evidence of the change of title or transfer of interest; (C) provide evidence of terms; (D) provide a written instrument that can be recorded.

113. A deed requires which of the following in order to be valid: (A) The grantee's signature; (B) A recital; (C) An acknowledgment; (D) A granting clause.

114. Jack sells his home to Barry who sets up his residency but fails to record the deed. Jack then gives a deed to Diane for the same home. What is the outcome? (A) Diane owns the property; (B) Barry and Diane are co-owners; (C) Diane has recourse over Barry; (D) Barry has title.

115. With a promissory note and trust deed signed by two or more co-borrowers, when one of the co-borrowers defaults, what is the liability? (A) personal and corporate liability; (B) all are together liable as individual borrowers; (C) each is jointly and severally liable; (D) each is individually and severally liable.

116. In making a decision to issue a standard title insurance policy, a title insurance company is most concerned with: (A) the trustor; (B) the grantee; (C) the chain of title; (D) boundary lines of the property.

117. In a standard title policy, what is not considered as one of the normal procedures? (A) the determination of the amount of insurance coverage; (B) investigation of title; (C) a survey of the property; (D) a review of prior deeds.

118. An "abstract of title" is: (A) A standard form; (B) An exact duplicate of the standard title policy; (C) Not available to the owner of the property; (D) A written summary of the chain of title.

119. Dolores is owner of a home which she has agreed to sell to David. A preliminary title report prepared during escrow shows: (A) exactly the same information as found in David's future standard title policy; (B) information about a deed of trust with Dolores as trustor; (C) the new trust deed with David as trustor; (D) title vested in David.

120. Most buyers get what type of title insurance? (A) certificate of title; (B) leasehold; (C) ALTA; (D) standard title insurance policy.

121. An ALTA title insurance policy guards against all of the following, **except**: (A) an unrecorded mechanic's lien; (B) an unrecorded easement; (C) zoning regulations; (D) rights of parties in possession.

122. A standard policy insures against: (A) encroachments; (B) claims of persons in possession; (C) prescriptive easements; (D) a recorded deed that was not properly delivered and accepted.

123. All of the following items are normally prorated at the close of escrow, **except**: (A) home-owner's insurance; (B) property taxes and assessments; (C) delinquent interest on unsecured loans; (D) interest and impounds.

124. An estate of inheritance or perpetual estate could also be described as a: (A) fee simple defeasible; (B) life estate; (C) less-than-freehold estate; (D) estate in fee.

125. Which of the following may a minor be able to undertake without court approval: (A) acquisition of real property through gift or inheritance; (B) give valid power of attorney to encumber property; (C) sell real estate through a guardian; (D) all of the above.

126. During escrow, the escrow officer received two structural pest control reports, the escrow officer should: (A) contact the inspection company to ask which report is best; (B) notify the buyer and seller and obtain written instructions as which report to use; (C) use the report which found the most infestation and damage; (D) use the report which found the least infestation and damage.

127. Mrs. Smith sold a home to Mr. Jones on an installment sales contract. Mr. Jones recorded the contract. Mr. Jones made a $1,000 down payment and after the sale made a few of the required monthly payments. One night Mr. Jones moved out and abandoned the house. Which of the following is true? (A) a deficiency judgment could be obtained by Mr. Jones; (B) a buyer who later bought the property for cash would have no concern about Mr. Jones; (C) there is a cloud on the title; (D) Mrs. Smith now has a marketable title which can be sold with no doubt in law.

128. The California Civil Code requires a transfer disclosure statement be delivered by the: (A) probate court; (B) trustee to trustor; (C) transferor to transferee; (D) husband to wife.

129. Capital improvements made to residential income property after 1986 may be depreciated: (A) by whatever type of depreciation the owner used on the original property; (B) by the 175% declining balance method; (C) over an estimated life of 27-1/2 years; (D) using accelerated depreciation.

130. Once recorded, a lis pendens is effective: (A) before the trial is held; (B) until the lawsuit is dismissed; (C) until a final judgment is rendered; (D) in any of the above situations.

131. A real estate broker included the following clause in her standard listing contract: "In consideration of execution of the foregoing, the undersigned broker agrees to use diligence in procuring a purchaser." This is: (A) superfluous and unnecessary in current contracts; (B) important to the creation of a bilateral contract; (C) important to the creation of a unilateral contract; (D) important according to the Statute of Limitations.

132. A voidable contract remains binding until it has been: (A) invalidated; (B) rescinded; (C) discovered; (D) qualified.

133. A contract has been executed when it has been: (A) signed, notarized and recorded; (B) entered into under the jurisdiction of the probate court; (C) completely and fully performed; (D) signed under threat of death.

134. All of the following are essential to the validity of a contract, **except**: (A) a meeting of the minds; (B) the adequate capacity of the parties to the contract; (C) the payment of money; (D) a legal purpose.

135. All of the following are essential to create a valid contract, **except**: (A) lawful object; (B) writing; (C) mutual consent; (D) consideration.

136. The Statute of Frauds requires which of the following contracts to be in writing? (A) an employment contract to represent the seller of a business opportunity; (B) a contract selling a business opportunity; (C) a contract which is not to be performed within one year of its making; (D) a nine month lease.

137. In order to have a binding contract between the buyer and seller, it must: (A) have been offered and accepted; (B) be recorded; (C) contain acknowledgment; (D) all of the above.

138. When damages are not adequate, each of the following may request specific performance, **except** the: (A) buyer from the seller; (B) attorney-in-fact for one of the principals; (C) seller of a large parcel of land; (D) broker from the principal.

139. An agent who acts exclusively as the agent for the buyer: (A) may present offers to the seller only; (B) may present offers to the seller and/or the seller's agent; (C) may present offers to the seller's agent only; (D) is acting illegally.

140. When a buyer gives the agent a postdated check to accompany an offer, it: (A) may not be accepted by the agent; (B) must be cashed immediately; (C) Must be delivered to the seller within one day; (D) may be retained, but must be disclosed to the seller.

141. A licensee who misrepresents property to the buyer while acting as an agent of the seller, is subject to: (A) discipline; (B) civil lawsuits; (C) criminal penalties; (D) all of the above.

142. The developer of a large time-share subdivision sent advertising offering prizes to over 100,000 potential buyers, but did not disclose that they were required to attend a sales presentation to be eligible to receive the prizes. Which of the following is true? (A) this is legal so long as the offer is made to all interested parties; (B) this is legal because a developer can give prizes if he wants to without limitation; (C) this is illegal because the developer failed to disclose the requirement that buyers must attend a sales presentation in order to receive a prize; (D) this is illegal because in addition to a prize, buyers were also awarded a partial ownership in the property.

143. The most detailed and accurate method of estimating the replacement cost new of an improvement is: (A) unit of comparison method; (B) cost per square foot method; (C) quantity survey method; (D) unit-in-place method.

144. An agent who pays part of the commission to the buyer: (A) must inform the seller; (B) is subject to criminal prosecution; (C) is subject to discipline by the Real Estate Commissioner; (D) is subject to a civil lawsuit by the seller, even if he disclosed everything to the seller.

145. When a licensee places an ad in the newspaper without the broker's name that reads, in total: "3 bdrm, 2 bath, den & spa, giant lot, $160,000 800-555-1212," this is: (A) a violation of the Truth in Lending Law; (B) misleading advertising; (C) false advertising; (D) a blind ad.

146. All of the following contribute to the stability of a residential neighborhood **except**: (A) location in the path of city growth; (B) many families with school children in the neighborhood; (C) conformity in uses, and occupations in the area; (D) increasing the population density and home sale turnover rate.

147. Why do many brokers open client trust fund accounts? (A) to commingle funds; (B) to avoid regulation; (C) to separate the client's money from broker's money; (D) to get those great free toasters the bank gives out.

148. Trust fund money can be withdrawn by whom? (A) any person employed by the broker; (B) an unlicensed person; (C) a corporate director; (D) any authorized employee of the broker.

149. Alice's license has been suspended. The Real Estate Education, Research, and Recovery Account (REERRA) has paid on claims by both the buyer and seller. When may Alice's license be reinstated? (A) when she pays the person the amount owed; (B) when she pays the Recovery Account for money paid plus 1/2 the interest; (C) a suspended licensee may never have his license reinstated; (D) when she pays the Recovery Account for money paid plus all interest.

150. A salesperson is using strong efforts to obtain listings in a nonintegrated community. He finds success by insinuating that, if minorities move in, the value of the property will decrease. His activities may be best described as: (A) steering; (B) panic peddling; (C) blockbusting; (D) both "B" and "C".

Answers to Salesperson Practice Exam #2

1. B The trustee's sale is the most expedient way to foreclose. The procedure takes about four months.

2. D A standby commitment is when a lender agrees to make a loan at some future date, typically for a future construction project.

3. C Under the FHA program, the interest rate on FHA loans is set by agreement between the buyer and the lender.

4. C A lien can be described as a charge on real property.

5. A The annual expenses are $936 interest ($15,600 x 6%), $50 weeds, $10 miscellaneous, and $450 taxes ($225 x 2), for a total of $1,446 per year. That amount times 5 years produces a total expense of $7,230. The gross profit was $2,340 ($17,940 - $15,600), but by subtracting the expenses of $7,230 from that amount, a loss of $4,890 is calculated.

6. B Real property is generally immovable.

7. A Mineral rights in land are automatically transferred with the land, unless expressly excluded by a grantor.

8. B "Estates or fees" describe the degree, quantity, nature and extent of interest or ownership one has in real property.

9. A A fee simple estate may have encumbrances; it is not always free of encumbrances.

10. B There can be more than one estate in real property. For example, a landlord holds a fee simple state, at the same time the tenant holds a less than freehold estate.

11. B When an existing note is used as the security for another loan, it is called a pledge agreement. The note is held by the lender as security for repayment of the new loan. The new borrower pledges the loan.

12. D A fee simple estate is the greatest interest one may hold in land.

13. B (1) 110 yds x 220 yds = 24,200 sq. yds;
(2) 24,200 sq. yds. divided by 4,840 sq. yds (in an acre) = 5 acres.

14. C An estate in fee is another name for an estate of inheritance.

15. D Personal property can be alienated, hypothecated or be changed into real property.

16. C A fee simple defeasible has a clause in the deed (such as "no alcohol" on property) which, if violated, causes the property to revert back to the grantor.

17. B If a property were listed at $100,000 and it was purchased at 20% discount (purchased for $80,000) and then sold for the list price ($100,000), this would be a profit of $20,000. Based on an investment of $80,000, there would be a profit of 25%.

18. B Leasehold estates in real property are the personal property of the lessee.

19. B Only the lessor is legally required to sign a written lease.

20. B A sublease transfers possession, but not ownership of real property.

21. B The words "time, title, interest, and possession" represent the four unities necessary to create a joint tenancy. Joint tenancy has the right of survivorship.

22. D (1) $2,400 x 12 = $28,800 gross annual income; (2) $28,800 x 10.72 GRM =$308,736.

23. B The law of intestate succession requires that separate property be divided one-third to the spouse and two-thirds divided equally among the surviving children.

24. D A landlord would bring an unlawful detainer action in court.

25. B The right of quiet enjoyment possession requires a landlord to defend a tenant from someone claiming "paramount title."

26. D All of these notices start the running of a limited period of time in which to file a mechanic's lien and are therefore very important.

27. B The Real Estate Commissioner may issue a desist and refrain order to stop violations of the subdivision law.

28. C The license is the personal and revocable permission to do something on the land of another.

29. B A general lien is a lien which encumbers all real property of the debtor in the county where it is recorded.

30. D A mechanic's lien is the only one of these documents which must be verified and recorded in order to be valid.

31. D A lis pendens is effective once it is recorded. This includes the time before trial is held, until the lawsuit is dismissed, or until final judgment is rendered.

32. B In construction loans, the lender holds the final payment until the lien period has expired to be sure that there will be no mechanic's liens filed against the property.

33. A The developer usually has the responsibility for completing the streets, utilities and curbs in a new subdivision.

34. C (1) $10,000 - $2,000 = $8,000 gain per lot; (2) $8,000 x 4 lots = $32,000 gain.

35. C A writ of execution is the court order to sell property after final judgment in a lawsuit has been made.

36. C This is Latin for "and wife."

37. D The major difference between an easement and a license is that a license can be revoked.

38. D (1) $18,000 x 2 = $36,000 cost of lots
       (2) $15,000 x 3 = $45,000 selling price
       (3) $45,000 - $36,000 = $9,000 profit
       (4) $9,000 divided by $36,000 = 25% profit

39. C Governments, not individuals, are given the power of eminent domain.

40. D The master plan usually shows all of these things and more.

41. B (1) $78,000 (selling price) divided by $690 (rent) = 113.04 GRM (gross rent multiplier);
       (2) $600 (rent) x 113.04 (GRM) = $67,826.09, "B" is the best answer.

42. A Both the owner of an unit in a condominium and a tenant renting an apartment have an estate in real property.

43. D The loss in the sale of residential income property may be deducted, subject to certain limitations.

44. D The owner's mortgage payment is not considered in the formula used to determine the gain or loss from the sale of real property.

45. B The trust deed is a specific lien.

46. D The property tax bill uses an assessor's number, not a legal description.

47. D The is to: standardize the methods for obtaining credit, regulate the total amount of credit given to the borrower and discourage discrimination in lending based on age, sex, race, marital status, color, religion or national origin.

48. B When you sell your primary personal residence and purchase and move into a less expensive replacement home within 24 months, you take your prior adjusted basis with you and report the amount you "moved down" as gain. $138,000 - $136,870 = $1,130 gain.

49. B $150,000 - $130,000 = $20,000 consideration. $20,000 divided by $500 = 40 taxable units. 40 x $.55 = $22.

50. D Under current tax law, commercial real estate can be depreciated over a minimum of 39 years.

51. A Conformity to land use objectives contributes to value.

52. D The principal of substitution assumes that no prudent person would pay more for something than other prudent people.

53. A The highest and best use is the use which will create the highest net return on money invested.

54. C Effective interest is what the buyer pays; nominal interest is what is specified in the note.

55. D These are all accepted definitions of value.

56. D (1) 50' x 100' = 5,000 square feet
       (2) 43,560 sq. ft. (acre) divided by 5,000 sq. ft. = 8.71 parcels

57. D A joint tenancy may be created by: joint tenants, deeding their property to themselves, and another person, as joint tenants, or tenants in common, deeding their property to themselves as joint tenants and/or husband and wife, deeding their property to themselves as joint tenants.

© 2013 John Henderson

58. D   The principle of substitution assumes that one property may be substituted for another in terms of income, use or structural design.

59. D   An attorney-in-fact is a legally competent person who has been given a power of attorney.

60. D   Before a broker may conduct business under a fictitious business name he must:
   1. Register the fictitious business name with the county recorder's office (not the secretary of state).
   2. Publish the fictitious business name statement in a paper of general circulation within the county where his office is located (not just any paper),
   3. Apply to the DRE for a new broker's license under the fictitious business name (not register the fictitious business name with the DRE). The broker may operate under the fictitious business name after he obtains a license from the DRE under the fictitious business name.

61. C   The appraiser adjusts the comparable to the subject property because two properties are rarely identical.

62. D   It is legal for an agent to advertise that she will give a $1,000 credit in escrow to any seller who lists with her and that she will pay one-half of her commission to any buyer who purchases a property through her, if the disclosure is made to all parties to the transaction.

63. A   This is the best available answer.

64. A   When a landlord and tenant mutually agreed to terminate a lease it is called surrender.

65. D   Assessed value has little or no impact on appraised value.

66. C   A bona fide listing to sell real property must contain: capable parties, mutual consent, lawful object, consideration, and be in writing.

67. C   An oversupply of like properties in the neighborhood is an example of economic obsolescence.

68. A   The cost approach to appraisal is most appropriate for appraising new property.

69. D   Fire insurance on the property may be short rated in escrow.

70. C   Plottage is an added value obtained when two or more contiguous lots come under common ownership.

71. B   "Depreciation" for appraisal purposes means a loss in value from any cause.

72. C   (1) $5,000 x 6% = $300 interest paid on the loan
       (2) $5,000 - $4,500 = $500 made by investor as a result of the discount
       (3) $300 + $500 = $800 total profit made by investor
       (4) $800 divided by $4,500 = 17.78% "C" 17.8% is the best answer

73. D   No title policy covers all risks.

74. C   An unearned increment is an increase in value due to no effort on the part of the owner, such as an increase in population.

75. A   The effective age of an improvement reflects how well it has been maintained by the owner. A well maintained structure may have an effective age which is far less than its physical age.

76. A Under an exclusive agency listing, the seller has retained the right to sell the property himself directly to a buyer without using any agent. When the seller in an exclusive agency listing sells the property himself, no commission is paid..

77. C The economic life of an improvement is the period of time in which the building earns sufficient income to justify its continued operation.

78. D The trustor (borrower) gives the trustee the power to sell the property in the event of default.

79. B The trustor has the right to reinstate the loan until 5 days before the trustee sale.

80. C Most real estate loans, such as home loans, are calculated using simple interest.

81. B This law is intended to protect prospective franchisees when they are considering purchasing a franchise.

82. D An "encumbrance" is defined as anything that affects or limits the title to property.

83. D A variable interest rate loan allows the interest rate to increase or decrease over time.

84. A Marketability and acceptability are the primary concerns.

85. D The Federal Reserve Board does not have authority to raise or lower interest rates on government insured mortgages.

86. C The trustor (borrower) signs the promissory note and trust deed, then gives them to the beneficiary (lender).

87. C A loan is discounted whenever it is sold for less than the face amount or current loan balance.

88. D When a loan is discounted, the loan amount does not change. Bob can foreclose for the full amount of the loan.

89. A A "straight note" is a note which requires no principal payments during the life of the loan.

90. B The salesperson should inform the seller that the earnest money deposit is a personal note, prior to the seller's acceptance of the offer.

91. D The beneficiary is the lender in a trust deed.

92. B The trustor (borrower) in a court foreclosure on a trust deed has a limited right of redemption after the property is sold.

93. B A tender is an offer of performance as part of a contract.

94. D When a lender accepts a deed in lieu of foreclosure, the lender assumes all junior liens against the property.

95. C The borrower's equity in the property is the most important concern to a lender making a junior loan.

96. D A counteroffer terminates the original offer. Since Sam had already issued a counter-offer, his counter-offer terminated the original offer. Therefore, there was no offer for him to later accept and there is no contract.

97. A When a buyer "assumes" the existing loan, the buyer becomes primarily liable for the debt. This relieves the seller from primary liability.

98. C   An exclusive loan listing may not exceed 45 days.

99. D   A clause in a trust deed that declares the total unpaid balance due and payable upon default is called an "acceleration clause."

100. C   A real estate broker may work out of his home. The other choices violate the law.

101. C   A joint tenancy requires equal ownership interests.

102. A   A joint tenant may not will his interest.

103. D   The only unity required for a tenancy in common is the unity of possession.

104. B   All joint tenants share one title.

105. B   A section contains 640 acres of land. 640 acres divided by 8 acres = 80 parcels of land.

106. B   Assuming she changed her name upon marriage, the different name on the deed would create a cloud on title.

107. C   Under the California Environmental Quality Act, any city or county agency having jurisdiction under the law would issue a negative declaration in the event that a subdivision proposes no significant effect on the environment.

108. B   The quitclaim deed contains no implied covenants.

109. B   The condition of title to personal property may not generally be determined by looking at the public records with the same accuracy as with real property.

110. C   An employee of a corporation which is buying real estate may take an acknowledgment from the grantor, so long as the employee is a notary and does not have a personal interest in the transaction.

111. B   Recording a judgment gives constructive notice.

112. B   The main purpose of a deed is to provide evidence of the change of title or transfer of interest in property.

113. D   A granting clause is one of the requirements of a valid deed.

114. D   The act of Barry's talking possession gives constructive notice of his rights.

115. C   Each of the co-borrowers on a loan will be held jointly and severally liable.

116. C   A title company would be most interested in the chain of title when issuing a standard title insurance policy.

117. C   A survey of the property is not one of the normal procedures when issuing a standard coverage policy.

118. D   An "abstract of title" is the written summary of the chain of title.

119. B   A preliminary title report will show the existing loan with Dolores as trustor.

120. D   Most buyers of homes get a standard title insurance policy

121. C   Neither a standard policy nor an ALTA policy protect against zoning.

122.	D	The standard title policy insures against a recorded deed that was not properly delivered and/or accepted. The other choices are only covered by an extended title policy.
123.	C	Interest on unsecured loans will not be prorated at close of escrow.
124.	D	An estate in fee is another name for the fee simple estate, estate of inheritance, or perpetual estate.
125.	A	A minor may acquire real property by gift or inheritance without court approval.
126.	B	The escrow officer must let the buyer and seller decide which termite report to use.
127.	C	When the land contract was recorded, it became part of the public record. There is a cloud on the title until something is done to have it removed.
128.	C	The transferor (seller) of four or less residential units must deliver the "transfer disclosure statement" to the transferee (buyer).
129.	C	For residential income property, any property purchased or capital improvements made after 1986 must be depreciated by the straight line method over a minimum of 27.5 years.
130.	D	Once recorded, a lis pendens is effective as long as the litigation is pending.
131.	B	A bilateral contract requires a promise given in exchange for another promise. This clause is the broker's exchanged promise to the seller.
132.	B	A voidable contract is valid until it is rescinded (voided).
133.	C	A contract has been executed when it has been completely and fully performed.
134.	C	Payment of money is not required for the validity of a contract. Promises can be the consideration.
135.	B	Most contracts do not require "writing."
136.	C	A contract which is not to be performed within one year of its making must be in writing in order to be enforceable under the Statute of Frauds.
137.	A	All contracts must have been offered and accepted in order to be binding.
138.	D	The broker may not seek specific performance from the principal. The broker's remedy is to sue for damages.
139.	B	An agent who is the exclusive agent for the buyer may present offers to the seller and/or the seller's agent.
140.	D	The agent may accept a postdated check from a buyer as deposit, but he must disclose this to the seller when presenting the offer.
141.	D	Licensees who make misrepresentations are subject to discipline, civil lawsuits, and or criminal penalties.
142.	C	The developer must disclose that attendance at a sales presentation is required.
143.	C	In the quantity survey method, an appraiser computes the cost of each component of a building and adds in the cost of labor, overhead, and profit.
144.	A	An agent may pay part of the commission to the buyer if he informs the seller.

145. D A "blind ad" is an ad that does not identify the broker.

146. D Increasing the population density and home sale turnover rate would tend to destabilize a residential neighborhood.

147. C A broker must keep a client's money separate from the broker's money. A trust account helps accomplish this goal.

148. D Any employee of the broker may make withdrawals from the client trust account, if authorized to do so by the broker.

149. D A license is suspended until the Real Estate Education, Research, and Recovery Account (REERRA) has been paid back, plus interest.

150. D This would be both "panic peddling" and "blockbusting."

Salesperson Exam Practice #3

1. Each of the following is considered personal property, **except**: (A) a corn crop prior to harvest; (B) oranges that have not been picked, but which have been sold under contract; (C) stock in a mutual water company; (D) gold which has been mined.

2. A riparian owner owns land which borders on: (A) a stream; (B) a lake; (C) the ocean; (D) any of the above.

3. An "estate" in real property is held by which of the following? (A) a trustee; (B) a beneficiary; (C) a life tenant; (D) none of the above.

4. The zoning for a subdivision said that each lot must contain a minimum of 15,000 square feet. The deed restrictions said that each lot must contain a minimum of 10,000 square feet. Which would control? (A) the most recent restriction; (B) deed restrictions; (C) zoning; (D) whichever restriction was created first.

5. Mary owns one parcel of land and is trying to show that exceptional circumstances exist which justify using the land in a way which is prohibited by current zoning laws. Her intended use would not be detrimental to the public. She would probably petition the planning commission for a: (A) rezoning agreement; (B) variance; (C) building permit; (D) redevelopment permit.

6. All of the following statements about covenants and conditions are false, **except:** (A) the violation of a covenant results in the loss of title; (B) a violation of a condition can result in the loss of title; (C) covenants and conditions must be for the benefit of the general public; (D) private covenants and conditions are usually enforced by local government.

7. The best way for the Federal Reserve Board to create a tight money market would be to: (A) sell government bonds; (B) lower the discount rate; (C) raise the discount rate and sell government bonds; (D) lower the discount rate and buy government bonds.

8. Copies of termite reports filed with the Structural Pest Control Board within the preceding two years can be obtained upon request and the payment of a fee by: (A) the seller involved in the transaction; (B) the buyer involved in the transaction; (C) any unlicensed person; (D) any of the above.

9. In the cost approach to appraisal, the phrase "reproduction cost" is different from "replacement cost" in that "replacement cost" measures: (A) the original cost to replace the building; (B) the original cost; (C) the present cost using utility; (D) the present cost to build an exact replica.

10. When a vendee in a land contract is paying the vendor impounds for taxes and insurance, those payments may not be disbursed for any other purpose without the consent of the: (A) trustee; (B) beneficiary; (C) vendor; (D) payor.

11. A "plot plan" is used by a builder for the purpose of: (A) showing the subcontractors what materials to used; (B) showing the details of the electrical wiring inside a structure; (C) showing placement of construction and related land improvements; (D) showing front and side views of homes in a subdivision.

12. When an appraiser arrives at the value of an income property by considering the income produced and the percentage rate of return which can reasonably be expected to be earned on the investment, she is applying a process called: (A) market data approach; (B) gross multiplier method; (C) capitalization approach; (D) cost approach.

13. If an investor were to restore a property to a former or improved condition without changing the plan, form, or style of the building this would be described as: (A) remodeling; (B) replacement; (C) reproduction; (D) rehabilitation.

14. What would be the total property value of a four unit apartment building if each unit rented for $206.25 per month, vacancies were 5% of gross rents, annual operating expenses were $4,140, and the net income represented an 8% capitalization rate: (A) $65,812.50; (B) $68,400; (C) $71,484; (D) $72,000.

15. When land is divided into districts according to use by police power, this is called: (A) zoning; (B) districting; (C) empowering; (D) eminent domain.

16. Which of the following would be defined as a fixture in the law? (A) a built-in stove in a mobile-home; (B) area rugs in a home; (C) crops after harvest; (D) something incorporated into the land.

17. What is a quiet title action? (A) purchasing property for a secret buyer; (B) a court action to remove a loud neighbor; (C) a foreclosure lawsuit; (D) a court suit to remove a cloud on the title.

18. Upon moving into the home he had just purchased, Mr. Jones discovered that his neighbors garage was four feet over on his property line. If a friendly settlement cannot be negotiated, Mr. Jones should: (A) sue the Real Estate Commissioner; (B) sue the neighbor; (C) sue the agent, for failure to disclose the encroachment; (D) sue the title company, that had issued a standard CLTA title insurance policy.

19. In typical economic times, investors who make long-term investments: (A) have less risk than those who make short-term investments; (B) have the same amount of risk as those who make short-term investments; (C) have more risk than those who make short-term investments; (D) have the best answer to worries about inflation.

20. Withdrawals from the real estate broker's client trust account can be made by the broker or by which of the following people, when authorized by the broker? (A) only salespeople in the broker's employ; (B) anyone employed by the broker; (C) only corporate officers; (D) anyone, when authorized by broker.

21. Which of the following is a violation of fair housing laws? (A) the landlord requires every tenant have a good credit rating and a steady source of income; (B) the landlord requires all tenants to furnish references from their previous landlords; (C) the landlord requires a cosigner exclusively for tenants who are single; (D) a landlord that requires all tenants pay first and last month's rent in advance.

22. Which of the following forms of ownership would commonly be subject to double taxation? (A) a partnership; (B) a corporation; (C) a joint tenancy; (D) community property.

23. In appraising real property, a separate site analysis is considered least important: (A) for calculating depreciation; (B) for applying the income approach; (C) when applying gross rent multiplier; (D) when applying the cost approach.

24. The "R-value" of insulation stands for its: (A) texture; (B) resistance to heat flow; (C) cost; (D) none of the above.

25. The United States Attorney General would likely act to enforce the Federal Open Housing Law when: (A) state officials fail to act; (B) a conspiracy exists to practice resistance to the Federal Fair Housing Law; (C) a complaint is filed with the Supreme Court; (D) the discrimination involves more than ten units.

26. When a lender makes a loan without a down payment and without a government guarantee, the lender would be best protected by: (A) a high unemployment rate; (B) low monthly payments; (C) a poor economy; (D) appreciation.

27. An owner of an apartment building is considering an extensive modernization program. In making his decision, he should put the most emphasis on: (A) cost; (B) history of vacancy; (C) potential increase in real property taxes; (D) net effect on income.

28. The recording of documents related to real estate transactions will accomplish all of the following, **except**: (A) give constructive notice of the contents of the documents to persons who have not searched the records; (B) give actual notice of the content of the documents to third parties who may be effected by the documents; (C) help title insurance companies maintain their title plants; (D) create a presumption of delivery of the transfer instrument.

29. The security of a trust deed may be impaired if: (A) the trust deed is recorded after a homestead; (B) a lis pendens is recorded after the trust deed is recorded; (C) a judgment lien is recorded after the trust deed is recorded; (D) it is recorded after work of improvement had commenced on the property.

30. When rent is based on a portion of the gross receipts of a business, the lease is called: (A) a gross lease; (B) a net lease; (C) a percentage lease; (D) a fixed lease.

31. Property can be transferred in all of the following ways, **except**: (A) court order; (B) public grant or dedication; (C) eminent domain; (D) executive sale.

32. Under federal income tax law, the "basis" of real property is the property's: (A) purchase price minus any existing assumed loans; (B) assessed value prior to sale; (C) fair market value; (D) cost.

33. Bob paid $4.40 per square foot to purchase a rectangular parcel of land containing 20,000 square feet. The land was 200 feet deep. What was the cost per front foot? (A) $222; (B) $440; (C) $880; (D) $1,000.

34. Property taxes are described as "ad valorem" taxes. "Ad valorem" most nearly means: (A) market value; (B) replacement value; (C) reproduction value; (D) according to value.

35. Under California law, when property taxes have not been paid real property is sold to the state on June 30. The most important aspect of this sale is that it: (A) starts the running of the redemption period; (B) gives notice to the owner that he must vacate the property with 180 days; (C) allows anyone to buy the property at that time by paying the back taxes plus interest; (D) all of the above.

36. Prepaid rent received by a landlord is treated as taxable income: (A) in the year collected; (B) only if it is actually applied toward rent in a later year; (C) only if it is for trade or business property; (D) none of the above.

37. A "water table" is defined as: (A) a chart showing water quality; (B) the depth at which water is found; (C) the speed of moving water; (D) a measurement of water.

38. What is a commercial acre? (A) any combination of 43,560 square feet; (B) any acre in an area zoned for commercial use; (C) an acre plus the space taken up by streets, alleys, sidewalks, etc.; (D) an acre minus deductions for streets, alleys, sidewalks, etc.

39. When title to real property passes by accession, the recipient receives title as the result of: (A) a valid deed; (B) a valid will or intestate succession; (C) the principal action of natural waters through accretion; (D) none of the above.

40. Certain sides of business streets are preferred by merchants because pedestrian traffic seeks the shady side of the street. The least desirable sides of the street are: (A) south and east; (B) south and west; (C) north and west; (D) north and east.

41. Generally, franchisors raise most of their funds from: (A) real estate investment trusts; (B) federal and state franchise loan programs; (C) financing from lenders, together with money from the sale of stock and service fees from franchisees; (D) public investment trusts and endowments.

42. When appraising the value of an older building using the replacement cost method, the appraiser would calculate all of the following, **except**: (A) cost to build improvements new; (B) the value of the land; (C) an appropriate capitalization rate; (D) accrued depreciation.

43. A percolation test is used to determine: (A) the topography of the land; (B) whether or not the house is in an earthquake zone; (C) capacity of soil to absorb water; (D) the quality of a coffee maker.

44. A buyer agreed to buy a home for $210,000. She deposited $6,000 into escrow. A lender agreed to lend 80% of the appraised value of $200,000, additionally, the settlement costs to be charged the buyer amount to 3% of the purchase price. How much additional money must the buyer deposit into escrow prior to closing? (A) $25,000; (B) $40,300; (C) $50,300; (D) there is insufficient information to arrive at an answer.

45. The first step of the appraisal process is to: (A) define the problem; (B) set the appraisal fee; (C) plan the appraisal; (D) look up comparable sales.

46. When using the market data approach, if a comparable property has a feature that is not present in the subject property, the value of that feature will be: (A) ignored since no two properties have identical features; (B) identified in the report and adjusted for inflation; (C) subtracted from the sales price of the comparable; (D) added to the sales price of the subject property.

47. "Backfill" used in construction can be described as: (A) soil to be used for planting; (B) cement used to cover a patio; (C) soil used to fill in excavations or brace foundation walls; (D) dirt used to re-grade a lot.

48. Fee schedules setting forth the cost of title policies and other services performed by title companies are set by the: (A) Department of Insurance; (B) Department of Real Estate; (C) title insurance companies; (D) Department of Corporations.

49. Which of the following factors are not considered a cause of obsolescence? (A) misplaced improvements; (B) obsolete equipment; (C) change of flight pattern at an airport; (D) wear and tear.

50. A valid written lease must include: (A) agreement to let and take; delivery and acceptance; (B) term, consideration and description of the premises; (C) a landlord and tenant with the legal capacity to enter a binding contract; (D) all of the above.

51. An appraiser who uses improper methods to appraise a property for a government backed loan may be guilty of: (A) violating appraisal ethics; (B) violating real estate licensing law; (C) a felony; (D) a misdemeanor.

52. In appraising income-producing property by the capitalization approach, if the property taxes go up $1,000 and all else remains equal, the property value will: (A) increase exactly $1,000; (B) increase more than $1,000; (C) decrease exactly $1,000; (D) decrease more than $1,000.

53. The major cause of loss of value in real property is due to: (A) wear and tear; (B) obsolescence; (C) deferred maintenance; (D) old age.

54. A high energy efficiency ratio (EER) on an air conditioning unit means: (A) the unit is more efficient; (B) the unit is less efficient; (C) the unit needs more electricity per BTU produced; (D) air conditioners do not use energy efficiency ratios.

55. When appraising real property by the income approach, the money invested in the improvements is recaptured by: (A) the unit-in-place method; (B) the cost-to-cure method; (C) a tax deduction in the year incurred; (D) accruals for depreciation.

56. Capitalization rates must provide for a return on, and a return of, the investment in an improvement. This is provided for by means of: (A) interest rates; (B) monthly savings; (C) depreciation methods; (D) principal investments.

57. An appraiser's narrative appraisal report of a single-family residence probably would contain no reference to: (A) the appraiser's qualifications; (B) the neighborhood amenities; (C) a special studies zone map; (D) a buyer's financing.

58. "Joist" is a construction term which means: (A) foundation; (B) conduit; (C) footing; (D) parallel beam.

59. A prospective buyer obtained a three-month option on a parcel of real property by paying $300 to the owner. All of the following are true, **except**: (A) the option is a unilateral contract; (B) the optionor is totally restricted by having received "valuable" consideration with the option; (C) the option imposes no obligation on the optionee to buy the property; (D) the optionee has created a legal interest in the property.

60. What is the basis of the market data approach to appraisal? (A) the principle of highest and best use; (B) the principle of substitution; (C) the principle of supply and demand; (D) the principle of conformity.

61. How many townships are in a ranch which is 36 miles square? (A) 12; (B) 18; (C) 24; (D) 36.

62. Which of the following statements is most correct? (A) property is deeded to the state on July 1, if the property taxes for the prior year were not paid; (B) the delinquent property taxpayer must make monthly payments to the state during the statutory redemption period; (C) the real effect of a "sale to the state" by the tax collector is to start the redemption period running, but the delinquent owner remains in possession for five years; (D) the property is automatically deeded to the state if the property is not redeemed within the first three years.

63. When Carr conveyed to Jim a portion of his fee estate for a term less than his own, Carr's interest would be identified as a: (A) fee defeasible; (B) vested severance; (C) reversionary interest; (D) leasehold.

64. What is usually considered to be the most crucial factor in planning a subdivision? (A) an accurate site analysis; (B) an accurate analysis of the community facilities; (C) an accurate market analysis; (D) an accurate construction analysis.

65. When the owner of a property believes that her property has been over-assessed by the county assessor, she should contact the: (A) State Controller's Office; (B) County Board of Supervisors; (C) Assessment Appeals Board; (D) County Tax Collector's Office.

66. Mike owns a 20-unit apartment building. He reports his income on a cash basis, therefore, he can deduct all of the following for tax purposes, **except**: (A) loss of income due to vacancies; (B) depreciation of improvements; (C) interest payments on the third trust deed; (D) the cost of painting three units.

67. The purpose of the property tax assessment roll is to: (A) set the tax rate; (B) establish the tax base; (C)   establish the actual tax amount; (D) average out the assessed values.

68. A prospective purchaser is interested in buying a lot in the desert from a subdivider. The buyer wishes to know about sewer assessments, liens, and utilities to his lot, blanket encumbrances, and maintenance of streets. The best source of this information is the: (A) county engineer; (B) Real Estate Commissioner; (C) county planning commissioner; (D) title insurance company.

69. The proper method to enforce private property restrictions on real property is: (A) an attachment lien; (B) an injunction; (C) an execution lien; (D) a desist and refrain order.

70. Which of the following would not be considered an appurtenance? (A) trees; (B) a trade fixture; (C) a house; (D) a swimming pool.

71. Recording a judgment gives what type of notice? (A) actual notice; (B) constructive notice; (C) incomplete notice; (D) no notice.

72. The impounding of purchase money, commonly required by the Commissioner when approving new subdivisions for sale, is primarily for the protection of: (A) the buyer of a lot in the subdivision; (B) the construction lender; (C) the builder; (D) the Real Estate Commissioner.

73. Who usually has responsibility for providing streets, utilities, sidewalks, and curbs in a new subdivision? (A) the county; (B) the city; (C) the builder/developer; (D) the local office of building and safety.

74. Real property in the State of California is assessed at: (A) 1% of the assessed value; (B) 10% of the taxable value; (C) 25% of the assessed value; (D) 100% of the taxable value..

75. In its broadest definition, the authority of local, state, and federal governments to regulate the use of or to purchase private property in order to achieve planning goals, is derived from: (A) escheat; (B) zoning; (C) condemnation power; (D) police power.

76. An abstract of judgment once recorded, creates: (A) an attachment lien; (B) a voluntary lien; (C) an involuntary lien; (D) an abstract lien.

77. A short form appraisal report includes all of the following information, **except**: (A) description of the site improvements; (B) an accurate market analysis; (C) a site analysis; (D) loans and financing terms.

78. When two properties are identical or highly similar, most buyers focus on lower price. This principle is called: (A) substitution; (B) highest and best use; (C) productivity; (D) diminished use.

79. A broker acting as agent for a principal has as much authority as: (A) other parties believe the agent to possess; (B) the agent chooses to accept; (C) the principal actually or ostensibly confers upon him; (D) he chooses to accept as limited by the statute of limitations.

80. Which of the following would be least likely to include a legal description of a parcel of real estate? (A) a grant deed; (B) a property tax bill; (C) escrow instructions; (D) a preliminary title report.

81. A farm measures 1/2 mile by 1/2 mile. How many acres does the farm contain? (A) 20 acres; (B) 40 acres; (C) 160 acres; (D) 320 acres.

82. In order to exist, an easement must: (A) be visible; (B) be recorded; (C) have a dominant tenement; (D) have a servient tenement.

83. Which of the following is not essential to the creation of an agency relationship: (A) consent of the principal; (B) competency of the principal; (C) a fiduciary relationship; (D) agreement to pay consideration.

84. When a real estate agent acts exclusively as a buyer's agent, he can do all of the following, **except**: (A) present offers directly to the seller; (B) present offers to the seller and seller's agent; (C) withhold confidential information about the buyer from the seller; (D) act as an exclusive agent of the seller.

85. Mrs. Smith listed a house with Broker Bob for $250,000. Mr. Jones submitted an offer of $210,000, with the offer to expire in three days. The next day, Mrs. Smith made a counter-offer with the sale price to be $230,000. When informed of the counter-offer, Mr. Jones would not accept it. Three days later, Mrs. Smith delivered to Broker Bob a signed acceptance of Jones' original $210,000 offer. When Broker Bob told Mr. Jones of Mrs. Smith's acceptance, Mr. Jones told him he had decided not to buy the property. Which of the following is true? (A) there is a valid contract; (B) there is a voidable contract; (C) there is a void contract; (D) there is no contract.

86. The homeowner can deduct all of the following costs for his primary residence each year on his federal tax return, **except**: (A) an uninsured casualty loss ; (B) local real property taxes; (C) painting the living room; (D) the portion of his monthly mortgage payment attributable to the payment of interest.

87. A rectangular parcel of land has an area of 540 square yards. It has a 45-foot frontage. How deep is the lot? (A) 60 feet; (B) 108 feet; (C) 1,080 feet; (D) 200 yards.

88. Which method of appraisal would a licensee most likely use to appraise a restaurant? (A) market data approach; (B) cost approach; (C) income approach; (D) any of the above.

89. In a real estate transaction, the term "reversion" would most nearly mean: (A) the interest held by the landlord in property which has been leased; (B) the interest held by the life tenant in a life estate; (C) the interest of a beneficiary under a trust deed; (D) the right of the state to acquire property by condemnation.

90. The buyer of a home was not informed that the house was on a septic tank system. The buyer has the right to: (A) sue the broker for his license; (B) rescind the contract; (C) sue the title company for failure to discover the problem; (D) remain silent.

91. What listing requires an owner to pay a commission, even though she sells the property herself? (A) exclusive right to sell listing; (B) exclusive agency listing; (C) open listing; (D) net listing.

92. Which of the following is the largest parcel? (A) 2 miles square; (B) 3 sections; (C) 6% of a township; (D) 2 miles by 1 mile.

93. Mr. Nelson made a written offer to purchase a home through Broker Starr. However, Nelson died in a car accident before Broker Starr could notify him of an unqualified, signed acceptance by the seller. Which of the following statements is most correct? (A) the death of Nelson constituted a revocation of the offer; (B) the acceptance does not have to be communicated to the buyer; (C) notification of acceptance to the executor would bind the Nelson estate; (D) the contract would not be binding because the deed had not been delivered into escrow.

94. Which of the following professions commonly use a benchmark? (A) an appraiser; (B) a surveyor; (C) a carpenter; (D) an assessor.

95. When a notice of default has been recorded on a trust deed, the borrower is given a period of time to reinstate the loan. During this time, the right of possession belongs to the: (A) trustor; (B) trustee; (C) beneficiary; (D) mortgagee.

96. The annual percentage rate (APR) is defined by the Federal Truth-in-Lending Law as: (A) the total of all costs which the borrower must pay to get the loan; (B) the total of only the direct costs of credit paid by borrower; (C) the total of only the indirect costs of credit which the borrower must pay; (D) the relative cost of credit expressed in percentage terms.

97. All of the following resulted directly or indirectly from the National Housing Act of 1934, **except**: (A) a method of allowing buyers to buy a home with a small down payment; (B) a method of insuring lenders against loss; (C) minimum construction standards; (D) maximum construction standards.

98. An acceleration clause is inserted into a note that is otherwise negotiable. Adding this clause: (A) makes the note nonnegotiable; (B) is required to be negotiable; (C) does not limit the negotiability of the note; (D) has no effect on negotiability, but also is of no benefit to the holder of the note.

99. Which of the following statements is most accurate concerning mortgage bankers? (A) they are regulated solely by federal law; (B) they never lend their own money; (C) they never make government backed loans; (D) they negotiate loans which are readily saleable in the secondary mortgage market.

100. Which of the following does not buy loans in the secondary mortgage market? (A) Federal Home Loan Mortgage Corporation; (B) Ginnie Mae; (C) Federal National Mortgage Association; (D) Federal Housing Administration.

101. The purpose of Regulation Z (Truth-in-Lending Law) is to: (A) control interest rates; (B) limit the annual percentage rate; (C) assure meaningful disclosure of credit terms; (D) limit consumer credit.

102. Reference to a monument in a legal description is usually considered to be less desirable because: (A) monuments are difficult to describe in writing; (B) monuments may be destroyed; (C) monuments may be hypothecated; (D) monuments are may not be mentioned in a recorded document.

103. The Federal Truth-in-Lending Law gives the borrower a 3-day right of rescission with which of the following loans? (A) a loan to purchase a duplex; (B) a loan to purchase land; (C) a loan to purchase a commercial building; (D) a loan to refinance the borrower's personal residence.

104. The unspecified maturity date on a construction loan, begins from what date? (A) from the date of construction begins; (B) from the date of the note; (C) when the money is placed in escrow; (D) from the date the escrow is formally closed.

105. When purchasing with FHA financing, a new buyer would normally do each of the following, **except**: (A) apply to a local FHA office for the FHA appraisal; (B) apply directly to a bank or savings and loan; (C) pay for mortgage insurance protection; (D) buy a home which conforms with FHA requirements and restrictions.

106. A primary effect of the deregulation of savings and loans has been: (A) there is now no governmental control of savings and loan associations; (B) there is no limit on the interest rate savings and loan associations can pay on money deposited with them; (C) savings and loans associations can only make home loans; (D) deposits in savings and loans have no government backing.

107. When a lender takes a deed in lieu of foreclosure from the borrower, the lender: (A) must get court approval; (B) must first obtain the written consent of all other lien holders; (C) will assume any junior liens; (D) none of the above.

108. The best investment hedge against inflation would be in: (A) saving accounts; (B) government bonds; (C) certificates of deposit; (D) equity assets such as real estate.

109. The measure of goods and services produced by the nation during any one calendar year is called: (A) national income; (B) gross domestic product (gross national product); (C) cost of living index; (D) national economic cycle.

110. "Equity" can be described as: (A) the difference between the value and the loans; (B) the owner's share of the total property value; (C) the initial down payment on the property; (D) any of the above.

111. The terms "index, net net net, and flat," are used to describe: (A) linkages; (B) leases; (C) rural land use; (D) freehold estates.

112. The usual ceiling height in a home purchased with FHA financing is: (A) 7-1/2 feet; (B) 8 feet; (C) 8-1/2 feet; (D) 10 feet.

113. The Truth-in-Lending Law allows borrowers a limited right of rescission. The time which is allowed for recession begins when the: (A) credit application is submitted to the lender; (B) lender gives loan approval; (C) loan documents are signed by the borrower; (D loan is funded by the lender.

114. The law of intestate succession is applied to the distribution of an estate when: (A) there is a holographic will; (B) there is no will; (C) some heirs are omitted from the will; (D) in any of these cases.

115. The purpose of a "release clause" in a mortgage is to: (A) allow a borrower to be released from liability; (B) release the title company from liability; (C) allow the release of some properties upon partial payment, when more than one property is used as security for the debt; (D) releases the lender from liability.

116. Before a title insurance policy is issued, the title insurance company examines various records affecting the title to the parcel. This is called the chain of title. It then develops a summary of the chain of title called: (A) a title guarantee; (B) an abstract of title; (C) a title insurance policy; (D) an acknowledgment of title.

117. The main purpose of "RESPA" (Real Estate Settlement Procedures Act) is to: (A) place a fixed limit on settlement costs in all real estate transactions; (B) place a fixed limit on settlement costs on residential property of four units or less; (C) standardize settlement services throughout the United States; (D) provide consumers with enough information to enable them to shop for settlement services.

118. Which of the following costs and fees are considered finance charges on the disclosure statement under the Federal Truth-in-Lending Law? (A) document preparation fees; (B) appraisal fees; (C) cost of title insurance; (D) assumption fees.

119. When an escrow is closed on the purchase of a home, the closing statements usually reveal that the seller has paid for certain items in advance, or may be in arrears in his payments on items which relate to ownership of that home. These items are usually prorated in escrow. All of the following would be prorated **except**: (A) homeowner's and fire insurance premiums; (B) property taxes and assessments; (C) interest and impounds on an existing loan which will be assumed by the buyer; (D) title insurance fees and nonrecurring fees.

120. Ace Escrow offers a $100 "referral fee" to any real estate agent who opens escrow during the month of May. Under the Real Estate Settlement Procedures Act (RESPA), such an offer is: (A) always permissible; (B) permissible only if both buyer and seller are informed; (C) not legal unless it is disclosed in the settlement statement; (D) not allowed under any circumstances.

121. A subordination clause in a loan works to the benefit of the: (A) trustor; (B) beneficiary; (C) trustee; (D) mortgagee.

122. If prices rise 20%, what has happened to the purchasing power of the dollar? (A) it has gone down 10%; (B) it has gone down 16-2/3%; (C) it has gone down 20%; (D) nothing, the purchasing power of the dollar is unchanged.

123. If a seller insists that a listing broker who is taking a listing discriminate against minority buyers, what should the broker do? (A) take the listing anyway, and hope it doesn't become a problem; (B) take the listing, but tell the seller that, as a real estate licensee, you may not discriminate; (C) refuse to take the listing and explain to the seller that his discrimination violates the law; (D) take the listing and assign it to a minority salesperson who works in the office.

124. A loan broker statement is more properly referred to as a: (A) mortgage loan disclosure statement; (B) regulation Z disclosure statement; (C) loan arranger's statement; (D) none of the above.

125. When a non-licensee performs acts for which a real estate license is required, the prosecution for violation of the law by the non-licensee is handled by: (A) the Real Estate Commissioner; (B) a deputy of the Department of Real Estate; (C) the District Attorney of the county in which the activity occurred; (D) the State Attorney General.

126. None of the following employees need a real estate license, **except**: (A) a clerical worker who only types sales reports for the agents in a real estate office; (B) a hostess at an open house who never tells the clients the prices, because all the information is contained in the data sheet she hands each client; (C) a resident property manager; (D) none of these people need a license.

127. Which of the following real estate disclosure laws went into effect January 1, 1987? (A) the Seller Transfer Disclosure Law; (B) the Agency Disclosure Law; (C) the California Lending Institutional Disclosure Act; (D) none of the above.

128. An offer said, "Seller to take back a second mortgage securing the note for $11,400, payable $240.00 or more per month, including interest at 7% per annum from May 15, 1989." If the first payment date on the second mortgage is June 15, 1989, how much of the regular payment will go to principal reduction? (A) $80.00; (B) $173.50; (C) $184.50; (D) $199.50.

129. The reciprocal of 8% is: (A) .125; (B) 1.25; (C) 12.5; (D) 125.

130. When a buyer withdraws an offer before the offer was legally accepted by the seller: (A) the seller may be entitled to one half of the deposit; (B) the broker may sue the buyer for specific performance; (C) The buyer is entitled to receive his deposit back; (D) the buyer may not legally withdraw an offer.

131. What is the general purpose of a building code? (A) assure utilization of skilled labor; (B) assure compliance with regulatory agencies; (C) provide minimum construction requirements; (D) guarantee cost effectiveness.

132. Mr. Buyer is considering purchasing an apartment property. He is given the following information by the agent: Listing price, $948,000; gross income, $143,000; expenses, $57,200; net income, $85,800. He wants an overall return of at least 8%. His agent should advise him in which of the following ways? (A) buy the property since the capitalization rate is approximately 1% greater than required; (B) buy the property since the capitalization rate is approximately 7% greater than required; (C) do not buy the property since the capitalization rate is approximately 5% less than required; (D) do not buy the property since the capitalization rate is approximately 1% less than required.

133. Broker Jane listed a home for sale for $100,000. Two weeks later she presented an offer that was 10% less than the listed price. The seller said he would accept the offer if Broker Jane agreed to reduced her 6% commission by 16-2/3%. If Broker Jane agreed, how much commission would she receive? (A) $2,000; (B) $4,500; (C) $5,000; (D) $6,000.

134. A real estate appraiser will determine the capitalization rate by: (A) band of investment; (B) summation; (C) market comparison; (D) any of the above.

135. The principal balance on a loan is currently $56,500. The scheduled monthly payment on the loan, including principal and interest, is $550. All of the payment goes toward interest, **except** for $43.85. What is the interest rate? (A) 9%; (B) 9-1/2%; (C) 10-3/4%; (D) 12-3/4%.

136. In which contract does one of the parties agree not to revoke? (A) exchange; (B) option; (C) open listing; (D) offer to purchase real property.

137. In construction terminology, the studs of an interior wall are supported by and rest on the: (A) i-beam; (B) joist; (C) soleplate; (D) sheeting.

138. Bruce bought a parcel of raw land in 2003 and subdivided it into four separate lots. Five years later, he sold each lot for $100,000. The adjusted basis for each lot was $20,000. Bruce's long-term capital gain on these transactions is: (A) $80,000; (B) $320,000; (C) $400,000; (D) $500,000.

139. When an appraiser is attempting to establish the value of a commercial building, in which of the following examples would changing economic conditions have the least impact on value? (A) cellophane manufacturing plant; (B) medical building; (C) computer electronics store; (D) automobile dealership.

140. Accession takes place when real property is acquired by: (A) will; (B) adverse possession; (C) quiet title action; (D) imperceptible addition of land by action of water through accretion.

141. A seller must provide a buyer with a real estate transfer disclosure statement in which of the following transactions? (A) a sale of a four unit residential building; (B) a bankruptcy sale; (C) a trustee sale; (D) a husband to wife transfer.

142. A residential purchase agreement says, "The seller will provide and pay for a structural pest control report on improvements and pay for corrective work, if any." The agent must be certain that the buyers receive a copy of the structural pest control report: (A) within 5 days of the date of the termite report; (B) within 10 days of opening escrow; (C) as soon as practicable before the close of escrow; (D) none of the above.

143. An easement may be created: (A) for the life of the grantor; (B) for a stated period of time; (C) for perpetuity; (D) for any of the above.

144. Joe sold his house to Mel, who did not record the deed, but moved in. Joe then sold the same property to Jane, who reviewed the county recorder's records, but did not look at the property. Joe gave Jane a deed, which she recorded. Which of the following would be true concerning title to the property? (A) Mel and Jane are co-owners of the property; (B) Jane now owns the property, because she recorded her deed and Mel did not; (C) Jane has recourse against Mel for failure to record; (D) Mel maintains title.

145. Scott executes a deed to Bob and records it. Later, Scott seeks to void the sale, claiming that there had been no delivery to Bob. Why will Scott lose? (A) Bob is in possession of the property; (B) delivery is presumed with recording; (C) a recorded deed is always valid; (D) recording establishes the priority of the deed.

146. A title company conducts a title search by searching the records of the: (A) county recorder's office; (B) county clerk's office; (C) federal land office; (D) all of the above.

147. Which of the following would have priority? (A) a first deed of trust recorded March 14, 1992; (B) a homestead recorded April 1, 1992; (C) as assessment lien for street improvement, recorded April 5, 1992; (D) an unrecorded mechanic's lien.

148. The added protection of an ALTA title insurance policy over a CLTA policy is in guarding against: (A) existing liens and encumbrances of record; (B) an invalid deed in the chain of title; (C) an error in the sequence of recording trust deed loans; (D) a dispute over property lines which would be disclosed by a survey.

149. Broker Sam took a listing providing for a 6% commission on the sale price of $300,000. A buyer offered the listed price, but failed to complete the transaction. The seller declared a forfeiture of the 3% deposit. A provision in the deposit receipt provides that the broker will receive half of the buyer's deposit in the event of the buyer's default. Under these circumstances, the broker is entitled to: (A) $1,125; (B) $2,250; (C) $4,500; (D) $9,000.

150. Loss of title results from: (A) erosion; (B) prescription; (C) accretion; (D) certiorari.

Salesperson Practice Exam #3 Answers:

1. C Stock in a mutual water company is always real property. Crops before harvest may be either real or personal property. Corn crops must be planted annually and are usually personal property. All corps mortgaged or sold prior to harvest, they become personal property. Minerals such as gold, when removed from the ground, become personal property.

2. A A riparian owner owns land touching moving water (a stream, watercourse or river). The water rights of a land owner adjacent to a lake or ocean are called littoral rights.

3. C A life tenant holds a freehold estate. A trustee receives the right to sell property in the event of a default on a trust deed, but does not have an "estate" in the property. The beneficiary (lender) has no estate in the property.

4. C Whichever restriction is most restrictive will control. In this case the zoning is more restrictive because larger lot sizes restrict the number of homes which can be built.

5. B When seeking an exception to the current zoning laws for one parcel of land, the owner must petition the planning commission for a variance.

6. B A violation of a condition can result in the loss of title.

7. C Raising the discount rate and selling government bonds would act to tighten the money supply. Lowering the discount rate and buying government bonds would act to increase the money supply.

8. D Anybody can obtain a copy of a structural pest control report filed within the last two years by paying a small fee.

9. C The "replacement cost" of a building is the present cost to build a comparable structure in terms of utility (comparable usefulness).

10. D The one paying the impounds (the payor/vendee) is the only one who can authorize a different expenditure of those impound funds..

11. C A plot plan shows the location of improvements, parking areas, and landscaping on the site.

12. C The capitalization approach divides the annual net income of the property by the expected rate of return on the investment (capitalization rate) to determine value.

13. D Rehabilitation is when the building is restored to a former or improved condition, usually without changing the plan, form or style of the building. Remodeling involves changing the design. Reproduction involves reproducing a duplicate building, not restoring the old building.

14. A (1) $206.25 x 4 x 12 = $9,900 Annual scheduled gross income;
(2) $9,900 x 5% = $495 loss due to vacancies;
(3) $9,900 - $495 = $9,405 adjusted gross income;
(4) $9,405 - $4,140 = $5,265 annual net income;
(5) $5,265 divided by 8% = $65,812.50 total property value.

15. A Zoning is an example of police power whereby land is divided into districts according to the use to which the land may be put.

16. D A fixture is something which has become attached or incorporated into the land and is now real property.

17. D Quiet title action is a court suit to clear up defects in or challenges to title, such as a cloud on title.

18. B A property owner would sue his neighbor to have an encroachment removed. The agent and Commissioner should not be held liable. The standard CLTA title policy does not include a survey and does not protect against an encroachment.

19. C Long term investments generally have a greater degree of risk. If interest rates and inflation increase, the investor would be locked into a low rate of return.

20. B Anyone employed by a broker who has authorization from the broker can make withdrawals from the trust account. If the employee does not have a license, the employee must also be bonded.

21. C Landlords may not require a co-signer for single tenants only.

22. B Ownership by a corporation be subject to double taxation.

23. C Gross rent multiplier determines value by multiplying gross income by a commonly accepted number. A separate site analysis would not be used.

24. B "R-value" measures the insulation's resistance to heat flow.

25. B The United States Attorney General has authority to enforce the Federal Fair Housing Law when there is evidence of a conspiracy to resist it.

26. D When property appreciates in value, the lender would then have some value in excess of the loan balance to cover foreclose expenses.

27. D The net effect on income is more important than the other factors.

28. B Recording of real estate related documents is a method of giving constructive notice, not actual notice, of the content of the documents.

29. D A mechanic's lien takes priority as of the time work first began or materials were first furnished. Therefore, the security of a trust deed recorded after work had commenced would be impaired if a mechanic's lien were filed.

30. C In a percentage lease, the rent is a percentage of the gross receipts of a business.

31. D There is no such thing as an executive sale.

32. D Under federal income tax law, the basis of real property would be what the current owner paid for it (the cost).

33. C (1) 20,000 square feet divided by 200 foot depth = 100 foot frontage
       (2) 20,000 square feet x $4.40 per square foot = $88,000 purchase price
       (3) $88,000 purchase price divided by 100 front footage = $880 per front foot

34. D "Ad valorem" is the Latin phrase for "according to value."

35. A The "sale to the state" merely starts the running of a five year redemption period. The owner gets to remain in possession for five years and can redeem it by paying the back taxes plus interest and penalties.

36. A Prepaid rent is reported as ordinary income in the year collected.

37. B Water table indicates the depth at which water is found beneath land.

38. D A commercial acre is the space left over after subtracting the area taken up by streets, alleys, sidewalks, etc., from a standard acre. Therefore, a commercial acre is always less than 43,560 sq. ft.

39. C Accession is the movement of land by the natural action of water or wind, resulting in the acquisition of title.

40. D The north and east sides of the street are the least desirable sides.

41. C Franchisors would normally raise money from loans, stock sales and franchise fees.

42. C Capitalization rate is not part of the replacement cost method.

43 C A percolation test is used to determine the capacity of soil to absorb water. You should certainly do this before installing a septic tank.

44. C (1) $200,000 x 80% = $160,000 loan amount
       (2) $210,000 - $160,000 = $50,000 total down payment
       (3) $210,000 x 3% = $6,300 settlement costs
       (4) $50,000 + $6,300 = $56,300 total of down payment and settlement costs
       (5) $56,300 - $6,000 (already in escrow) = $50,300

45. A An appraiser must first define the problem.

46. C In the market data approach to appraising, when the comparable has a feature missing in the subject property, the appraiser subtracts the value of the feature from the sales price of the comparable.

47. C Backfill is soil used to fill in excavations and to brace foundations.

48. C Fee schedules setting forth the cost of title policies and other services performed by title companies are set by the title insurance companies, not by state agencies.

49. D Wear and tear is a cause of physical deterioration. Misplaced improvements, obsolete equipment, and the change of flight pattern at an airport are causes of obsolescence.

50. D Each of the choices describes a necessary element of a valid lease.

51. C An appraiser using improper methods on a government appraisal is committing a felony.

52. D When expenses (taxes) go up, annual net income is reduced. A small reduction in annual net income creates a large reduction in value.

53. B Obsolescence includes both economic and functional obsolescence. Obsolescence causes more loss in value than the physical deterioration of choices A, C, and D.

54. A The energy efficiency ratio (EER) measures the efficiency of the air conditioner. The higher the EER, the more efficient the unit.

55. D Depreciation compensates the investor with a "return on" and "return of" money invested in improvements.

56. C In calculating capitalization rates, a factor for the depreciation of the improvement is figured into the return given the investor. This allows for a "return of" in addition to a "return on" the investment.

57. D Appraisal reports do not normally include information about financing.

58. D A joist is one on several parallel beams used to support ceilings and floors.

59. D An option does not create a legal interest in the property for the optionee.

60. B The principle of substitution is the basis of all appraisal theory to some extent. The market data approach applies this principle directly.

61. D 36 miles square means a square that is 36 miles on each side. Since a township is 6 miles on each side, there would be 6 townships on each side of the ranch. 6 X 6 = 36 townships.

62. C The real effect of a "sale to the state" by the tax collector is to start the redemption period running; however, the owner can remain in possession for five years.

63. C Carr (lessor) has granted a leasehold interest to Jim (lessee). Carr holds a reversionary interest in that the possession will revert to Carr upon termination of the lease.

64. C An accurate market analysis is critical if a profit is to be made.

65. C The Assessment Appeals Board is the correct agency to contact.

66. A A vacant unit generates no income to report, but is likewise not a deduction. The other expenses are deductible from income.

67. B The purpose of the tax assessment roll is to establish the tax base.

68. B The final public report issued by the Real Estate Commissioner would be the best source for information of this type.

69. B An injunction is a court order restraining a party from violating private restrictions. An attachment lien is where property is held pending the outcome of a lawsuit. An execution lien is a method of collecting a monetary judgment. A desist and refrain order can be used by the Real Estate Commissioner to halt a violation of the real estate law.

70. B Trade fixtures are the personal property of an owner of a business and therefore are not appurtenances.

71. B Recording gives constructive notice.

72. A The buyer of a lot in the subdivision benefits because an unethical builder might take the buyer's money without removing the lot from the blanket encumbrance.

73. C The builder usually has responsibility for installing these items in a new subdivision.

74. D Property is assessed at 100% of the taxable value or fair market value.

75. D In the broadest definition of the "police power" of government, local, state and federal governments can regulate the use of or purchase private property for the health, welfare, and safety of the general public.

76. C A recorded abstract of judgment creates an involuntary lien (money encumbrance) upon all real property of the debtor located in that county.

77. D The loans and financing terms are not usually included on the short form appraisal, the other items are.

78. A The principle of substitution says the buyer will not pay more for a property than other similar properties sell for in the area. Where two properties are similar, most buyers focus on the lower price.

79. C An agent has as much authority as his principal actually or ostensibly confers upon him.

80. B Property tax bills use an assessor parcel number, not a legal description. The other documents will contain a legal description.

81. C The farm is 1/4 of a section. A section contains 640 acres. 1/4 of 640 acres is 160 acres.

82. D All easements must have a servient tenement.

83. D Agency does not require consideration. A broker could act as an agent without getting paid.

84. D When the licensee is the exclusive agent of the buyer, he may not be the exclusive agent for the seller.

85. D A counter-offer terminates the original offer, so there is no contract whatsoever.

86. C The homeowner may deduct some uninsured casualty losses, property taxes, and interest payments on the home's mortgage. The homeowner cannot deduct maintenance expenses such as painting.

87. B (1) 540 x 9 (sq. ft. in a sq. yd.) = 4,860 sq. ft.;
       (2) 4,860 sq. ft. divided by 45 = 108 feet

88. C The income approach to appraisal is the best method to appraise a restaurant.

89. A "Reversion" indicates that one party's interest will revert, go back, to another. The right of possession will revert to the landlord.

90. B A septic tank is a material fact which must be disclosed. The buyer could rescind the contract.

91. A The broker gets the commission no matter who sells the property, if it sells during the term of the exclusive right to sell listing.

92. A Two miles square is a square which is 2 miles by 2 miles, containing 4 square miles. The other choices each contain less than 4 square miles.

93. A Death of the offeror constitutes a revocation of the offer. Legally, if the acceptance had been communicated to buyer before the accident, the contract would have been binding on his estate.

94. B A bench mark is a monument used by a surveyor to establish the elevation at a particular point on land.

95. A The borrower (trustor) has the right to possess the property during the reinstatement period.

96. D The annual percentage rate (APR) is the relative cost of the credit expressed in percentage terms. The total of the direct costs of credit which the borrower must pay is the definition of the finance charge.

97. D The National Housing Act of 1934 created the FHA, allowed buyers to buy with a small down payment; insured lenders against loss, and establish minimum, not maximum, construction standards.

98. C An acceleration clause allows the lender to call the loan upon the happening of a certain event. This benefits the holder of the note and does not limit negotiability. The loan can still be sold to another lender.

99. D Mortgage bankers are regulated by state law, sometimes lend their own money, and commonly make government backed loans. They typically structure loans for resale in the secondary mortgage market.

100. D The Federal Housing Administration (FHA) does not buy loans on the secondary market. The FHA insures loans in the primary mortgage market.

101. C Regulation Z (Truth-in-Lending Law) requires lenders to disclose the cost of credit in terms of annual percentage rate (APR) in order to assure a meaningful disclosure of credit terms.

102. B Monuments are not desirable in a legal description or land because monuments may be destroyed.

103. D A loan used to refinance owner-occupied residential property does include the 3-day right of rescission.

104. B The date of the note determines the maturity date on construction loans.

105. A A buyer does not apply to the FHA.

106. B Under deregulation saving and loan associations may pay any amount of interest on deposits.

107. C If a lender accepts a deed from the borrower in lieu of foreclosure, existing liens would stay against the property.

108.	D	Historically, equity producing assets such as real estate, are the best hedge against inflation.
109.	B	The measure of goods and services produced by the nation during any one calendar year used to be called Gross Domestic Product (Gross National Product).
110.	D	Equity can be used to describe any of the answers.
111.	B	The terms "index, net net net, and flat," are used to describe leases.
112.	B	The usual ceiling height in a home purchased with FHA financing is 8 feet. Note: the minimum ceiling height is 7-1/2 feet.
113.	C	The borrower usually has until midnight of the third business day after the promissory note is signed to rescind the agreement.
114.	B	The law of intestate succession is applied to the distribution of an estate when there is no will.
115.	C	When a blanket mortgage is used to secure a debt, there is a clause which will release some of the properties upon partial payment of the debt.
116.	B	An abstract of title is a summary of the records relating to the title of that particular property.
117.	D	The Real Estate Settlement Procedures Act requires certain disclosures be made to the buyer. This information would allow her to shop for settlement services when buying real property.
118.	D	Assumption fees are included in the finance charge. The other choices are not.
119.	D	Title insurance fees and nonrecurring fees are not prorated in escrow.
120.	D	According to RESPA, kickbacks for referral of services are not allowed.
121.	A	A subordination clause in a loan allows the borrower (trustor) to get additional financing. The holder of the loan (beneficiary or mortgagee) containing the subordination clause allows a later loan to take priority over his loan. This works to the borrower's advantage, not the lender's.
122.	B	Example: Six apples that used to sell for $1.00 now sell for $1.20 (20 cents each). The dollar which used to buy six apples now only buys five apples, a decrease in purchasing power of 1/6 or 16-2/3%.
123.	C	The broker must refuse to take the listing and should explain to the seller that his discrimination violates fair housing law.
124.	A	A mortgage loan disclosure statement is also called a loan broker statement.
125.	C	The prosecution for violation of the law by the non-licensee is handled by the local District Attorney of the county in which the activity occurred.
126.	B	The hostess at an open house who hands out information sheets about the home must have a license.

127. A   As of January 1, 1987, sellers of one-to-four residential units must disclose defects to the buyer. This law is the Seller Transfer Disclosure law. (Note, the Agency Disclosure took effect January 1, 1988).

128. B   (1) $11,400 loan amount x 7% annual interest rate = $798 annual interest
(2) $798 annual interest divided by 12 months = $66.50 first month's interest
(3) $240 monthly payment - $66.50 first month's interest = $173.50 first month's principal

129. C   (1) To find the reciprocal of a number, you first convert it into a fraction (8% = 8/100).
(2) You then reverse the numerator and the denominator of the fraction (100/8).
(3) 100 divided by 8 = 12.5.

130. C   A buyer may withdraw his offer before acceptance by seller. The broker must return the deposit to the buyer.

131. C   The general purpose of a building code is to provide minimum construction standards.

132. A $85,800 divided by $948,000 = 9.1%. If he buys for the listed price he would have a return of 9.05%. Since he will settle for a 8% return, he should buy the property because the cap rate is approximately 1% greater than he is asking for.

133. B   (1) $100,000 x 10% = $10,000
(2) $100,000 - $10,000 = $90,000 (amount of the offer)
(3) 16-2/3% = 1/6 (memorize this)
(4) 6% reduced by 1/6 = 5% commission
(5) $90,000 x 5% = $4,500 commission to Broker Jane.

134. D   Capitalization rate is determined by: market comparison, band of investment, or summation (C.B.S.).

135. C   (1) $550 - $43.85 principal payment = $506.15 interest payment
(2) $506.15 x 12 months = $6,073.80 annual interest.
(3) $6,073.80 divided by $56,500 loan balance = .1075 = 10-3/4% interest rate

136. B   In the option contract, the optionor agrees not to revoke his offer to sell the property.

137. C   The studs rest on the soleplate.

138. B   (1) $20,000 x 4 lots = $80,000 adjusted basis
(2) $100,000 x 4 lots = $400,000 total selling price
(3) $400,000 - $80,000 = $320,000 capital gain

139. B   People get sick even when the economy slows down.

140. D   Accession is when title to land is acquired by accretion.

141. A   The transfer disclosure statement is required in the sale of one to four residential units, except when the sale is a bankruptcy, probate, trustee or husband/wife transfer.

142. C   The agent must be certain that the buyers receive a copy of the structural pest control report as soon as practicable before the close of escrow.

143. D   An easement may be created for the life of the grantor; for a stated period of time; or for perpetuity. Perpetuity means an easement may be created in such a way as to run for an indefinite period of time, possibly forever.

144. D   Although Mel did not record his deed, he took possession by moving-in. Possession of the property by Mel gives constructive notice. Since Jane recorded after Mel took possession, she had constructive notice of Mel's rights.

145. B   Recording a deed creates a legal presumption of delivery and acceptance. Scott will l lose the argument unless he can overcome this presumption.

146. D   All of these offices are searched by a title company when conducting a title search.

147. C   Government liens (assessment, property tax, etc.) may have priority over all other liens.

148. D   An ALTA policy includes a survey and would protect against a property line dispute.

149. C   (1) $300,000 x 3% = $9,000;
          (2) $9,000 divided by 2 = $4,500.

150. A   Erosion results in loss of title. Accretion is the addition of land by depositing, due to action of water.

Salesperson Practice Exam #4

1. Personal property is most commonly distinguished from real property in that personal property: (A) is always less valuable; (B) can become real property, but real property can never become personal property; (C) is generally immovable; (D) is generally movable.

2. What happens to the value of a parcel of land when the depth of that parcel increases beyond the depth of other lots in the area? (A) the value per front foot remains the same; (B) the value per square foot increases; (C) the value per front foot increases; (D) the total value of the lot decreases.

3. If a lease requires a tenant to pay certain expenses, such as taxes or insurance in addition to the rent, the lease may be called: (A) a gross lease; (B) a net lease; (C) a percentage lease; (D) a flat lease.

4. Private restrictions on real property can be created: (A) only by deed; (B) only by zoning; (C) by deed or by written agreement; (D) by deed, written agreement, or zoning ordinances.

5. Mr. Smith is the vendor in a land contract selling his home. One day, shortly after entering into the contract, he noticed that a plumber was installing new plumbing in the home. To protect himself, he should: (A) post a notice of completion; (B) record a notice of non-responsibility once the job has been completed; (C) post and record a notice of non-responsibility within ten days; (D) do nothing, since he has already sold the home.

6. The primary purpose of city building codes is to establish minimum: (A) ceiling heights; (B) fees paid to the city; (C) construction standards for buildings within the city; (D) sewer pipe diameters.

7. A real estate broker must hold all real estate documents for how long? (A) one year; (B) two years; (C) three years; (D) four years.

8. A "hard money" loan secured by a note and trust deed most nearly means: (A) a purchase money first trust deed; (B) a purchase money second trust deed; (C) a signature loan; (D) a cash loan.

9. A real estate salesman tried to obtain listings by warning owners that minority groups were moving into the area and values would decline. This behavior is: (A) not a violation of any legal or ethical standards; (B) grounds for discipline by the Real Estate Commissioner; (C) unethical, but not grounds for discipline by the Real Estate Commissioner; (D) standard practice and acceptable behavior.

10. Which of the following state agencies acts to prevent discrimination in housing accommodations based on race, color, sex, national origin, or ancestry? (A) Department of Housing; (B) Labor Commission; (C) Department of Fair Employment and Housing; (D) Real Estate Commission.

11. Why do brokers have client trust accounts? (A) in order to earn interest on client money; (B) in order to impress clients; (C) in order to commingle client's funds; (D) in order to separate trust fund money from the broker's money.

12. A broker who keeps a buyer's cash deposit in his office safe and refuses to release the money to escrow, the seller, or the buyer, is: (A) acting properly; (B) wrong in refusing to release the money to the seller, but acting properly when keeping the buyer's cash in his safe; (C) probably going to be subject to discipline by the Commissioner; (D) none of the above.

13. Property is technically defined as: (A) less than freehold estates; (B) things owned by buyers and sellers; (C) rights or interests which a person has in the thing owned; (D) fee simple absolute.

14. An appraiser determining the value of a commercial site would consider which of the following as the most important factor in determining value? (A) zoning; (B) accessibility to airports; (C) purchasing power of the community; (D) convenience of transportation systems for the labor force.

15. The Real Estate Commissioner would most likely issue a final public report even if the subdivision plan lacked: (A) copies of contracts used in the purchase of the lots; (B) subdivision maps; (C) finance documents; (D) proof of completion of community recreational facilities, even though financial arrangements to assure completion were provided.

16. In order to legally transfer fee estate to a parcel of real property encumbered by a trust deed, it is always necessary to do which of the following? (A) secure the consent of all lenders; (B) completely pay off all existing loans; (C) deliver a valid deed from the grantor to the grantee; (D) record a reconveyance deed from the trustee.

17. Carson purchased one of 40 lots in a subdivision and signed a contract which stated, "No owner of a lot in this subdivision shall put a 'for sale' sign on his lot until all of the lots owned by the subdivider are sold." If Carson wants to sell his lot before the subdivider has sold all of his lots, he may: (A) not use a "for sale" sign because of the statement in the contract; (B) use a reasonably sized "for sale" sign because the statement in the contract is illegal; (C) use a "for sale" sign of any size if he pays a fee to the developer; (D) be sent to jail for violation of the contract.

18. Who has primary regulatory responsibility for approvals under the Subdivision Map Act? (A) local city and/or county agencies; (B) the Department of Real Estate; (C) the Department of Labor; (D) the Federal Housing Administration.

19. The effective gross income found in the capitalization approach to appraisal, requires a deduction to be made for: (A) real property taxes; (B) repairs; (C) federal income taxes; (D) vacancies.

20. In the financing of real estate, the cash provided by the buyer as part of the purchase price, or by a tenant in real estate as an acquisition cost, is commonly known as: (A) commercial equity loans; (B) equity funds; (C) highly leveraged funds; (D) borrowed funds.

21. When real estate is sold, property taxes are set at: (A) 1% of the tax assessor's appraised value; (B) 100% of the tax assessor's appraised value; (C) 1-1/2% of full cash value plus an amount for the existing bonded indebtedness; (D) 1% of full cash value plus an amount for the existing bonded debt.

22. Mr. Brown purchased an apartment building for $1,000,000. The listed price was $1,200,000. Mr. Brown put $200,000 down and acquired a new first trust deed for the difference. Mr. Brown's cost basis for income tax purposes would be: (A) $200,000; (B) $800,000; (C) $1,000,000; (D) $1,200,000.

23. Which of the following federal entities would most likely be involved in buying and selling government securities in the open market? (A) the Securities and Exchange Commission; (B) the Federal Housing Administration; (C) the Federal Open Market Committee; (D) the Federal Truth-in-Lending Committee.

24. Depreciation, when taken, is subtracted from: (A) the salvage value; (B) the appraised value; (C) the cost basis; (D) none of the above.

25. The annual property taxes a property owner must pay are determined by: (A) assessing the land and improvements separately, then multiplying the total by one tax rate; (B) assessing the land and improvements together, then multiplying them each by different tax rates; (C) assessing the land and improvements separately, then multiplying by different tax rates; (D) none of the above.

26. Which of the following basic economic characteristics is the best expression of why real estate has inherent value? (A) maximum utility of available resources; (B) proximity to high rents; (C) possibility of speculative gain; (D) high replacement cost.

27. A real estate appraisal is valid for what period of time? (A) for the term of the loan; (B) a year; (C) as of a given date; (D) for any period of time.

28. Conditions of a sale will affect the: (A) highest and best use of the subject property; (B) demand for the subject property; (C) scarcity of the subject property; (D) price of a subject property.

29. When an appraiser refers to the "orientation" of a structure, he is describing: (A) the process of connecting adjoining structures together; (B) the amenities found in the structure; (C) the position of a building on land in its relationship to exposure to the sun, privacy from the street, prevailing winds, views, etc.; (D) none of the above.

30. A real estate licensee may handle the sale of a mobilehome when the mobilehome: (A) is new; (B) has been registered; (C) is 32 feet long; (D) is sold with a deed.

31. The word "tenancy" in real property law, most nearly means: (A) the method or mode of holding title to real property by lessee or owner; (B) the interest in property held by a life tenant; (C) the landlord-tenant relationship; (D) none of the above.

32. The upper limits of value are determined by which approach to appraisal? (A) market data: (B) reproduction; (C) income; (D) substitution.

33. The appraisal of real property is made as of a "given date" to indicate: (A) the true age of the improvement; (B) the market conditions influencing the value of the property at that point in time; (C) the date the price was agreed upon; (D) the loan balance as of a given date.

34. In arriving at an estimate of value, an appraiser is most interested in the date: (A) the purchase price was agreed upon; (B) the escrow was opened; (C) the escrow was closed; (D) the loan application was submitted.

35. The value arrived at by an appraisal of real property is: (A) based upon the reproduction cost; (B) based upon an analysis of facts as of a specific date; (C) income data covering the last five years; (D) based on new replacement cost.

36. Rental schedules for income property are established by: (A) market comparison; (B) cost of construction; (C) gross multiplier; (D) capitalization of annual net income.

37. Capitalization: (A) Establishes the value of an asset by dividing the annual net income by the desirable rate of return; (B) Is the effective interest return of and on an investment in a first trust deed; (C) Is based on gross income only; (D) Results in net asset value.

38. In the capitalization approach to appraisal, which of the following is not deducted to determine the annual net income? (A) maintenance expense; (B) management expense; (C) interest expenses on the loan; (D) vacancies.

39. The gross rent multiplier is arrived at by dividing: (A) net monthly rental by market value; (B) gross monthly rental by market value; (C) sales price by gross monthly rental; (D) sales price by annual net income.

40. The main reason that signatures on a deed are acknowledged is to make the deed acceptable for recording. A secondary reason for having the grantor's signature acknowledged is: (A) an acknowledged signature protects the grantee's rights in the property, even though the deed is not recorded; (B) an acknowledged deed may be accepted as prima facie evidence in court; (C) an acknowledged deed cannot be disputed by the courts; (D) acknowledgment gives constructive notice concerning the grantee's rights.

41. The square foot, cubic foot, and unit-in-place methods of real estate appraisal are most commonly used in what approach? (A) the market data approach; (B) the income approach; (C) the cost approach; (D) none of the above.

42. In the capitalization approach, when capitalization rates go up: (A) values go up; (B) values go down; (C) values are unchanged; (D) the money supply increases.

43. A roof which slopes or inclines on all four sides is called a: (A) gambrel roof; (B) gable roof; (C) hip roof; (D) flat roof.

44. Who has the right of possession of a home during the redemption period following a judicial foreclosure sale on a mortgage? (A) mortgagee; (B) beneficiary; (C) court appointed trustee; (D) mortgagor.

45. Sheet metal used to protect a building from water seepage is called: (A) sheeting; (B) gutter; (C) flashing; (D) none of the above.

46. The relationship between the thing desired and the potential purchaser is best defined as: (A) supply and demand; (B) value; (C) depreciation; (D) the present worth amortized.

47. While appraising a home an appraiser observes cracks in the foundation and notices that the doors and windows do not close properly. The appraiser would probably recommend that which of the following be ordered? (A) a termite report; (B) a soil engineer's report; (C) a special studies zone report; (D) a home warranty protection policy.

48. A "turnkey project" describes: (A) a planned unit development; (B) new construction which is ready for immediate occupancy; (C) a subdivision at the end of a long road; (D) a subdivision with high security standards.

49. Which of the following items would be warranted by the seller in a grant deed, but not covered by a standard policy of title insurance? (A) that there are no defects in the chain of title; (B) that the grantor actually signed the deed; (C) that there are no undisclosed liens against the property placed there by the grantor; (D) that the grantor is legally competent to convey title.

50. The first thing to do when appraising vacant land is to determine: (A) soil conditions; (B) the original purchase price; (C) the prices of recent sales in the area; (D) the highest and best use of the land.

51. What is shown on a plot map? (A) views of exteriors of homes; (B) location of the improvement on the lot and relationship to surrounding structures; (C) topography; (D) all of the above.

52. Each of the following is an example of functional obsolescence, **except**: (A) no air conditioning in a commercial building in a desert community; (B) the proximity of noxious fumes from an adjoining property; (C) obsolete or outlandish design; (D) improvements which have lost their functionality.

53. An "advance fee" contract must be approved in advance by the DRE and must include all of the following, **except**: (A) a complete description or the services to be rendered; (B) the total amount of the advance fee; (C) guarantees that the sale, lease or exchange will be completed; (D) the date the fee is to be paid.

54. The term "deciduous" describes which of the following? (A) the condition of the plumbing in an old structure; (B) a new style of wiring a home for cable television; (C) a type of soil condition; (D) trees which lose their leaves in winter.

55. In the capitalization approach to appraisal, which of the following would be subtracted from gross income to determine annual net income? (A) annual depreciation; (B) vacancies; (C) federal income taxes; (D) loan payments.

56. "Economic rent" is defined as the: (A) rent necessary to allow the owner to break-even; (B) rent the property would produce in a perfectly informed marketplace; (C) rent received under a contract; (D) rent received for comparable space in the current economic marketplace.

57. When comparing the economic life and the physical life of an improvement, the economic life is usually: (A) shorter than the physical life; (B) the same as the physical life; (C) longer than the physical life; (D) none of the above.

58. The method which is most commonly used to value land or sites is: (A) the residual method; (B) the developmental method; (C) the unit-in-place survey method; (D) the comparative method.

59. Which of the following do appraisers find most difficult to measure accurately? (A) capitalized income; (B) accrued depreciation; (C) comparable sales data; (D) new replacement cost.

60. The cause of depreciation which gives us the phrase "more buildings are torn down than fall down," would be described as: (A) wear and tear; (B) physical deterioration; (C) social obsolescence; (D) deferred maintenance.

61. An elevation sheet for a subdivision shows: (A) front and side views of the homes as they will appear when finished; (B) topography of the land; (C) interior views of the homes as they will appear when finished; (D) aerial views of the homes as they will appear when finished.

62. A standard policy of title insurance protects the insured against: (A) defects known to the buyer, but undisclosed to the insurance company; (B) the power of eminent domain; (C) lack of capacity of a party in the transaction; (D) zoning.

63. An investor purchased a home for $72,000, with a $20,000 down payment and financing the balance with a $52,000 straight note. The investor then sold the property for double the purchase price. If the investor had made no principal or interest payments on the loan, each dollar invested would now be worth: (A) $2.20; (B) $4.00; (C) $4.60; (D) $6.60.

64. The reciprocal of 12.5 is: (A) .8%; (B) 8%; (C) 80%; (D) 8.

65. When may a real estate broker, acting as agent for the seller, refuse to submit a buyer's offer? (A) when the owner has already accepted an offer; (B) when the owner has already accepted a better offer; (C) when the owner has given broker express instructions not to submit any further offers; (D) never, all offers must be presented.

66. The property tax rate is set each year by: (A) the city councils within the county; (B) the county board of supervisors; (C) the county tax assessor; (D) the county board of equalization.

67. Which of the following best describes an estate of indefinite duration? (A) a life estate; (B) an estate for years; (C) an estate of periodic tenancy; (D) an estate of inheritance.

68. When a broker takes an exclusive loan listing to negotiate a loan secured by real property, the listing is limited to a term of not more than: (A) 10 days; (B) 365 days; (C) 45 days; (D) 180 days.

69. A buyer purchased a home for $80,000 putting up a good down payment of 21.25% of the purchase price, and financing the balance on a 30-year amortized loan with interest at 10.25% per annum. The lender requires monthly impounds for property taxes of $800 per year and casualty insurance costing $978 for a three year policy. Assuming that the first monthly payment on the principal is $119, the total amount the buyer will have to pay the first month will be approximately: (A) $250; (B) $357; (C) $751; (D) $827

70. All of the following statements about a lis pendens are false, **except**: (A) only a court order may remove it; (B) it can be used in any lawsuit; (C) based on the outcome of the lawsuit, it may affect title to real property; (D) "lis pendens" means listen patiently.

71. An easement differs from a license in that a license: (A) must be in writing; (B) is assignable; (C) is an estate in the land of another; (D) may be revoked.

72. An attachment lien is good for: (A) 6 months; (B) 2 years; (C) 3 years; (D) 6 years.

73. An owner of an income property deducted $6,000 from the gross income for depreciation on his federal income tax return. His basis of the property is therefore: (A) raised by $6,000; (B) unchanged; (C) lowered by $6,000; (D) adjusted only when the property is sold.

74. When a piece of land is washed away by a flood or a dam giving way, this is called: (A) accretion; (B) alluvion; (C) avulsion; (D) erosion.

75. Who establishes deed restrictions? (A) the Master Plan of the city; (B) the planning commission; (C) the grantor in a deed; (D) zoning laws,

76. The major difference between mechanic's liens and judgment liens is: (A) judgment liens must be recorded; (B) judgment liens are voluntary liens; (C) mechanic's liens may take priority earlier than the date of recording; (D) mechanic's liens are statutory liens.

77. The action by which the city or county permits an owner to use property in violation of zoning or building codes is known as: (A) an exemption; (B) a variance; (C) an exception; (D) a permit.

78. Investors want to build an apartment house which will have a gross income of $2,500 per month and annual expenses of $6,000. The investors require a 12% capitalization rate on the investment. If the improvements cost $150,000, how much can the investors pay for the land? (A) $24,000; (B) $50,000; (C) $150,000; (D) $200,000.

79. The interest acquired in real property through adverse possession is different from the interest acquired by prescription in that the interest acquired by prescription is: (A) a legal title to the property; (B) an equitable title to the property; (C) the right to use land which belongs to someone else; (D) acquired by payment of taxes.

80. A seller sued an agent for making a false promise. In her defense, the agent proved that her listing contract to sell the seller's home was oral. What will the judge rule? (A) the Statutes of Frauds protects the agent; (B) the Statute of Frauds does not apply to listing contracts; (C) the seller is as much at fault as the agent, case dismissed; (D) the agent is liable for any damages as a result of the false promise.

81. Mrs. Johnson told Broker Bob, "While I will not sign a listing for my home, if you can find a buyer who will pay at least $250,000 for it, I'll pay you a 6% commission." Three weeks later, Broker Bob found a buyer who gave him a $1,000 deposit on the purchase price of $255,000, along with a signed offer to purchase. When the offer was presented to Mrs. Johnson, she accepted it and then demanded that the deposit be given to her. Which of the following is true? (A) once the offer is accepted, the deposit belongs to the seller, Broker Bob must give it to her upon demand; (B) Broker Bob may not give the buyer's deposit to the seller without the buyer's written consent; (C) because the listing was not in writing, Broker Bob is not obligated to follow the seller's orders; (D) Broker Bob should deposit the money into escrow and then let the escrow officer worry about it.

82. "Drywall" construction, uses all of the following, **except**: (A) fiberboard; (B) plywood; (C) gypsum board; (D) plaster.

83. How many square miles does a section contain? (A) 1; (B) 6; (C) 36; (D) 180.

84. Upon inspection, a pest control company finds no evidence of termite infestation. However, they do find conditions which may lead to infestation. Whose responsibility is it to pay for correcting these conditions? (A) the seller in all cases; (B) the buyer in all cases; (C) the seller and the buyer, each paying half; (D) the buyer, only if he chooses to have the condition corrected.

85. A buyer must bring a lawsuit for breach of written contract against a seller within: (A) 6 months; (B) 1 year; (C) 3 years; (D) 4 years.

86. On April 2 a buyer gave a broker a personal check as a deposit to accompany an offer. The buyer told the broker to hold the check uncashed until after April 15. What should the broker do? (A) the broker cannot legally accept the check; (B) the broker should present the offer and hope the seller does not ask about the check; (C) the broker should present the offer to the seller, but must tell the seller about buyer's instruction to hold the check until after April 15; (D) the broker should immediately deposit the check in his trust account.

87. Mr. Gray sold an apartment building for $137,000. This was 20% more than what he paid for it. His original cost was approximately: (A) $114,200; (B) $119,600; (C) $144,176; (D) there is insufficient information to arrive at an answer.

88. Harry sold two parcels of land for $9,430 which was 15% more than their cost four years prior. While Harry owned the parcels, he paid taxes each year at a rate of $8.00 per $100 on an assessed value of 25% of the purchase price. Assuming an annual loss of 5% imputed interest on Harry's original investment as an expense, how much did Harry lose on the transaction? (A) $650; (B) $885; (C) $1,066; (D) None of the above, because Harry made money on the transaction.

89. A contract obtained through duress, is: (A) good; (B) voidable; (C) void; (D) valid.

90. For a broker with a nonexclusive listing to be legally entitled to a commission, she must first prove that: (A) she was duly licensed at the time of the sale; (B) she found a buyer ready, willing, and able to buy; (C) she was the procuring cause of the transaction; (D) all of the above.

91. Which of the following loans is exempt from the Federal Truth-in-Lending Law on the basis of the type of loan itself? (A) an agricultural loan; (B) an FHA loan to buy a home; (C) a VA loan to refinance the veteran's home; (D) a $25,000 loan from a credit union for home improvement purposes.

92. Which of the following contracts must be in writing to be enforceable? (A) a lease for one year; (B) a listing to lease for one year; (C) an agreement by a buyer to assume an existing loan secured by a deed of trust; (D) an agreement between brokers to share a commission.

93. The usual listing contract authorizes a broker to: (A) find a purchaser and bind the seller to a contract to sell; (B) find a purchaser and accept a deposit with an offer to purchase; (C) guarantee prospective purchasers that the home is defect free; (D) convey the real property upon the receipt of a perfect offer.

94. A subdivision of new homes is encumbered by a blanket construction loan. As each of these encumbered homes are sold, the beneficiary should issue which of the following? (A) a request for partial reconveyance; (B) a reconveyance deed; (C) a partial reconveyance deed; (D) all of the above.

95. Which of the following contracts must be in writing in order to be enforceable? (A) a listing to sell a business opportunity; (B) a lease of real property for six months; (C) a listing to lease real property for one year; (D) an agreement which is not to be performed within one year of the making.

96. An investor paid $300,000 for an apartment building, making a $30,000 cash down payment. One year later, the property increased 10% in value. This resulted in a $30,000 or 100% gain on the $30,000 equity. This is an example of: (A) contribution; (B) escalation; (C) substitution; (D) leverage.

97. Which of the following advertisements would be permitted under the Federal Truth-in-Lending Law? (A) "assume a 7-1/2% annual interest rate mortgage..."; (B) "assume a 7-1/2% annual percentage rate mortgage..."; (C) "assume a 7-1/2% interest mortgage..."; (D) "assume a 7-1/2% annual rate mortgage...."

98. To earn $200 per month, the amount an investor would have to invest at 8% is: (A) $15,000; (B) $20,000; (C) $22,000; (D) $30,000.

99. An ad offering "secured" loans for sale would be regarded as misleading unless: (A) the ad was placed by a licensed loan broker; (B) each purchaser were offered a standard title insurance policy covering the encumbered properties; (C) the broker secured the borrower's signature on the loan broker statement; (D) the ad fully explained how and to what extent the funds would be secured.

100. When commercial banks consider "liquidity" and "marketability" of loans, they are referring to: (A) commercial property loans; (B) the discount rate; (C) the secondary mortgage market; (D) regulation by the Federal Reserve Board.

101. Who is usually responsible for providing streets, utilities, sidewalks, and curbs in a new subdivision? (A) the county; (B) the city; (C) the builder; (D) the local office of building and safety.

102. A seller in a land contract would not likely file a lawsuit based upon which of the following: (A) an agreement not to record; (B) damages; (C) specific performance; (D) any of the above.

103. Life insurance companies normally deal with borrowers through the services of: (A) banks; (B) savings and loans; (C) mortgage companies; (D) all of the above.

104. A buyer and seller initial the liquidated damages clause in a deposit receipt and then the buyer defaults. The deposit is: (A) given to the seller when escrow opens; (B) limited to 3% of the selling price; (C) divided equally between the seller and the listing agent; (D) used to pay any costs incurred and then returned to the buyer.

105. Under the Federal Truth-in Lending Law, the cost of credit is expressed as: (A) the annual interest rate; (B) the annual percentage rate; (C) the annual premium rate; (D) the monthly percentage rate.

106. A trust deed in the County Recorder's Office, refers to standard clauses contained in a previously recorded trust deed. The previously recorded trust deed is called a: (A) short form trust deed; (B) invisible trust deed; (C) fictitious trust deed; (D) primary deed of trust.

107. A mortgage loan disclosure statement must be given to the borrower: (A) within three days of receipt of a completed loan application or before the borrower is obligated to take the loan; (B) within two days of the time the borrower signs it; (C) within one week of the time the borrower signs it; (D) before the close of escrow.

108. All of the following tend to increase the available supply of real estate loan funds, **except**: (A) an increase in the national income; (B) an increase in deposits in savings and loans; (C) an increased demand for a investment liquidity; (D) an increased desire to provide for old age.

109. Which of the following would usually be true concerning a hard money second trust deed? (A) it always has a lower than normal interest rate; (B) it must always be repaid in 4 years; (C) it is seller financing; (D) it is secured by real estate and given to a third party to obtain a cash loan.

110. The property taxes on homes are determined annually by the: (A) county treasurer; (B) county assessor; (C) county board of supervisors; (D) state board of equalization.

111. Under the Federal Truth-in-Lending Law, which of the following does not need to be included in the "finance charge" portion of the disclosure statement? (A) loan arranger's commission; (B) the cost of a credit report and appraisal fee necessary to make the loan; (C) credit life insurance premiums; (D) the loan origination fees for FHA or VA loans.

112. Generally, as the employment rate and the GNP (Gross National Product or GDP - Gross Domestic Product) rise: (A) the personal income rises; (B) new residential developments will increase; (C) sales of existing homes will increase; (D) all of the above will probably occur.

113. Who sets the county property tax rate? (A) the state board of equalization; (B) the county board of supervisors; (C) the county tax assessor; (D) the governor.

114. Which cycle has the phases of "depression, expansion, prosperity, and recession?" (A) life; (B) mortgage; (C) real estate; (D) business.

115. If the current highest and best use of a parcel is expected to change, the current use is referred to as: (A) the interim use; (B) the temporary use; (C) the transitional use; (D) the possible use.

116. Jack wants to purchase Bill's property for $200,000 with a deposit of $40,000. He wants Bill to carry back a first trust deed on the property for the balance with payments of $1,290 or more per month. He wants the interest rate to be no more than 9% per annum. He wants to be able to pay off the loan at any time with no penalty. The finance terms portion of the deposit receipt should be completed in which of the following ways? (A) the buyer to deposit $40,000 in escrow and the seller to accept the balance at $1,290 per month; (B) the buyer agrees to execute in favor of the seller a note to be secured by a first trust deed secured by the property in the amount of $160,000, payable $1,290 or more per month including interest of 9% per annum; (C) it is hereby agreed that a first trust deed and note in the amount of $140,000 will be executed; the payment of this note will be $1,290 per month including interest; (D) the seller agrees to take back a note and second trust deed in the amount of $160,000, payable $1,290 per month including 9% interest per annum.

117. Which of the following would most likely provide an investor with the best hedge against inflation? (A) ownership of real estate: (B) United States savings bonds; (C) a passbook savings account at a bank; (D) trust deeds and mortgages held as an investment.

118. A subdivider is selling new homes, using land contracts for financing. The subdivider places into the contract a clause whereby the purchaser agrees not to prepay any part of the debt. Which of the following statements is true? (A) the vendee is bound by the clause; (B) the clause is binding on subsequent purchasers; (C) the vendee can disregard the clause; (D) the entire contract would be void because of the clause.

119. When a buyer buys property "subject to" an existing loan, rather than "assuming" the loan, the buyer will: (A) have any loss limited to his equity in the property should it go into foreclosure; (B) become a substitute trustor, in place of the seller; (C) eliminate the possibility of a trustee's sale; (D) will not lose the property if the debt goes unpaid.

120. No title insurance policy offers protection against: (A) legal expenses incurred in defending a title; (B) defects in the chain of title; (C) lack of capacity of grantor; (D) zoning.

121. The relationship between the parties to a real estate transaction and the escrow officer is usually described as which of the following? (A) independent contractor; (B) employee; (C) mediator; (D) agent.

122. Companies that issue private mortgage insurance (PMI) normally raise money from: (A) the Federal Reserve Board; (B) premiums earned on pooled insurance policies and stock or debt issue; (C) the Federal Savings and Loan Association; (D) the Federal Housing Administration.

123. Broker Barbara listed a home for sale for $400,000. The seller told her he would take anything over $350,000. Broker Barbara then found a buyer willing to pay $380,000, but instead of presenting the buyer's offer, she wrote up her own offer for $350,000, which the seller accepted. She then sold the home to the buyer for $380,000 without informing the seller. Such action would properly be classified as: (A) false promise; (B) secret profit; (C) commingling; (D) good business practice.

124. An agreement to sell community real property signed by only one spouse is: (A) enforceable; (B) unenforceable; (C) binding; (D) void.

125. Accretion would result in the acquisition of land by: (A) a prescriptive easement; (B) a neighbor who acquired land by natural causes; (C) the city government following a condemnation action; (D) none of the above.

126. Broker John took a listing on a commercial office complex and also received an option to purchase the property within 30 days. On the 28th day of the listing, John decided to buy the property. Before buying the property, he was required to: (A) disclose any outstanding offers; (B) disclose all material information to the seller; (C) obtain written consent from the owner which acknowledges any profit or anticipated profit; (D) all of the above.

127. A house sold for $345,000, which was 9% more than the cost of the house. The original cost of the house was most nearly: (A) $300,300; (B) $306,500; (C) $310,150; (D) $316,500.

128. Which of the following is necessary for a deed to be valid? (A) a granting clause; (B) consideration; (C) an acknowledgment; (D) the grantee is of legal age.

129. Under RESPA, the uniform settlement statement must be delivered: (A) five calendar days after the loan commitment is made; (B) three business days prior to the close of the transaction; (C) one calendar day prior to the settlement date; (D) at or before the settlement date.

130. Usually, an escrow officer is authorized to: (A) determine which financing is best for the buyer; (B) change the escrow instructions when asked to by the selling agent; (C) call for the funding of buyer's loan; (D) choose the pest control company.

131. Which of the following loans may be described as a "balloon loan?" (A) a partially amortized loan; (B) a fully amortized loan; (C) a non-assumable loan; (D) an adjustable rate loan.

132. Of the following, who would most likely pay for the mortgage insurance premium? (A) a purchaser of a home with a conventional loan from a savings and loan association; (B) a purchaser of a large commercial building; (C) a veteran who buys a fourplex using VA financing; (D) a homeowner who assumed an FHA loan.

133. If a broker delegates specific authority to a salesperson to supervise, review, and initial real estate contracts prepared by other salespersons, the delegated salesperson must have: (A) accumulated at least 2 years experience as a full-time salesperson during the preceding 10 years; (B) accumulated at least 2 years full-time experience as a real estate salesperson during the preceding 5 years; (C) been employed by the same broker for at least 5 years; (D) accumulated 2 years experience as a real estate salesperson and completed 2 years of college courses related to real estate.

134. Lenders commonly charge points to: (A) increase effective yields; (B) close the gap between fixed interest rates and market rates; (C) help defray the costs of the loan; (D) all of the above.

135. Each of the following would be subject to property taxes, **except**: (A) possessory interest of the lessee in oil, and gas rights in real property owned by the government; (B) a mobilehome installed on a permanent foundation system; (C) intangible personal property; (D) vacant land in an unincorporated section of the county.

136. When a seller of property allows the buyer to owe him a portion of the purchase price and charge zero interest, the Internal Revenue Code considers: (A) an interest rate of 12% to be imputed to the seller; (B) interest payments to be imputed to the seller and deductible by the buyer; (C) all payments made by the buyer to be deductible interest; (D) the entire amount paid as part of the purchase price with no deduction for interest.

137. "Kiosk" is a term used to identify: (A) an information booth in a mall; (B) a storage warehouse; (C) a bridge linking two parts of a shopping center; (D) a special type of crane, used in very tall construction.

138. Which of the following parties would be most likely to file an unlawful detainer court action? (A) a real estate broker enforcing a listing contract; (B) a defaulting trustor; (C) a subagent of the selling agent; (D) an offended lessor.

139. When a river suddenly changed course, it tore away a strip of land from the river bank. Such an event is called: (A) alluvion; (B) erosion; (C) avulsion; (D) accretion.

140. Title to personal property is transferred with a bill of sale. A valid bill of sale must: (A) be dated; (B) contain an acknowledgment; (C) have the seller's signature; (D) be verified and recorded.

141. Which of the following can be considered as a hidden cost of home ownership? (A) depreciation of land; (B) loss in value as a result of adverse zoning; (C) loss of interest on the owner's equity; (D) improvement appreciation.

142. All of the following are common types of misrepresentation, **except**: (A) innocent misrepresentation; (B) malicious misrepresentation; (C) negligent misrepresentation; (D) fraudulent misrepresentation.

143. An offer which is made contingent upon the buyer's first obtaining a satisfactory lease on another property is: (A) an illusory offer; (B) a valid offer; (C) a unilateral contingent offer; (D) unenforceable.

144. When preparing an appraisal of a home, how does the appraiser calculate the square footage of the improvements? (A) measure the interior dimension of each room; (B) measure the exterior dimensions of the structure; (C) multiply the length x the width x the height of the improvement; (D) appraisers never measure, they rely totally upon the tax assessor records.

145. A parcel of land which makes a 36 mile square would contain how many townships? (A) 1; (B) 18; (C) 36; (D) 72.

146. When prospective buyers of a home request a real estate broker's assistance in obtaining an FHA loan, the broker would most likely contact: (A) the Federal Housing Administration; (B) an FHA appraiser; (C) an institutional lender, such as a bank or savings and loan; (D) the Federal Reserve Board.

147. When does the cost of real property most likely equal its value? (A) in a neighborhood where there is a supply and demand imbalance; (B) when the improvements are new; (C) when improvements on the property represent the current highest and best use of the land; (D) when both (B) and (C) are true.

148. When deciding whether or not to make a proposed real estate loan, most institutional lenders try to minimize the: (A) lender's overall net yield; (B) loan-to-value ratio; (C) the borrower's difficulties which may arise in the future, such as a divorce or illness; (D) likelihood of a substandard loan becoming a part of their loan portfolio.

149. When a real estate auction is held, the auctioneer usually is acting as the agent for: (A) the buyer; (B) the seller; (C) the trustee; (D) none of the above.

150. When the student got every answer correct on the real estate salesperson exam, the California Department of Real Estate will assume: (A) the student cheated; (B) the test was too easy; (C) the student got lucky; (D) the student completed all the questions in the Real Estate Centre's Salesperson's Prep book.

Salesperson Practice Exam #4 Answers:

1. D Personal property is generally moveable; real property is generally immovable.

2. C The deeper the lot, the greater the front foot value. The value per square foot usually goes down.

3. B The net lease requires the tenant to pay certain expenses such as taxes, insurance or maintenance.

4. C Private restrictions are created by deed or by written agreement, not by zoning. Zoning is a public restriction.

5. C As vendor in a land contract, Mr. Smith has retained legal title to the home. He should post and record a notice of nonresponsibility within ten days of obtaining knowledge of the work to protect his interest from mechanic's liens.

6. C The primary purpose of city building codes is to establish minimum construction standards.

7. C All real estate documents must be kept three years. Note: If the question had asked about "loan documents," they must be kept four years.

8. D A "hard money" loan is a loan where the borrower receives cash using a new note, secured by a trust deed. Typically, when a home owner borrows against the equity in his home, he receives "cash in his hand." There are limits on the commissions and costs loan brokers can charge to negotiate such loans.

9. B Such behavior is called panic selling or block busting. It violates fair housing laws and would subject the licensee to discipline by the Commissioner.

10. C Housing complaints are submitted to the Department of Fair Employment and Housing under the Rumford Act.

11. D A broker uses a client trust fund account to separate clients' money from the broker's money.

12. C Once an offer is accepted, if the seller demands it, the broker must give the cash deposit to him. The broker also violated the law by placing the buyer's cash deposit in his safe, this is called commingling.

13. C The legal definition of property is the rights that a person has in the thing owned. It is called the "Bundle of Rights" theory.

14. C The purchasing power of the community would be the most important factor of those given. If a community has little purchasing power, the commercial business would do poorly in that locale.

15. D Contracts, maps, and finance documents must be submitted. The Commissioner would issue a final report even though community recreational facilities had not been completed, as long as there was proof that financial arrangements had been made to assure completion.

16. C Fee title can only be transferred with a valid deed. A valid deed must be delivered to be effective. The other choices are sometimes necessary, but not always.

17. B The courts have held that a prohibition of "for sale" signs is unconstitutional. However, the signs must be a reasonable size.

18. A Local city and/or county agencies have the primary regulatory responsibility for approvals under the Subdivision Map Act.

19. D In the capitalization approach to appraisal, scheduled gross income minus vacancies equals effective gross income.

20. B The cash provided by the buyer or by a tenant can be called "equity funds."

21. D Property taxes are set at 1% of the full cash value plus an amount to cover any bonded debt approved by taxpayers.

22. C For income tax purposes, the cost basis is the purchase price of the property.

23. C The Federal Open Market Committee of the Federal Reserve Board buys and sells existing government securities to control the money supply and inflation.

24. C Depreciation, when taken, is subtracted from the cost basis of the property.

25. A The land and improvements are assessed separately. However, one tax rate is applied to the total assessed value.

26. A Real estate has inherent value when it represents the maximum utility of available resources.

27. C The appraisal is valid as of the date of the appraisal only.

28. D Conditions of sale such as favorable financing or a forced sale would directly affect the price.

29. C Orientation refers to the location of an improvement on the land.

30. B A real estate licensee may handle the sale of a mobilehome once it has been initially sold and registered with the Department of Housing and Community Development.

31. A In real property law, "tenancy" is the method or mode of holding title to real property.

32. B The "reproduction" approach generally sets the upper limit on value.

33. B The appraisal of real property is made as of a given date to indicate the market conditions influencing the property at that particular point in time.

34. A The date purchase price was agreed upon is the date of valuation and would be of most interest to an appraiser.

35. B When appraising real property, the appraiser determines the value of the property as of a given date.

36. A Market comparison would be the best method of establishing rental schedules.

37. A Capitalization arrives at the value of an asset by dividing the annual net income by the desirable rate of return.

38. C Loan expenses, such as interest, are not deducted when calculating annual net income in the capitalization approach.

39. C Gross rent multiplier = sale price divided by the gross monthly rent.

40. B Once a deed has been acknowledged it is accepted as prima facie evidence in court.

41. C The first step of the cost approach is to determine replacement cost of improvements. This is done by the square foot, cubic foot, unit-in-place, or quantity survey methods.

42. B Values go in the opposite direction of capitalization rates.

43. C A hip roof slopes or inclines on all four sides.

44. D The mortgagor (borrower) remains in possession for one year after the court foreclosure sale on a mortgage.

45. C Flashing is the name of this sheet metal.

46. B This is a definition of "value."

47. B The cracking in the foundation and the shifting of the house would probably be caused by improperly compacted soil.

48. B New construction projects which are ready for immediate occupancy are called "turnkey projects" because, once the tenant has the key, he can move in.

49. C A grant deed contains two implied warranties. One of them is that there are no undisclosed liens against the property placed there by the grantor. The standard title insurance policy carries no such protection.

50. D The first thing to do when appraising vacant land is to determine its highest and best use. The other choices would be done later.

51. B A plot map shows the location of the improvement on the lot.

52. B Noxious fumes coming from the adjoining property describes a loss in value from an external cause and is an example of economic obsolescence.

53. C An "advance fee" contract may not include any guarantees that the sale, lease or exchange will be completed.

54. D Deciduous refers to trees which lose their leaves in autumn or winter.

55. B Vacancies or a "vacancy allowance" is the only choice offered that is factored into the calculation of annual net income.

56. D This is the definition of "economic rent". No marketplace is perfectly informed.

57. A The economic life of an improvement is the length of time that it can be used profitably. A building may be able to stand (physical life) for fifty years, but it may be more economical to knock it down after thirty years (economic life).

58. D Land is most commonly appraised by comparison (comparative method).

59. B Accrued depreciation is most difficult to measure accurately because it always requires an appraiser to use her subjective opinion. The other choices may be ascertained by objective data.

60. C Social or economic obsolescence refers to the fact that neighborhoods change and buildings become socially or economically unacceptable. Therefore, a building is commonly torn down before it has used up its physical life.

61. A Elevation sheets show the outside of the homes as they will appear when finished.

62. C Lack of capacity is covered by all title policies. Known defects which are undisclosed, eminent domain and zoning are not covered by any policy.

63. C (1) $72,000 x 2 = $144,000 new selling price;
       (2) $144,000 - $52,000 Loan = $92,000 equity;
       (3) $92,000 (equity) divided by $20,000 (invested) = 4.60.

64. B To find the reciprocal of a number, you first convert it into a fraction (12.5 = 12.5/1). You then reverse the numerator and the denominator of the fraction (1/12.5).
       1 divided by 12.5 = .08; .08 converts to 8%

65. C A broker must present all offers unless they are frivolous, seller has expressly instructed broker to submit no further offers or the escrow has closed.

66. B The county tax rate is set each year by the County Board of Supervisors.

67. D An estate of inheritance is another term for a fee simple estate. A fee simple estate is of an indefinite duration. The other choices have some fixed duration.

68. C An exclusive loan listing cannot exceed a period of 45 days.

69. C (1) $80,000 x 21.25% = $17,000 cash down payment
       (2) $80,000 - 17,000 = $63,000 loan amount
       (3) $63,000 x 10.25% = $6,457.50 annual interest
       (4) $6,457.50 divided by 12 = $538.13 monthly interest
       (5) $978 divided by 36 = $27.17 monthly insurance
       (6) $800 divided by 12 = $66.67 monthly taxes
       (7) $538.13 + $27.17 + $66.67 + $119 principal = $750.97 total first month payment.

70. C A lis pendens means litigation is pending concerning title or possession of real property.

71. D A license is the revocable, nonassignable permission to do something on the land of another.

72. C An attachment lien is good for three years.

73. C The basis is adjusted each year to reflect the depreciation claimed on the income tax return.

74. C The sudden violent tearing away of land by water is called avulsion. Accretion is when land slowly builds up along a river. Alluvion is the dirt that builds up. Erosion is the gradual wearing away of land.

75. C Deed restrictions are private restrictions placed in a deed by a grantor.

76. C Mechanic's liens take priority as of the day the work began or materials were first furnished. This date is usually earlier than the date of recording.

77. B A variance is when the city or county allows an owner to build something and/or use the land in a manner which is inconsistent with the existing laws.

78. B (1) $2,500 x 12 = $30,000 gross annual income
(2) $30,000 - $6,000 (expenses) = $24,000 annual net income
(3) $24,000 divided by 12% (cap rate) = $200,000 total property value (land and improvements)
(4) $200,000 - $150,000 (cost of improvements) = $50,000 (available to pay for the land)

79. C Prescription creates an easement which is the right to use the land of another, but it does not transfer title. Adverse possession acquires title to property.

80. D A judge would not allow an agent to escape liability for wrongful acts because of the agent's failure to put the contract in writing.

81. B Broker Bob may not give the deposit to the seller unless he has first obtained the written consent of the buyer.

82. D Plaster is applied wet, the other materials are dry.

83. A A section is one mile by one mile (one mile square) and contains one square mile.

84. D The seller is responsible only for termite damage present at the time of inspection. Any preventative action is the responsibility of the buyer.

85. D The Statute of Limitations requires law suits for breach of a written contract to be filed within four years of the breach.

86. C The broker must present the offer and disclose the hold on the check, because it is a material fact.

87. A Divide $137,000 by 120% to produce an answer of $114,167. Choice "A" is the best available answer.

88. C (1) $9,430 divided by 115% = $8,200 original cost
(2) $8,200 x 25% = $2,050 assessed value
(3) $2,050 x .08 = $164 annual property taxes
(4) $164 x 4 = $656 taxes
(5) $8,200 x 5% x 4 = $1,640 loss of interest
(6) $8,200 + $656 + $1,640 = $10,496 total cost
(7) $10,496 - $9,430 = $1,066 loss

89. B The injured party has the option to void the contract; therefore, it is voidable.

90. D A broker must have an active license, produce a ready, willing, and able buyer, and show that she was the procuring cause of the transaction.

91. A Business loans and agricultural loans are exempt from the Federal Truth-in-Lending Law.

92. C An agreement to answer for the debt of another must be in writing.

93. B A listing is an employment contract which usually authorizes the broker to find a purchaser and accept a deposit as the seller's agent. The broker is not authorized to do the acts described in the other choices.

94. A As each parcel is sold, the beneficiary (lender) will issue a "request for partial reconveyance" to the trustee. The trustee then records a "partial reconveyance deed," which removes that home from the construction loan encumbrance.

95. D The Statute of Frauds lists the contracts which must be in writing in order to be enforceable. Included in the Statute of Frauds is "an agreement which is not to be performed within one year." The other agreements would be enforceable even if oral.

96. D Leverage is the use of borrowed money to the maximum extent possible. In this case, a 10% increase in value resulted in a 100% increase in equity.

97. B The Federal Truth-in-Lending Law requires the interest rate to be quoted as "annual percentage rate" (APR).

98. D (1) $200 income x 12 months = $2,400 annual income
       (2) $2,400 annual income divided by 8% rate of return = $30,000 (total investment required)

99. D The DRE requires that an ad offering "secured" loans discloses to what extent they are secured.

100. C The terms "liquidity" and "marketability" refer to the ability to sell the loans on the secondary mortgage market.

101. C The builder is usually responsible for installing these items in a new subdivision.

102. A California law allows the buyer (vendee) to record the land contract. A seller (vendor) would not be successful in a lawsuit based upon an agreement not to record.

103. C Life insurance companies usually work through mortgage companies to arrange and service their loans.

104. C The standard deposit receipt provides that if buyer defaults, seller and agent shall split whatever seller actually recovers from the buyer, but never to exceed the agreed upon commission. Since buyer initialed liquidated damages, seller should recover the deposit and split it with the agent.

105. B The Truth-in-Lending Law (Regulation Z), requires lenders to state interest rates in annual percentage rate (APR).

106. C A fictitious trust deed contains standard clauses which are then referred to by subsequent trust deeds.

107. A A mortgage loan disclosure statement must be given to the borrower within three days of receipt of a completed loan application or before the borrower is obligated to take the loan.

108.	C	Real estate loans are not very liquid. An increase in the demand for liquidity decreases the money available for real estate loans.
109.	D	A hard money loan, is where the borrower gets cash from a third party and uses real estate to secure the loan.
110.	B	The County Tax Assessor determines the assessed value of homes and therefore determines the amount of the property tax.
111.	B	Fees for a credit report or appraisal need not be included in the finance charge portion of the disclosure statement.
112.	D	Generally, increases in these factors indicate an improving economy. All the choices should occur.
113.	B	The county property tax rate is set each year by the County Board of Supervisors.
114.	D	These terms describe the business cycle.
115.	A	Interim use describes the current use, when the highest and best use is expected to change.
116.	B	These terms best represent the agreement of the parties.
117.	A	Historically, real estate is the best hedge against inflation.
118.	C	A clause prohibiting prepayment is called a "lock-in" clause. California law does not allow a vendor (seller/lender) to "lock-in" a land contract for the sale of four or less residential units. The contract is still valid, but the vendee (buyer) may disregard the clause.
119.	A	When a buyer takes title "subject to" an existing loan, the seller as original borrower remains on the loan documents. The buyer would not have any personal liability. His loss would be limited to any equity he had in the property, should it go into foreclosure.
120.	D	No title policy offers protection against governmental regulations, such as zoning.
121.	D	The escrow officer is an agent for the buyer and seller.
122.	B	These are private companies who insure high loan-to-value ratio loan with programs similar to FHA. They receive money from the PMI payments (premiums) and sale of stock or debt issues.
123.	B	This would be classified as making a secret profit. A broker may not make any undisclosed profit in a real estate transaction.
124.	B	An agreement to sell real property signed by only one spouse is unenforceable. It could be voided within one year by the nonconsenting spouse.
125.	B	Accretion is the acquisition of title to land when soil builds up along a river bank.
126.	D	A broker who has an option to purchase his own listing must disclose any outstanding offers; disclose all material information to the seller and obtain written consent from the owner which acknowledges any profit or anticipated profit..
127.	D	Divide $345,000 (selling price) by 109% (100% cost plus 9% profit) = $316,513.76. "D" ($316,500) is the best answer.

128. A The granting clause is also called the action clause and is considered one of the essential elements to a valid deed.

129. D Although the lender must allow the borrower to inspect the uniform settlement statement one day prior to the close of the transaction, the statement must be delivered at or before the date of settlement.

130. C Typical escrow instructions authorize the escrow officer to call for the funding of the buyer's loan in order to close escrow. Escrow officers are not authorized to do the other choices.

131. A A loan can be called a "balloon loan" when it calls for a payment that is more than twice the amount of the smallest installment. A partially amortized loan would always call for a balloon payment.

132. D Mortgage Insurance Premium (MIP) is found only in the FHA loan program.

133. B A broker can designate a salesperson to supervise, review, initial, and date contracts, if that salesperson has at least 2 years full-time experience during the preceding 5 years.

134. D Lenders commonly charge points to increase effective yield, close the gap between fixed interest rates and market rates, and help defray the costs of the loan.

135. C Intangible personal property, such as the good will of a business opportunity, is not subject to property taxes.

136. B When the seller carries back a loan for part of the purchase price and charges no interest, the IRS will consider part of each payment as interest. This is reported as interest income to the seller and an interest expense of the buyer. This imputed rate will vary depending upon current interest rates.

137. A A kiosk would describe the typical information booth in a mall.

138. D An "offended lessor" describes an angry landlord. A landlord evicts a tenant with an unlawful detainer court action.

139. C Avulsion is the sudden and violent tearing away of land by the action of water.

140. C A bill of sale must have the signature of the seller.

141. C A hidden cost of home ownership is loss of any interest income which could have earned on the owner's equity.

142. B Innocent misrepresentation, negligent misrepresentation and fraudulent misrepresentation are common types of misrepresentation. Malicious misrepresentation is relatively rare.

143. B An offer made contingent upon the happening of a certain event (obtaining a lease) is a valid offer. It is quite common for an offer to have contingencies.

144. B Appraisers measure the exterior dimensions of the structure to calculate square footage of the improvement.

145. C There are 36 townships is a 36 mile square.

146. C The broker should contact the lender, not the FHA.

147. D   The cost of real property will most likely the value, only when the improvements are new and they represent the highest and best use of the land.

148. D   A substandard loan is one that is more likely to go into default. A lender would try to reduce the possibility of any new loan being substandard.

149. B   The auctioneer in a real estate auction is the agent for the seller.

150.   Both "C" and "D" are correct.

Bonus Questions for the Salesperson Exam

1. A salesperson is using strong efforts to obtain listings by telling owners that members of another racial group are moving in and property values will decrease. His activities may be best described as: (A) blockbusting; (B) panic peddling; (C) both A and B; (D) neither A or B.

2. Which of the following, would most likely be a cause of economic obsolescence? (A) an unpopular architectural design on the property; (B) a change in nearby zoning, (C) poor manage-ment of the property; (D) an increased demand for larger units.

3. A broker who advertises using the term "Realtor" and who is not a member of the organization that owns the name is guilty of: (A) unethical conduct; (B) unlawful conduct; (C) both A and B; (D) neither A nor B.

4. Short rate refers to: (A) property tax bill; (B) insurance; (C) interest; (D) loan documents.

5. A sheriff's sale results from enforcement of which of the following? (A) adverse possession; (B) judgment lien; (C) lis pendens; (D) injunction.

6. Which of the following building codes controls construction when they are in conflict? (A) local building codes; (B) state housing laws; (C) Uniform Building Code; (D) whichever code sets the highest construction standard.

7. Trust deeds and mortgages differ in all of the following ways, **except:** (A) parties; (B) security; (C) title; (D) rights of redemption.

8. Real estate licensees who originate loans must provide borrowers with the federal RESPA booklet and disclosures when a federally related real estate loan is secured by a first lien and the proceeds are used for financing: (A) the purchase of four or less residential units; (B) a room addition to the borrower's home; (C) the purchase of 40 or more acres of raw land; (D) the construction of 5 or more residential units.

9. When a real estate broker advertises real estate and/or real estate loans through the Internet, the broker is required to do which of the following? (A) return all messages promptly and correctly within 24 hours of receipt; (B) employ only real estate licensees to respond to queries about properties and loan terms; (C) exercise proper supervision over licensees and non-licensees responding to queries; (D) report all international inquiries to the DRE.

10. Carol, a licensed real estate broker presented an offer to a seller which met the terms of the listing. The offer was from a financially-qualified African American. Later, one of her salespersons presented the seller an offer at a lower price from Caucasian buyers. The seller did not accept either offer, but instead, sold the property to a neighbor through the same salesperson. The neighbor wanted to buy the property to prevent a minority person moving into the neighborhood. Which of the following parties has not violated the Civil Rights Act of 1968? (A) seller; (B) neighbor; (C) Caucasian buyers; (D) salesperson.

11. Which of the following conditions would not cause a building to be declared a "substandard" structure? (A) lack of a heating system; (B) electrical wiring does not comply with the present code, but it was "up to code" when it was installed and is currently safe and working properly; (C) dampness in habitable rooms; (D) lack of weather stripping.

12. A licensed real estate broker; who owned a large real estate firm operating under the name ABC Realty Company, listed a property for sale at $400,000. The broker and many of his salespersons were the owners of an investment company operating under the name of Realty Income Investment Company. The investment company decided to purchase the property and the broker presented an all cash offer to the owner for the full price, without disclosing to the seller who the purchaser was. The seller accepted the offer and opened escrow. Under these circumstances: (A) the broker's actions were perfectly legal since he made a full price cash offer; (B) the broker's action was improper because he did not reveal the true identity of the purchaser; (C) the broker acted properly provided he agreed to waive any commission; (D) the broker's action would be legal, provided he added to the escrow instructions the fact that the company buying the property was comprised of brokers and salespersons.

13. What happens to the licensees who work for a broker when the broker dies? The agents: (A) must stop real estate activity immediately; (B) may continue working for up to 30 days; (C) may continue working if there is an office manager appointed by the broker with two years experience within the last five years. (D) may continue working until another broker takes over the office or the office is closed.

14. When lenders charge points on FHA insured loans, this is done to: (A) close the gap between market rates and fixed rates; (B) increase the effective yield; (C) obtain the market yield; (D) all of the above.

15. For property tax purposes, when is property assessed? (A) when sold; (B) every year; (C) every two years; (D) twice per year.

16. Who pays the points on a Cal-Vet loan? (A) buyer; (B) seller; (C) agent; (D) none of the above.

17. A real estate broker wrote an offer for his buyers. The offer was made contingent on the approval of the home by the buyer's uncle. The buyers informed the broker that their uncle was currently in Europe and they were unsure when he would return. The broker replied that the uncle's being out of the country would be no problem. The broker then presented the offer to the seller without disclosing that the buyer's uncle was out of the country. The seller accepted the offer. Under these circumstances, the broker's conduct was: (A) lawful; (B) unlawful; (C) ethical; (D) unethical.

18. A buyer and a seller entered into a contract for the sale of the seller's home. The buyer backed out. The seller exercised his right of rescission. Which of the following is true? (A) the seller can sue the buyer; (B) the seller must return the deposit to the buyer; (C) the seller can try to sell the property to someone else in order to limit the damage; (D) all of the above.

19. The amount of a security deposit a landlord may collect from a prospective tenant is limited depending upon: (A) competition from other apartments in the area; (B) the term of the lease and whether the apartment is furnished or unfurnished; (C) the number of children occupying the unit; (D) the total number of tenants who plan to occupy the premises.

20. The owner of a parcel of land granted an easement to the local telephone company to erect telephone poles across his land. This would create an: (A) encroachment; (B) encumbrance; (C) appurtenance: (D) estate at sufferance.

21. The law requires the county recorder to index deeds by: (A) a street address, and by a legal description; (B) a street address and by the parcel number; (C) the names of the grantor and the grantee; (D) the date and time of recording.

22. Flooding will be described as frequent in a flood hazard report when the flooding occurs:(A) once in three years; (B) twice in five years; (C) on average two or more times in ten years; (D) three or more times in ten years.

23. The reason an appraiser determines the value of an income producing property as of a "given date" is to indicate: (A) the age of the improvements as of a given date; (B) the date the appraiser inspected the property; (C) the market conditions influencing the value of the property as of a given point in time; (D) the value of the seller's equity as of a given date.

24. When is a real estate licensee relieved of his obligation to present an offer to purchase real property to a seller? (A) when the offer is patently frivolous or the agent is acting on written instructions of his seller; (B) when the offer contains more than two contingency clauses; (C) when the offer is for the purchase of commercial property; (D) when the agent notifies the seller in writing of his decision not to present the offer.

25. FHA will, but VA and Cal Vet will not, provide loans for: (A) agricultural land; (B) farming equipment; (C) duplex purchased for rental; (D) business.

26. Which of the following is the largest parcel of land? (A) 2 sections; (B) 10% of a township; (C) 5,280 ft. by 10,000 ft.; (D) 4 sq. miles.

27. An apartment building and a condominium project have certain things in common; these things include: (A) occupants of both have a fee interest; (B) occupants of both have an estate in real property; (C) after building two units, both would come under the subdivided lands law; (D) separate tax bills are sent to each tenant.

28. Which of the following must be given to every buyer of a condominium unit? (A) copy of the C.C.& R's; (B) copy of the bylaws; (C) copy of the most recent financial statement of the association; (D) all of the above.

29. Acknowledgment of the signature on a deed taken by a notary is usually accomplished in order to: (A) Determine the validity to the deed; (B) Enable the deed to be recorded at the county recorder's office; (C) Give actual notice to others of the grantee's rights in the property; (D) All of the above.

30. Seller Houton listed a parcel of vacant land with Broker Jack. Broker Jack placed the listing in the local multiple listing service (MLS). The land was shown to buyer Barton by Salesperson Clinton who is employed by Live Oak Realty. Salesperson Clinton is directly responsible to: (A) Broker Jack; (B) Seller Houton; (C) Buyer Barton; (D) Live Oak Realty.

31. Broker Johnson sold a property owned by Mr. and Mrs. Guzman to Buyer Wong. Four months later, when the first rains of the season arrived, Buyer Wong found that the roof leaked badly in many places. The buyer sued both the sellers and the broker for the cost of the necessary repairs. In the same action, the sellers sued Broker Johnson, because the sellers had informed the broker several times that the building needed a new roof. Broker Johnson's testimony in court revealed that she was aware of the leaky roof, but had not mentioned it to Buyer Wong, because, "they never asked." Based on the foregoing information, the most likely result of the court action would be: (A) on the basis of the principle of caveat emptor, the buyer was not entitled to recover from either the broker or the sellers; (B) the buyer recovered from the broker, but the sellers would not be considered liable; (C) the buyer recovered from the sellers, but the broker would not be liable; (D) the buyer would be successful in the suit against both the sellers and the broker; the sellers were successful in the suit against the broker.

32. On January 13th, a prospective buyer gave a deposit to a broker to accompany his offer. The offer included the statement, "this offer is irrevocable for five days." On January 14th, before the offer had been accepted by the seller, the buyer contacted the broker, withdrew his offer and demanded the return of his deposit. The broker: (A) has until January 18th to obtain the seller's acceptance; (B) must return the remainder of the deposit to the buyer after retaining enough of the deposit to pay the liquidated damages to the seller; (C) must return the entire deposit to the buyer as demanded; (D) must place the deposit in a neutral escrow until the five day period expires.

33. A homeowner needed $9,000 to pay for his child's college education. A loan broker arranged a home equity loan for $9,600. The broker must provide the borrower with which of the following? (A) broker closing statement; (B) mortgage loan disclosure statement; (C) loan balance statement; (D) beneficiary statement.

34. One of the main purposes of the Real Estate Settlement Procedures Act (RESPA) is: (A) to set limits on settlement costs in real estate transactions; (B) to fix all settlement costs on the sale of four or less family dwellings; (C) to standardize settlement costs in different regions of the nation; (D) to provide a prospective borrower with an opportunity to shop for settlement services.

35. The market data approach to appraisal would be least effective as a result of which of the following: (A) different financing terms of comparable property; (B) similar types of property that are regularly sold; (C) economic conditions that rapidly change; (D) physical differences in the comparable properties.

36. A real estate broker has a management contract with the owner of an apartment building complex. The broker collects rents and deposits them into his trust fund account. He also acts as a broker on other real estate sales transactions and puts the buyer's deposits into the same trust fund account. Which of the following is correct regarding this practice? (A) it is legal if a separate record for each trust fund deposit and disbursement is properly maintained by the broker; (B) it is legal only if the broker is bonded for the maximum amount of the trust fund account; (C) it is legal only if the broker doesn't deposit more than $3,000 into the trust fund account; (D) under no circumstances can funds from different types of real estate activities be deposited into the same trust fund account.

37. The distance measurement of a parcel of land along a street or thoroughfare is called: (A) front foot; (B) frontage; (C) width; (D) street line.

38. Agent Donald listed a ranch for sale under an exclusive right to sell listing. Agent Haney, working through the local multiple listing service, presented an offer which the seller accepted. During escrow, Agent Donald discovered that Agent Haney's buyer had recently purchased many similar ranches in the area at a far higher cost per acre than had been offered in this transaction. What should Agent Donald do? (A) inform the seller, but insist the deal stay in escrow; (B) do nothing because the deal is in escrow; (C) disclose all information to the seller and let the seller decide what to do; (D) tell the seller to rescind the agreement and try to resell the property for a higher price.

39. Jim leased a single family dwelling from Mr. McDowell and moved in. Mr. McDowell then demanded that Jim sign a contract agreeing to make substantial capital improvements to the property. This requirement by the lessor would render the lease contract: (A) valid; (B) voidable by the lessor; (C) voidable by the lessee; (D) void.

40. Broker Bob presented an offer to purchase real property for the full listed price from a ready, willing, and able, African American buyer. The offer was refused by the seller because of the buyer's race. Broker Bob may: (A) sue the seller for his commission; (B) advise the African American buyer of his right to complain to the Department of Housing and Urban Development; (C) warn the seller that his refusal is a violation of the Fair Housing Act of 1968; (D) do all of the above.

41. When someone who has passed the real estate exam pays the fee to obtain a real estate license, there is a certain amount that is credited to the Real Estate Education, Research, and Recovery Account (REERRA). A portion of that money is allocated for recovery purposes and is used: (A) to help offset damages caused by licensees against the general public; (B) so a salesperson can recover lost commissions due to the broker's negligence; (C) for research projects only; (D) for none of the above.

42. The home sold for $212,000. The buyer applied for a 80/20 LTV loan. The appraisal came in at $205,000. How much cash will the buyer have to put up? (A) 20% of $205,000 + $7,000 ; (B) 20% of $205,000 - $7,000; (C) 20% of $212,000; (D) 20% of 212,000 - $7,000.

43. Mr. Gonzalez sold ten previously unencumbered properties to Mr. Long. Part of the purchase price was a loan made by Mr. Gonzalez that was secured by a trust deed on the ten properties. This trust deed may be described as: (A) a reconveyance deed; (B) an all-inclusive trust deed; (C) a blanket encumbrance; (D) a quitclaim deed.

44. Which of the following characteristics are present in FHA and VA loans but are not present in most conventional loans? (A) no acceleration clauses; (B) no prepayment penalty clauses; (C) a restraint on alienation of title; (D) an escalator clause.

45. Whenever a home is sold, the property tax rate under Proposition 13 will be set at: (A) 1% of the purchase price; (B) 1.5% of the purchase price; (C) 2% of the purchase price; (D) 2.5% of the purchase price.

46. Every lease has an implied covenant to place the tenant in quiet enjoyment of the property for the purpose for which it was leased. This means the tenant has a right to be free from disturbances caused by: (A) nuisances inflicted by adjoining property owners; (B) a loud air conditioning unit; (C) the landlord or another who has paramount title; (D) all of the above.

47. The term "potable" refers to: (A) sewers systems; (B) water; (C) natural gas; (D) backfill.

48. For appraisal purposes, "capitalization" is a process used to: (A) establish current market value; (B) determine annual net income; (C) find interest rate; (D) convert income into value.

49. Mr. and Mrs. Lee had a real estate agent write up an offer to purchase a home. The offer had a contingency, making the offer contingent upon the sale of Lee's existing home. The seller made a counter-offer accepting the Lee's offer, but reserved the right to continue marketing the home, seeking higher offers and granting the Lees a right of first refusal to remove their contingency if a better offer came in. The Lees accepted the seller's counter-offer and immediately listed their existing home for sale. Shortly thereafter, the seller notified the Lee's agent that a better offer had been received without contingencies. What should the agent advise the Lees to do?
(A) immediately advise the Lees to remove their contingency and open escrow with the seller;
(B) advise the Lees to get a short term bridge loan so that they can purchase the home without first selling their existing home; (C) advise the Lees of the advantages and disadvantages of removing the contingency and buying the home before the sale of their existing home; (D) the Lees' agent should not offer advice to the Lees on this issue.

50. Which of the following is a true statement regarding fair housing and discrimination? (A) a real estate licensee is not liable in a fair housing lawsuit if he/she had no intent to discriminate; (B) the landlord renting a single family dwelling can discriminate without liability; (C) the owner renting out one room in a home where he/she resides can discriminate; (D) apartment complexes must be built to accommodate people with physical disabilities or handicaps.

51. A lender would likely not enforce the "due on sale" clause in a promissory note under which of the following circumstances? (A) when a new loan could be made at a higher rate of interest than the existing loan; (B) when inflation causes the value of real estate to rise rapidly; (C) when there are more buyers than sellers; (D) when deflation occurs and there are more houses for sale than there are buyers.

52. When appraising real estate, appraisers attempt to estimate value. The value arrived at by appraisers is: (A) based solely upon the replacement cost; (B) based upon an analysis of facts as of a given date; (C) derived from income data covering the preceding nine months; (D) projected from original cost minus depreciation and inflation.

53. The appraisal of income producing property is usually: (A) determined by a gross multiplier; (B) determined by the structural soundness of the structure; (C) directly proportional to the remaining economic life of the building; (D) based on the capitalization of net income.

54. The most essential document to establish the relationship between a property management company and a property owner is: (A) a lease; (B) a maintenance agreement; (C) a broker license; (D) a written property management agreement.

55. A typical subordination clause contained in a loan: (A) allows early payment of the loan without an additional charge; (B) permits an adjustment in the rate of interest paid on a loan as influenced by the availability of investment mortgage money; (C) authorizes the lender to demand, at its option, the immediate payment of the remaining balance of a note secured by a trust deed; (D) grants the borrower authority to issue additional security devices on the property which automatically receive higher classification over the mortgage or trust deed.

56. Bob is beneficiary of a $150,000 deed of trust on a single-family home located in Costa Mesa, California. Mike, the trustor, made $20,000 in principal payments, then defaulted. At a trustee's sale, the property sold for $100,000, resulting in a $30,000 deficiency. In California, a deficiency judgment cannot be obtained: (A) if the loan was secured with a purchase-money trust deed; (B) if foreclosed through a trustee's sale; (C) if the fair market value of the property exceeds the loan balance; (D) in any of the above situations.

57. In May, 2003, Mr. Sanchez leased a unit in his apartment building to a tenant for a one-year term. The tenant prepaid the last month's rent at the time he entered into the lease agreement. For federal income tax purposes, that amount will be considered as income for Mr. Sanchez: (A) as of May, 2003; (B) as of May, 2004; (C) will be prorated equally throughout the term of the lease; (D) when it is actually applied toward the last month of the rent.

58. When someone acquires property as the result of intestate succession, he acquires the property through the direction of which of the following? (A) holographic will; (B) nuncupative will; (C) probate court; (D) formal witnessed will.

59. Conversion of apartments to community apartment projects and condominiums come within the provisions of the California Real Estate Subdivided Lands Law when they contain how many units? (A) two or more; (B) three or more; (C) five or more; (D) all subdivisions come within that law.

60. Many investors believe, stocks and bonds, when compared with real estate, are usually: (A) more difficult to sell; (B) more difficult to properly value; (C) less inclined to change in value; (D) more liquid when it is time to sell.

61. In residential real estate, when the market turns from a buyer's market to a seller's market, which of the following would be true? (A) prices rise because there is now a shortage of properties available for sale; (B) prices fall because there are more buyers; (C) there is no change in prices because all real estate is unique; (D) interest rates go up.

62. In which of the following ways is the Federal Housing Administration different from conventional lending programs? (A) FHA insures loans, rather than making loans; (B) FHA handles loans for veterans only; (C) FHA interest rates are always 2% to 3% lower than conventional loans; (D) FHA's maximum loan amount is 80% of the appraised value.

63. When leasing industrial space, a landlord and/or property manager is required to make sure the property: (A) complies with the Americans With Disabilities Act (ADA); (B) complies with all applicable building codes; (C) is in perfect shape; (D) has no encumbrances.

64. A real estate investor who wished to utilize the principle of leverage, would do which of the following? (A) use his own funds as much as possible; (B) use borrowed money and his own personal money on an equal basis; (C) use borrowed money to the maximum extent possible; (D) invest in rental properties with declining values.

65. John purchased Blackacre from Ben, using a land sales contract. John recorded the contract. Six months later John failed to make payments as provided in the agreement. Finally, John abandoned the property, relocating to Hawaii, vowing never to return. Since Ben cannot now locate John, what should Ben do to remove the cloud on title? (A) proceed with a trustee sale of the property; (B) execute a quitclaim deed in favor of John; (C) institute a quiet title action; (D) none of the above.

66. Withdrawals from the broker's trust account may be made by: (A) any employee of the broker; (B) any officer and director of the broker's corporation; (C) an unlicensed employee of the broker who is authorized by the broker and fidelity bonded; (D) any of the above.

67. Conditions affecting interest rates and the availability of loan funds vary over time. When would it be advantageous for a lender to waive a prepayment penalty clause contained in a promissory note? (A) when the Federal Reserve Board lowers the discount rate: (B) in a tight money market where there is a lack of funds available for real estate loans; (C) in a deflationary economy where home prices are falling; (D) when money is readily available for real estate loans at low interest rates.

68. Which of the following items would be least likely to appear as a debit on a buyer's closing statement? (A) proration of property taxes; (B) interest on an assumed loan; (C) discount points for an FHA loan; (D) prorations of insurance premiums.

69. A property sold for $150,000. The taxable value is $125,000. The tax rate is $.55 per $500 of taxable value. The documentary transfer tax is: (A) $55; (B) $138; (C) $325; (D) $750.

70. On the local level, compliance with the State Housing Law and minimum construction standards will usually be enforced by: (A) the city engineer; (B) the local district attorney; (C) the city planning commission; (D) the local building inspector.

71. In real estate finance, the term "impounds" refers to: (A) moratorium; (B) reserves; (C) attachments; (D) penalties.

72. A real estate salesperson hired an unlicensed assistant. Which of the following actions taken by the unlicensed assistant would be improper? (A) selected a licensed pest control inspector from a list provided by the real estate salesperson; (B) met the pest control inspector at the property and let him in to perform the inspection; (C) answered questions and provided the termite inspector with information about the property; (D) picked up the finished termite report from the inspector and delivered it to the escrow.

73. A real estate broker would look at which of the following to find the size and dimensions of the footings, concrete piers and details of the subfloor area? (A) floor plan; (B) plot plan; (C) elevation plan; (D) foundation plan.

74. Which of the following statements is correct concerning a load bearing wall? (A) it is usually left intact and not disturbed during remodeling; (B) it is constructed of stronger support members than other walls; (C) it can be built at any angle to doorways; (D) all of the above.

75. A tenant entered into a two year lease. The lease made no mention of assignment or subleasing. The tenant: (A) may assign or sublease to another tenant, because the lease made no mention of assignment or subleasing; (B) may sublease to another tenant, but only with the prior consent of the landlord; (C) cannot sublease to another tenant; (D) may assign the lease, but not sublease.

76. What section is due north of section 8? (A) section 1; (B) section 5; (C) section 7; (D) section 17.

77. In the capitalization approach to appraisal, the appraiser arrives at an effective gross income figure by making a deduction for: (A) interest payments on the loan; (B) repairs; (C) vacancy; (D) depreciation.

78. Rental schedules for various units of housing space are realistically established on what basis? (A) capitalization of annual net income; (B) comparative cost of construction; (C) market comparison; (D) average housing costs for the county where the property is located.

79. A benefit to the broker of having a salesperson as an independent contractors is? (A) not paying for workers compensation insurance; (B) secure desk cost income; (C) not paying social security for the salesperson; (D) no liability for a salesperson employed as an independent contractor.

80. Davidson, a licensed Real Estate Broker, listed a home for sale for 9 months without any success. He knew that it needed some major structural repair and that it was overpriced by 10%. He wrote the following ad in a local newspaper. "Charming cute Victorian home, move right in, you will not believe the price. Call Davidson, 410-9718." What was wrong with this advertisement? (A) it doesn't specify the asking price and therefore violated the Truth-in-Lending law; (B) the ad was misleading and deceptive because Davidson knew the home needed major repair: (C) it is unethical to overprice and advertise a home for sale; (D) the newspaper will be held liable if someone purchases the home and relies on the advertisement.

81. When using the cost approach to determine the value of a building built in 1901, an appraiser would: (A) determine the cost to build the building in 1901; (B) determine labor costs for 1901 and then adjust to current year based upon the CPI; (C) use current prices to build a building with the same utility, then subtract accrued depreciation; (D) average labor costs over the lifetime of the building.

Answers to Bonus Questions for the Salesperson's Exam

1. C   When a real estate licensee attempts to obtain listings by telling owners that members of another racial or ethnic group are moving in and property values will decrease, it is called blockbusting and/or panic peddling. This same activity is also described as inducing "panic selling."

2. B   Economic obsolescence is loss in value caused by things happening outside of the property lines of the property being appraised. A change in zoning nearby the property (think sewage treatment plant) could lower the property value.

3. C   A broker who advertises using the term "Realtor" without being a member of the organization is guilty of both unethical conduct and unlawful conduct.

4. B   Short rate refers to insurance.

5. B   A judgment lien is enforced by a sheriff's sale.

6. D   The most restrictive restriction controls, therefore the code setting the highest standards controls.

7. B   Trust deeds and mortgages both are used to create the security for a debt.

8. A   RESPA is primarily concerned with loans made by federally regulated lenders for the purchase of four or less residential units.

9. C   When a real estate broker advertises real estate and/or real estate loans through the internet, the broker must exercise proper supervision over licensees and non-licensees responding to queries.

10. C   The Caucasian buyers apparently were not involved in the discrimination in this question.

11. B   Electrical wiring which does not comply with the present code, but it was "up to code" when it was installed and is currently safe and working properly will not cause a building to be declared a substandard structure.

12. B   The broker's action was improper because he did not reveal the true identity of the purchaser.

13. A   The licensees of an office must stop real estate activity immediately when the employing broker dies.

14. D   Most lenders charge points in connection with FHA insured loans to close the gap between market rates and fixed rates, increase the effective yield, and to obtain the market yield.

15. B   Property is assessed every year for property tax purposes.

16. D   There are no points on a Cal-Vet loan.

17. B   A real estate broker must disclose material facts to the seller. The broker's failure to disclose the absence of the uncle was withholding material facts and was unlawful.

18. D   When a buyer breaches the contract and the seller exercises his right of rescission, the seller can sue the buyer for damages, must return the deposit to the buyer and can try to sell the property to someone else in order to limit the damage.

19. B   The amount of a security deposit a landlord may collect from a prospective tenant is limited depending upon the term of the lease and whether the apartment is furnished or unfurnished.

20. B   An easement is an encumbrance.

21. C   The law requires the county recorder to index deeds by the names of the grantor and the grantee.

22. C   Flooding is considered "frequent" if a flood occurs on **average** more than once in 10 years. Answer "C" is the best answer because it includes "average." The other answers could be isolated events.

23. C   An appraiser determines the value of an income producing property as of a "given date" is to indicate the market conditions influencing the value of the property as of a given point in time.

24. A   A real estate licensee is relieved of his obligation to present an offer to purchase real property when the offer is patently frivolous or the agent is acting on written instructions of his seller not to present the offer.

25. C   FHA will, but VA and Cal Vet will not, provide loans for rental property.

26. D   (1) 2 sections = 2 square miles.
        (2) 10% of a township = 36 square miles x 10% = 3.6 square miles.
        (3) 5,280 ft. x 10,000 = 52,800,000 sq. ft = 1.89 square miles.
        (4) 4 sq. miles is the largest parcel of land.

27. B   Both tenants of an apartment building and the owners of the units in a condominium have an estate in real property.

28. D The seller of a unit in a condominium must give the buyer a copy of the C.C.& R's, a copy of the bylaws, and a copy of the most recent financial statement of the association.

29. B A deed must be acknowledged in order to be recorded at the county recorder's office.

30. D Salesperson Clinton is directly responsible to his employing broker.

31. D Broker Johnson had a duty to the buyer to disclose material facts, even if not asked by the buyer. The buyer was successful in his suit against both the seller and the broker. The seller would then recover from the broker.

32. C A buyer may revoke an offer at any time, and for any reason, prior to the seller's acceptance of the offer. The broker must return the entire deposit to the buyer as demanded.

33. B The mortgage loan disclosure statement must be given to the borrower for all loans negotiated by a loan broker.

34. D One of the main purposes of the RESPA is to provide a prospective borrower with an opportunity to shop for settlement services.

35. C The market data approach to appraisal would be least effective in times of rapid economic changes.

36. A A real estate broker needs only one trust account. Both real estate sales and property management trust funds can be placed in one account, as long as a separate record for each trust fund deposit and disbursement is properly maintained by the broker.

37. B The distance measurement of a parcel of land along a street or thoroughfare is called frontage.

38. C An agent for the seller must disclose all material facts to the seller, including the buyer's purchase of other similar properties at a higher price.

39. C A contract entered into under duress is voidable by the injured party. In this question, the contract is voidable by Jim, the lessee.

40. D Real estate licensees may not be involved in discrimination.

41. A A portion of the license fee is placed in the real estate fund which contains a Real Estate Education, Research, and Recovery Account (REERRA) designed to help offset damages caused by licensees against the general public.

42. A (1) The loan will be 80% of the appraised value of $205,000;
(2) $212,999 (selling price) - $205,000 (loan amount) = $7,000;
(3) The buyer will have to put up the 20% $205,000 (appraised value) + $7,000 (difference between the selling price and the amount of the appraisal).

43. C The blanket encumbrance covers more than one property.

44. B FHA and VA loans have no prepayment penalty clauses.

45. A Under Proposition 13 the property tax is set at 1% of the purchase price (assessed value taxable value, full cash value, fair market value), plus an amount to cover existing bond debt. Answer "A" is the best answer.

46. C The landlord must protect the tenant from disturbances or claims made by another person claiming paramount title to the premises.

47. B Potable, refers to water which is suitable for drinking.

48. D Capitalization is the process used to convert income into value.

49. C Agents should always advise their clients of the advantages and disadvantages of removing the contingency and let the client decide.

50. C The Fair Employment and Housing Act applies to all housing accommodations but does not apply to renting or leasing to a roomer or boarder in a single-family house, provided that no more than one roomer or boarder lives in the household.

51. D A lender would likely not enforce the "due on sale" clause in a promissory note when deflation occurs and there are more houses for sale than there are buyers. The lender might be unable to re-loan the money to another borrower.

52. B When appraising real estate, appraisers attempt to estimate value based upon an analysis of facts as of a given date.

53. D The appraisal of income producing property is usually based on the capitalization of net income.

54. D The most essential document to establish the relationship between a property management company and the property owner is a written property management agreement.

55. D A typical subordination clause contained in a loan grants the borrower authority to issue additional security devices on the property which automatically receive higher classification over the mortgage or trust deed.

56. D In California, a deficiency judgment cannot be obtained if the loan was secured with a purchase-money trust deed or, if foreclosed through a trustee's sale or, if the fair market value of the property exceeds the loan balance.

57. A Prepaid rent is treated as income to the owner of income property in the year received.

58. C   When someone dies intestate, there is no will. The court determines which heirs get the property of the deceased.

59. C   Conversion of apartments to community apartment projects and condominiums comes within the provisions of the California real estate Subdivided Lands Law when it contains five or more units.

60. D   When compared to real estate investments, some investors prefer stocks and bonds because they have greater liquidity.

61. A   In residential real estate, when the market turns from a buyer's market to a seller's market, prices rise because there is now a shortage of properties available for sale.

62. A   The unique feature of FHA is that FHA insures, rather than making, loans.

63. B   The lessor has an obligation to make sure the property is suitable for the purpose for which it is leased, including compliance with all applicable building codes.

64. C   Leverage involves using borrowed money to the maximum extent possible.

65. C   The recorded installment sales contract clouds the title until it is removed with a quiet title action in court.

66. C   An unlicensed employee of the broker who is authorized by the broker and is fidelity bonded, may make withdrawal from the trust account.

67. B   A lender might waive a prepayment penalty clause contained in a promissory note in a tight money market where there is a lack of funds available for real estate loans. By waving the prepayment penalty, the lender encourages the borrower to pay off an older low interest rate loan and would receive funds which the lender could then lend out at a higher rate of interest.

68. B   Interest on an assumed loan would not appear as a debit on a buyer's closing statement.

69. B   The taxable value under the documentary transfer tax is based on consideration (selling price - existing loans assumed by the buyer).
   (1) The taxable value is $125,000
   (2) The tax rate is $.55 per $500 of consideration.
   (3) $125,000 divided by $500 = 250.
   (4) 250 x $.55 = $137.50. "B" is the best answer.

70. D   On the local level, compliance with the State Housing Law will usually be enforced by the local building inspector.

71. B   In real estate finance, the term "impounds" refers to "reserves."

72. A It is a violation of the law for either the licensee or an unlicensed assistant to select the licensed pest control inspector for the parties to a transaction.

73. D The foundation plan shows the location, size and dimensions of the footings, concrete piers and details of the subfloor area.

74. D A load bearing wall is usually left intact and not disturbed during remodeling, is constructed of stronger support members than other walls, and can be built at any angle to doorways.

75. A A tenant may assign or sublease the property if the lease does not prohibit it.

76. B Section 5 is due north of section 8.

77. C The appraiser subtracts vacancy from the scheduled gross income to arrive at the effective gross income.

78. C Rental schedules for various units of housing space are realistically established on the basis of market comparison.

79. C A benefit to the broker of having a salesperson as an independent contractor is not paying social security for the salesperson.

80. B An ad saying "move right in" is misrepresentation when the home needs major repair.

81. C When using the cost approach to determine the value of a building built in 1901, the appraiser would use current prices to build a building with the same utility, then subtract accrued depreciation.

Notes:

Notes:

Notes:

Notes:

Notes:

Notes: